Domination and Emancipation

Reinventing Critical Theory

Series Editors: Gabriel Rockhill, Associate Professor of Philosophy, Villanova University and Jennifer Ponce de León, Assistant Professor of English, University of Pennsylvania

The *Reinventing Critical Theory* series publishes cutting-edge work that seeks to reinvent critical social theory for the twenty-first century. It serves as a platform for new research in critical philosophy that examines the political, social, historical, anthropological, psychological, technological, religious, aesthetic, and/or economic dynamics shaping the contemporary situation. Books in the series provide alternative accounts and points of view regarding the development of critical social theory, put critical theory in dialogue with other intellectual traditions around the world, and/or advance new, radical forms of pluralist critical theory that contest the current hegemonic order.

Commercium: Critical Theory from a Cosmopolitan Point of View
Brian Milstein

Resistance and Decolonization
Amílcar Cabral—Translated by Dan Wood

Critical Theories of Crisis in Europe: From Weimar to the Euro
Edited by Poul F. Kjaer and Niklas Olsen

Politics of Divination: Neoliberal Endgame and the Religion of Contingency
Joshua Ramey

Comparative Metaphysics: Ontology After Anthropology
Pierre Charbonnier, Gildas Salmon, and Peter Skafish

The Invention of the Visible: The Image in Light of the Arts
Patrick Vauday—Translated by Jared Bly

Metaphors of Invention and Dissension
Rajeshwari S. Vallury

Technology, Modernity and Democracy
Edited by Eduardo Beira and Andrew Feenberg

A Critique of Sovereignty
Daniel Loick—Translated by Amanda DeMarco

Democracy and Relativism: A Debate
Cornelius Castoriadis—Translated by John V. Garner

Democracy in Spite of the Demos: From Arendt to the Frankfurt School
Larry Alan Busk

The Politics of Bodies: Philosophical Emancipation With and Beyond Rancière
Laura Quintana

Domination and Emancipation: Remaking Critique
Edited by Daniel Benson

Domination and Emancipation

Remaking Critique

Edited by Daniel Benson

ROWMAN & LITTLEFIELD
Lanham • Boulder • New York • London

Published by Rowman & Littlefield
An imprint of The Rowman & Littlefield Publishing Group, Inc.
4501 Forbes Boulevard, Suite 200, Lanham, Maryland 20706
www.rowman.com

86-90 Paul Street, London EC2A 4NE

This English translation copyright © 2021 by The Rowman & Littlefield Publishing Group, Inc.

Originally published in French: Boltanski, Luc, Fraser, Nancy, and Corcuff, Philippe. *Domination et émancipation: Pour un renouveau de la critique sociale* © Presses universitaires de Lyon, 2014.

This volume contains the following previously published material:
Sánchez, Rosaura. "On A Critical Realist Theory of Identity" in L. M. Alcoff et al. (eds.), *Identity Politics Reconsidered*. New York: Palgrave Macmillan, 2006.

"Like a Riot: The Politics of Forgetfulness, Relearning the South, and the Island of Dr. Moreau," by Françoise Vergès, originally published in South as a State of Mind: The documenta 14 Journal, Issue #1, Fall/Winter 2015, edited by Quinn Latimer and Adam Szymczyk.

Citton, Yves. "Politiques de la tension" in *Contre-courants politiques*. Paris: Librairie Artheme Fayard, 2018.
All rights reserved. No part of this book may be reproduced in any form or by any electronic or mechanical means, including information storage and retrieval systems, without written permission from the publisher, except by a reviewer who may quote passages in a review.

British Library Cataloguing in Publication Information Available

Library of Congress Cataloging-in-Publication Data

Name: Benson, Daniel, 1985– editor.
Title: Domination and emancipation : remaking critique / edited by Daniel Benson.
Other titles: Domination et émancipation. English.
Description: Lanham : Rowman and Littlefield, [2021] | Series: Reinventing critical theory | "Originally published in French: Boltanski, Luc, Fraser, Nancy, and Corcuff, Philippe. Domination et émancipation: Pour un renouveau de la critique sociale © Presses universitaires de Lyon, 2014." | Includes bibliographical references and index. | Summary: "This volume presents a series of dialogues and articles by leading thinkers, scholars, and activists on contemporary events and theoretical developments in the social sciences, humanities, political/social philosophy, and critical theory."— Provided by publisher.
Identifiers: LCCN 2021023890 (print) | LCCN 2021023891 (ebook) | ISBN 9781786606990 (hardback) | ISBN 9781538199176 (paperback) | ISBN 9781786607010 (epub)
Subjects: LCSH: Sociology—Philosophy. | Critical theory.
Classification: LCC HM588 .B655 2021 (print) | LCC HM588 (ebook) | DDC 301.01—dc23
LC record available at https://lccn.loc.gov/2021023890
LC ebook record available at https://lccn.loc.gov/2021023891

Contents

Acknowledgments vii

Note on Translations ix

Introduction xi
Daniel Benson

PART I: DIALOGUES 1

1 Domination and Emancipation: For a Revival of Social Critique 3
  Luc Boltanski and Nancy Fraser

2 Domination and Emancipation in the Current Conjuncture 31
  Philippe Corcuff and Gabriel Rockhill

PART II: EMANCIPATORY SUBJECTS 67

3 Emancipation, Political, and Real 69
  Asad Haider

4 On a Critical Realist Theory of Identity 89
  Rosaura Sánchez

PART III: COUNTER-HISTORIES 115

5 Critical and Revolutionary Theory: For the Reinvention of
  Critique in the Age of Ideological Realignment 117
  Gabriel Rockhill

6   Like a Riot: The Politics of Forgetfulness, Relearning
    the South, and the Island of Dr. Moreau   163
    Françoise Vergès

PART IV: CRITICAL TENSIONS   183

7   Emancipation, Domination, and Critical Theory in
    the Anthropocene   185
    Ajay Singh Chaudhary

8   Renewing Critical Theory in an Ultra-Conservative Context:
    Between the Social Sciences, Political Philosophy, and
    Emancipatory Engagement   229
    Philippe Corcuff

9   Politics in Tensions. Counter-Currents for a Postcritical Age   259
    Yves Citton

Index   287

Notes on Contributors   293

Acknowledgments

This book began as a translation of *Domination et émancipation: Pour un renouveau de la critique sociale* (Presses universitaires de Lyon, 2014), the written version of a debate between Nancy Fraser and Luc Boltanski, moderated and presented by Philippe Corcuff, that originally took place on November 27, 2012 in France at the Maison de la Culture de Grenoble in the "Mode d'emploi" festival organized by the Villa Gillet. I would like to thank Philippe Corcuff for all his support and encouragement that allowed the translation to be completed and included in the present volume. I would also like to thank Jacob Carlson for reading an early draft of the translation and for our many stimulating discussions over the years.

Over the course of bringing the above dialogue into English, the book has taken on a broader scope by including newly written, translated, or republished contributions from several additional authors. Grateful acknowledgment is made to the original publishers for permission to reproduce or translate the following previously published material. The chapter by Françoise Vergès "Like a Riot: The Politics of Forgetfulness, Relearning the South, and the Island of Dr. Moreau" was originally published in *South as a State of Mind: The documenta 14 Journal*, Issue #1, Fall/Winter 2015, edited by Quinn Latimer and Adam Szymczyk. The contribution by Yves Citton "Politics in Tensions. Counter-Currents for a Postcritical Age" originally appeared as the conclusion to his book *Contre-courants politiques* by Yves Citton (c) Librairie Arthème Fayard, 2018. It has been augmented and modified by the author for inclusion in the present volume and translated into English. Rosaura Sánchez's chapter "On a Critical Realist Theory of Identity" was originally published in *Identity Politics Reconsidered,* edited by Linda Martín Alcoff, Michael Hames-García, Satya P. Mohanty, and Paula M. L. Moya (Palgrave Macmillan, 2006). I would also like to thank the New York Public

Library for its expanded services during the COVID-19 pandemic, which were instrumental to the completion of the book.

Finally, I would like to thank all the contributors to this volume, some whom I've known for a long time, others whom I've never met in person. All have generously provided work of the highest quality, which, I hope, is able to collectively resonate in what follows. A special thanks to Gabriel Rockhill, whose writing has been a constant inspiration and whose friendship has provided steadfast support for many years.

Note on Translations

Unless otherwise noted, all translations of works cited in French are my own. I have translated the entirety of chapters 1, 8, and 9 from the French, except where noted.

Introduction
Daniel Benson

"In the beginning was defeat. Anyone who wishes to understand the nature of contemporary critical thinking must start from this fact."[1] So begins Razmig Keucheyan's recent cartography of critical theory. He is not alone in his assessment: a litany of other recent works could be cited to convince the reader of the contemporary defeatism that marks critical thought and leftist politics.[2] A consequence of this has been an exaggerated focus on domination among critical theorists, leaving emancipation—along with questions of political organization and strategy—undertheorized at best, or disregarded as delusional, at worst. If emancipation still plays a role in critical reflection, it is most often in a "domesticated" form, made into a bedfellow of centrist liberalism.[3] There is a need, then, to rebuild the emancipatory pole of critique and bring forward theoretical work that is more in step with the struggles and aspirations of the moment. These struggles are legion, especially since the financial collapse of 2008 and the movements—emancipatory as much as reactionary—it has spawned throughout the world. Within this context, the present volume seeks to contribute to remaking critical analysis and militancy.

---

[1] Razmig Keucheyan, *Left Hemisphere: Mapping Contemporary Theory*, trans. Gregory Elliott (New York: Verso, 2014), 7.
[2] Already in 1976, Perry Anderson affirmed that all of "Western Marxism" was marked by defeat, after the failure of the Russian Revolution of 1917 to spread outward, and theory has essentially been severed from practical politics following WWII. *Considerations on Western Marxism* (New York: Verso, 1987).
[3] Speaking of Habermas' immanent and normative conception of critique, Stathis Kouvelakis writes: "From there, the project of emancipation consists in working on the untapped potentialities of today's society . . . . In the end, through critique, society cannot fail to conform to its concept and give substance to its promises." *La Critique défaite: Émergence et domestication de la théorie critique* (Paris: Amsterdam, 2019), 10.

The modern notion of "critique" originated in the German philosophical tradition, from Kant to Marx and beyond to other thinkers within and outside of Europe. In the Marxist lineage, the theoretical critique of domination is attached to a practical political project of emancipation that aims to free individuals and societies from the structural oppressions generated by capitalist production. But critique also needs to be recognized as arising from individuals in their daily experiences—critiques of predatory landlords, of corrupt and/or incompetent politicians, of police violence, of femicides, of imperialism, of fuel taxes, of too-expensive subway fares, of homophobia, of grossly underfunded hospitals—the list is long. Out of the hardships and "organized passivity"[4] of everyday life, critique signifies both a consciousness of domination and the desire for emancipation. At a basic level, then, this book provides a forum for theoretical critique that is in solidarity with the hopes, aspirations, movements, and sometimes inchoate forces that are already critiquing, challenging, and contesting domination in its various manifestations.

However, the emancipatory horizon of critique is no longer clearly visible today, and the very practice of critique is facing scrutiny. Didier Fassin has recently provided a diagnostic of critique in the United States and France from the 1960s/1970s to the 2000s/2010s. He notes a major shift in terms of its radicality, legitimacy, and impact, in the first period, and its marginalization, in the second. The reasons for this are multiple, chiefly due to the loss of the political hopes and possibilities of the 1960s that fueled critique, and the stifling political and economic effects of neoliberalism on the public sphere and academia, where positivism is valued at the expense of critique.[5] Fassin notes that his analysis of the "conditions of possibility" of critique is distinct from, but partly instigated by, the "postcritical" turn in the social sciences and humanities. This movement is oriented toward an internal analysis of critique, questioning its methods, its techniques, or its epistemological suppositions, and some call to abandon it altogether.[6] Bruno Latour's article of 2004, "Why Has Critique Run Out of Steam?," is the most cited reference point in the postcritical turn, since he polemically attacks several cherished notions of critical thought.[7] Latour notes how critical theorists place themselves above other people, content to show them how they are supposedly

---

[4] Henri Lefebvre, "The Everyday and Everydayness," *Yale French Studies*, no. 73 (1987): 10.
[5] Didier Fassin, "How is Critique?," in *A Time for Critique*, ed. Didier Fassin and Bernard E. Harcourt (New York: Columbia University Press, 2019).
[6] For a useful overview of postcritique, See Elizabeth S. Anker and Rita Felski, "Introduction," in *Critique and Postcritique*, ed. Elizabeth S. Anker and Rita Felski (Durham: Duke University Press Books, 2017).
[7] Bruno Latour, "Why Has Critique Run Out of Steam? From Matters of Fact to Matters of Concern," *Cultural Inquiry* 30, no. 2 (Winter 2004): 225–48.

trapped in illusions through the effects of domination. The same effort to demystify people's taken-for-granted notions leads, in his account, to a rejection of scientific facts more generally, such that the critical attitude has been weaponized by the right in such instances as climate denial and conspiracy theories of all sorts. Latour seeks to move critical energies in a more positive direction and create "new critical tools" to "retrieve a realist attitude."[8] Other postcritical theorists are less nuanced, and flatly assert that critical thought "makes us stupid."[9]

Yet the basis for critique is exteriority, which allows for an alternative viewpoint on a given situation.[10] Calls to abandon critique risk abandoning this exteriority and jettisoning any conceptualization of an alternative. What is at stake is keeping open a space for critical distance and political difference. Between the exterior conditions limiting critique's scope and the internal questioning of its usefulness, critique needs to be remade in the material and practical sense of making: to build as well as to produce an effect. "Remaking" rather than "rethinking," because the question of critique today is not primarily an epistemological question, but a practical one.[11] Thus, if critique has "run out of steam," it is because the forces, movements, and cultures constituting an emancipatory alternative to the existing order have been decimated, delegitimized, or simply ignored, from Cuba to Kerala.

Indeed, the impasse facing critique—its marginalization and limited political effectiveness in the world—arose from the explicit dismantling of very concrete organizations, experiences, memories, theories, and international linkages of past emancipatory movements. The most recent of which were the anti-capitalist, anti-imperialist, and anti-authoritarian movements that permeated global culture from the 1950s to the 1970s. Christopher Leigh Connery has written that the "long Sixties" were driven above all by a politics of "we," with equality as the watchword.[12] This politics supported feminist movements, movements for racial equality, and decolonization movements,

---

[8] Latour, *Critique*, 243.
[9] Laurent de Sutter, "Ouverture," in *Postcritique*, ed. Laurent de Sutter (Paris: Presses Universitaires de France, 2019), 8.
[10] Luc Boltanski has written that "In the final analysis, exteriority is what defines critiques. To critique is to disengage oneself from an action so as to occupy an external position allowing the action to be considered from a different viewpoint." *Love and Justice as Competences,* trans. Catherine Porter (Malden, MA: Polity, 2012), 29.
[11] Bernard E. Harcourt has written that while critical theory has been productive over the last decades, critical *praxis* has been marginalized. "Critical Praxis for the Twenty-First Century," in *A Time for Critique,* ed. Didier Fassin and Bernanrd E. Harcourt (New York: Columbia University Press, 2019). However, in my view, critical theories that are incapable of having practical effects are *also* deficient as theories.
[12] Christopher Leigh Connery, "The World Sixties," in *The Worlding Project: Doing Cultural Studies in the Era of Globalization*, ed. Rob Wilson and Christopher Leigh Connery (Santa Cruz, CA: New Pacific Press, 2007).

among others, and included political ideologies such as socialism, communism, or third-worldism as an emancipatory horizon. This horizon has slowly been obscured, sometimes with the complicity of critical theorists themselves. According to the dominate narrative, the overarching emancipatory project of these decades received its coup de grâce with the fall of the Berlin Wall in 1989 and the dismantling of the Soviet Union two years later. Emancipation—from capitalism, from racism, from patriarchy, from imperialism—has become suspect.[13]

Even Jacques Rancière, who is among the few contemporary thinkers to have continued to promote emancipation during the theoretical and political quagmire of the 1980s, acknowledges the defeat of the politics of "we" that was able to link diverse geographies, temporalities, and struggles in the 1960s. He notes that the strength of the 1960s was the way various shared experiences—from the Bandung conference of 1955, to the Cuban Revolution, to decolonization, to the revolutionary movements in Latin America and the West at the end of the 1960s—were understood theoretically and practically through the global framework of Marxism. This framework has come apart, according to Rancière, with the series of defeats over the last half century.[14] Reflecting on the protests and occupation movements that arose since 2011, he writes, not without a sense of pessimism: "there is no we that carries within it the memories of everything that's happened since the great hopes of the 60s, which could draw up the balance sheet and inscribe it into the dynamic of recent struggles and draw plans of action from them."[15]

Critique thus needs to be remade from the standpoint of a positive project of cultural, social, economic, ecological, and political transformation. While books such as the present volume can only play a very small part in such a larger collective project, I think it is important to note its horizon. The goal is not to go backward in time, to the global 1960s, for example, which would be impossible in any case (and the period had its fair share of forms of domination). Rather, it is to construct a similarly multifaceted project and theoretical framework for the contemporary period. Such a project is already underway, if we consider the reverberations of the Arab Spring revolutions, the occupy movements, and the newfound labor militancy that occurred throughout the world in 2011, from Tunisia, to Egypt, to Wisconsin, to Madrid and beyond.[16]

---

[13] Susanne Lettow writes that "Although liberation and emancipation became ubiquitous terms in [the 1960s and 1970s], they almost vanished from political language and theory in the late 1980s and early 1990s." "Editor's Introduction—Emancipation: Rethinking Subjectivity, Power, and Change," *Hypatia* 30, no. 3 (2015): 501.

[14] Jacques Rancière and Eric Hazan, *En quel temps vivons-nous?* (Paris: La Fabrique Editions, 2017), 37.

[15] Rancière and Hazan, *En quel temps*, 41.

[16] It is worth recalling the extraordinary sequence of events that arose in 2011: "The struggle over the Budget Repair Bill [in Wisconsin] began just as the Egyptians began celebrating the fall of the

These events should be seen as marking the beginning of a revolutionary sequence, not necessarily coordinated, but one which gathers momentum and inspiration from events across diverse situations and geographies.[17] Critical intellectuals have their parts to play in amplifying the voices of the participants in such events, participating themselves in them, constructing blueprints of action, creating institutions of international solidarity, and in linking various times and places into larger histories and struggles.

I have specifically avoided naming this book one of "Critical Theory." Of course, some contributors to this volume use the term and anchor their reflection in the tradition of critical theory, an expression coined by Max Horkheimer in 1937.[18] Domination, emancipation, and critique certainly are addressed in works associated with this tradition, which has made important contributions to transformative politics. However, to be in a position to remake critique, operating under the label of critical theory is, I think, unhelpful. It is all too easy to be weighed down by schools or proper names associated with the term—"the Frankfurt School," "Poststructuralism," "Deconstruction," "Foucauldian," "Lacanian," etc.—labels that are more likely to lead us astray of questions of political and social importance than to guide thinking and action. Critical theorists operating under such labels too often produce what Luc Boltanski provocatively calls "critique for critique's sake," an echo of past condemnations of works of "art for art's sake" that are self-referential and politically and socially useless.[19]

Given the current global conjuncture that is marked by uncertainty and possibility, there is a need to recenter critique within the poles of emancipation and domination, rather than within academic or philosophical labels. Especially since critique is not a purely intellectual activity, but already exists in society, in social movements, as part of everyday life. Intellectual critique, if it wants to be politically, culturally, and socially relevant for the contemporary moment, needs to be linked to (and read by participants in) social movements of all sorts, political parties, within the labor movement, and within

---

U.S.-backed dictator Hosni Mubarek. And it was just as the mass demonstrations in Wisconsin were subsiding that the call for 'Real Democracy Now' sparked a mass movement of *'indignados'* in Spain, itself inspiring anti-austerity protests across Europe." Connor Donegan, "Disciplining Labor, Dismantling Democracy: Rebellion and Control in Wisconsin," *Wisconsin Uprising: Labor Fights Back* (New York: Monthly Review Press, 2010), 43.

[17] Regarding the particular case of the Arab Spring, Gilbert Ashcar has noted that despite the counter-revolutionary reaction that has reinstated authoritarian regimes or led to ongoing civil wars in Yemen and Syria, the continued social struggles in the Middle East and North Africa, such as recent movements in Sudan, Algeria, and Iraq, indicate that the event is the beginning of a long revolutionary process that is likely to last years or decades. "Le Soudan et l'Algérie reprennent-ils le flambeau du 'printemps arabe'?," *Le Monde Diplomatique*, no. 783 (June 2019): 6–7.

[18] Max Horkheimer, "Traditional and Critical Theory," in *Critical Theory: Selected Essays* (New York: Continuum, 2002), 188–243.

[19] See interview in the present volume,16.

networks of international solidarity: linked to positive projects of emancipation and institution building. This is not to blissfully ignore the myriad negative constraints of domination that make emancipation difficult and perilous today. However, to renounce emancipation and revolutionary transformation altogether—as illusory, as impossible, as utopian, as inevitably destructive, as always already caught up in the inescapable functioning of power—means acquiescing from the start.[20] It means operating under the horizon of defeat.

I cannot speak for the specific orientations of the contributors to this volume, whose intellectual coordinates and political positions vary widely (some going so far as to question the very vocabulary of "emancipation" and "critique" altogether). I have nonetheless attempted to assemble texts by thinkers, scholars, and activists that work toward a different horizon. The reader can judge the success or failure of such an endeavor, but they will at least know its intent.

*

This book took its inspiration from a debate of 2012 between Nancy Fraser and Luc Boltanski, moderated by Philippe Corcuff.[21] Staged in the aftermath of the 2008 housing crash, and touching on fundamental questions of theoretical and political concern—such as the relationship between capitalism and the state, the future of social protection after decades of neoliberalism, and how to make critique relevant for emancipatory movements in the contemporary conjuncture—the debate has lost none of its pertinence. It appears here newly translated into English as the opening text of this volume, in Part I: Dialogues. The cross-border dialogue between the French sociologist and the American political philosopher sets the stage for the fundamentally multidisciplinary nature of the book and the Franco-American geography of the contributions that follow. It also lays out the terms of domination, emancipation, and critique that structure the volume as a whole.

While we are still in the same historical process that framed the above debate of 2012, new events have taken place since then: the Yellow Vests movement in France, a multi-tendency uprising that forcefully challenged the authoritarian neoliberalism of President Emmanuel Macron; the police murder of George Floyd, which led to the largest sustained demonstrations in U.S. history; the revolt against extreme inequality in Chile begun in 2019 triggered by a rise in subway fares; and many other movements throughout the globe, from Sudan to Algeria. All solidify the sentiment that neoliberal hegemony continues to weaken, bringing forth new desires and possibilities for emancipation.

---

[20] For a concise summary of the supposed illusions of emancipation and the impossibility, and undesirability, of revolution, see, among many others, Wendy Brown, "Feminism Unbound: Revolution, Mourning, Politics," in *Edgework: Critical Essays on Knowledge and Politics* (Princeton: Princeton University Press, 2009).

[21] Published in 2014 under the title of *Domination et émancipation. Pour un renouveau de la critique sociale* (Lyon: Presses Universitaires de Lyon, 2014).

But reactionary forces are on the rise as well: from vigilante white-supremacist terrorism in the United States, the consolidation of fascistic authoritarian governments in India and Brazil, to the authoritarian power grabs in Poland and Hungary during the ongoing COVID-19 pandemic that continues to ravage the health and economy of peoples across the world. To take stock of some of the new elements of the current conjuncture, the next chapter in this volume is a dialogue between Philippe Corcuff and Gabriel Rockhill. Their debate, which took place via email from December 2020 to February 2021, updates the context of the first dialogue and expands into other thematics, such as intellectual intervention and participation in ongoing social movements, questions of political organization and political parties, and revolution. The debate also has the added interest of reviving the socialist/anarchist debates of yore in the context of twenty-first century issues, with Rockhill's committed revolutionary socialism at times clashing with Corcuff's pragmatic anarchism.

The next parts of this book involve a number of individual contributions from a diverse range of thinkers. Asad Haider provides a situated theory of emancipation to open Part II: Emancipatory Subjects. Grounding his argument in a lexical, historical, and conceptual analysis, Haider's theory of emancipation implies understanding the constraints and forces in play in a given situation of domination, in order to encounter "the subjectivities that exceed them." He makes use of Marx's early distinction between political and real emancipation to analyze the paradoxical status of the proletariat in his work—the political subject of the historical process, the negation of the existing society, and the human kernel comprising the goal of the new social order to be achieved. Drawing on certain insights of Louis Althusser and Alain Badiou, he shows how the late Marx revised his early accounts of emancipation that followed a teleological philosophy of history to one in which organization plays the key role in creating an emancipatory subject "which does not exist prior to its organization." He thus circumvents the tired assertions in so much postmodern and poststructuralist theory that emancipation in its Marxist variant is necessarily caught up in teleology.[22] Moreover, his reappraisal of emancipation is politically important, since the disappearance of a clearly identifiable "subject of emancipation" (such as the working class) is all too often used as an excuse to give up on emancipation tout court in favor of identity politics in one or another of its guises.[23]

---

[22] See for instance Jean-François Lyotard, *The Postmodern Condition*, trans. Geoff Bennington and Brian Massumi (Minneapolis: University of Minnesota Press, 1984), 60; and Ernesto Laclau, *Emancipation(s)* (New York: Verso, 1996), 10.

[23] Razmig Keucheyan writes that "the concept of 'identity' is today prioritized in the context of the crisis of the 'subject of emancipation' that has been brewing since the 1960s. Generally speaking, a 'recoding' of the social world in terms of 'identities' is noticeable from the 1980s." *Left Hemisphere*, 24.

Of course, identity and emancipation needn't be seen in opposition, as Rosaura Sánchez argues in her contribution. Challenging liberal and post-structuralist ideas of identity that emphasize "difference" and neglect questions of how identity is structurally grounded in class, political economy, and by the state, Sánchez provides a materialist understanding of identity politics. While acknowledging that identity claims tend to be reformist in nature, they are certainly not opposed to emancipation, in her view. In particular, Sánchez points to the long-term organizational construction of political subjects: organizing for claims that are not revolutionary in the short term does not foreclose the construction of revolutionary subjects. Moreover, Sánchez provides an extremely useful conceptual typology, distinguishing positioning (a subject's place in a given structure) and positionality (how one sees oneself or acts from one's given position in a structure); and identification (which imposes a category on individuals by placing them into a given collective) from identity (formed by social agents as a self-reflexive affiliation or disaffiliation with a collective). She thus points to a multilayered theory of agency, such that subjects are not mere effects of structures, nor are they completely unmoored from them. She terms her approach "critical realist," drawing from Roy Bhaskar's philosophical work, and elaborates it with the aid of Tomás Rivera and Helena María Viramontes' literary writings. While the literary protagonists of these writers are able to achieve a critical consciousness of their positioning within the social structure, they are unable to take the next step and work to change it: only collective struggle is able to do that.

Part III: Counter-Histories continues the reorientation of critique away from defeatism and moves toward a wholesale replacement of critical theory with revolutionary theory in Gabriel Rockhill's contribution. Taking aim at Frankfurt School critical theory, he marshals a scathing critique of the most prominent members associated with this tradition, from Max Horkheimer and Theodor Adorno, to Jürgen Habermas, Axel Honneth, and Nancy Fraser. But beyond proper names, his critique aims more broadly at the function of the Frankfurt School in the "international political economy of ideas": that of anti-revolutionary conformism. Beginning with Horkheimer's tenure as director of the Frankfurt Institute for Social Research in 1930, through its exile in the United States, to its return to West Germany in the 1950s, Rockhill considers the dubious sources of the Institute's funding, the reactionary political positions held by its most prominent members, its Eurocentrism, and the generalized eradication of all association with communism, anti-imperialism, and emancipation beyond capitalism. Despite its radical appearances, Frankfurt School critical theory is theory made palatable to liberal-democratic-capitalist societies by purging any elements that would actually challenge the capitalist order. In its place, Rockhill argues for the revolutionary theory of historical materialism, understood as a fallibilistic science based on class struggle. He reminds the reader that Marx and the Marxist lineage have always been attuned to the racialized, gendered, nature of the international working class, and to the capitalist exploitation of the workforce outside of the official economy, from slavery to unpaid domestic work—very far from a rigid, class-reductionist, dogmatic, teleological doctrine that so many "critical" theorists have leveled against Marxism. Rockhill's "counter-history of critical theory" provides an opening for other names, traditions, and geographies of critique to appear.

Françoise Vergès' contribution maps out such an alternative geography. Her upbringing in the French overseas department of Réunion Island imbued her with an emancipatory cartography of the South: of exchanges between Africa and Asia, of the Bandung conference and the Cuban Revolution, of wars of liberation from Algeria to Mozambique. This counter-hegemonic map was one on which Europe was on the periphery. She considers how the forgetting of this map structures contemporary capitalism and imperial politics in the creation of a surplus humanity. Vergès provides an example of this by staging an encounter between H. G. Wells' fictional Doctor Moreau and his perhaps more insidious historical double, Doctor Moreau of Réunion Island, who engaged in forced abortions and sterilizations of Reunionese women from 1966 to 1970 with the complicity of the colonial government—at a time when abortion was illegal in the metropole. This is part of longer, global story of how "disposable peoples and forgotten territories" are produced in the "Capitalocene," Jason Moore's term for the generalized destruction of peoples and the environment brought about by capitalism. Combating it means piecing together a palimpsest of the traces of the vanquished: the enslaved, the colonized, women, workers, peasants, and migrants the world over. In the struggle for a "politics of lives that matter," an "ethics of emancipation" is needed. In such an ethics, reconstructing the traces of the forgotten is not about filling in the gaps of a linear historical narrative in order to achieve recognition for them according to the terms set by Western democracies: it is to provide a "source of images, texts, and songs that constitute a counter-hegemonic library for present battles."

Part IV: Critical Tensions concludes the book. It provides space for reworking themes brought up in the first three parts of the volume, challenging them, expanding on them, or otherwise reformulating them in terms of the unavoidable tensions present in contemporary theoretical and practical undertakings.

Ajay Singh Chaudhary confronts the environmental crisis discussed in the previous chapter in his spirited defense of Frankfurt School critical theory. He notes how the impeding environmental catastrophe hearkens back to the crises that generated the original "Critical Theoretical project" in the interwar period, with World War II (WWII) looming on the horizon. However, far from advocating a dogmatic return to the main thinkers associated with the Frankfurt School, he argues that critical theory must change: firstly, through a dialogue with climate scientists. In fact, climate science increasingly contains what Chaudhary calls an "intuitive critical theory," since it sees any response to the climate crisis as dependent on a wholesale transformation of social, economic, and political structures. Secondly, critical theory needs to be supplemented by a practical politics, a "left-wing climate realism." The relative distrust of praxis by thinkers such as Theodor Adorno, which may have made a certain amount of sense in the post-WWII period, is no longer operative. The critical theorist of today, for Chaudhary, must be both a "media studies scholar" and a "radio technician," twisting Adorno's comparison meant to discourage Angela Davis—scholar and communist/Black Panther Party militant/prison abolitionist—from engaging in practical politics. Indeed, Chaudhary considers the path of Davis as exemplary in this regard. To face the climate crisis, the negative critique of the Frankfurt School cannot be abandoned, nor can we revert to an anti-intellectual activism. To arrest progress that is leading to disaster, what is needed is more critique, not less; but this must be attached to a "brutal, instrumental" zero-sum politics in order to keep open the narrowing window of emancipation.

Philippe Corcuff also argues for the need to reassociate the critical and the emancipatory today. Indeed, his contribution starts from the hypothesis that emancipation and critiques of domination have been severed in the contemporary period. This leaves critical theory and leftist politics in disarray, since both were traditionally based on the association critique/emancipation. What remains is, on the one hand, uncritical social sciences supposedly based on Weberian "ethical neutrality"; and on the other, extreme-right forces around the world adopting a social critique that has been abandoned by the left. To counter this trend, Corcuff reconstructs social critique and emancipation not by privileging one or the other of the terms, but by keeping them in an irresolvable tension. He analyzes other tensions, including that between critical sociology (Pierre Bourdieu) and a philosophy of emancipation (Jacques Rancière); individuality versus the social question; or academic research versus militant engagement. Such tensions constitute the basis for a "renewed critical theory" against the dominant modes of conceptualization that, in Corcuff's view, remain beholden to resolving contradictions in a Hegelian-inspired synthesis. At the political level, he sees a similar perspective at play in contemporary identitarian, right-wing movements, which fix individuals and collectives into singular, closed, identities. Corcuff thus proposes a "politics of open being" that re-establishes an emancipatory horizon for both critical theory and leftist politics, drawing from a diverse list of thinkers, including Emmanuel Levinas, Judith Butler, and Miguel Abensour. Political and theoretical tensions will always remain, though, and cannot be "overcome": antinomies and oppositions can only be "balanced" following the anti-Hegelian formulation by the early anarchist thinker and militant, Pierre-Joseph Proudhon.

Tensions are also foundational in Yves Citton's concluding contribution, which builds on the previous chapter in interesting ways. Like Corcuff, he sees leftist politics without a stable rudder due to the disruption of the critique of domination/emancipation model of social progress that traditionally supported it. But he further questions the very desirability of using terms such as "critique" and "emancipation," and proposes a postcritical politics of tensions. Using an electromagnetic imaginary, he draws a highly original cartography of eighteen polarities that structure politics: just as positive and negative poles structure electromagnetic currents, he identifies polarities that structure political currents and counter-currents. Navigating important contemporary issues, such as the rise of so-called populism, right-wing extremism, the general disorder of traditional political parties, the increasing dominance of the economy of attention, and the impeding ecological catastrophe, he ultimately sees political action as constituted by a world based on ubiquitous hinges that open or close to let in desirable elements (e.g., citizens of a country) and shut out others (e.g., unwanted migrants). Citton asks us to situate ourselves in such a world of "hingery," and presents a final polarity that consists of binarists who see the world in terms of on or off, all or nothing, and the potentialists, who see the world in terms of an infinite gradation of partial openings and closings. He thus allows us to consider the various tensions between the contributions that make up this book, from revolutionary anti-capitalism, emancipatory Marxism, critical realist identity politics, decolonial feminism, left-wing climate realism, pragmatic anarchism, to postcritical politics of tensions.

Such tensions cannot be resolved here and synthesized in this project of remaking critique and of re-establishing an emancipatory horizon for political action. Not all the contributors agree in their analyses of the contemporary moment and on the path forward for social transformation. But since action is always begun in medias res, never made under freely chosen circumstances, "but under circumstances directly encountered,"[24] tensions may be an unavoidable part of any theory and practice of emancipation.

BIBLIOGRAPHY

Anderson, Perry. *Considerations on Western Marxism*. New York: Verso, 1987.
Anker, Elizabeth S., and Rita Felski. "Introduction." In *Critique and Postcritique*, edited by Elizabeth S. Anker and Rita Felski, 1–28. Durham: Duke University Press Books, 2017.

---

[24] Karl Marx, *Selected Writings*, ed. Lawrence H. Simon (Indianapolis: Hackett Publishing Company, 1994), 188.

Ashcar, Gilbert. "Le Soudan et l'Algérie reprennent-ils le flambeau du 'printemps arabe'?" *Le Monde Diplomatique*, no. 783 (June 2019): 6–7.

Boltanski, Luc. *Love and Justice as Competences*. Translated by Catherine Porter. Malden, MA: Polity, 2012.

Boltanski, Luc, Philippe Corcuff, and Nancy Fraser. *Domination et émancipation. Pour un renouveau de la critique sociale*. Lyon: Presses Universitaires de Lyon, 2014.

Brown, Wendy. *Edgework: Critical Essays on Knowledge and Politics*. Princeton: Princeton University Press, 2009.

Connery, Christopher Leigh. "The World Sixties." In *The Worlding Project: Doing Cultural Studies in the Era of Globalization*, edited by Rob Wilson and Christopher Leigh Connery, 77–107. Santa Cruz, CA: New Pacific Press, 2007.

Donegan, Connor. "Disciplining Labor, Dismantling Democracy: Rebellion and Control in Wisconsin." In *Wisconsin Uprising: Labor Fights Back*, edited by Michael D. Yates, 29–45. New York: Monthly Review Press, 2010.

Fassin, Didier. "How is Critique?" In *A Time for Critique*, edited by Didier Fassin and Bernard E. Harcourt, 13–35. New York: Columbia University Press, 2019.

Harcourt, Bernard E. "Critical Praxis for the Twenty-First Century." In *A Time for Critique*, edited by Didier Fassin and Bernanrd E. Harcourt. New York: Columbia University Press, 2019.

Keucheyan, Razmig. *Left Hemisphere: Mapping Contemporary Theory*. Translated by Gregory Elliott. New York: Verso, 2014.

Kouvelakis, Stathis. *La Critique défaite: Émergence et domestication de la théorie critique*. Paris: Amsterdam, 2019.

Laclau, Ernesto. *Emancipation(s)*. New York: Verso, 1996.

Latour, Bruno. "Why Has Critique Run Out of Steam? From Matters of Fact to Matters of Concern." *Cultural Inquiry* 30, no. 2 (Winter 2004): 225–48.

Lefebvre, Henri. "The Everyday and Everydayness." *Yale French Studies*, no. 73 (1987): 1–11.

Lettow, Susanne. "Editor's Introduction—Emancipation: Rethinking Subjectivity, Power, and Change." *Hypatia* 30, no. 3 (2015): 501–12.

Lyotard, Jean-François. *The Postmodern Condition*. Translated by Geoff Bennington and Brian Massumi. Minneapolis: University of Minnesota Press, 1984.

Marx, Karl. *Selected Writings*. Edited by Lawrence H. Simon. Indianapolis: Hackett Publishing Company, 1994.

Rancière, Jacques, and Eric Hazan. *En quel temps vivons-nous?* Paris: La Fabrique Editions, 2017.

Sutter, Laurent de, ed. *Postcritique*. Paris: Presses Universitaires de France, 2019.

Part I

DIALOGUES

Chapter 1

Domination and Emancipation

For a Revival of Social Critique

Luc Boltanski and Nancy Fraser
Interviewed by Philippe Corcuff

Translated by Daniel Benson

HISTORICAL PERSPECTIVE

Each in their own way, Nancy Fraser and Luc Boltanski situate their critique of the contemporary world within a historical framework. Fraser privileges the history of social protection and Boltanski that of capitalism. In each case, statism is radically questioned, as both thinkers take their distance from crude critiques of neoliberalism that more often than not harbor a nostalgia for a strong state.[1]

Philippe Corcuff:

Today, the critique of the social destruction wrought by the neoliberal moment of capitalism is often supported by, at least implicitly, a certain nostalgia for the social state, usually called the "welfare state." Nancy Fraser's approach appears more nuanced, though it still keeps its radically critical edge. She achieves this by addressing the problem of social protection through a series of historical displacements that allow for a better view of current problems.

---

[1] The italicized summaries that begin each section are by Philippe Corcuff.—Ed.

Nancy Fraser:

There's a certain tendency to simply oppose a good social democracy to a bad neoliberalism, the good public to the bad private sector, the good French republicanism to the bad American approach... However, these simplistic binaries don't help us at all. Such easy definitions lead us to sentimentalize our analyses of capitalism by referring to its earlier phases, which of course had their own problems and were haunted by crises; but in any case they're past. We can't go backward and revive previous phases of capitalism. We have to think differently today. Moreover, social protection has evolved over time and its varied forms were often criticized by social movements.

First off, let's take the pre-neoliberal form of social protection, which was based on multiple forms of domination. There were, for example, sexist approaches to the understanding of work and contributions: it was very often presumed that a single salary was sufficient for a family, and that a family was constituted by a man who made money and a woman who took care of the household. This setup I call *heterosexism*. It was an approach that was dominated by *heteronormativity*, and social protection was strongly tied to it. This reading went together with the idea that everyone was supposed to work toward the interest of the community as conceived by the culturally dominant majority, which severely penalized people who were part of religious or ethnic minorities or various other groups. There is a feminist and, more broadly, anti-discriminatory critique of the welfare state, and this critique is necessary. Such forms of social protection were justly criticized by social movements in favor of emancipation in the 1960s and 1970s. They were seen as oppressive forms of protection—and indeed, in an emancipatory logic, it's not desirable to go back to this sort of social protection. Whatever forms of social protection are advocated for today, they must be linked to the imperatives of emancipation, and we must be vigilant in order to avoid the resurgence of past forms of domination.

The second point to discuss is the statist aspect of pre-neoliberal social democracy. It is an approach that is bureaucratic, *expertocratic*, and uses a mode of protection that is oppressively coded and constrictive. I remember very clearly the criticism, used in the 1960s and 1970s by what was called the "New Left," of such a mode of protection that removed all agency from its beneficiaries and made them into passive users. This is not the kind of social protection we want if we adopt an emancipatory perspective. There is perhaps a grain of truth in the liberal critique of social protection as an impediment to freedom, even if we can't follow liberals all the way in their thinking.

The third point that I'd like to raise is the national question. Personally, I think that the welfare state and the forms of social protection that have arisen since WWII were financed on the backs of postcolonial peoples in the

Global South. This form of protection was poorly framed. Which is to say that an entire group that was exposed to risks and needed protection—and such a group was much larger than the people of any one nation-state—was sacrificed for the benefit of a small circle of citizens. Faced with transnational or global forms of risk, we can't be satisfied with protecting people through national programs. We must assume a larger, more global approach. Such is the argument I tried to develop in my work *Scales of Justice*.[2] In our globalized world, there are transnational injustices that are erroneously reduced to the national level: for example, the effects of delocalizing jobs on unemployment and low salaries, or North/South inequalities that are the true source of migration movements, leading to zones of lawlessness for those who don't have access to citizen rights within the scope of Western nation-states, etc.

The three points above allow us to develop the question of social welfare by escaping the most Manichean shortcomings of contemporary critiques of neoliberalism.

Philippe Corcuff:

In a stimulating way, Nancy Fraser's approach makes it possible to integrate the critique of the social welfare state developed by the "New Left" in the 1960s and 1970s, which contested its bureaucratic logic and the forms of domination that were associated with it, such as sexist domination, without putting social protection into question—on the contrary! This prevents our critique from being hijacked by the neoliberal turn of capitalism. Moreover, the perspective of reinventing a type of social protection that is more firmly anchored to emancipation allows us to rescue the theme of protection from conservative forces, or indeed from the extreme right, who tend to confine the question of protection to the question of national security.

Luc Boltanski, for his part, speaks little of social protection. Yet, in *On Critique*,[3] he develops a rather original conception of institutions through a semantic approach that relates to the question of protection, insofar as he proposes a critique of the state without abandoning the question of institutions. We can thus identify an analogous approach in the two thinkers. They have many similarities, not at the level of content, but in the logic of their two analyses: critique of the social state and defense of social protection, in Fraser's account, critique of the state and defense of institutions, in Boltanski's work. Both authors, moreover, contest the national limitations of statism.

---

[2] Nancy Fraser, *Scales of Justice: Reimagining Political Space in a Globalizing World* (New York: Columbia University Press, 2009).
[3] Luc Boltanski, "The Power of Institutions," chap. 3 in *On Critique: A Sociology of Emancipation*, trans. Gregory Elliot (Malden, MA: Polity Press, 2011).

Beyond the analogy, Boltanski's contribution to the historicization of a renewed social critique is more specific and proposes a reading of the historical movements common to both capitalism and the state.

Luc Boltanski:

We need to develop analyses of the relationship between capitalism and the state since the end of WWII, following the long-term historical work of Michael Mann[4] and Saskia Sassen.[5] But let's go back a bit. At the end of the nineteenth century, the state took up the rather misguided, even demiurgic, project of completely stabilizing and formatting reality for a given population on a given territory. In *Mysteries and Conspiracies*,[6] I was able to capture this element through the birth of two literary genres: the detective novel and the spy novel, each of which deals with the tensions brought about by the state's attempt, aided by science, to manage social reality in its principal aspects. This statist project goes hand in hand, moreover, with a certain xenophobia, a rejection of those who don't belong to a supposedly homogenous population. Such a rejection was, in the twentieth century, the origin of the most terrible form of insecurity, for it led to the most monstrous wars that humanity has ever known.

In the years between 1945 and 1950, a compromise is found that is partly a punishment of capitalism for the crisis of the 1930s, partly a measure taken in reaction to the massive involvement of business executives in European fascism. Such a compromise between capitalism and the state roughly takes on the following form: the state's role is to reproduce, educate, and care for the workforce and look after infrastructures, while capitalist businesses pay taxes and recognize to a certain degree worker representation through unions, state planning, and its committees, as well as through other joint organisms (between employers and unions) or tripartite ones (including representatives of the state), etc.

This compromise is put into question, after 1968, by the actors occupying positions of power in large firms. Though it should be noted that the compromise was already in crisis in the 1960s, when capitalism was marked by a decline in productivity, the increasing power of unions, the extension of social struggles to so-called tertiary workers, the development of student

---

[4] For a synthesis of this work, see Michael Mann, "The Autonomous Power of the State: Its Origins, Mechanisms and Results," *European journal of sociology* 25, no. 2 (1984): 185–213.

[5] Saskia Sassen, *Territory, Authority, Rights: From Medieval to Global Assemblages* (Princeton, NJ: Princeton University Press, 2008).

[6] Luc Boltanski, *Mysteries and Conspiracies: Detective Stories, Spy Novels and the Making of Modern Societies*, trans. Catherine Porter (Malden, MA: Polity Press, 2014).

contestation, and especially by a decline in stockholders' share of surplus value that continued until the middle of the following decade.

A kind of redeploying of capitalism takes place from 1975 to 1985—and continues thereafter. A number of displacements occur, not fully coordinated, which will be integrated into what Eve Chiapello and I have called the "new spirit of capitalism."[7] This "new spirit of capitalism" expressed itself in business management during the 1990s by rehashing the themes of 1968 in capitalist language. An attempt was made to liberate capitalism from the double constraint weighing on it: the worker constraint and the fiscal constraint that arose during the period of compromise with the social state. For the state is essentially about taxation, as several historical sociological studies have shown, such as those of Michael Mann that I mentioned earlier.[8] The various neocapitalist maneuverings involve a complete restructuring of businesses, outsourcing, and lobbying for the deregulation of finance, the goal being to create profit without needing to employ the working class, at least not the local working class. These different logics have the corollary effect of reducing the capacities of states to assure the upkeep of the workforce or the multiple functions of the welfare state.

The excellent thesis of Jeanne Lazarus, published under the title *L'Epreuve de l'argent* (The ordeal of money),[9] shows that in the middle of the 1960s only a quarter of the French population possessed a bank account. People were often paid by the week, sometimes even by the hour, not monthly. This changed just after 1968 when the monthly salary became widespread under the Chaban-Delmas/Delors government (which was essentially the heyday of the welfare state before it began to be dismantled) and pressure grew for everyone to own a bank account.

Consequently, people who had a certain flexibility and a certain autonomy, whether in the form of struggle at the workplace or in managing their money, ultimately exchanged this flexibility and autonomy for the state's promise of greater security. But after the period of 1973–1975, a whole series of phenomena, related to the reorganization of capitalism that aimed at raising stockholder profits, greatly altered people's level of security without providing them with a corresponding autonomy to help them confront this increased insecurity. Today, whoever doesn't have a bank account or who has problems with their bank is considered—forgive the bankers' jargon—to be a *"cas soc,"* a good-for-nothing. Such people are really doubly stigmatized:

---

[7] Luc Boltanski and Eve Chiapello, *The New Spirit of Capitalism*, trans. Gregory Elliott (New York: Verso, 2018).
[8] Michael Mann, *States, War and Capitalism: Studies in Political Sociology* (Oxford: Blackwell, 1988).
[9] Jeanne Lazarus, *L'épreuve de l'argent: banques, banquiers, clients* (Paris: Calmann-Lévy, 2012).

by the difficulties that they encounter and from the fact that new financial agencies of control have appeared in their lives. In this situation, it is certainly necessary to try to "preserve what's left" and defend the remnants of social security—I think that most leftist social movements would agree with that. But there is no credible perspective in which we could think that states are actually capable of modifying the situation to their advantage, nor even, indeed, that they are really inclined to do so beyond pious vows delivered at big international forums. In short, state interventionism, in the context of contemporary capitalism, does not appear to be the best path to curb the further erosion of social security. Moreover, there's an entirely different neoconservative discourse that is very widespread, I'm sure you're familiar with it, which consists in punishing individuals, *blaming the victim*—to use the title of a famous American book[10]—by considering that those who don't succeed according to capitalist rules are responsible for their plight and don't deserve social protection.

FORCES OF POLITICAL CONFRONTATION AND DANGEROUS LIAISONS

How can we think through the principal political/ideological forces operating in the neoliberal phase of capitalism? What are the dangerous liaisons between them? Which perspectives appear desirable from the point of view of emancipation? Nancy Fraser and Luc Boltanski outline different scenarios in the United States and France, between which we can observe certain intersections.

Philippe Corcuff:

By putting the question of autonomy and protection into the historical perspective of capitalism's development since WWII, we can begin to formulate a type of social protection that would not necessarily be nationally localized and state based. This would mark a step forward from the rigidity of leftist responses in France that are stuck in such statist or nationalist schemas in the face of capitalism's crisis. As a way to resist nation-centric statism, Fraser and Boltanski share a common element in their most recent thinking, which consists in recuperating part of political liberalism as a dimension of emancipation. Political liberalism thus becomes one of the resources that can be used to counter state domination and the exclusionary consequences of

---

[10] William Ryan, *Blaming the Victim* (New York: Vintage Books, 1976).

national borders. Such a perspective flies in the face of fashionable theses—
I'm thinking of the philosopher Jean-Claude Michéa, among others—which
conflate political liberalism and economic liberalism and thus associate both
with capitalism and the right.[11] This move is analogous, and conceptually
related, to what I call the "collectivist programing"[12] that dominates the left
in France following the 1914–1918 World War. That is, an unquestioned
presupposition became dominant in which everything related to the collective
is seen as leftist, and everything individual is right wing and capitalist; such
a politico-intellectual robotism persists to this day.

Nancy Fraser understands the question of the liberal dimension of emancipation through the idea of "negative liberty"[13] in the tradition of Isaiah Berlin.[14] How can we define more precisely this liberal element, which is a (non-exclusive) part of emancipatory logic?

Nancy Fraser:

Luc Boltanski and I use different terms, but we have an analogous perspective. To put it simply, there are essentially three main forces in play today. First of all, a neoliberal faction that aims to extend markets as far as possible and dispossess states of their protective capacity, while defending other aspects of the state such as, for example, the repressive element. Next, there are other forces that try to resist this faction and defend or establish a form of social protection. These forces can be harmful, racist, xenophobic, etc. It's not the case for all of them, but even the best of them are heavily centered on the idea of the nation-state. There exists, finally, a third group of forces, perhaps in more embryonic form, that Luc Boltanski groups under the banner of the libertarian left. I would define them in more general terms as forces seeking emancipation.

From there, several combinations are possible between two of these forces which would pit them against the third. Luc Boltanski warns us of the danger of an alliance in which emancipatory forces of the left adopt conservative uses of social protection that tend to marginalize or even eliminate the possible emancipatory tendencies already present in political liberalism (which we need to distinguish from economic neoliberalism). Nevertheless, I analyzed the nearly exact opposite phenomenon in the United States, and I think that

---

[11] Philippe Corcuff, "Michéa et le libéralisme: hommage critique," *Revue du MAUSS permanente*, April 22, 2009, http://www.journaldumauss.net/spip.php?page=imprimer&id_article=495.
[12] Philippe Corcuff, *La gauche est-elle en état de mort cérébrale?* (Paris: Textuel, 2012), 45–48.
[13] Nancy Fraser, *Fortunes of Feminism: From State-Managed Capitalism to Neoliberal Crisis* (New York: Verso, 2013), 5.
[14] Isaiah Berlin, "Two Concepts of Liberty," in *Liberty: Incorporating Four Essays on Liberty* (Oxford: Oxford University Press, 2002).

France could also be confronted with a similar logic. In the United States, we are dealing with a different dangerous liaison: emancipatory forces joining up with neoliberal forces, a scenario in which social protection passes from a leftist demand to the right. These two types of dangerous liaisons are very different, but both are problematic, because, in my view, each of the three forces we are dealing with is oriented toward different values or principal objectives.

In the case of emancipation, the principal objective is evidently to overcome domination. In the case of social protection, it is a matter of validating social security, social stability, or social solidarity in one form or another. Whereas for economic neoliberalism, negative liberty and freedom of choice in markets are the motivating factors. This is why I say that we need a modest conception of emancipation. Emancipation must not be an objective that dominates all the others. Each force has its legitimate values and these values can be ambivalent; each of the three groups can unite with one of the others (emancipation could combine with neoliberalism but also with social protection). These coalitions can turn out badly, if, neglecting the third party, they are too skewed or oriented to one side or the other.

In order to solve this problem, we need to try to develop a new analysis that consists in establishing connections between the best of emancipation and the best of social protection, without sacrificing the value of negative liberty. The latter must not be surrendered to economic neoliberalism, just as social protection must not be left to nationalists and neoconservatives. Social protection does not exist without emancipation, without a form of legitimate recognition of negative liberty—or without participatory democracy. I concluded my book *Fortunes of Feminism* with an analysis of this "new alliance."[15]

Moreover, the frame of the nation-state is not necessarily the correct frame in which social security should be conceptualized. It is necessary to provide a plurality of scales of reflection and to work on the relation between the scales. Security and protection can be assured on an entirely different level beyond the nation-state, but also on smaller levels that focus on cooperation among living spaces, work places, cities, regions ... For it is impossible to correctly understand social protection without the correct framing of the dangers and the risks situated at different levels, from the local, to the national, to the global. We must think about protection on several scales: there are many types of public authorities just as there are many levels of social protection.

---

[15] Fraser, *Fortunes of Feminism*, 240–41.

Philippe Corcuff:

Aided by the disarray of the political and intellectual references formulated in the nineteenth and twentieth centuries, several dangerous liaisons are imperceptibly forming within today's ideological fermentation. Nancy Fraser and Luc Boltanski help us to elucidate them in the present moment—evidence that the distance provided by theoretical tools can also be used to see through the haze and ambiguity of unfolding contemporary events.

In the U.S. context, Nancy Fraser identifies the dangerous liaison between the emancipatory left and neoliberalism. A similar dangerous liaison already occurred in the 1980s in France when the "Second Left"[16] (which backed the CFDT (Confédération française démocratique du travail) labor union and gave political support to Michel Rocard) contributed, largely unintentionally, to foster the neoliberal movement through its partially justified critique of the bureaucracy of the social state and more generally of the rigidities of statism—but also through its re-evaluation, much more contestable, of the market. The Saint-Simon Foundation (1982–1999), under the triple auspices of François Furet, Pierre Rosanvallon, and Alain Minc, set up one of the main cauldrons in which part of the "New Left" of the 1960s and 1970s was made into a pitiful neoliberal soup.

Today, the dangerous liaisons have shifted in France: they've taken up the anti-liberal critique, which had legitimately questioned the ideas propagated by the Saint-Simon Foundation. They can now be found orbiting a simplified version of "French republicanism." In a recent work, I identified a galaxy of reified attitudes associated with the left: "republicanists," [*républicards*] "secularists," [*laïcards*] and "nationalistes."[17] Such intellectual reflexes are equally present in what Luc Boltanski calls "French neoconservatism." This dangerous liaison is "new" in our contemporary context, even if it has a whiff of the 1930s.

Luc Boltanski:

In France, political positions have long differentiated themselves on the question of liberalism, but there is a huge variety of different critiques of liberalism. There is, on the one hand, a socialist position with statist undertones that is essentially opposed to economic liberalism. There is also an anarchic, non-statist socialist position (ultimately very little developed in France but extremely present, as we know, in Spain), oriented against economic liberalism though adopting a range of characteristics of political liberalism, such as

---

[16] The "Second Left" was the non-Marxist left that joined the French Socialist Party after the disbanding of the SFIO (the French Section of the Workers' International) in 1969.—Ed.
[17] Corcuff, *mort cérébrale*, 64–71.

emphasizing the importance of rights and of the differences of individual subjects. And then there exist a series of anti-liberal traditionalist currents since the nineteenth century, very often Catholic, regionalist, and nationalist, which stress the organic character of the nation and tradition. These currents are in opposition to a different right-wing movement, the fully fledged liberal right (that is, the politically liberal and especially economically liberal position).

The shifting allegiances between these different positions are what give political color to an era. When a social movement appears dangerous, or seems to be going in favor of the left, the liberal right wing, ordinarily little interested in national values and more concerned with satisfying the business world through the mechanisms of capitalism, all of a sudden allies with the traditionalist and moralistic right wing. When, on the contrary, traditionalist movements become strong and verge on fascism, the same liberal right might ally itself with socialist movements. These are some examples of historical coalitions that have formed.

Using this frame of analysis, it's worth considering that the 1930s in France witnessed the appearance of intellectuals, thinkers, or even politicians who declared themselves to be "neither left nor right"[18]—they were called "non-conformists"[19]—and who also used an anti-capitalist discourse. We find a similar phenomenon today. Consider the numerous texts published in the past few years, at the interstices of the social sciences or social and political philosophy, that emphasize the necessity of "limits"; or the demands of "living together" considered uniquely from a moral point of view (that of "politeness"), and not from the perspective of the conditions under which we might actually arrive at it; or the deleterious effects of critique ("of everything and nothing"). Or else the necessary identification of "our true values"—the "our" in question often left very hazy, implicitly referring now to "we the West," now to "we the nationals," now to "we the intellectuals, guardians of an ancestral heritage" or "we the heterosexuals in a world of depravity"... Such expressions aren't far from the lamentations of the "decline of the West"[20] by Oswald Spengler, often invoked by the fascist right in the 1930s in France. Today, we find various associations between these types of positions. The non-conformists of the 1930s were often found near Marshal Pétain five or ten years later. I don't know what will happen to the "neither left nor right" non-conformists of today.

---

[18] Zeev Sternhell, *Neither Right Nor Left: Fascist Ideology in France*, trans. David Maisel (Princeton: Princeton University Press, 1995).
[19] See Jean-Louis Loubet del Bayle, *Les Non-conformistes des années 30* (Paris: Éditions du Seuil, 1969).
[20] Oswald Spengler, *The Decline of the West*, 2 vols., trans. Charles Francis Atkinson (New York: Alfred A. Knopf, 1922).

Among those who adopt this discourse (which isn't a discourse of reconciliation, but simply one of being "neither left nor right," of an anti-capitalism associated with traditionalism), there are indeed many leftists, or those who come from a leftist background, who subscribe to republicanism and the ideas popularized over the last two decades, beginning with Jean-Pierre Chevènement. As for the right, the principal themes of the French neoconservatives (who need to be distinguished from the American "Neocons" ideologically close to neoliberalism) have scarcely changed since the 1930s: it's still a question of defending *true* values and *true* culture in, for example, educational curriculum—as a way to stay in favor with teachers and literary professors. Thus, *La Princesse de Clèves*, which symbolized the most archaic aspects of the educational system for the critics of the 1970s, today has become a symbol of the struggle of *true* culture against capitalist commodification. More generally, it is a question of opposing the *true* people (today, workers threatened by deindustrialization) to the *false* people (that of suburban immigrants or the precarious urban population). A similar situation arose in 1930s, when the peasants stood for the good, true people against the bad, red population of the suburbs…

Additionally, there are several examples of left/right intermingling. I'm thinking particularly of the infamous headscarf debate, which has become an object of extraordinary interest over the past twenty years for the French people. If the headscarf didn't exist, people would find work again, shale gas would no longer be drilled, the balance of payments would be re-established, etc. Everything hinges on the headscarf! This unfortunate headscarf has created very interesting bridges between feminist positions, secular and republican positions, and xenophobia. The latter phenomenon was always a trait of the French right, but has moved away from anti-semitism, widespread in France from 1880 to 1950, toward hostility toward immigrants, especially those of the Arab-Islamic world. Of course, the two forms of xenophobia are far from incompatible, as the return of anti-semitism is on the rise with the increasing power of the extreme right.[21]

---

[21] For a more systematic view of "French neoconservatism" that is part of the current ideological and political extreme-right movement, see Luc Boltanski and Arnaud Esquerre's collaborative work *Vers l'extrême: extension des domaines de la droite* (Bellevaux: Éditions Dehors, 2014). For a continuation of this view, see Philippe Corcuff, *Les années 30 reviennent et la gauche est dans le brouillard* (Paris: Textuel, 2014).

A CRITIQUE OF INHIBITED CAPITALISM

The financial crisis of 2007–2010 has again revealed the destructive character of capitalism. And yet the slogan "There is no alternative" or TINA, attributed to the ex-prime minister of Britain Margaret Thatcher, still appears ideologically and politically strong. To shed light on this issue, Nancy Fraser emphasizes the fall of so-called communist countries, while Luc Boltanski highlights how critique has been paralyzed in the contemporary context.

Philippe Corcuff:

I would like to ask you about an initial paradox. The harmfulness of capitalism was again revealed during the recent financial crisis. And yet capitalism continues to impose its demands over human well-being and ecological equilibrium. How can we understand this troubling observation?

Nancy Fraser:

It's true that whenever the question comes up about who is going to pay for the crisis, everything is done to protect investors at the expense of people and the environment. At this stage, we need to understand why political elites throughout the world have become neoliberal agents—with the exception perhaps of Latin America, which we should discuss. Even politicians who claim to be "social democrats," but who in fact have become social liberals, insist on austerity policies, on the reduction of the deficit, and on ensuring that the loss for investors is less than for everyone else. Democracy is demoralized, incapable of presenting any clear alternative. On this point, the United States and France are in a similar situation. On both sides of the Atlantic, we've recently elected a new president[22] and lawmakers on the basis of a strong rejection of brutal neoliberalism, and yet all of them have revealed themselves to be nothing but "neoliberalism *light*."

What has happened at the political level? To answer this, we need to understand the expansion of finance. Capitalism, in the past based on production, is today dominated by finance. There is an accumulation of more and more capital, but this is no longer due to the exploitation of workers. Accumulated capital is linked to state debt. There are several factors that can explain the decline of real wages, which leaves capitalist societies without consumers, without a working class that has the purchasing power to buy enough products. This is what has left a gaping hole of debts, whether they are linked to

---

[22] Barack Obama in the United States and François Hollande in France.—Ed.

credit cards or real estate ... Lack of consumption has only got worse in the crisis of 2008 and its toxic loans. Capitalism has managed to overcome the crisis by transferring it to states, whose sovereignty is curtailed by the necessity that forces them to resort to borrowing from financial markets.

What I'm trying to say is that whichever thread you follow, everything comes back to capitalism, inevitably. It's difficult to see things differently. Capitalism, considered in its entirety, must be seen as a form of life in which the economic part depends on all the other parts, while at the same time endangering and literally eroding them. I think that this is the true object of contemporary critique. On the other hand, there's a very simple question, a fundamental one, which needs to be asked in order to judge capitalism: to what degree does capitalism respond to human needs?

Even if we respond negatively to this question, we need to confront another discouraging characteristic of today. Here I join the paradox you mentioned. In earlier periods, critique as well as leftist and emancipatory forces had a sort of self-confidence because they were truly convinced that there existed another path, another way to support social needs beyond capitalism. We should not underestimate the importance of the collapse of "actually existing socialism," whose legitimate fall unfortunately pulled along with it all new social programs. The movement toward an emancipatory socialism was never completed and the failure to reform and leave behind Stalinist terror in all those political regimes who wrongly claimed to be communist has been disheartening. Today, we are in the grips of this incertitude, this lack of confidence. Does another realizable solution exist? This is the question that an increasingly fragmentary critique is asking.

Philippe Corcuff:

The feeling of no alternative to capitalism that Nancy Fraser highlights is undeniable, and weighs on critical thought as well as on social movements, creating a lamentable environment. For Luc Boltanski, this feeling also relates to a certain ineffectiveness of critique in the particularities of the current context. That said, there has been a revival of critique in comparison to the listless atmosphere of the 1980s. Is this a second paradox?

Luc Boltanski:

Indeed, on this subject, the principal question that we need to address, in my opinion, is the negligible effect of critique in the historical situation that we live in. This ineffectiveness is particularly evident in the case of the critique of capitalism. The latter, to which the social sciences contributed a great deal, was very active in the 1960s and 1970s before being reduced to near silence in the following two decades. Nevertheless, this reduction to silence was of a short duration. At the end of the 1990s and even more so in the 2000s, the critique of capitalism became very active again. And yet we must recognize that it only marginally affected the procedures and measures that contribute to the formatting of historical reality, whether in the political, economic, or cultural domain. And this is true whether one looks *up* or *down*.

Looking down, critique hasn't found any real echo in social movements. The latter have either maintained the inherited positions of the past that accompanied their decline, or else they haven't managed to constitute themselves in original and offensive forms. We only need to look at the difficulties encountered by the associations and movements for precarious workers in their attempts to put in place a system to establish an identity, a collective force that would increase their capabilities in the power struggles with employers (including the state). We've seen moments of collective effervescence, but these haven't brought about stable oppositional structures for the moment.

Looking up, that is, to governing bodies, whether they claim to be on the left or right, the themes and terms of critique have frequently been adopted, but without reorienting given policies in any real and durable way. In the mouths of power-holders, critical terms have remained "empty talk." Witness the weakness of so-called heterodox economic currents, which, even if they rarely take on a radical form, have not managed to disrupt the strength of mainstream economics.

However, there cannot be any true revival of critique if the reasons for its current ineffectiveness are not analyzed. I will offer up a few suggestions.

Let's mention, with respect to social mobilization, the disconnect between critical thinkers (at least most of them) and social movements, something that is quite novel in the last 200 years of history. The long period in which critical thought attempted to formulate the demands of social movements has given way to an academic autonomization of critique, an intellectual activity that is now almost considered an end in itself: "critique for critique's sake," just as one speaks of "art for art's sake," often haughty and confined to internal debates, where tensions play out among competing thinkers within the field of critique. Such obscure critique has taken the paradoxical form of an "avant-garde" of master thinkers (a form largely questioned already in the aftermath of May 68), but without a rearguard or troops.

Regarding governing authorities, in order to understand the current status of critique, we should probably be attentive to new forms of governmentality, to borrow Michel Foucault's concept, that have established themselves over the course of the last decades. One of the specificities of the *managerial mode of domination* that arose in Europe is, perhaps, its ability to tolerate critique, provided that the latter is confined to the order of discourse without leading to any practical consequences. Opposed to older forms of power that feared critique, and thus sought to block it, new modes of governance have arisen, capable of incorporating certain carefully selected elements of critique and manipulating its vocabulary. Moreover, criticism is constantly submitted to the supposedly realist demands of *necessity*, that is, of a reality governed by forces whose nature is so totally systematic and impersonal that to resist it would be irresponsible folly. In marked contrast to classical forms of domination, more brutal in nature, the new forms of domination are instead characterized by a much more refined comprehension of the mechanisms of power, aided in part by some of the most sophisticated analyses in the social sciences, which are often incorporated in management strategies. This allows the various powers in play to make changes, rather than oppose them, by considering them as an external necessity and as the expression of the will of expert-backed competence: the most effective instrument of domination.

EMANCIPATION AND INSTITUTIONS

If capitalism and the state are obstacles on the road to individual and collective emancipation, we may still have a need for institutions. Such in any case is the path that Luc Boltanski and Nancy Fraser take, each in their own way, in the last part of their dialogue. Both adopt a perspective of rupture with the capitalist structure. Luc Boltanski even conceives of going beyond the nation-state, while Nancy Fraser maintains a place for the constitutional state.

Philippe Corcuff:

While the left has willingly adopted the idea of self-emancipation—in the sense of the pronominal verb *to emancipate oneself* [*s'émanciper*]—, it often surreptitiously substitutes a tutelary vision of emancipation and adopts the transitive verb *to emancipate others*.[23] This happens through the bureaucratic weight of parties, through the institutional forms of hierarchy and violence that are reproduced in organizations with an emancipatory aim, through the unequal social relations that are replicated within them, etc. But the radical critique of the tutelary excesses of emancipation does not imply the rejection of institutions, according to Luc Boltanski.

---

[23] On this point, see Philippe Corcuff, *Où est passé la critique sociale? Penser le global au croisement des savoirs* (Paris: La Découverte, 2012), 33–46, and Corcuff, *mort cérébrale*, 72–75.

Luc Boltanski:

Emancipatory politics is not politics from on high. Otherwise, it would be like the *double bind* imposed on children.[24] Saying "I want you to be free" to your son or daughter rarely works, and sometimes leads to some fine neuroses. Emancipatory politics comes from the actors, from people themselves. Emancipation, for me, thus presupposes self-emancipation. And it can't come about unless people reappropriate their lived environment. In general, such a reappropriation happens when one can say no. I think that it's totally illusory to talk about emancipation or about the future of critique without looking into power relations [*rapports de force*]—a notion that most contemporary sociology finds completely offensive, I know. Without modifying power relations, first of all by saying no, there is little chance of taking control of one's environment. Which doesn't necessarily mean resorting to violence. Forms of opposition from the citizenry exist, of passive resistance, of civil disobedience, etc. What matters is the ability to say no.

There is moreover an extremely interesting point that should be explored in much greater detail than it usually is: the question of rules and sanctions, or to be more precise, the question of inequalities with respect to rules and sanctions—whether "laws" issued by the state or norms of "good behavior" encouraged by managerial entities. When you work on these questions, you quickly realize that there are extremely profound inequalities in play, related to many other asymmetrical relationships brought about by organizations that determine social selection. We can describe the arbitrary nature of rules by distinguishing between the *spirit* of the rule and the *letter* of the rule. Those on the bottom of the hierarchy are asked to carry out very precise tasks determined beforehand by research departments, while those on the upper echelons have objectives that are not bound to specific criteria of accomplishment. On the contrary, to achieve the latter objectives, it's thought that room for maneuver is needed with respect to the letter of the rule, while the spirit of the rule is to be closely followed. But since those in dominant positions make the rules, it's rather easy for them to stay within the spirit of the rule.

Faced with this problem, there is a moralistic, fundamentalist response that says: "Everyone must obey the same rules," forcing the important, the rich, the strong, to strictly obey the rules just like those on the bottom. However, I think moral indignation is a bad advisor in politics. A very fine book by Svend Ranulf on the rise of Nazism shows that beginning in the 1930s, Nazis spent their time being morally outraged.[25] It would be much more fruitful to

---

[24] On the double bind, see Gregory Bateson et al., "Toward a Theory of Schizophrenia," *Behavioral Science* 1, no. 4 (1956): 251–64.

[25] Svend Ranulf, *Moral Indignation and Middle Class Psychology: A Sociological Study* (Copenhagen: Levin and Munksgaard, 1938).

take the massive inequality with respect to rules as a starting point to think about a social world in which the possibilities for negotiating and adjusting rules would be equally distributed among all social classes, rather than reserved to the elite.

This point can lead to a re-evaluation of the place of institutions within the perspective of emancipation. While we must combat the symbolic and physical violence exerted by institutions, I don't think it's wise to abandon their very idea, which would mean giving up the positive functions they assume. I'm thinking specifically of the task of providing people with a minimal semantic security—that is, with relatively stable bounds faced with the uncertainty of existence—so as to allow for their reidentification regardless of the situation they're in, partially protecting them from the arbitrariness that arises from losing their points of reference. Jean Searle quite rightly emphasized, based on the philosophy of language, the semantic functions of institutions.[26] That said, we must leave a place for uncertainty and fragility, and acknowledge that the meaning of institutions is provisional and reversible through democratic processes. Moreover, preserving transformed and open institutions does not mean that the nation-state should be maintained in its nineteenth-century form: as the prime mover that seeks to embody the point of view of totality, encompassing the entire field of experience by hierarchically integrating different institutions, and delimiting the range of acceptable definitions of reality.

Philippe Corcuff:

The first anti-capitalist phase of social democracy, whether revolutionary or reformist, ended in 1959 with the congress of Bad Godesberg of the German Social Democratic Party. This opened the next phase of social democracy, which involved the search for a social compromise favorable to workers within the framework of capitalism. This phase has in turn disappeared, as the neoliberalization of political elites, including those on the left, became generalized in the 1980s. This disappearance hasn't really been theorized or positively affirmed in France, excepting a few marginal instances. In Britain it was, when the great sociologist Anthony Giddens, close to the prime minister of the epoch, Tony Blair, conceptualized social liberalism as the "third way" that was to realize an alliance between the previous form of social democracy and economic neoliberalism.[27] In France, we can only see this shift through specific actions, beginning with the "austerity turn" [*tournant de la rigueur*]

---

[26] John R. Searle, *The Construction of Social Reality* (New York: Free Press, 1997).
[27] Anthony Giddens, *The Third Way: The Renewal of Social Democracy* (Cambridge: Polity Press, 1999).

of 1983; there wasn't really any intellectual work within the socialist party to think about this movement.

However, this shift of social democracy toward neoliberalism wasn't the only possible route. A few years ago, I participated in the attempt to outline the idea of a *libertarian social democracy*,[28] which sought to renovate social democracy by discussing the question of social protection in dialogue with the anarchist tradition rather than with neoliberal logic. Such an approach has affinities with Nancy Fraser's attempt to tie together the emancipatory left, social protection, and political liberalism in a postcapitalist perspective, though rooted in specifically American intellectual and political debates.

Nancy Fraser:

As Luc Boltanski mentioned, emancipation must be self-emancipation, it must come from the person and not be imposed from above. Struggle is necessary in order to reach emancipation. However, whatever the new order will be like, if such an order exists, it must be institutionalized. It can't be based solely on a movement that would demand our mobilization every minute of our lives. Emancipation must be able to establish itself within the framework of the new order. That said, there will always be people who find the established order a bit too regulated, a bit too governed, a bit too structured, and who will struggle against it. It's at this point that the question of domination becomes important. There will always be an insurmountable tension between individual liberty, collective autonomy, and the institutionalized order governed by rules. However, it is crucial to determine whether or not this institutionalized and regulated order is structurally attached to domination. Are there forms of domination, for instance, that lead to profound disparities in the way people interact, in their relationship to rules, in their access to resources or recognition, in their ability to express themselves, whether politically or through civil society? Emancipation proceeds by dismantling the social order that supports such structural inequalities. If the social order is based on domination, it should be replaced by another social order that, even if it's burdensome, provides an equitable basis for interactions. For the moment, the problem is that the rules are biased in such a way that there's no possibility for just competition. In the context of the present social order, we have no possibility whatsoever to correct things, which for me means that we must take an outside route in order to radically change the existing order, rather than attempt to improve it.

---

[28] Philippe Corcuff, *La société de verre: pour une éthique de la fragilité* (Paris: Armand Colin, 2002), 220–51; and *La question individualiste: Stirner, Marx, Durkheim, Proudhon* (Latresne: Le Bord de l'eau, 2003), 63–73.

But we must not let the perspective of overcoming domination be our only leitmotiv, our only goal, however important it is. While this would certainly lead to a society freed from profound disparities, no longer governed by a dominating force, it would be a world in which each person would be subject to all kinds of insecurity, continually thrown left and right by diverse, abrupt changes... With this in mind, I developed the idea of a modest and non-exclusive conception of emancipation. Though we often see them as restrictive, security, stability, and solidarity have their specific value. This is why, I wanted to propose a new synthesis, a new alliance between emancipation and social protection. Social protection implies reinforcing institutions, rules, and the logic of the constitutional state. This is problematic from a libertarian perspective, but I don't think we can dispense with it.

We also can't do without markets. I can't imagine a desirable society in which markets and consumer goods were abolished. The main issue is the following: where are markets necessary, and where are they not? There are at least three domains in which consumer products must have a market: the environment, social protection, and finance. These are areas in which robust markets are required, heavily regulated and restricted, markets that impose rules. The most important question to address is the question of the social surplus. Who decides what to do with it? Who controls it? Markets must not be able to decide these questions. Capitalism considers that this social surplus is subject to the decisions of private actors. This is the worst aspect of capitalism, for it means losing collective and democratic control over essential questions such as: what to do with the surplus? Should social earnings be reinvested? Should we work less, or work differently, to slow down the rate of accumulation of capital? Defining, localizing, and regulating the role of markets is fundamental in order to think about different possible alternatives to capitalism.

CONCLUSION

Philippe Corcuff:

In their provisional concluding remarks, Luc Boltanski and Nancy Fraser converge tellingly around the logic of self-emancipation, whose meaning is clearly captured by the pronominal verb *to emancipate oneself*. One problem of the left has been to move, without being totally conscious of it, from the verb *to emancipate oneself* (in the logic of the slogan of the First International: *The emancipation of the laborers must be the work of the laborers themselves*) to the transitive verb *to emancipate*, as if it were a question of emancipating slaves. Like the republican and later socialist professor who sought to emancipate minds trapped in Plato's cave and bring them into the light of Reason... or the professor of ATTAC (Association for the Taxation of financial Transactions and Aid to Citizens) who emancipates people mystified on neoliberal "propaganda" today, or the feminist militant of the past who sought to emancipate the prostitute or the veiled woman, or the ecological prophet who seeks to emancipate alienated consumers, etc.

Both Luc Boltanski and Nancy Fraser emphasize the imperative of self-emancipation against the tutelary deviations possible within the democratic relationship to politics. With this objective in mind and by working around the questions associated with it, new paths can be taken to think through notions that are often seen as incompatible, such as emancipation and security, movement and institution, mobility and stability, risk and protection, or individual autonomy and collective solidarity, all within the perspective of a postcapitalist framework. However, as we bring our attention to emancipatory possibilities by reinventing past critical traditions, in our rush toward a supposedly radiant future, we must not be blinded to the present and neglect the actions of the here and now, notably the capitalist constraints that curb and disturb it, such as neoconservative threats. We can't afford to look the other way in the face of current crises and imminent dangers, however exciting our current task is, both intellectually and practically, as we proceed through trials, errors, and experimentation.

POSTSCRIPT: SOCIOLOGY AND SOCIAL CRITIQUE: DOWNWARD TURN OR REVIVAL?

by Luc Boltanski

A Certain Return of Critique

After the lethargy of the 1980s and 1990s, the 2000s witnessed a revival of critique as understood by leftist currents. Its task was to understand the new globalized managerial structures and their associated modes of governmentality, including at the local level. It took the particular form of a critique of economic liberalism and especially neoliberalism, considered as a pathology of capitalism, rather than a critique of capitalism as such or a reflection on alternatives to it. This new critique of neoliberalism was substantiated and stimulated by the crisis of 2007–2008.

One of the positive effects of the critique of neoliberalism, as it was deployed over the last decade, has been to highlight the changes brought about by the importation of managerial logics into the functioning of the state and public services (such as benchmarking, cost accounting, the contractualization of the relations between actors, temporary and precarious employment, etc.). These practices, first invented and executed in large, globalized corporations, often of Anglo-Saxon origin, were adapted to public administration in Great Britain under the government of Margaret Thatcher, and later in France, predominately since the 2000s.[29]

However, it is legitimate to reproach this critique for too often identifying the changes underway by contrasting the neoliberal abuses of the state with an idealized vision of state forms, reconstructed after the fact, that preceded the importation of "new public management" in France. In so doing, this critique neglects the numerous and often very pertinent criticisms of the state which had been proposed, particularly within the social sciences, in the 1960s and 1970s—that is, before the neoliberal turn.[30]

This selective amnesia and the reconstruction of an idealized model of the French "republican" state—seen as the embodiment of collective good, supposedly preceding the current deviations of the state that arose after its "colonization" by neoliberal logics imported from Anglo-Saxon countries via Brussels and European institutions—have led to at least two types of negative effects.

Firstly, the critique of capitalism has become focused on the opposition between the private and the public, between managerial logics, largely vilified, and statist logics, believed to be a source of redemption: not by opposing capitalism, of course, but by "regulating" it or even by "moralizing" it (as if one of the specificities, and strengths, of capitalism wasn't precisely to rely on a strictly mathematical logic and consequently to disregard those questions often considered to be of a "moral" character). This overlooks the fact that the current crisis is both a crisis of capitalism and a crisis of the state form.[31] For the moment, capitalism seems to have overcome the crisis situation in which it has been floundering for several decades by transferring it to societies—leading to the current conjunction of a flourishing capitalism and increasingly unequal societies, eroded by unemployment and insecurity.

The Wayward Critique of Economic Liberalism Toward Neoconservatism

Secondly, the critique of neoliberalism has often had another consequence. It opened the possibility of shifting critique from economic liberalism toward a critique of political liberalism more generally; the latter, however, constitutes a partially indispensable heritage of modern democracies and indeed of the

---

[29] See Pierre Lascoumes and Patrick Le Galès, eds., *Gouverner par les instruments* (Paris: Presses de Sciences-Po, 2005).

[30] For an overview of such criticisms, see Pierre Bourdieu, *On the State: Lectures at the Collège de France, 1989–1992*, ed. Patrick Champagne et al., trans. David Fernbach (Malden, MA: Polity Press, 2014).

[31] See Fraser, *Scales of Justice*.

left, including its most radical expressions. In France, this anti-liberalism has often been disguised in the language of *republicanism*. Liberalism has thus been attacked by two different types of critiques that have mutually supported each other. The first, from the left, highlights the social inequalities brought about by the rationales of liberal economics. The second comes from the traditionalist right, which criticizes individual liberties in the name of moral and/or nationalist imperatives, usually expressed in a language—forged in the nineteenth century in reaction to the Enlightenment and the French Revolution—that stresses the supposedly "organic" relation uniting the true "people" and the "nation," the latter conceived as a prior and superior entity to the state, including (or especially) in its republican forms. There's a paradoxical way in which certain statements today that promote "republicanism" are inspired by currents of thought that have ceaselessly attacked the republic for two centuries.

A strange mix is emerging from this encounter that we could qualify as the new dominant ideology or as French neoconservatism. It is anti-capitalist (which distinguishes it from American neoconservatism), moralist, and xenophobic. It is focused, in a quasi-obsessional way, on the question of national identity, opposing the true (good) people of France to the emigrants of the *banlieues* who are amoral, violent, dangerous and who above all are keen on abusively taking advantage of the "public goods" that remain of the welfare state. It calls for the reinforcement of the most "noble" cultural forms (opposed to the "ramblings" of counter-culture) and denounces the weakness of democracies, whose tolerance borders on laxity, and consequently calls for a reinforcement of police authority.

This ideology, in its most visible expressions, is of course propagated by the parties of the extreme right, like the National Front.[32] But we have to acknowledge that it tends to contaminate, in more euphemistic forms, numerous discourses and practices that lay claim not only to the traditional right but also, in a significant number of cases, to the left. And this comes not only from party advocates, eager to seduce potential electors who might vote otherwise, but also from certain intellectual currents of the left, something that is perhaps even more worrisome.

For a True Revival of Social Critique

Rebuilding critique on a more radically emancipatory foundation must, in my opinion, begin by deepening the above diagnostic of the limits of the

---

[32] Now called the National Rally.—Ed.

critique of neoliberalism and the dangerous liaisons that it formed with rising neoconservatism.

The revival of critique implies, furthermore, that critical reflection connects with the most innovative and radical contemporary social experimentations, that is, those which engage people in the pursuit of new forms of life, of cooperation (like co-ops), and of struggle. Such experiments exist, certainly, even though they are rarely discussed in the media or scholarly essays. This means that scholars and analysts who want to accompany critical projects need to abandon their contemplative fascination with their television set, where the "misery of the world" finds a deformed reflection, and go straight to the source. They might take up or pursue empirical studies not only of the condition of the most impoverished, but especially of the new structures of power and those who are invested in them. Concretely, this means developing research on the new contours of the dominant classes, both locally and globally—a task that is more and more difficult to accomplish, it should be noted, faced with increasingly enclosed centers of power.

Such an effort can only succeed if it undertakes the joint critical analysis of the two forces which, since the nineteenth century, have historically played a preponderant role. That is, on the one hand, capitalism and its recent evolutions, and, on the other, the nation-state form. These two interacting modes of governance are at the height of their power but also profoundly in crisis. The priority of critical reflection should be to take on the project of outlining the contours of a livable world that could emerge out of these crises.

The task above is difficult, particularly for sociology, given that the original forms of the discipline, its conceptual framework, and even its project were connected, at the end of the nineteenth century, to the development of nation-states and of industrial methods of capitalism. This means that if sociology wants to become, or become again, a truly critical discipline, it must engage in self-reflection. It must do so, first of all, to free itself from expertise-oriented tasks in which governing bodies hope to confine it. But it must do so especially in order to profoundly re-elaborate its concepts and language in such a way as to reacquire the necessary instruments—both in terms of its technical capacity and of its intellectual legitimacy—for re-elaborating global frameworks of analysis.

Frameworks of this type are indispensable to move beyond the simple description of empirically observed situations, in order to be able to critically assess them. We may never have needed "grand narratives" more than we do today.

POSTSCRIPT: CRITIQUE, DOMINATION, EMANCIPATION[33]

by Nancy Fraser

Necessary Conceptual Clarifications

The time is right for renewing discussion of critique, domination, and emancipation. The current crisis of neoliberal capitalism has put these questions squarely back on the agenda and given them a new urgency. No wonder, then, that we are currently witnessing a revival of critique and of the passion for emancipation.

Nevertheless, it is by no means clear that the forms of critique in fashion today are adequate for the task at hand. The same is true for our received understandings of domination and emancipation. Formed in an earlier period, during which the crisis tendencies inherent in capitalist society were relatively latent, these ideas developed in an abstract, moralistic form, disconnected from any large-scale, systematic understanding of our how our society works, where its principal fault lines lie, which actors might conceivably transform it, and to what ends.

Today, accordingly, it is worth revisiting these concepts, considering which understandings are best able to clarify our present situation. To this end, I want to suggest an *ambitious* conception of critique and a *modest* conception of emancipation.

An Ambitious Critique

Let me begin by suggesting that the object of critique should be society as a whole: its deep structural sources of domination, its crisis tendencies or contradictions, its characteristic forms of social conflict, and its historically specific potentials for emancipation. Only such an ambitious conception has the chance to uncover connections among apparently discrete "social problems," to disclose their deep structural causes, and to discover the extent to which they arise accidentally or necessarily, as a result of systemic features of the society.

For our present purposes, I propose that we conceive our society as a whole, first and foremost as *capitalist society*. I do not mean capitalism in the narrow sense of a specific subsystem of society, equivalent to its system of wage labor, private enterprises, commodity production processes, and markets. I mean rather capitalism as a larger form of life, which encompasses not only the official monetized economy but also the unofficial, non-monetized

---

[33] This section by Nancy Fraser was originally written in English.—Ed.

forms of activity and sources of value on which the official economy depends. Call these the necessary background conditions for the official economy.

Let me mention two absolutely indispensable background conditions, although there are more. The first is the natural biosphere, which sustains life and supplies the necessary material inputs for commodity production. The second is the realm of "social reproduction," which includes household carework and associational activities in neighborhoods and communities, activities that serve to create, maintain, and transform social bonds, while also supplying the appropriately socialized and skilled "labor power" that capitalism needs. Each of these background conditions is absolutely necessary for the operation of capitalism in the narrow economic sense. And each should therefore be included in the conception of capitalist society that forms the object of our critique.

It follows that critique should not confine itself to the official economy. Rather it must situate monetized forms of injustice, such as the exploitation of wage labor, in relation to other, non-monetized forms, such as ecological depredation and free-riding on women's carework and household labor. Only such a broad understanding can capture the actual mechanisms that generate domination. These include capitalism's sharp, structural separation of waged from unwaged labor, a separation unknown in other societies, and its specific forms of human-nature metabolism, above all industrial manufacturing premised on fossil fuels.

In addition, the broad view of capitalist society allows us to grasp the deep sources of instability in capitalist society, which lie behind the present crisis. Too often the crisis is understood one-dimensionally, as pertaining chiefly to finance or finance plus the "real" (monetized) economy. Equally important, however, and equally related to capitalism, are the ecological dimension of the crisis and the social reproduction dimension of the crisis, both of which share a common grammar. In both cases, the crisis arises because capitalism's drive for limitless expansion necessarily erodes its own background conditions of possibility. In the case of ecological crisis, what is being eroded are the natural processes that sustain life and provide the material inputs for social provisioning. In the case of social reproduction crisis, what is at stake are the socio-cultural processes that supply the solidary relations, affective dispositions, and value horizons that underpin social cooperation, as well as the appropriately socialized and skilled human beings who constitute "labor." With its intensified push to commodify nature and social reproduction, neoliberalism is eroding the very supports on which capitalism depends.

I am suggesting here that practitioners of critique return to the question of capitalism, which many had abandoned in previous decades—but not in the same old orthodox way. By adopting an expanded understanding of capitalism, rather, we can incorporate the insights of newer critical paradigms, such as feminism, postcolonial theory, and ecological thought. The result is not only an expanded understanding of domination, but a critique of capitalism as inherently crisis-prone.

In general, the sort of critique I envision would interweave an expanded "crisis critique" of capitalist society with an expanded "fairness" critique of the relations of domination it necessarily generates and with a "grammar of life" critique that problematizes the quality of relations to which it gives rise—self-relations, social relations, and human-nature relations. This, as I said, is an ambitious understanding of critique, whose work must somehow be shared by critical theorists and social actors, including social movements.

A Modest and Open-Ended Approach to Emancipation

Interestingly, I think this ambitious view of critique goes best with a modest conception of emancipation. I mean "modest" not in the sense that we should aim low in our efforts to transform society, but in the sense that critical theorists should not rush to fill in the specific content of emancipation. That should rather be kept open, to be filled in historically and politically. We should content ourselves with the modest definition that emancipation means overcoming domination. But the forms of domination are not given all at once. Rather, they unfold historically, through the medium of social struggle, often in unpredictable ways. Who could have imagined fifty years ago, when I was a teenager, that there was such a thing as heterosexist domination, rooted in the structural organization of capitalist society? And why shouldn't it be the case that people living fifty years from now will recognize other forms of domination, which are unimaginable to us now.

A modest view of emancipation valorizes this open-ended historical process by which the understanding of domination unfolds. Wary of overly specific definitions that would foreclose that process, it contents itself with the thin and seemingly tautologous idea that emancipation means overcoming domination—in whatever form the latter arises.

BIBLIOGRAPHY

Bateson, Gregory, Don D. Jackson, Jay Haley, and John Weakland. "Toward a Theory of Schizophrenia." *Behavioral Science* 1, no. 4 (1956): 251–64.

Berlin, Isaiah. *Liberty: Incorporating Four Essays on Liberty.* Oxford: Oxford University Press, 2002.

Boltanski, Luc. *Mysteries and Conspiracies: Detective Stories, Spy Novels and the Making of Modern Societies.* Translated by Catherine Porter. Malden, MA: Polity Press, 2014.

Boltanski, Luc. *On Critique: A Sociology of Emancipation.* Translated by Gregory Elliot. Malden, MA: Polity Press, 2011.

Boltanski, Luc, and Eve Chiapello. *The New Spirit of Capitalism*. Translated by Gregory Elliott. New York: Verso, 2018.

Boltanski, Luc, and Arnaud Esquerre. *Vers l'extrême: extension des domaines de la droite*. Bellevaux: Éditions Dehors, 2014.

Bourdieu, Pierre. *On the State: Lectures at the Collège de France, 1989–1992*. Edited by Patrick Champagne, Remi Lenoir, Franck Poupeau, and Marie-Christine Rivière. Translated by David Fernbach. Malden, MA: Polity Press, 2014.

Corcuff, Philippe. *Les années 30 reviennent et la gauche est dans le brouillard*. Paris: Textuel, 2014.

Corcuff, Philippe. *La gauche est-elle en état de mort cérébrale?* Paris: Textuel, 2012.

Corcuff, Philippe. "Michéa et le libéralisme: hommage critique." *Revue du MAUSS permanente*, April 22, 2009. http://www.journaldumauss.net/spip.php?page=imprimer&id_article=495.

Corcuff, Philippe. *Où est passé la critique sociale? Penser le global au croisement des savoirs*. Paris: La Découverte, 2012.

Corcuff, Philippe. *La question individualiste: Stirner, Marx, Durkheim, Proudhon*. Latresne: Le Bord de l'eau, 2003.

Corcuff, Philippe. *La société de verre: pour une éthique de la fragilité*. Paris: Armand Colin, 2002.

Fraser, Nancy. *Fortunes of Feminism: From State-Managed Capitalism to Neoliberal Crisis*. New York: Verso, 2013.

Fraser, Nancy. *Scales of Justice: Reimagining Political Space in a Globalizing World*. New York: Columbia University Press, 2009.

Giddens, Anthony. *The Third Way: The Renewal of Social Democracy*. Cambridge: Polity Press, 1999.

Lascoumes, Pierre, and Patrick Le Galès, eds. *Gouverner par les instruments*. Paris: Presses de Sciences-Po, 2005.

Lazarus, Jeanne. *L'épreuve de l'argent: banques, banquiers, clients*. Paris: Calmann-Lévy, 2012.

Loubet del Bayle, Jean-Louis. *Les Non-conformistes des années 30*. Paris: Éditions du Seuil, 1969.

Mann, Michael. "The Autonomous Power of the State: Its Origins, Mechanisms and Results." *European journal of sociology* 25, no. 2 (2009): 185–213.

Mann, Michael. *States, War and Capitalism: Studies in Political Sociology*. Oxford: Blackwell, 1988.

Ranulf, Svend. *Moral Indignation and Middle Class Psychology: A Sociological Study*. Copenhagen: Levin and Munksgaard, 1938.

Ryan, William. *Blaming the Victim*. New York: Vintage Books, 1976.

Sassen, Saskia. *Territory, Authority, Rights: From Medieval to Global Assemblages*. Princeton: Princeton University Press, 2008.

Searle, John R. *The Construction of Social Reality*. New York: Free Press, 1997.

Spengler, Oswald. *The Decline of the West*. 2 vols. Translated by Charles Francis Atkinson. New York: Alfred A. Knopf, 1922.

Sternhell, Zeev. *Neither Right Nor Left: Fascist Ideology in France*. Translated by David Maisel. Princeton: Princeton University Press, 1995.

Chapter 2

Domination and Emancipation in the Current Conjuncture

Philippe Corcuff and Gabriel Rockhill
Interviewed by Daniel Benson

IDEOLOGY, HEGEMONY, AND CRITIQUE

Gabriel Rockhill frames his analysis of the current conjuncture in terms of a resurgent revolutionary socialism, while Philippe Corcuff highlights the dangers of employing past political concepts to understand the murkiness of today's socio-political situation. Their respective analyses of the Yellow Vests movement in France reveal their differing approaches, but both are highly critical of the intellectual disengagement evident among supposedly "critical" theorists.

Daniel Benson:

Firstly, let's begin with a broad question relating to the current conjuncture. The interview between Luc Boltanski and Nancy Fraser took place shortly after the financial crisis of 2008 and the Arab Spring revolutions and occupy movements that occurred across the world in 2011. Many significant events have occurred since then, such as the Yellow Vests movement in France begun in 2018 for economic and political change, the ongoing Movement for Black Lives in the United States, including the massive popular uprisings for racial justice in 2020 after the police killing of George Floyd, and the recent electoral success of the indigenous and socialist MAS party in Bolivia, democratically reinstated after a military coup removed it from power. On the other hand, extreme right-wing forces have consolidated themselves throughout the world, from India to Brazil, including resurgent white supremacy spurred on by Donald Trump's presidency in the United States, to say nothing of the COVID-19 pandemic that continues to ravage the already fragile social, political, and economic global order. There is a widespread sentiment that the current period is one of crisis, where neoliberal hegemony is no longer entirely functioning, yet still persists, leaving the world in a state of interregnum where "the old is dying and the new cannot be born," to quote Antonio Gramsci's expression of 1930 that seems particularly apt to characterize the moment.[1]

I would like to ask you both for your analysis of this moment of crisis or shifting hegemony. How has the contemporary conjuncture evolved over the past decade, in terms of creating new possibilities for emancipation or of consolidating structures of domination, either in France or the United States, or globally?

Gabriel Rockhill:

We are currently living through what is perhaps the most acute crisis of neoliberal capitalism, which has led to an intensification and radicalization of global class struggle. Neoliberalism originally emerged as a new phase of capitalist accumulation in the wake of the economic crisis of the early 1970s, and it simultaneously functioned as a counter-insurgency tactic against the anti-systemic movements of the 1960s. It sought to solve the economic and political crisis at the time by reorganizing the capitalist economy through the globalization of production, the digitalization and financialization of the economy, the dismantling of the welfare state, etc.[2] With the collapse of the Soviet Union in 1991, this project of capitalist restructuring went into overdrive, no longer held back by the need to maintain the appearance of offering a better alternative to Soviet-style socialism with its guaranteed education, healthcare, and employment.

Through rampant privatization and the dismantling of the welfare state, neoliberalism has thus been destroying the material basis for hegemonic rule for some fifty years. An increasing number of people simply do not have stable employment and access to affordable food, housing, and healthcare, and they are therefore less likely to lend their consent to the capitalist system

---

[1] Antonio Gramsci, *Selections from the Prison Notebooks of Antonio Gramsci* (New York: International Publishers, 2014), 276. For contemporary resonances of the expression, see Nancy Fraser's recent book *The Old Is Dying and the New Cannot Be Born: From Progressive Neoliberalism to Trump and Beyond* (New York: Verso, 2019) or Cornell West's intervention at the inaugural summit of the Progressive International, September 18, 2020, https://www.youtube.com/watch?v=ZIZTQW8gQV0.

[2] William I. Robinson has provided one of the most coherent and systematic accounts of neoliberalism in books like *Global Capitalism and the Crisis of Humanity* (New York: Cambridge University Press, 2014) and *The Global Police State* (London: Pluto Press, 2020).

(though this is, of course, always mediated by ideology).³ The global pandemic has only intensified this crisis, bringing into stark relief the failings of the capitalist system when compared to socialism.⁴ Moreover, given the ecological crisis, the stakes of global class struggle are arguably higher than at any point in history because it is clear to anyone paying attention that capitalism is destroying the very conditions of possibility of life on Earth.

Given the context of our current discussion, I should also mention the profound intellectual crisis of the globalized Euro-American world. Whereas much of the Western intelligentsia was once well versed in revolutionary theory and practice, the era of neoliberalism has been accompanied by a global theory industry that is overwhelmingly anti-communist (with the minor exception of the clownish forms of metaphysical Marxism that cast a long shadow over the work of actual materialists). The so-called postmodernists, on the one hand, have been the grand sophists of neoliberal capitalism, well paid and promoted to peddle discursive pyrotechnics in the place of theories with actual transformative use-value. Contemporary critical theorists of the Frankfurt School lineage, on the other hand, have attempted to shore up anti-communist liberalism, sometimes with a piquant dose of radical democracy, as the dominant ideology of the "politicized" intelligentsia.

The driving force behind emancipatory struggles in the current conjuncture is not to be found in the Western intelligentsia, but in the working and toiling masses, as they continue to organize and build power. Many lessons have been learned from the Occupy Movement and the so-called Arab Spring, both of which were important insurgencies that had very mixed results. One of the most important lessons, which many knew prior to these uprisings, is that mass mobilization is a necessary but not a sufficient condition to win the struggle against the state and para-state forces driving the neoliberal project. Strong anti-capitalist parties and organizations are necessary to coordinate, sustain, and provide leadership to the mobilization of the masses. The good news is that these forms of organizing are on the rise, as we've seen as of late with the proletarian uprisings against the U.S. racist police state and many other insurgent movements around the world. Revolutionary socialism is very

---

[3] Robinson has provided a concise summary of Oxfam's recent study of global inequality: "the richest 1 percent of humanity in 2017 controlled more than half of the world's wealth; the top 30 percent of the population controlled more than 95 percent of global wealth, while the remaining 70 percent of the population had to make do with less than 5 percent of the world's resources." William I. Robinson, "Introduction: Who Rules the World?," in Peter Phillips, *Giants: The Global Power Elite* (New York: Seven Stories Press, 2018), 15.

[4] See "CoronaShock and Socialism," *Tricontinental*, July 8, 2020, https://www.thetricontinental.org/studies-3-coronashock-and-socialism/.

much on the agenda in the early twenty-first century, and intellectuals should heed its call to arms.[5]

Philippe Corcuff:

It's useful to begin by clarifying some of the terms in your questions in order to navigate the complex problems of a composite socio-political reality in motion, and about which we should not be too hasty in providing answers.[6]

First of all, the Gramscian notion of hegemony may have become a misleading commonplace of critical thought, warn out from overuse, at least in its dominant usages on the left (but also on the right and extreme right in France, as certain right-wing sectors took up the term at the end of the 1960s). Perry Anderson noted already in 1976 that "the price of so ecumenical an admiration" for Gramsci's writings was "ambiguity."[7] In this respect, I will follow the hypothesis formulated by Luc Boltanski concerning the notion of "dominant ideology": the latter is not to be understood as a set of ideas shared widely among a population, serving dominant interests, but, more modestly, as a way of attempting to "maintain a relative cohesion" between different more or less divergent sectors of the dominant classes.[8] However, notions of "dominant ideology" and "hegemony," as well as degraded forms of these, such as Noam Chomsky's notion of "propaganda" (since it includes conspiracist tones) implicitly harbor an intellectual arrogance vis-à-vis the supposed passivity of the amorphous "masses" on which "dominant ideas" would be imposed without any critical distance. In a little-known 1963 article, anticipating the studies of media reception against the assumptions of the "mass-mediologists" of the 1960s, Pierre Bourdieu and Jean-Claude Passeron lucidly noted:

> And why ignore the protections that the masses arm themselves with against the onslaught of mass media? . . . But intellectuals still find it hard to believe in defenses, that is to say, in the freedom of others, since they willingly claim a professional monopoly on freedom of thought.[9]

---

[5] According to a 2019 poll, 70 percent of millennials in the United States said they were likely to vote socialist, and 36 percent said they supported communism. Moreover, only one in two millennials said they had a favorable opinion of capitalism. See https://victimsofcommunism.org/annual-poll/2019-annual-poll/.

[6] All responses by Philippe Corcuff are my translations.—Ed.

[7] Perry Anderson, *The Antinomies of Antonio Gramsci* (New York: Verso, 2017), 29.

[8] Luc Boltanski, *On Critique: A Sociology of Emancipation*, trans. Gregory Elliot (Malden, MA: Polity Press, 2011), 41.

[9] Pierre Bourdieu and Jean-Claude Passeron, "Sociologues des mythologies et mythologies des sociologues," *Les Temps modernes* 211 (December 1963): 1009–1010.

The success of "hegemony" among critical intellectuals and the radical left is often revelatory of a characteristic of the period that still prevails today: while frequently disavowing avant-garde "Leninist" postures, the critical thinkers most engaged in public debates and organizations of the radical left have not finished with a miserabilist perspective on the dominated.

Regarding another aspect of your questions, is it fair to speak of the Yellow Vests in France as a movement "for economic and political change" (and what sort of economic and political change)? Yes, if we follow the overwhelming majority of critical intellectuals who have expressed themselves publicly on it, and most of the organizations of the radical left. But precisely these positions tell us less about the Yellow Vests themselves than about the double crisis of critical intellectuals and the radical left in France, ready at the slightest movement to mistake their desires for reality in order to try to escape from a quadruple ethical, political, strategic, and intellectual quagmire; or rather a growing difficulty in linking intellectual tools, ethical guidelines, political projects, and strategic blueprints that make it possible to mark out the "how" of emancipatory social and political transformation. Thus, critical thinkers and radical leftists tend to juxtapose, without really thinking about them, two opposing postures: intellectualist elitism (as we have seen with the frequent use of the notion of "hegemony") and demagogic conformism (in the case of the "Yellow Vests"). Between the two, a conceptual passageway can be established from the unassumed residues of a teleological philosophy of history: critical intellectuals and militants on the radical left implicitly constituting themselves as bearers of the "meaning of history."

Returning to the Yellow Vests movement, which emerged in October–November 2018, let us recall first of all that in the first weeks of their mobilization they were supported by the main political forces (the extreme right, the classical right, the moderate left, and the radical left), excluding the supporters of President Emmanuel Macron (who constitute a minority of voters), and that both the extreme right and the radical left continue to support the movement today. It should also be noted that opinion polls have shown that both participants and supporters of the Yellow Vests voted in greater numbers for the far-right list of the National Rally in the May 2019 European elections. As for their supposed anti-neoliberal orientation, it is not self-evident, considering the neoliberal themes that have been bannered about by mediatized figures of the movement such as "the reduction of compulsory contributions" and the stigmatization of "handouts" to the most marginalized sectors of the working classes. This movement should rather be seen as a composite social movement overmediatized in a confusionist context, which should have elicited neither such adherence on the left nor, conversely, unilateral reprobation, but rather an effort at critical understanding. For it has expressed demands for dignity scorned by neoliberal capitalism as well as aspirations for radical forms of democracy, but its social critique is often saturated with conspiracy theories and strongly fetishizes the nation, with, moreover, ultra-conservative minority components (xenophobia, anti-semitism—including the resurgence of the fantastical figure of "Rothschild" who has nourished an anti-semitic anti-capitalism in France since 1830—, homophobia...).

One can surmise that this social movement was significantly affected by the ultra-conservative and confusionist context in which it developed. I distinguish neoliberal conservatism from the ultra-conservatism active in France and in different countries of the world since the 2000s, marked by xenophobia (anti-migrant, Islamophobic, negrophobic, and/or anti-semitic), sexism, and homophobia within a nationalist framework; the two ideological poles have variable tensions and intersections depending on the situation and the individual who is speaking. The notion of confusionism identifies the development of rhetorical and ideological interferences between positions and themes that circulate between the extreme right, the right, the moderate left, and the radical left. The Yellow Vests could then be a harbinger: we may have to get used to social movements bringing together in the same processions people who yesterday would have joined those of the Popular Front in 1936, others who would have demonstrated on February 6, 1934 with the extreme right-wing leagues, and others, even more numerous, for whom the left/right cleavage and the symbolic distinction from the extreme right no longer make sense.

These two distinct plans—the dominant uses of the notion of "hegemony" and pronouncements on the "Yellow Vests"—introduce us indirectly to characteristic features of the period, in any case in the French context. First of all, they help us to better grasp a certain exhaustion, maybe even willful deception, of the most committed critical intellectuals and organizations of the radical left in the face of the ideological and political issues of a particularly composite moment, filled with contradictions, about which the expression "shifting hegemony" tells us something, as long as we are careful to avoid the most common simplifications contained in the notion of "hegemony." Their blindness can then be instructive to us in terms of what is not seen or badly seen, on the negative side as well as in terms of emancipatory possibilities. As far as the negative pole is concerned, what gets missed is the interplay between ultra-conservatism and confusionism, the left focusing its demonizing attention on neoliberalism in its parareligious quest for an absolute evil rather than trying to apprehend the interactions and tensions between a plurality of ills. As far as emancipatory potentialities are concerned, several years ago, through a survey of the reception in France of the American TV series Ally McBeal, I highlighted how anti-capitalists were inattentive to, even contemptuous of (because of the prejudice of the "generalized alienation of the masses by television"), the critical discrepancy between the values of capitalism and the dreaming and wounded intimacy of the television viewers of the series.[10]

This confused era is particularly conducive to a Benjamin-inspired melancholy, open to the future but without the progressive drum rolls of blissful optimism.

Daniel Benson:

I'd like to bring in Gabriel's thoughts on the Yellow Vests. Since you've also written on the movement—and were also highly critical of the intellectual response to it—, let's use this as the starting point for a larger discussion of how theoretical work needs to be recalibrated or reimagined today in order to become an active element of popular struggles rather than a sidelined spectator to them.

Could you speak, firstly, to the importance of the Yellow Vests uprising, its broader implications or shortcomings, in regard to the current French social and political context; and, secondly, how critical theory can productively respond to unforeseen events and popular movements more generally?

Gabriel Rockhill:

Before addressing these questions directly, I would like to briefly demarcate my approach from what appear to be the general intellectual coordinates of Philippe's response. While I do not know the extent to which he accepts these coordinates or might subjectively distinguish certain features of his work from them, his comments resonate very strongly with one of the most fashionable anti-Marxist discourses in France, which we can heuristically refer to as "the critique of critique." It has been developed in different and sometimes slightly opposing ways by figures as diverse as Michel Foucault, Pierre Bourdieu, Jacques Rancière, Jacques Derrida, and Bruno Latour. Relying on straw-person representations of historical materialism (and actually existing socialism), this strategy consists in attacking its supposed intellectual presuppositions as boorish and naïve, either since "times have changed" and our "old concepts" no longer work, or simply because things are more complex, heterogenous, singular, etc. In its most extreme forms, which I assume Philippe would reject, it is assumed that any claim to know anything useful about the social totality is somehow totalitarian, presumably because the words sound the same, particularly for academic beautiful souls content with

---

[10] Philippe Corcuff, "De l'imaginaire utopique dans les cultures ordinaires. Pistes à partir d'une enquête sur la série télévisée Ally McBeal," in *L'ordinaire et le politique*, ed. Claude Gautier and Sandra Laugier (Paris: PUF, 2006), 71–84.

being passively enchanted by the endless play of signifiers.[11] While having a lot of exchange-value in the symbolic economy of the global theory industry, this idealist intellectual practice has very little use-value.

Historical materialism is not an idealist science based on a set of dogmatic principles subject to purely theoretical refutation (this is a classic case of liberal intellectual projection). It is a concrete science with real use-value outside of the academy—and it is one of the major contributions that intellectuals have made to anti-systemic movements, to begin to address Daniel's second question first—because it strives to provide the most coherent and rigorous account of the social totality. Any refutation of its claims would need to provide a better scientific explanation, not simply repeat the hackneyed postmodern mantra that "things are more complicated" or patently false claims like "the working class no longer exists" or "all revolutions fail."[12] Moreover, unlike the doctrinaire schools developed around figures like Foucault, Derrida, and others, historical materialism is a dynamic and collective science that continues to refine itself rather than simply indulge in cults of personality and arguments from authority as an ersatz for analysis.

In this regard, I have been advocating for a multiscalar methodology, which recognizes that conceptual and discursive mappings, when they are rooted in materialist analysis, are not "misrepresentations." They are concrete abstractions in the precise sense that they are at once moored in the empirical world and are deliberate changes in scale that abstract from its immediacy in order to foster a different—and more useful—apprehension of it. If every blade of grass were perfectly depicted to scale on a road map, for instance,

---

[11] In a classy performance of petty-bourgeois intellectuality, Derrida went so far as to proclaim that the signifier "social class" is meaningless for him: "I cannot construct finished or plausible sentences using the expression social class. I don't really know what social class means." Derrida Negotiations: Interventions and Interviews, 1971–2001, ed. and trans. Elizabeth Rottenberg (Stanford: Stanford University Press, 2002), 170). In this exchange, he suggests that his subjective experience as a palavering intellectual would of necessity coalesce with objective reality, viz. social class has no meaning. Although he might not be able to construct finished sentences with this expression, however, others certainly can, particularly when it comes to analyzing the relationship between his own social class and statements such as these.

[12] To take but one glaring example of this specific "critique of critique," Gilles Deleuze, who had pushed back against Foucault's support for the rabid anti-Marxist *Nouveaux Philosophes*, later attempted to outflank Foucault to the right by universalizing André Glucksmann's reactionary position on the Russian Revolution. After a rambling series of baseless and incoherent claims about the history of bourgeois and proletarian revolutions (and non-revolutions), Deleuze indignantly proclaimed: "All revolutions fail [*foirent*]. Everyone knows it: we pretend to rediscover it here [with the writings of Glucksmann and Furet]. You have to be a complete idiot [*débile*]!" "Gilles Deleuze: Qu'est-ce qu'être de gauche?," *Œuvres ouvertes*, accessed January 25, 2021, https://www.oeuvresouvertes.net/spip.php?article910 (my translation). I have provided a detailed critique of Foucault's anti-Marxism, including his peremptory condemnation of the entire socialist tradition, in Gabriel Rockhill, "Foucault: The Faux Radical," *The Philosophical Salon*, October 12, 2020, http://thephilosophicalsalon.com/foucault-the-faux-radical/.

you would have a lot of trouble navigating because you would, in effect, be doing so without a map. By scaling out from the grass in order to apprehend the relationships between roads, you are not "misrepresenting" the grass, but rather changing the scale of abstraction in order to maximize its use-value. A multiscalar materialist analysis allows us to develop different levels of concrete abstraction in order to avoid the false binary of either "totalitarian thinking" or pseudo-ethical, petty-bourgeois "respect for differences" (in which nothing concrete could ever be said because it would be an "oversimplification"). I have also attempted to develop a multi-agential analysis that foregrounds all of the complex forms of agency—including economic forces, state institutions, the media and culture industries, technologies, social agents, etc.—operative in any conjuncture. As Lenin explained, "the actual unfolding of the class struggle is infinitely richer than the most advanced theory."[13] One of the tasks of materialist analysis is to develop the most coherent and systemic account of all of these forces, drawing up conceptual maps at different scales that have real use-value, while simultaneously recognizing that these are heuristic abstractions open to revision based on new data. In this regard, intellectuals can play—and have sometimes played—the important role of serving as concrete cartographers of class struggle.

In the case of the Yellow Vests, to pivot to Daniel's first question, it is helpful to distinguish between different scales of analysis, such as the conjunctural, the structural, and the systemic. We know that rising fuel prices and the high cost of living were important conjunctural sparks for the movement, and it is true that a wide array of ideological positions were present, particularly at the beginning. Structurally, however, it is an—ideologically mediated—response to decades of neoliberalization and the destruction of the materialist basis for hegemony that I was discussing earlier. It has also been an attempt, through the creative labor power of the masses, to develop innovative modes of struggle as a response to the relative failures of the square movements as well as some of the workers' organizations and parties in France. A militant research collective I'm involved with, Radical Education Department (RED), developed a detailed list of these tactics as a contribution to the struggle and a form of international solidarity.[14] Unfortunately, but unsurprisingly, a significant portion of the French intelligentsia, including

---

[13] Cited in Bay Area Socialist Organizing Committee, "Confronting Reality/Learning from the History of Our Movement," accessed December 23, 2020 https://www.marxists.org/history/erol/ncm-7/basoc/ch-5.htm. In *"Left-Wing" Communism: An Infantile Disorder*, Lenin writes: "History generally, and the history of revolutions in particular, is always richer in content, more varied, more many sided, more lively and 'subtle' than even the best parties and the most class-conscious vanguards of the most advanced classes imagine." (Peking: Foreign Languages Press, 1970), 82.

[14] See "Ten Lesson from the Yellow Vests," *RED*, December 28, 2018, https://radicaleducationdepartment.com/2018/12/28/ten-lessons-from-the-yellow-vests-ed/.

self-stylized radicals, stood on the sidelines and haughtily ridiculed the movement rather than getting involved in order to use their agency to try and push it in what they considered to be the optimal direction.[15]

If we scale out and relate the Yellow Vests' fight back against the structural phase of capitalist accumulation known as neoliberalism to the deeper history of class struggle, some of its shortcomings become readily apparent. While it has been able to mobilize the masses around a few significant economic and political issues, and it has demonstrated the insurgent courage of the dispossessed to confront the extremely repressive state apparatus of neoliberal managers like Macron, there has not yet been a clear and centralized form of leadership that could help guide the masses to victory. When we look back at the last 100 years or so of global class struggle, it should be clear that mass mobilization without sustained leadership—which listens and responds to the needs of the masses, but also struggles against reactionary ideologies—is like a ship without a rudder. It can be a very powerful force, but it is easily batted about by counter-insurgent elements and has trouble staying course.

If you are going to fight and win against the disciplined and overfunded armies of the capitalist ruling class, you need well-coordinated organizations of the working masses. At the level of materialist analysis, there should be nothing surprising about this. However, a rampant anti-party and anti-leadership ideology, as well as false historical narratives about the supposed failure of socialism, has incessantly denigrated the organized fight back as "authoritarian," precisely because it has proven to be the most successful tactic historically. We need to study the past and ask ourselves very basic questions like: How did the Vietnamese defeat the most powerful imperialist army in the world? Why did the Cuban Revolution succeed against all odds? How did Thomas Sankara wrest control of a structurally underdeveloped country from the death grip of French colonialism? Was it because they conformed to a defeatist principle disguised as a moral dictate, which ultimately serves the interests of the capitalist ruling class, namely that any opposition to the armies of capitalism needs to be bereft of leadership, discipline, hierarchy, and centralized organization?

---

[15] See Gabriel Rockhill, "The Failure of the French Intelligentsia? Intellectuals and Uprisings in the Case of the Yellow Vests," *The Philosophical Salon*, April 29, 2019, http://thephilosophicalsalon.com/the-failure-of-the-french-intelligentsia-intellectuals-and-uprisings-in-the-case-of-the-yellow-vests/.

POLITICAL PARTIES AND EMANCIPATORY ORGANIZATION

The discussion turns to the often neglected question among critical theorists of strategy and organization. Philippe Corcuff's more eclectic theoretical constellation contrasts with Gabriel Rockhill's historical materialist approach, but both thinkers are firmly committed to the need to organize to achieve any lasting social and political transformation.

Daniel Benson:

My next question is related precisely to political organizing today, since both of your responses touched on it. Addressing the issue of strategy and organization head on will serve to bring into sharp relief the divergences visible in your respective analyses above, but also to work toward overcoming the deep-seated defeatism among many critical theorists who have all but abandoned the terrain of practical politics.[16]

In the context of societies that have been deeply depoliticized by decades of neoliberalism in many countries of the world, how can we re-establish an anti-capitalist, anti-imperialist, feminist, and anti-racist internationalism that was so vital in fueling emancipatory struggles in the past? How to avoid the sectarianism that has so often marginalized leftist parties, where irrelevance is the price to pay for ideological purity; or, conversely, how to avoid the dangers associated with a big tent approach to party organization, which all too often involves capitulating to meager capitalist reforms in exchange for a few seats in parliament?

Philippe Corcuff:

In order to formulate some possible responses to this question, it's worth situating my atypical political career in relation to other French critical theorists. Since 1976, at the age of 16, I have been a member of a series of political organizations, leading me, contrary to the dominant tendency of my generation and of the previous generation of 1968, to move more and more to the left and remain in continuous contact with concrete militant practices. I began in a Marxist current of the Socialist Party, harboring illusions about the possibility of a revolutionary transformation of social democracy. From

---

[16] There have been many critiques of the distance between critical theory and concrete political engagement, from Perry Anderson's classic *Considerations on Western Marxism* (New York: Verso, 1987), to more recently Razmig Keucheyan, *Left Hemisphere: Mapping Contemporary Theory*, trans. Gregory Elliott (New York: Verso, 2014) or Stathis Kouvélakis, *La Critique défaite: émergence et domestication de la théorie critique* (Paris: Amsterdam, 2019).

the end of the 1990s to the beginning of the 2000s, I was a militant of the Trotskyist Revolutionary Communist League (now the New Anticapitalist Party), along with the great political and intellectual figure and friend, the late Daniel Bensaïd. Although no longer strictly speaking a "Marxist," I felt that it was here that the most promising dynamics of the radical left were to be found. Since 2013, dissatisfied with the organizational possibilities of the moment, I have taken "refuge" in an old and very small organization: the Anarchist Federation.

Contact with Pierre Bourdieu's "post-Marxist" critical sociology led me to break with an exclusively Marxist identity in the mid-1980s. Since then, I have felt close to Maurice Merleau-Ponty's pioneering pronouncement on Marxism, written in 1960: "By placing Marxism in the order of *secondary truth*, recent experience gives Marxists a new posture and almost a new method, which make it useless to call them into court."[17] That's why I continue to defend Marxian[18] and Marxist elements (I'm thinking in particular of the anti-Leninist approach to revolutionary processes of Rosa Luxemburg, including the place and form of political organizations) for a pluralist and hybrid *emancipatory left* of the future. In this galaxy, the anarchist tradition as well as feminist, anti-racist, anti-colonial, queer, or intersectional critiques have their place, as well as cross-fertilizations between the theoretical contributions of John Dewey, Hannah Arendt, Emmanuel Levinas, Maurice Merleau-Ponty, Frantz Fanon, Michel Foucault, Edouard Glissant, Pierre Bourdieu, Jacques Rancière, Luc Boltanski, Nancy Fraser, Axel Honneth, and Judith Butler. It's a galaxy open to historical contingencies and periodic redefinitions in the face of the new, in search of a global vision that rejects both nostalgia for the totalities of yesteryear and the vain dissipation of meaning from postmodernist "deconstructors."[19] I could here metaphorically follow Harry Bosch, Michael Connelly's hero: "Bosch knew that in a murder case, or in any case, for that matter, there were always unanswered questions."[20]

In this perspective, I reject the "anti-organizational" political prejudices that all too often accompany the double crisis currently confronting the radical left and critical intellectuals, especially in France. And I agree with Gabriel in this respect. And, beyond that, as far as critical intellectuals more specifically are concerned, we are witnessing a crisis of the linkages between critical thought and political praxis, as Daniel's question rightly points out. In

---

[17] Maurice Merleau-Ponty, *Signs*, trans. Richard C. McCleary (Evanston, IL: Northwestern University Press, 1964), 9.
[18] See Philippe Corcuff, *Marx XXIᵉ siècle* (Paris: Textuel, 2012).
[19] See Philippe Corcuff, *Où est passée la critique sociale?* (Paris: La Découverte, 2014).
[20] Michael Connelly, chap. 39 in *The Night Fire* (New York: Little, Brown and Company, 2019).

the case of the "Yellow Vests," for example, it wasn't a lack of support for the movement that was the main problem for me—the overwhelming majority of critical intellectuals who have spoken publicly on the movement have even fully supported it, unlike me for the reasons I indicated earlier—; rather, it was both the uncritical character of this support, avoiding the troubling and ambivalent aspects that were also part of it, and a lack of any substantive, practical implication in it, thus extending a benevolent but ultimately paternalistic intellectualism.[21]

Three types of spaces seem to me to be important to explore in order to overcome the partial paralysis of our time. First of all, we should participate in developing spaces of *democratic intellectuality*, hybrid spaces that assume the tensions between the demands of "the equality between any speaking being with every other," according to Rancière's radically democratic presupposition, and those of professional intellectual work (in the social sciences, philosophy, critical theory...), with their specific competencies and rigor. We've sketched out something like this, though on a scale that is still far too microscopic, beginning in June 2013 with the founding of a seminar for activist and libertarian research called ETAPE (Explorations Théoriques Anarchistes Pragmatistes pour l'Emancipation) and its associated website Grand Angle,[22] which brings together activists, academics, and "hybrids" like me. Next, we should invent new political organizations that are not political parties. The "party" form has historically been far too calibrated to the modern nation-state, between the statism of its functioning and its constrained imaginary by national borders. And yet we need organized common spaces, endowed with a certain stability over time, able to counteract the effects of neoliberal zapping on struggles by creating a critical memory of past defeats and advances, and by elaborating strategic compasses that can draw bridges between the short, medium and long term toward desired socio-political transformations. Finally, we should explore the reconstruction of a cosmopolitics based on intercultural dialogue at the local level, while at the same time forging links between associations, unions, local political groups, etc. around the world. This also means being involved in solidarity struggles with migrants wherever we live. On each of these three levels, the existing political organizations of the radical left and the anarchist milieu in France are largely missing, while critical intellectuals remain immured in their bubbles and their essentially discursive practices. It is a major task of intellectual and

---

[21] For a detailed analysis, see Philippe Corcuff, "Les 'gilets jaunes': un mouvement social composite surmédiatisé en contexte confusionniste," chap. 6 in *La grande confusion. Comment l'extrême droite gagne la bataille des idées* (Paris: Textuel, 2021), 309–51.

[22] http://www.grand-angle-libertaire.net/.

organizational reconstruction that lies ahead of us, supported by real expectations but facing considerable resistance as well.

Gabriel Rockhill:

I agree with Philippe that the disconnect between "critical theory" and transformative political practice is one of the fundamental problems with the professional intelligentsia. When it is politicized in some way, it largely operates within the parameters of "radical" liberal ideology, even in the case of some self-declared socialists and anarchists (such as many of the authors cited by Philippe). The neoliberal era, particularly within the Euro-American world, has been a veritable dark age for communist consciousness. It followed on the heels of decades of anti-communist purges and a partially clandestine campaign to destabilize and attempt to overthrow every socialist country in the world, and it continued or intensified many of these counter-insurgent tactics of the capitalist ruling class, while shattering workers' organizations and important sites of political agitation through the globalization of production chains. When Eastern Europe and the Soviet Union collapsed, many—including those on the anti-capitalist left—came to accept the neoliberal mantra that "socialism failed" or "never worked."

What this overlooks is the fact that socialism did work for literally millions of people, who had—or do have, in the case of actually existing socialist or socialistically oriented countries—access to housing, healthcare, education, and employment in a much more egalitarian manner than in capitalist countries.[23] It worked for the masses of humanity, not just for the ruling elite, and that's of course why the idea that it "didn't work" has been peddled so forcefully by the professional managerial class working for the bourgeoisie. If we dig deeper into this history, as I have done for one of my current book projects that examines the history of the U.S. national security state, we learn that

---

[23] Among the most rigorous assessments of the successes of socialism, which include some important criticisms and contextualization, see Minqi Li, "The 21st Century: Is There an Alternative (to Socialism)?" *Science & Society* 77, no. 1 (January 2013): 10–43; Vicente Navarro, "Has Socialism Failed? An Analysis of Health Indicators under Capitalism and Socialism," *Science & Society* 57, no. 1 (spring 1993): 6–30; and Michael Parenti, "Reflections on the Overthrow of Communism" (recorded lecture), accessed on January 20, 2021 https://archive.org/details/ReflectionOnTheOverthrowOfCommunismNLSubtitlesDutch. Parenti provides one of the best summaries of the most rigorous research on the actual history of socialism: "To say that "socialism doesn't work" is to overlook the fact that it did. In Eastern Europe, Russia, China, Mongolia, North Korea, and Cuba, revolutionary communism created a life for the mass of people that was far better than the wretched existence they had endured under feudal lords, military bosses, foreign colonizers, and Western capitalists. The end result was a dramatic improvement in living conditions for hundreds of millions of people on a scale never before or since witnessed in history." Michael Parenti, *Blackshirts & Reds: Rational Fascism and the Overthrow of Communism* (San Francisco: City Lights Publishers, 1997), 85.

capitalist countries and their security forces have been tirelessly deploying every dirty trick imaginable to make it look like socialism doesn't work (and ultimately destroy it in the process). This includes brutal imperialist wars and deadly economic blockades, of course, but it also involves clandestine terrorist campaigns, sabotage, targeted assassinations, biological and chemical warfare, election rigging, diplomatic isolation, stultifying propaganda campaigns, and much more.[24] The principal reason why socialist countries have had to maintain a strong state—which has led to the disingenuous portrayal of them as "authoritarian"—is precisely in order to mitigate the systematic economic and military warfare being waged against them by capitalist states and their intelligence services.[25] As Ernesto Che Guevara—who was later assassinated after being captured in a global Central Intelligence Agency (CIA) manhunt—poignantly explained regarding Cuba: "our two principal problems are: imperialism and imperialism."[26] These massive and constant counter-revolutionary operations would not be necessary if the threat of socialism wasn't real, or if it organically collapsed due to its own internal logic.

This means, then, that we already have a deep and ongoing revolutionary socialist tradition to learn from and draw on for the revitalization of anti-capitalist, anti-imperialist, feminist, and anti-racist internationalism in the current moment. Part of the labor of organizing, at least in the regions of the world where my activism is concentrated—the United States and, more tangentially, France—is to tap into this tradition and mine it for all of its rich resources in order to bring it to bear on the present, while also drawing on

---

[24] William Blum has provided the most in-depth overview of the global war on communism, which he summarizes as follows: "Every socialist experiment of any significance in the twentieth century—without exception—has either been crushed, overthrown, or invaded, or corrupted, perverted, subverted, or destabilized, or otherwise had life made impossible for it, by the United States. Not one socialist government or movement [. . .] was permitted to rise or fall solely on its own merits. [. . .] It's as if the Wright brothers' first experiments with flying machines all failed because the automobile interests sabotaged each test flight. And then the good and god-fearing folk of the world looked upon this, took notice of the consequences, nodded their collective heads wisely, and intoned solemnly: Man shall never fly." *Killing Hope: US Military and CIA Interventions since World War II* (London: Zed Books, 2014), 20.

[25] As V.I. Lenin wrote during the ongoing imperialist invasion of the Soviet Union by fourteen capitalist countries, in order to "strangle the Bolshevik baby in its crib" according to Winston Churchill: "Certainly, almost everyone now realizes that the Bolsheviks could not have maintained themselves in power for two and a half months, let alone two and a half years, unless the strictest, truly iron discipline had prevailed in our party, and unless the latter had been rendered the fullest and unreserved support of the whole mass of the working class . . . The dictatorship of the proletariat is a most determined and most ruthless war waged by the new class against a *more powerful* enemy, the bourgeoisie." *"Left-Wing" Communism*, 4.

[26] This statement was given in an interview on *ABC News*, cited on the Twitter account @Gabrielgiussi, May 23, 2020, accessed January 20, 2021, https://twitter.com/gabrielgiussi/status/1264278131642335236?s=20.

the heritage of historical materialism to develop new tools of analysis and tactics for activism.

The short answer to Daniel's question, then, is that we need to build a revolutionary socialist movement for our historical moment, while also developing organs of leadership that can help guide the movement to victory. And, make no mistake about it: this is exactly what we are doing, and the movement has been growing at a record pace as of late. To do this successfully does take time, however, particularly given the reactionary political culture that dominates the United States and much of Western Europe. Each phase of this process has its own trials and tribulations, and it can require different tactics, as well as shifting allegiances. If A is the current state of the American Empire in decline as the guard dog of global capitalism, and Z is communism, then there is no way of going from A to Z other than working through the alphabet in a step-by-step fashion, even if there are moments of intensification when several steps might be moved through more quickly. Moreover, each step in this process is itself multifaceted and requires different types of work. In my own case, I have been deeply involved in political education, the development of educational and cultural counter-institutions, and revolutionary socialist organizing. More specifically, I founded the Critical Theory Workshop/Atelier de Théorie Critique years ago as a counter-hegemonic educational institution that offers courses and workshops on the international traditions of revolutionary socialism, and I was one of the founders of RED, a Marxist militant research collective. I am also an activist with the Philadelphia Liberation Center and a member of the Party for Socialism and Liberation, both of which connect local grassroots community organizing to the international struggle against capitalism.

I agree with Daniel about the dangerous bullhorns of ideological purity and big tent approaches. The former has always been one of the pitfalls of certain intellectual responses to the crises of capitalism. It can be found in many Trotskyist and anarchist circles, and radical liberals are usually "right" about everything because they're not actually involved in doing anything other than condescendingly occupying the cutting edge of woke consensualism. The big tent approach tends to pitch to the lowest common denominator, meaning indoctrinated subjects, without actually taking on the difficult and gradual labor of real political education. It also usually assumes that the ruling class will—miraculously—allow itself to be voted out of power if we can just get enough people under the same tent. Social democrats generally prefer this approach, and we've seen its consequences spelled out yet again with Sanders' presidential campaigns (even though he represents a rightward leaning, Yankee version of social democracy). In spite of the fact that many believed that a self-stylized progressive candidate could work through the Democratic Party and win, it is important to recognize that, from the point of view of the ruling class, Sanders' primary social function has been a pressure release valve: he allowed the youth and certain progressives to get excited about "real change" within the system, helped funnel all of their political energies and money into the graveyard of the Democratic Party, and then delivered the goods by ultimately lining up on the party position and supporting neoliberal reactionaries, leaving his base in disarray.

To avoid sectarianism, however, those who seek to fight and win against the capitalist world system can and should form tactical alliances with Trotskyists, anarchists, social democrats, and even liberals at times. Each stage of the struggle has different features, and tactical support for the Sanders campaigns, without an overinvestment in electoral politics, is a perfectly coherent position for communists. After all, his campaigns did help make socialism an acceptable word in the United States, and his positions on issues like healthcare, education, wages, and the environment were generally more progressive than the other capitalist candidates. However—and this is a very important point for revolutionary Marxists—tactics should never to be confused with strategy. At the end of the day, it is essential to recognize that we need coordinated workers' organizations and revolutionary party leadership to wrest control of the means of production from the ruling class. The strategies proposed by these other orientations have historically proven themselves to be insufficient, unrealistic, or ideologically confused, in spite of the fact that they have, at times, made important contributions to the struggle for a socialist future. If the revolutionary Marxist tradition is superior, this is not because it simply has the "right line" in some dogmatic or abstract, theoretical sense. It is, on the contrary, because it is the tradition that has constantly been putting its ideas to the test of material practice, learning from practical challenges and adjusting its theoretical framework accordingly, and proving time and again its concrete ability to fight and make real gains in the ongoing struggle to defeat capitalism before it completely destroys life as we know it on planet Earth.[27]

REVOLUTIONARY INTERNATIONALISM TOWARD AN EMANCIPATORY HORIZON

The concluding section of the dialogue addresses the need for a revolutionary perspective in order to avoid the pitfalls of a nation-state-centered approach to emancipation. Philippe Corcuff proposes rethinking the revolutionary/

---

[27] Mao Tse-tung provided one of the most cogent accounts of Marxism's materialist epistemology in "On Practice," in *Collected Writings of Chairman Mao*, vol. 3, *On Policy, Practice and Contradiction*, ed. Shawn Conners (El Paso, TX: El Paso Norte Press, 2009).

reformist dichotomy, noting the failures of previous socialist regimes to promote emancipation, the gendered language of revolutionary action, and the trap of identity politics. Gabriel Rockhill is also attentive to the dangers of identity politics, in particular as it is used to divide the global working classes. However, he is committed to positively re-evaluating previous and current socialist experiments as resources for any revolutionary internationalism today.

Daniel Benson:

My last question is on revolution. Given the continued unrest following the 2008 financial crisis, the notion of revolution has a newfound currency in intellectual debate as well as in mainstream political culture more generally: from Bernie Sanders' call for a "political revolution" in the United States to Emmanuel Macron's autobiography entitled none other than *Revolution*.[28] Ironically, Sanders' vision of revolution aimed to bolster the decrepit U.S. welfare state, whereas Macron's revolution has been one of pure neoliberalism seeking to dismantle the French welfare state. Of course, both evocations of "revolution" are limited to the ballot box, and their political horizon remains squarely in a statist imaginary, severely curtailing emancipatory possibilities.

I would like to ask you to elaborate on your conceptions of revolutionary transformation, since you both allude to it in your last responses. How might a renewed perspective on or reconceptualization of revolution provide current social movements and political organizations with an expanded imaginary beyond the nation-state and its associated exclusions and hierarchies?

Philippe Corcuff:

First of all, reinventing emancipation—attentive to the challenges of the beginning of the twenty-first century, after the authoritarian excesses of Bolshevism and the totalitarian radicalization brought about by Stalinism in the twentieth century—implies re-examining categories such as the "revolutionary"/"reformist" dichotomy that gradually imposed itself after the Revolution of 1917. This opposition initially concerned the methods needed to achieve a social revolution: were dominant representative institutions to be used, or was an insurrectionist logic needed to subvert them? But neither "the reformists" nor "the revolutionaries" achieved a lasting social revolution from capitalism based on emancipatory principles. And the social

---

[28] Emmanuel Macron, *Revolution*, trans. Jonathan Goldberg and Juliette Scott (Carlton: Scribe Publications, 2017).

democratic "reformists" gradually abandoned any postcapitalist horizon for their actions and ended up joining the neoliberal counter-revolution from the 1980s onward. I remain revolutionary insofar as I maintain the objective of a social revolution aimed at building a non-capitalist society and, beyond that, one that challenges all forms of domination; but I'm not revolutionary in the post-1917 strategic sense, according to which there would be clear methods leading to that revolution.

I am rather a perplexed revolutionary from this point of view. Such perplexity does not mean fatalism, and an ethic of curiosity orients me toward the reconstruction of strategic guideposts to maintain openings toward a revolutionary horizon. The paths taken by John Holloway in his book *Crack Capitalism*[29] appear useful to mention here, as they help us decant the old recipes that have had so little success up to now. The strategy of "cracks" that he outlines does not start from the solidity of the capitalist wall, as it does for those who make the seizure of state power—whether by "revolutionary" or "reformist" directives—the heart of the process; rather, it begins with the capacities of the oppressed to bring out the frailties and contradictions of the wall.

However, we should be more attentive than Holloway is to the constitution of organized and stabilized spaces for the coordination of sites of struggle and alternative experimentations. In this perspective, we must be aware that while we do not need "directives" per se, because of the oligarchic tendencies they harbor, we cannot do without active minorities, since the vast majority of the masses are rarely in a state of coordinated, emancipatory self-activity. To this end, the Russian anarchist revolutionary Volin, in his libertarian critique of Bolshevik authoritarianism after October 1917, suggestively left a place to the organizing spirit of the "collaborators" of the masses in order to "help" them in their dynamic of self-organization.[30] Thus, active minorities *with* the masses, not in front of them or above them!

Avoiding the statism and the "directives" of classical "revolutionary" strategies, without dodging the inevitable tensions between active minorities and the majority of the oppressed, constitutes an initial step forward that could be deepened by a critique of the strategic machismo that has often been associated with revolutionary language. For the gendered nature of the military-inspired vocabulary that has nourished the strategic imaginaries of the left is obvious: "the rise of class struggle," "class warfare," "conquest," "relations of force" (an omnipresent expression), "accumulating forces," "combat," "confrontation," "overthrow," and so on. This vocabulary fully resonates with the values that are socially and historically constituted in our societies as

---

[29] John Holloway, *Crack Capitalism* (London: Pluto Press, 2010).
[30] Voline, *La Révolution inconnue. Russie 1917-1921* (Paris: Les Amis de Voline, 1947).

belonging to a dominant definition of the "masculine." Revolutionary action seems above all to want to show that "we have balls," and such a politics has repressed what other metaphors—those socio-historically constituted in a dominant way as "feminine," and therefore dominated—could tell us about other possible relationships to emancipatory politics. Such criticism is not an invitation to abandon the strategic vocabulary of "relations of force" and "combat," but to blend it with the words of imagination, exploration, trial and error, experimentation and creation, thus enlarging the mental space for thinking strategy in emancipatory politics. To sow "gender trouble" in such a way, in line with Judith Butler's destabilizing feminism, would lead, by ricochet, to the sowing of trouble in the dominant definitions of politics, and thus also of revolutionary politics.

Some of the components to be re-evaluated in emancipatory discourses and practices include the experimental logics already present in the practical prefigurations of localized alternatives to capitalism and domination, which serve both to stimulate political imaginaries against fatalistic dead ends and to provide concreteness to the hopes they carry. It is at this point that the radically democratic pragmatist politics of John Dewey[31] can join the processual and organic vision of revolution (whereby the masses learn from their own mistakes) defended by Rosa Luxemburg against the mechanistic tendencies of Leninism.[32] This pragmatist component is already alive and well at the local level in the United States, whereas in France it has historically been greatly restricted by the political centralization of Paris.

Opting for the strategy of self-emancipation by the subaltern masses themselves (lucid about the oligarchic pitfalls of the left over the course of the twentieth century) must not, however, lead us to a simplistic fetishization of the masses as the sole bearers of individual and collective emancipation. The historian Marc Ferro has pointed out in the case of the Russian Revolution a double mythology among the ranks of emancipatory forces: the Leninist legend, which disregards the "Bolshevik absolutism" that gradually monopolized power by eliminating other revolutionary organizations; and the anarchist legend that disregards the "popular absolutism" which in some soviets suppressed pluralism even without the presence of Bolshevik militants.[33] This historical observation should lead us to reassess political liberalism as one of the components of an emancipatory constellation. Socialists such as

---

[31] See John Dewey, *The Public and Its Problems*, ed. Melvin L. Rogers (University Park, PA: Pennsylvania State University Press, 2012).

[32] See Rosa Luxemburg, "Organizational Questions of Russian Social Democracy," in *The Rosa Luxemburg Reader*, ed. Peter Hudis and Kevin B. Anderson (New York: Monthly Review Press, 2004), 248–65.

[33] Marc Ferro, *Des soviets au communisme bureaucratique: les mécanismes d'une subversion* (Paris: Gallimard/Julliard, 1980).

Proudhon, Marx, Bakunin, or Rosa Luxemburg critically appropriated the liberal heritage, notably by getting rid of its overly monadic approach to the individual by reintegrating them into social relations. And the liberal attention to political pluralism, individual rights, and the reciprocal limitation of powers (following Montesquieu) also proves to be an asset in the struggles against the current authoritarian tendencies of economic neoliberalism.

The last route for rethinking revolutionary processes is to become aware of the risks of identitarian fetishization that arose out of "identity politics" at the end of the twentieth century, particularly in the United States. There is the danger of moving from the legitimate search for identitarian reference points for individuals and subordinate groups to the *inversion* of the dominant discourse into an *identitarianism* that fixes individuals and groups into a single, closed identity under the watchful eye of often sectarian gatekeepers. This impedes the strategic possibilities opened up by intersectional thinking in the search for common spaces able to ground specific and autonomous struggles, and instead fragments subaltern groups into non-communicating identities. There are even certain uses of intersectionality that paradoxically favor the promotion of increasingly smaller self-sustaining identities, as if in an infinite dissipation... Against such temptations, new emancipatory strategies should start from the plural, shifting, hybrid and open character of individual and collective identities. This is where Emmanuel Levinas' philosophy of "getting out of being"[34] joins the creolization of identity open to the *Whole-World* elaborated by the West Indian poet Edouard Glissant.[35]

The renewal of revolutionary strategies therefore also requires a renewal of the words to say them, but not only, because if such paths are not confronted with praxis, they will be reduced to discourse with little effect on the world: something that intellectual circles are all too comfortable to remain doing.

Gabriel Rockhill:

Internationalism is a hallmark of the revolutionary Marxist tradition. It recognizes nationalist—as well as culturalist—imaginaries and geographies as formidable weapons in the hands of the ruling class, which it uses to divide and conquer the global working class.[36] The same is true regarding racialization,

---

[34] See Emmanuel Levinas, *On Escape*, trans. Bettina Bergo (Stanford: Stanford University Press, 2003).

[35] See Edouard Glissant, *Treatise on the Whole-World*, trans. Celia Britton (Liverpool: Liverpool University Press, 2020).

[36] The Third International made a major contribution in this regard. As Ho Chi Minh pointed out on numerous occasions: "Lenin was the first to realize and assess the full importance of drawing the colonial peoples into the revolutionary movement. He was the first to point out that, without the participation of the colonial peoples, the socialist revolution could not come about." Ho Chi Minh, *Selected Writings (1920-1969)* (Honolulu, Hawaii: University Press of the Pacific, 2001), 37.

as well as gender and sexual oppression, and this is one of the reasons why liberal identity politics has been such a powerful tool for splintering the left in the neoliberal era, siloing it into distinct battles for representation that are unmoored from class struggle. The internationalist perspective of the revolutionary socialist tradition therefore needs to be recognized for what it is: a powerful antidote to the ideological divisions of the left and the proletariat (which take on concrete material forms), as well as a theoretical and practical framework for understanding how phenomena like nationality, race, gender, and sexuality are constructed and weaponized in specific ways within the social totality of global capitalism.

Regarding the question of revolution, there is no fixed blueprint because the complexity and dynamism of the social world are irreducible to dogmatic theoretical formulas. However, there are road maps that have been developed in the past, in very distinct situations (from the Soviet Union to China, Cuba, Vietnam, Burkina Faso, and beyond), and there is much to learn from them. It is here, moreover, that we should call out for what it is the petty-bourgeois reflex of crying foul as soon as a revolution succeeds in pushing back imperialism and capitalism, thereby browbeating onlookers into the reactionary position that revolutionary social change is "authoritarian" any time it gets organized enough to fight and win. This sidelined politics is content to continue to theoretically criticize the capitalist system from the inside—and it is not surprising that it is often rooted in relatively comfortable class positions within this very system—while never accepting the high stakes of the practical commitment necessary to make real, fundamental change. The practical perpetuation of capitalism thereby seamlessly merges with its ongoing theoretical critique, in a parasitic relationship that is common in certain Trotskyist and anarchist circles.[37]

In relation to these positions, we should fearlessly engage in an examination of what it really means, at a practical level, to struggle to the point of victory against the best equipped and overfunded armies in the world: those of the capitalist ruling class. This simply is not possible by "thinking otherwise," developing some idiosyncratic idea about social change based on an amalgamation of heteroclite intellectual references, or doing purely interstitial work within the capitalist system. By tapping into and learning from the history of actual social revolutions, not hollow appeals to "what needs

---

[37] The anti-capitalism of Trotskyists and most anarchists sometimes means that they can be significant allies in the negative project of criticizing capitalist social relations, particularly when compared to liberals. However, they fall short when it comes to the positive project, meaning the practical task of developing, in the here and now of *this* concrete world, forms of socialism that can successfully defend themselves against the imperial armies of capital. In this regard, there is room for both unity and division with them—and hence ongoing class struggle—from the point of view of revolutionary socialists.

to be done," we can draw on these resources—in a collective endeavor that depends on a process of constant verification, and subsequent modification, through practice—to produce new road maps to revolution for our current conjuncture.[38]

Based on my work with a number of organizations, here are a few things that, in my opinion, would need to be taken into account for these road maps in the case of the United States, where I'm based. To begin with, the restructuring of the capitalist economy has had a very significant impact on social organization and the very coordinates of activism. The globalization of production chains, the digitalization and financialization of the economy, and the expansion of the service and distribution sectors have all led to a substantial reconfiguration of the working class within the United States. One of the challenges of organizing in this context is how to build real proletarian power through anti-capitalist parties and organizations that bring a fragmented working class together around a common project of social transformation, and which provide the focused leadership and cadre training necessary for a vanguard that is accountable to—and respected by—the working masses. Secondly, the expansion of forced immigration and the increased surplussing of certain sectors of humanity, which are no longer primarily targeted for wage labor, have shifted some of the logic of capitalist accumulation.[39] Finding ways of organizing the global surplus population is therefore of the utmost importance, which requires forging deeper ties with the populations caught in the dragnet of the prison-industrial complex, as well as with immigrants and the lumpenproletariat more generally. Thirdly, many of the unions have been taken over by years of CIA infiltration, financial manipulation, and the creation of a labor aristocracy content to mitigate conflicts between labor and capital. This has led to insurgent wildcat strikes on the part of the rank and file, but ultimately stronger, revolutionary labor unions would help us put more power squarely in the hands of workers.

This material battle, which of course has many other aspects to it, needs to be conjoined with ideological struggle. "Today," writes Alan Macleod, "just five gigantic corporations control over 90 per cent of what America reads, watches or listens to."[40] The fight to establish real, alternative media that actually informs the public is therefore incredibly important. Fortunately,

---

[38] "Discover the truth through practice," Mao writes, "and again through practice verify and develop the truth. Start from perceptual knowledge and actively develop it into rational knowledge; then start from rational knowledge and actively guide revolutionary practice to change both the subjective and the objective world. Practice, knowledge, again practice, and again knowledge. This form repeats itself in endless cycles, and with each cycle the content of practice and knowledge rises to a higher level." Mao Tse-tung, *Collected Writings*, 38.

[39] On the global surplus population, see William I. Robinson's *The Global Police State*.

[40] Alan Macleod, ed., *Propaganda in the Information Age: Still Manufacturing Consent* (London and New York: Routledge, 2019).

there are already a number of platforms doing excellent work, but these need to receive additional funding and support, be given greater visibility within the media landscape, and their efforts need to be further expanded.[41] Educational institutions are another crucial site of ideological struggle, and we should do everything in our power to leverage them in the direction of producing knowledge with real, transformative use-value. It is also essential to recognize some of their limitations and develop alternative institutions for popular education, like the People's Forum and other platforms with a similar orientation. Finally, I would add that culture—in the broadest sense of the term—is an extremely important locus of class struggle. It produces the social cement that bonds people to the dominant ideology, but it also has the power to rend this bond and introduce people to an alternative world of sense: one in which the socio-economic order would actually *make sense* for the majority of us.[42]

The struggle for the revolutionary transformation of society is multifaceted, and there are many different contributions that people can make. "The task of communism cannot be fulfilled without effort," Lenin writes, "and our efforts must be devoted to fulfilling *practical* tasks, ever more varied, ever more closely connected with all branches of social life, *winning* branch after branch and sphere after sphere *from the bourgeoisie*."[43] This battle also plays itself out over interlocking spatial and temporal scales, meaning that there is work to be done locally, regionally, nationally, and internationally, as well as in the short, medium, and long term. Capitalism will continue to produce contradictions that it is incapable of resolving, the most extreme of which is the contradiction between capital and life on planet Earth. We need to build ideological and material power for the working and toiling masses on all of these fronts so that we can resolve these contradictions by abolishing the very system that produces them in the first place.

---

[41] RED has established a resource list with many of the more reliable alternative media platforms: https://radicaleducationdepartment.com/resources/.

[42] I am currently working on a book with Jennifer Ponce de León, entitled *Revolutionizing Aesthetics*, which examines the role of culture as a crucial weapon in class struggle. This project draws on and further develops my work in *Radical History & the Politics of Art* (New York: Columbia University Press, 2014) and Jennifer's incisive analyses in *Another Aesthetics Is Possible: Arts of Rebellion in the Fourth World War* (Durham, NC: Duke University Press, 2021).

[43] V.I. Lenin, *"Left-Wing" Communism*, 85.

POSTSCRIPT: A FEW TRAPS ON THE WAY TOWARD EMANCIPATORY SOCIAL CRITIQUE, BETWEEN *THE MATRIX, TERMINATOR, KUNG FU,* CAROLE KING, AND JAMES TAYLOR.

by Philippe Corcuff

The debate with Gabriel Rockhill, with stimulating incitement provided by Daniel Benson, allowed me to tackle a whole series of questions around the critical linkages between domination and emancipation, questions which, moreover, I would not have spontaneously formulated in the same way. Of course, one can never be completely exhaustive, but I would like to take advantage of this final moment of the discussion to point out a few more pitfalls to avoid on our way to reconstruct critical theories adjusted to the twenty-first century. I will quickly and unevenly point out four problems that I believe to be important.

Presentism, Nostalgism, and Benjaminian Melancholy

The historian François Hartog has pointed out a tendency within current neoliberal capitalism to change our relationship to time: *presentism*.[44] In the context of a crisis of "Progress" and its principle orientation toward the future, we tend to lock ourselves into a present that is increasingly disconnected from the past as well as from the future. Presentism is a kind of implicit cult of the perpetual present, with its submission to an immediacy that forever begins and forever disappoints. It does not affect all areas of social life in a uniform way, but it particularly affects the economic field under the constraint of neoliberal demands, corporate neomanagement, advertising and media logics, dominant uses of the internet and social networks, the temporal rhythms of professional political arenas, or the zapping culture within militant circles, including critical ones.

The *nostalgism* of "it was better before" is one of the reactions to the development of presentism: we look back on a mythical past as the main response to the challenges of the present. Indeed, the French left has experienced a strong upsurge of national-republican nostalgism since the end of the 1980s. A fantasy republic, forgetting the "dark sides of the Force" (sexism, antisemitism, colonial and postcolonial racism...), is then erected as *the* solution, claiming in a farcical hexagonal way to hold *a priori* the keys to the universal. The historian of ideas Mark Lilla has identified a North American variant of this temptation.[45] But classical forms of socialism can also be subject to such

---

[44] François Hartog, *Regimes of Historicity: Presentism and the Experiences of Time*, trans. Saskia Brown (New York: Columbia University Press, 2015).
[45] Mark Lilla, *The Once and Future Liberal: After Identity Politics* (New York: HarperCollins, 2017).

nostalgism. This is evident in the case of the philosopher Alain Badiou's blind nostalgism toward Maoist totalitarianism.[46]

Both presentism and nostalgism contribute to the loss of a perspective in which to situate present actions with respect to the past as well as to possible futures, within a particularly messy, and even perilous, ideological, and political conjuncture. However, if we follow Walter Benjamin, heretic in both Judaism and Marxism, in his 1940 theses on the concept of history, written a few months before committing suicide on the France–Spain border as he was fleeing from Nazism, it is "at a moment of danger" that we must make a special effort to fan "the spark of hope" by reviving "the tradition of the oppressed."[47] Present action has a decisive role to play, from this point of view, if it knows how to find resources in the past while remaining open to the future, in a different configuration than that of presentist zapping. Benjaminian melancholy, by re-evaluating the past that had been flattened into "prejudices" by the Enlightenment of the eighteenth century, and by remaining connected to the possibilities of the future, thus gives present action a renewed basis.

Three Traps: Conspiratorial Hypercritique, the Forgetting of Individuality, and the Primacy of Ecology

Even after establishing a better temporal footing, traps still remain on the paths leading to the renewal of critical emancipatory action. Three areas appear particularly significant.

On the internet and social networks, a vaguely "anti-system" conspiratorial hypercritique is increasingly taking the place of the structural social critique of anarchism, Marxism, and/or contemporary social sciences. It is a *hyper*critique, for a seemingly radical critique is deployed in all directions; but only superficially and without a compass, because any analysis of the structural constraints generated by social relations tends to be replaced by an analysis of deliberate manipulation, either at the individual or collective level. Drawing analogies from cinema, such hypercritique shares affinities with spy thrillers with conspiratorial themes such as the *James Bond* films. Structural social critique, for its part, is more in tune with science fiction cinema attentive to impersonal mechanisms of domination, as for example in the case of computers that escape human control in the form of The Matrix (in *The Matrix* series) or Skynet (in the *Terminator* series).

---

[46] See especially Alain Badiou, *The Communist Hypothesis*, trans. David Macey and Steve Corcoran (New York: Verso, 2015).

[47] Walter Benjamin, "Theses on the Philosophy of History," *Illuminations*, ed. Hannah Arendt, trans. Harry Zohn (New York: Mariner Books, 2019), 196–209.

Secondly, in Europe and Latin America, radical-critical traditions and leftist organizations have often marginalized the individual component of social transformation over the course of the twentieth century. It was thus forgotten that for nineteenth-century revolutionaries like Marx or Bakunin, individuality—though reintegrated into social and historical relations, unlike political or economic liberalism—had great importance as a support for the critique of capitalism and the state. North American critical traditions, with figures such as Ralph Waldo Emerson, Henry David Thoreau, and, in a more sociological sense, John Dewey, have been more resistant to the trend; and the feminist, gay, or queer movements extended such resistance. In the case of France in the 1970s, when I was a high school student, one had to choose between the binary of "changing the world," and doing politics, and "changing oneself," usually by practicing Eastern spiritualisms. At the time, I chose to "change the world" through Marxist politics... I had no idea that it was possible to try to associate the two perspectives! It's true that, as a teenager, I was attracted by the character played by David Carradine in the TV series *Kung Fu* ... Since then, the possibility of such a reassociation has arguably become one of the key issues of emancipatory politics in the twenty-first century, if we consider the contradiction between capital and individuality as one of the main contradictions of our individualist-capitalist societies.[48] To leave the question of the individual to economic neoliberalism would lead us to miss the anti-capitalist potentialities opened by the expectations and disappointments of contemporary relationships generated by this capital/individuality contradiction.

The global threats of climate change, the loss of biodiversity, various forms of pollution, and techno-scientific dangers constitute the other major challenge that critical theory must confront. This entails, in particular, taking the capital/nature contradiction more seriously than it was for the productivism that dominated the left in the nineteenth and twentieth centuries, and rethinking the question of progress. It is very tempting to make ecology into the main paradigm for the recomposition of politics, in the manner, for example, taken by the anthropologist of science, Bruno Latour.[49] That would be a mistake. For, despite the real importance of ecological dangers, such an approach, by focusing on a single axis, can be considered as a *revival* of the Marxist tendency to erect the capital/labor contradiction as the primary motor of emancipation. The errors of the past and the complexities of contemporary issues should rather incite us to break with politics that are organized

---

[48] See Philippe Corcuff, "Individualité et contradictions du néocapitalisme," *SociologieS*, October 22, 2006, http://sociologies.revues.org/document462.html.

[49] For example in Bruno Latour, "L'Anthropocène et la destruction de l'image du Globe," *De l'univers clos au monde infini*, ed. Emilie Hache (Paris: Editions Dehors, 2014), 29–56.

around a central pivot, in order to confront more radically the plurality of domination—and the inevitable tensions it generates—far removed from homogenizing Christmas stories. In the perspective of a libertarian pluralism, the ecological question presents itself as an important axis, which prompts a major revamping of the problematic of emancipation, but in articulation and in tension with other axes (the class question, the democratic question, the feminist question, the postcolonial question, the question of individuality, the multicultural question, the question of open identities…); each of these different axes should not be conceived in isolation, but through their intersections.

To End, Tentatively … with Carole King and James Taylor

Much remains to be said about critiques of dominations and emancipatory actions, and about their reproblematizations. From yesterday's dead ends, to today's perils and ambiguities, to tomorrow's uncertainties, our melancholy journey remains open to the *perhaps*. A bit like in Carole King's song beautifully interpreted by James Taylor, *You've Got a Friend* (1971). As a storm appears on the horizon, with winds circling and clouds darkening, the singer tells the listener that despite the forbidding sky, you only need to call out and a friend will soon be "knocking at your door." A melancholy ballad, not nostalgically closed to the past, but open to the future through the richness of ordinary friendships… Avoiding the absolute certainties of the Enlightenment or of various socialisms (and the nostalgia for such certainties), distrustful of the overarching lessons given by self-proclaimed avant-gardes and/or by the intellectual arrogance of the tragicomedy of their historical failures, we have at best only a compass in our hands, with individual itineraries and the clatter of historical experiences as guides, redefining ourselves along the way. This is not insignificant, but it does not give any definitive guarantee before the passage of time. The friends of emancipation who will come "knocking at our door" so that we are not alone under these stormy skies are welcome.

POSTSCRIPT

by Gabriel Rockhill

In looking back over this dialogue, as well as the one between Nancy Fraser and Luc Boltanski, it strikes me that there are a number of objective factors that function as the overall coordinates for some of the subjective positions that are taken. The most important of these is the great Western ideological realignment, by which I mean the project of shifting the overall political spectrum of the professional intelligentsia to the right, thereby distancing it from the communist left. This has been a gradual process, which has now succeeded in becoming fully institutionalized, and it is therefore largely invisible to those who are not familiar with earlier phases of class struggle in theory. If one tracks out, however, from the contemporary conjuncture in the Euro-American academic world, the rightward drift of the intelligentsia becomes immediately visible.

Postwar intellectuals in Western Europe—and, to a lesser extent, in the United States—were somewhat versed in historical materialism, at least when compared to the contemporary situation, and a number of thinkers in the 1960s and 1970s were engaged in studying and supporting global struggles for actually existing socialism, as well as anti-colonial liberation movements. Now it is generally acceptable, within academic settings, to simply dismiss Marxism out of hand, with no knowledge base whatsoever regarding actual Marxist theory and practice, including its stalwart commitment to anti-imperialism. In fact, it has even become a badge of academic and moral honor to indulge in the ritualistic incantation of purely ideological descriptors—such as "totalitarian," "authoritarian," "masculinist," "violent," "conspiratorial," etc.—as soon as there is any reference to actually existing socialism, or even socialist aspirations.

To take but one concrete example, I would like to briefly return to one of Philippe's misrepresentations of the Marxist tradition, which he shares to a certain extent with Nancy Fraser, namely the idea that it is entrapped in a "strategic machismo" and, at least for him, an anti-revolutionary liberal theorist like Judith Butler might be able to help us overcome this pitfall.[50] The idea that revolutionary socialism is somehow "masculinist," or rooted in some "patriarchal authoritarianism," because it directly confronts the armies of the capitalist ruling class, is not only the epitome of metaphorical thinking, but it is also the vehicle for a specific form of misogyny. Rather than examining the material history of women's struggles and socialist victories, this approach indulges in idealist abstraction in order to move from concrete reality into the realm of theoretical free association. For it is here, and only here, that the very real, concrete gains for and by women under socialism magically disappear, vanishing into the thin air of supposedly "masculine ideas." Lest we forget through the metaphorical free associations of radical liberal ideology, here is what actually occurred under the leadership of Alexandra Kollontai in the first successful socialist revolution

---

[50] See, among other sources, Ben Norton, "Postmodern Philosopher Judith Butler Repeatedly Donated to 'Top Cop' Kamala Harris," December 18, 2019, accessed on March 2, 2021, https://bennorton.com/judith-butler-kamala-harris-donations/, and Ben Norton, "Coup-Supporting Academics Spread Lies to Censor The Grayzone Reporting Exposing Ecuador's Pseudo-Left Candidate Yaku Pérez," *The Grayzone*, March 1, 2021, accessed on March 3, 2021, https://thegrayzone.com/2021/03/01/academic-letter-censor-grayzone-ecuador-yaku-perez/.

(others would follow similar developments, mediated of course by gender class struggle):

> labor legislation was passed to give women an eight-hour day, social insurance, pregnancy leave for two months before and after childbirth, and time at work to breast-feed. It also prohibited child labor and night work for women. The early months of the revolution also saw legislation to establish equality between husband and wife, civil registration of marriage, easy divorce, abolition of illegitimacy, and the wife's right not to take her husband's name or share his domicile .... The Bolsheviks also stressed the need for political participation of women .... The Bolsheviks strongly supported "free union" and therefore legalized divorce.[51]

This erasure of the concrete gains for the masses of women who have fought for and lived under socialism seamlessly merges with a misogynist elimination of their agency. For if they are not to be duped into "acting like men" and trying to prove they "have balls" by engaging in revolutionary struggle, which is assumed to be "masculine," then women, it follows, should conform to their socio-historically constituted role by being non-confrontational. Kathleen Neal Cleaver addressed this anti-revolutionary, misogynist ideology head on when she identified the assumption underlying a question that was regularly addressed to her, namely "What is the woman's role in the Black Panther Party?" "The assumption," she wrote, "held that being part of a revolutionary movement was in conflict with what the questioner had been socialized to believe was appropriate conduct for a woman."[52] Fortunately, not all women accept their socialized role under capitalism, nor do they embrace the attendant idealist ideology that mobilizes metaphorical abstraction to affiliate revolutionary action with men and passive acquiescence with women.

There is, of course, a long and deep history of anti-communism in the so-called Western world, and these are just some of its manifestations in the era of identity politics, so I am not at all suggesting that there was once a golden age in the capitalist apparatus of knowledge production. However, I would like to insist on the fact that the neoliberal era, within which I have been trained in institutions of higher learning, is dominated by a particularly reactionary intellectual culture. In my own case, I spent decades studying philosophy, history, and the social sciences at so-called prestigious institutions in

---

[51] Valentine M. Moghadam, *Modernizing Women: Gender and Social Change in the Middle East* (Boulder: Lynne Rienner Publishers, 1993), 78.

[52] Kathleen Neal Cleaver, "What Is the Woman's Role in the Black Panther Party?," *Liberation, Imagination, and the Black Panther Party,* ed. Kathleen Cleaver and George Katsiaficas (New York: Routledge, 2001), 124.

France and the United States, including with some of the leading luminaries of French theory like Jacques Derrida, Luce Irigaray, and Alain Badiou. The various student communities I was part of were never educated, in any serious way, in historical materialism. For the most part, Marxism was simply dismissed or ignored as passé and irrelevant. In the few cases when it was mentioned, it was often simply to attack a straw-person version of it as naïve and unsophisticated when compared, for instance, to Foucauldian-style anti-Marxism (Rancière), Bourdieusian-inspired sociology or Heideggerianism with a French facelift.[53] Even those rare intellectuals who openly embraced a Marxist conceptual framework presented it as one discourse among others, which could—and in fact should—be combined with other theoretical models in order to enhance its symbolic cachet, if it be that of Lacan (Badiou), Derrida (Balibar), Deleuze (Negri) or other idealist discourses unmoored from international class struggle. It was never taken seriously—at least in the circles that I was in at the time—as a materialist tradition of theory and practice that had real use-value for transforming the world outside of the symbolic economy of the global theory industry. In short, it was never sexy enough, as a commodity, to be embraced on its own or simply studied—along with actually existing socialism—in a serious and rigorous fashion.

It is interesting, in this light, to compare the contemporary moment to the history of Western Marxism provided by Perry Anderson in his 1983 book *In the Tracks of Historical Materialism*. He charted its emergence in the early twentieth century by highlighting the immediate context of failed revolutions in the West, the development of a concomitant pessimism, the steady drift of Marxist intellectuals away from parties and unions and into universities, the investment in culture and the arts as the privileged terrains of investigation (and potential emancipation), and the tendency to meld Marxism with non-Marxist systems of thought (from Weber and Croce to Heidegger and Lacan). Regardless of any issues that one might have with Anderson's account, or with the work of Western Marxists like Gramsci and Lukács, or Sartre and Althusser, it is nonetheless clear that this group of thinkers was anchored in Marxist theory and practice to varying degrees. With the promotion of anti-Marxist French theory in the global theory industry beginning around 1966, as well as the elevation of the Frankfurt School as perhaps the only academically legitimate intellectual movement that is vaguely Marxian, the most prominent developments of the Western intelligentsia in the neoliberal era are decisively further to the right than one hundred, or even fifty, years ago.

It might be true that figures like Badiou, Žižek, and Negri have helped maintain some interest in Marxism within the petty-bourgeois intelligentsia,

---

[53] On Foucault and the Foucauldian heritage, see my article "Foucault, Genealogy, Counter-History," *Theory & Event* 23, no. 1 (January 2020): 85–119.

for what it's worth, and their political writings have occasionally brought to the fore some of the strengths of the historical materialist tradition. This is particularly true when compared to the Habermasian, anti-communist trajectory of the Frankfurt School. However, it is nevertheless symptomatic of the contemporary situation that the revived interest in communism in certain intellectual circles is largely a concern with what Badiou calls the "Idea" of communism rather than the concrete social practice. It is as if Marxism—at least in its most visible forms in the academy—could only survive in the context of the neoliberal intelligentsia by going metaphysical and becoming largely idealist, while simultaneously merging itself with various reactionary strains of French theory.[54]

It is within these objective coordinates of the capitalist apparatus of knowledge production that radical liberals have been promoted as the world's greatest critical theorists, in order to police the left border of critique and foreclose the communist alternative (if it cannot be transformed into a metaphysical abstraction, a buffoonish joke, incoherent prose devoid of use-value, or all three at the same time). The reinvention of critical—and, dare I say, revolutionary—theory in the twenty-first century requires that we unflinchingly engage in what Karl Marx called a ruthless critique of everything. The academic protocols of obsequious decorum, which enshrine the top commodities of the global theory industry in order to shelter them from revolutionary criticism, should not stand in the way of incisively diagnosing material reality and seeking to change it. In order to do so, we need to come to terms with these objective coordinates of contemporary intellectual life, identify their primary social function, reject all of the crass misrepresentations of historical materialism and actually existing socialism, and contribute to the deep and rich tradition of revolutionary theory and practice, which is a creative, collective, and dynamic practice of knowledge production with real use-value. In other words, we have to recognize that these coordinates are set by the bourgeois apparatus of knowledge, whose ultimate goal is to eliminate theory with real use-value and replace it by theory whose primary purpose is to generate exchange-value.

---

[54] Since the reactionary, anti-communist orientation of much of French theory has been obscured due to its free association with the events of 1968 and its promotion as a form of critical theory, I take the liberty of referring the reader to my forthcoming article, which debunks the myth according to which French theory was somehow a revolutionary force: "May 68: Historical Commodity Fetishism and Ideological Rollback," *Oxford Handbook of Modern French Philosophy*, ed. Mark Sinclair and Daniel Whistler (Oxford: Oxford University Press, forthcoming).

BIBLIOGRAPHY

Anderson, Perry. *The Antinomies of Antonio Gramsci.* New York: Verso, 2017.
Anderson, Perry. *Considerations on Western Marxism.* New York: Verso, 1987.
Badiou, Alain. *The Communist Hypothesis.* Translated by David Macey and Steve Corcoran. New York: Verso, 2015.
Bay Area Socialist Organizing Committee. "Confronting Reality/Learning from the History of Our Movement." Accessed December 23, 2020, https://www.marxists.org/history/erol/ncm-7/basoc/ch-5.htm.
Benjamin, Walter. "Theses on the Philosophy of History." In *Illuminations*, edited by Hannah Arendt, translated by Harry Zohn, 196–209. New York: Mariner Books, 2019.
Blum, William. *Killing Hope: US Military and CIA Interventions since World War II.* London: Zed Books, 2014.
Boltanski, Luc. *On Critique: A Sociology of Emancipation.* Translated by Gregory Elliot. Malden, MA: Polity Press, 2011.
Bourdieu, Pierre, and Jean-Claude Passeron. "Sociologues des mythologies et mythologies des sociologues." *Les Temps modernes* 211 (December 1963): 998–1021.
Chi Minh, Ho. *Selected Writings (1920-1969).* Honolulu, Hawaii: University Press of the Pacific, 2001.
Cleaver, Kathleen, and George Katsiaficas, eds. *Liberation, Imagination, and the Black Panther Party.* New York: Routledge, 2001.
Connelly, Michael. *The Night Fire.* New York: Little, Brown and Company, 2019.
Corcuff, Philippe. *La grande confusion. Comment l'extrême droite gagne la bataille des idées.* Paris: Textuel, 2021.
Corcuff, Philippe. "De l'imaginaire utopique dans les cultures ordinaires. Pistes à partir d'une enquête sur la série télévisée Ally McBeal." In *L'ordinaire et le politique*, edited by Claude Gautier and Sandra Laugier, 71–84. Paris: PUF, 2006.
Corcuff, Philippe. "Individualité et contradictions du néocapitalisme." *SociologieS*, October 22, 2006, http://sociologies.revues.org/document462.html.
Corcuff, Philippe. *Marx XXIe siècle.* Paris, Textuel, 2012.
Corcuff, Philippe. *Où est passée la critique sociale?* Paris: La Découverte, 2014.
"CoronaShock and Socialism." *Tricontinental*, July 8, 2020, https://www.thetricontinental.org/studies-3-coronashock-and-socialism/.
Deleuze, Gilles. "Gilles Deleuze: Qu'est-ce qu'être de gauche?" *Œuvres ouvertes*, accessed January 25, 2021, https://www.oeuvresouvertes.net/spip.php?article910.
Derrida, Jacques. *Derrida Negotiations: Interventions and Interviews, 1971-2001.* Edited and translated by Elizabeth Rottenberg. Stanford: Stanford University Press, 2002.
Dewey, John. *The Public and Its Problems.* Edited by Melvin L. Rogers. University Park, PA: Pennsylvania State University Press, 2012.
Ferro, Marc. *Des soviets au communisme bureaucratique: les mécanismes d'une subversion.* Paris: Gallimard/Julliard, 1980,
Fraser, Nancy. *The Old Is Dying and the New Cannot Be Born: From Progressive Neoliberalism to Trump and Beyond.* New York: Verso, 2019.

Glissant, Edouard. *Treatise on the Whole-World.* Translated by Celia Britton. Liverpool: Liverpool University Press, 2020.

Gramsci, Antonio. *Selections from the Prison Notebooks of Antonio Gramsci.* New York: International Publishers, 2014.

Hartog, François. *Regimes of Historicity: Presentism and the Experiences of Time.* Translated by Saskia Brown. New York: Columbia University Press, 2015.

Holloway, John. *Crack Capitalism.* London: Pluto Press, 2010.

Keucheyan, Razmig. *Left Hemisphere: Mapping Contemporary Theory.* Translated by Gregory Elliott. New York: Verso, 2014.

Kouvélakis, Stathis. *La Critique défaite: émergence et domestication de la théorie critique.* Paris: Amsterdam, 2019.

Lenin, Vladimir Ilyich. *"Left-Wing" Communism: An Infantile Disorder.* Peking: Foreign Languages Press, 1970.

Levinas, Emmanuel. *On Escape.* Translated by Bettina Bergo. Stanford: Stanford University Press, 2003.

Luxemburg, Rosa. "Organizational Questions of Russian Social Democracy." In *The Rosa Luxemburg Reader*, edited by Peter Hudis and Kevin B. Anderson, 248–65. New York: Monthly Review Press, 2004.

Latour, Bruno. "L'Anthropocène et la destruction de l'image du Globe." In *De l'univers clos au monde infini*, edited by Emilie Hache, 29–56. Paris: Editions Dehors, 2014.

Li, Minqi. "The 21st Century: Is There an Alternative (to Socialism)?" *Science & Society* 77, no. 1 (January 2013): 10–43.

Lilla, Mark. *The Once and Future Liberal: After Identity Politics.* New York: HarperCollins, 2017.

Macleod, Alan, ed. *Propaganda in the Information Age: Still Manufacturing Consent.* London and New York: Routledge, 2019.

Macron, Emmanuel. *Revolution.* Translated by Jonathan Goldberg and Juliette Scott. Carlton: Scribe Publications, 2017.

Merleau-Ponty, Maurice. *Signs.* Translated by Richard C. McCleary. Evanston, IL: Northwestern University Press, 1964.

Moghadam, Valentine M. *Modernizing Women: Gender and Social Change in the Middle East.* Boulder: Lynne Rienner Publishers, 1993.

Navarro, Vicente. "Has Socialism Failed? An Analysis of Health Indicators under Capitalism and Socialism." *Science & Society* 57, no. 1 (Spring 1993): 6–30.

Norton, Ben. "Coup-Supporting Academics Spread Lies to Censor The Grayzone Reporting Exposing Ecuador's Pseudo-Left Candidate Yaku Pérez." *The Grayzone,* March 1, 2021, accessed on March 3, 2021, https://thegrayzone.com/2021/03/01/academic-letter-censor-grayzone-ecuador-yaku-perez/.

Norton, Ben. "Postmodern Philosopher Judith Butler Repeatedly Donated to 'Top Cop' Kamala Harris." Personal website (blog), December 18, 2019, accessed on March 2, 2021, https://bennorton.com/judith-butler-kamala-harris-donations/.

Parenti, Michael. *Blackshirts & Reds: Rational Fascism and the Overthrow of Communism.* San Francisco: City Lights Publishers, 1997.

Parenti, Michael. "Reflections on the Overthrow of Communism." Recorded lecture, accessed on January 20, 2021. https://archive.org/details/ReflectionOnTheOverthrowOfCommunismNLSubtitlesDutch.

Phillips, Peter. *Giants: The Global Power Elite*. New York: Seven Stories Press, 2018.

Ponce de León, Jennifer. *Another Aesthetics Is Possible: Arts of Rebellion in the Fourth World War*. Durham, NC: Duke University Press, 2021.

Robinson, William I. *Global Capitalism and the Crisis of Humanity*. New York: Cambridge University Press, 2014.

Robinson, William I. *The Global Police State*. London: Pluto Press, 2020.

Rockhill, Gabriel. "The Failure of the French Intelligentsia? Intellectuals and Uprisings in the Case of the Yellow Vests." *The Philosophical Salon*, April 29, 2019, http://thephilosophicalsalon.com/the-failure-of-the-french-intelligentsia-intellectuals-and-uprisings-in-the-case-of-the-yellow-vests/.

Rockhill, Gabriel. "Foucault: The Faux Radical." *The Philosophical Salon*, October 12, 2020, http://thephilosophicalsalon.com/foucault-the-faux-radical/.

Rockhill, Gabriel. "Foucault, Genealogy, Counter-History." *Theory & Event* 23, no. 1 (January 2020): 85–119.

Rockhill, Gabriel. "May 68: Historical Commodity Fetishism and Ideological Rollback." In *Oxford Handbook of Modern French Philosophy*, edited by Mark Sinclair and Daniel Whistler. Oxford: Oxford University Press, forthcoming.

Rockhill, Gabriel. *Radical History & the Politics of Art*. New York: Columbia University Press, 2014.

"Ten Lesson from the Yellow Vests." *RED*, December 28, 2018, https://radicaleducationdepartment.com/2018/12/28/ten-lessons-from-the-yellow-vests-ed/.

Tse-tung, Mao. *Collected Writings of Chairman Mao*. Vol. 3, *On Policy, Practice and Contradiction*. Edited by Shawn Conners. El Paso, TX: El Paso Norte Press, 2009.

Voline. *La Révolution inconnue. Russie 1917-1921*. Paris: Les Amis de Voline, 1947.

Part II
EMANCIPATORY SUBJECTS

Chapter 3

Emancipation, Political, and Real

Asad Haider

To be emancipated is to be set free from a power. This statement, despite being etymologically valid, should be distinguished from a definition. It is rather a "thesis of existence"—it says that *there is* emancipation, that being set free from a power can be conceived.[1] We can conceive of it because it is real, not in the sense that a free state exists or could be constructed in the mind, but in the sense that the demand for freedom has been and remains a matter of irrepressible fact. In my manner of proceeding, these facts cannot be reduced to secondary, merely empirical manifestations of a category which has already been defined. Actually, politics only exists and becomes thinkable in those singular moments which bring about new possibilities. To think politically means that we must see these singular moments of invention as altering what is possible and thus allowing us to have new thoughts. As the result of a lexical history which we will explore, the word emancipation has come to name these moments of invention, each of which constitute a singular politics.

It is for this reason that I say that this statement on the existence of emancipation is not a definition, which would say *what it is* and be capable of describing its nature. This is clear first of all because emancipation can only be said to exist with reference to *specific situations* of domination. Indeed, there are only specific situations, and it is in these specific situations that emancipation is real. To define emancipation in general would not tell us about their specificity. Furthermore, the more we fill the term with substantial content, the farther we drift from the singularity of politics. In this sense I go as far as to claim that there can be no general theory of emancipation.

---

[1] Sylvain Lazarus, *Anthropology of the Name*, trans. Gila Walker (New York: Seagull Books, 2015), 24.

Since we are concerned with politics, the difficulties only multiply, and our next difficulty pertains to the category of freedom. To conceive of being set free assumes a starting point of domination. If we were to invert the procedure, and begin with a definition of freedom, we would be once again departing from the reality of emancipation: to observe that *there is* emancipation means observing that there is domination preceding it. Yet the starting point of domination is an obstacle to thinking emancipation. Concretely, freedom cannot simply be conceived as a gift from the power from which one is supposed to be freed—a scenario which presents us with something like a paradox. To be free, I have to answer first and foremost to myself. So emancipation must exist in itself—except insofar as it only exists in specific situations with reference to a specific domination. The broader point illustrated by the paradox of power is that there must be something in emancipation which is irreducible to the situation of domination, despite the fact that this situation is the starting point.

This line of reasoning, with its seeming paradox and circularity, calls for theoretical elaboration. How do we move from the study of a specific situation to a conception of freedom which necessarily goes beyond it? A great deal is at stake in this question, which revolves around the problem of the *subject* of emancipation. Where does the emancipatory subject come from—or to put it differently, what is the relation between the political subject and the objective conditions of its emergence? What, furthermore, makes this subject emancipatory?

We can track these conceptual problems in the etymological accretion of meanings. In the laws of Ancient Rome, emancipation referred to freedom from paternal power, the legal authority of the father. The freeing of slaves, who had no legal personhood, was called manumission. The Roman father used the legal fiction of selling, or alienating his son three times to grant him the status of an independent legal personality. Daughters, it should be noted, only needed to be sold once, though they also had the option of being transferred to the power of the husband through marriage.[2] This difference reveals that the ambiguity in the *word* "emancipation"—a freedom which appears to be subjugated to the external authorities which grant it—represents *historical* ambiguities. As Joan Scott puts it: "Historically, the word has often been synonymous with liberation or freedom, but not necessarily with equality. For a Roman son or wife, emancipation would more often mean disinheritance than the possibility of assuming equal standing with a father or husband."[3]

---

[2] George Long, "Emancipatio," in *A Dictionary of Greek and Roman Antiquities*, ed. William Smith (London: John Murray, 1875).

[3] Joan Wallach Scott, "The Vexed Relationship of Emancipation and Equality," *History of the Present* 2, no. 2 (2012): 149.

The question, then, is not only whether being set free from a power can be done through transfer to another power, through alienation to another authority, but whether freedom can be *granted* at all. In the Middle Ages, the possibility of another conception of emancipation emerged when the term developed beyond the strictly Roman meaning of a legal act by the paternal authority, and came to signify the independence gained automatically upon reaching the age of maturity. As the term was adopted in western European vernaculars from the fourteenth to the seventeenth centuries, it took on a reflexive usage, indicating, as Reinhart Koselleck writes in his conceptual-historical sketch of the concept, "an act performed on one's own authority." While the premise that "one could emancipate oneself was unthinkable in the Roman tradition," in the modern development of the concept "the act of being declared free was always overtaken by the move toward self-authorization."[4]

Koselleck argues that it is only since the Enlightenment that the concept of emancipation extends to "the fundamental eradication of domination by humans over humans." "Only since the Enlightenment," writes Koselleck, "does the privilege of exercising power over human beings, a privilege previously limited only to free citizens or lords, become a general right: that rule could henceforth only be self-rule by mature human beings (first men and, then later, women too) over themselves."[5] Enlightenment, in Kant's presentation, was an exit from immaturity, which would not simply be "automatically realized by each succeeding generation," but instead "became a historical perspective on the future of a politically self-ruling humanity."[6] The subsumption of "the Kantian philosophy of history under the new and fashionable concept of emancipation," Koselleck continues, is what frames the extension of the term at around 1800 to "the legal liberation coming to pass with self-emancipation."[7] Thus, the historical perspective of non-domination is attached to the historical movements against specific dominations, extending to freedom from persecution for religious minorities, of which Catholic and Jewish emancipation are the exemplary cases, to the freedom of women from not only familial but also social domination, and ultimately to slaves.

Yet the specific word "emancipation," with this precise etymological foundation, frequently does not appear in the documents which are now understood to address the question historically. It is not used with reference to the emancipation of Jews in France in 1791, or the emancipation of Catholics in Ireland in 1829. It appears neither in the 1793 emancipation of

---

[4] Reinhart Koselleck, *The Practice of Conceptual History: Timing History, Spacing Concepts* (Stanford: Stanford University Press, 2002), 252–53.
[5] Koselleck, *Conceptual History*, 249–50.
[6] Koselleck, *Conceptual History*, 253.
[7] Koselleck, *Conceptual History*, 254.

Saint-Domingue by Sonthonax, which refers more literally to enfranchisement, nor in Lincoln's 1863 proclamation, which refers simply to freedom. As Koselleck speculates, "we can suspect that the strict and narrow Roman law meaning was just as much present to the lawyers formulating the laws as the sense that more claims were expressed behind every emancipation than at the time seemed purely juridically possible to concede."[8]

The transmission of the Latin term does not appear to be continuous but rather operates according to lag and retrojection. The question of this word is not its precise etymological continuity but rather its resurgence and attraction in constellation with other terms specific to situations. But the tension between the act of the external authority and self-authorization persists. Whether emancipation can be proclaimed by another, and whether its maintenance can come from being externally recognized, is not resolved with reference to the classic cases of emancipation. In the example of American history, we are confronted with a historiographical debate over whether slaves won their own freedom, or it was conferred by Union armies. That is, was it what W.E.B. Du Bois characterized as the "general strike" of the slaves, their autonomous activity and departure from the plantations, or necessarily the action from above, at the level of the state, which should be understood as the ultimate historical *cause* of the abolition of slavery? And indeed, this question of historical causality gives way to a conceptual question, which is whether the abolition of slavery can be understood as the realization of freedom in isolation from the autonomous activity of the slaves—that is, even if the formal achievement of abolition is understood as the consequence of maneuvering at the level of state, can it be characterized as emancipatory in isolation from the self-authorizing action of those whose freedom is in question? However, it is difficult to even pose these questions given what followed emancipation, as Martin Luther King implied when he said, standing in front of the Lincoln Memorial, "one hundred years later the Negro still is not free." It is with reference to this continuing unfreedom in American history that, as Saidiya Hartman puts it, "emancipation appears less the grand event of liberation than a point of transition between modes of servitude and racial subjection."[9] As Hartman elaborates:

> As a consequence of emancipation blacks were incorporated into the narrative of the rights of man and citizen; by virtue of the gift of freedom and wage labor, the formerly enslaved were granted entry into the hallowed halls of humanity,

---

[8] Koselleck, *Conceptual History*, 255.
[9] Saidiya V. Hartman, *Scenes of Subjection: Terror, Slavery, and Self-Making in Nineteenth-Century America* (New York: Oxford University Press, 1997), 6.

and, at the same time, the unyielding and implacable fabrication of blackness as subordination continued under the aegis of formal equality.[10]

In the United States, after slavery had been legally abolished, freedom had not been achieved. Yet a century later, emancipation would again be invoked by mass movements. King would declare in a tribute to Du Bois on the commemoration of his 100th birthday in 1968: "People deprived of their freedom do not give up—Negroes have been fighting more than a hundred years and even if the date of full emancipation is uncertain, what is explicitly certain is that the struggle for it will endure."[11] I suggest that this enduring quality requires us to propose new conceptions of emancipation.

To conceive of being set free is to begin with the fact of subjection to a power, and being set free does not mean being alienated to another power. However, whether it is possible to be set free by the very power to which one is subjected remains unclear. For freedom to be proclaimed, recognized, and maintained by an external power, in the words of the Emancipation Proclamation, does not historically appear to realize freedom. It is in response to this problem that the term "self-emancipation" takes on its significance, by emerging within a situation of subjection and yet making freedom refer to itself. King alluded to this by writing in 1967, in a complex discussion of the "psychological freedom" aimed at by "Black Power":

> No Lincolnian Emancipation Proclamation or Kennedyan or Johnsonian civil rights bill can totally bring this kind of freedom. The Negro will only be truly free when he reaches down to the inner depths of his own being and signs with the pen and ink of assertive selfhood his own emancipation proclamation.[12]

The consequence of this recursivity is that while we cannot conceive of emancipation outside of the situations in which freedom must be demanded, and it thus only exists in those concrete sequences in which it is pursued, the subject of emancipation is both in excess of these situations and self-founding. We are no longer in the domain of the state, but in that of the political activity which, while it is represented and contained by external powers, necessarily exceeds them if the movement toward freedom persists.[13]

Hartman alludes to Marx's "On the Jewish Question" in her discussion of the "double bind of freedom."[14] With Marx's 1843 text, which appears in the

---

[10] Hartman, *Scenes of Subjection*, 119.
[11] Martin Luther King, Jr., *The Radical King*, ed. Cornel West (Boston: Beacon Press, 2016), 120.
[12] King, Jr., *The Radical King*, 198–99.
[13] Michael Neocosmos, *Thinking Freedom in Africa* (Johannesburg: Wits University Press, 2016), 40–41, 46.
[14] Hartman, *Scenes of Subjection*, 115.

historical moment just after the term emancipation has been generalized to refer to various social groups, the general fact of different emancipations is expressed in terms of an internal limit constitutive of the concept, represented by the famous line of demarcation between political and real emancipation.

Marx's thought begins not with political economy, but with the philosophical problem of emancipation. This is chronologically evident in "On the Jewish Question," which we can consider his first major theoretical text, which is followed immediately by his "Introduction to A Contribution to the Critique of Hegel's *Philosophy of Right*," and then the *1844 Manuscripts*. As we shall see, in drawing a line of demarcation between different emancipations, and criticizing the partial nature of political emancipation, Marx has to pose the question of the relation between the subject of the emancipation and the historical process.

The problem Marx inherits is religious emancipation, the emancipation of the Jews, which Bruno Bauer had used to express his theory of political emancipation. For Bauer the emancipation of a religious minority circumscribes the emancipation of everyone, which consists in emancipation from religion itself and thus the movement toward a universal state. Religion, according to Bauer, is based on exclusion, and it is the essence of the state. As long as there is a privileged religion, religious prejudice exists; but if no religion is privileged, then there can be no religion at all. That is, if the dynamic of exclusion which is represented by religion is overcome at the level of the state, exclusiveness is also overcome, and there can be no more religion.

All this is why secularization is equivalent to emancipation, that is, the overcoming of exclusion and the development of the state into its most universal form. Bauer asserts the self-consciousness of the individual against every form of privilege, hierarchy, or exclusion; the fully developed republic would be a realization of this self-consciousness in social life. Following Hegel, the state is seen as the expression of reason and the space for the realization of freedom, rather than a limit on freedom; but in Bauer's conception, this is a secular republic.[15]

The problem remains that for Bauer, the self of self-emancipation is an individual, and thus, Marx argues in his critique, Bauer remains stuck in the dichotomies of modern society. Marx here first criticizes the egoism of the civil society produced by the separation of the economic and the political occasioned by the dissolution of the feudal estates, and further, by making use of Rousseau, begins to integrate a critique of the state *itself*, that is, the

---

[15] Massimiliano Tomba, "Exclusiveness and Political Universalism in Bruno Bauer," in *The New Hegelians*, ed. Douglas Moggach (Cambridge: Cambridge University Press, 2006); "Emancipation as Therapy: Bauer and Marx on the Jewish Question," in *Die linken Hegelianer*, ed. Michael Quante and Amir Mohseni (Paderborn, Germany: Wilhelm Fink, 2015).

secular state as the separation and exclusion from power. Marx inverts Bauer: for Bauer, the state was potentially the expression of freedom, but religion with its structure of exclusion had created a state that remained in the thrall of feudal privilege. For Marx, it is rather the separateness of the state from human beings and their lives that is the basis for belief in religion, which turns God, who is in actuality an expression of human nature, into a separate power. In this turn, Marx uses the ideas of Ludwig Feuerbach to argue that religion operates not simply by exclusion, but by inversion, which, Marx adds, has a secular basis in the inversion of the state: the alienation of powers into the separate form of the state, and the subordination of human beings to their own alienated power. His argument suggests that separateness of the state has as its basis the relations of civil society, though he is not yet prepared to elaborate this argument.

Marx's critique of rights in this text is at a certain level a skeptical response to the way that real social inequalities are masked by the formal equality of abstract individuals. But it is not only that real social inequalities are masked by formal equality, but also that the abstract individuality of formal equality is itself constituted by the egoism of civil society. Therefore, Marx famously states:

> None of the so-called rights of man... go beyond egoistic man, beyond man as a member of civil society, that is, an individual withdrawn into himself, into the confines of his private interests and private caprice, and separated from the community. In the rights of man, he is far from being conceived as a species-being; on the contrary, species-life itself, society, appears as a framework external to the individuals, as a restriction of their original independence.[16]

Now, Bauer had already pointed out that rights were not natural, but cultural, insofar as they resulted from struggles against feudal privileges. Marx cites Bauer's point without commenting on it, and proceeds to demonstrate through his reading of the various declarations of the rights of man that abstract rights are the rights of abstract persons, the individual of civil society. We might attempt to synchronize these arguments by concluding that what rights represent is something concrete but internally antagonistic: the insurgency of those excluded, and the pacifying powers of the state in response. As a consequence of the struggles to limit the state's power, to change the relation of power such that those who are excluded are active agents, rights are formed and granted to abstract persons. Florence Gauthier goes as far as to suggest that the institutionalization of inequality that comes with the Thermidor and the

---

[16] Karl Marx and Frederick Engels, *Collected Works*, vol. 3 (London: Lawrence and Wishart, 1975), 164.

re-establishing of slavery in the French colonies represents "the defeat of the Revolution of the rights of man and the citizen... accompanied by the defeat of the Enlightenment." This defeat was "the triumph of the specific interest of the possessing classes, of the politics of money, of the despotism of economic power," through which "the possessing classes, conquerors in Europe and colonialists outside Europe, carried through a counter-revolution."[17]

Of course, Marx argues that we can consider the rights of man and political emancipation to be a great step forward, suggesting something of the conflictual nature of this process. However, he remains ambiguous on this point, implying that rights are a stage in the teleological unfolding of the origin. As Wendy Brown points out, "while Marx counted on a progressive dialectical process" for overcoming the limits of rights, this is in fact a question of struggles for which the "parameters are invented rather than secured in advance and whose outcome is never guaranteed."[18]

Nevertheless, Marx's text presents us with a logic of division, not only of synthesis. Emancipation divides into political and real emancipation. The latter represents, first of all, the moment "when the real, individual man reabsorbs in himself the abstract citizen, and as an individual human being has become a *species-being* in his everyday life." But it is also the moment when "man has recognized and organized his *forces propres* as *social forces*, and consequently no longer separates social power from himself in the shape of *political* power." Only at this moment "will human emancipation have been accomplished."[19] Political emancipation is not equivalent to real emancipation, because it is the emancipation of the bourgeois individual. Real emancipation is "human"—the meaning of this term is yet to be established—and can only result from the reabsorption of powers into the human community.

In the immediately subsequent text, the "Introduction to A Contribution to the Critique of Hegel's *Philosophy of Right*," Marx "discovers" a foundation for this real emancipation, which is nevertheless not clearly a foundation. This discovery is the proletariat, though it is not yet theorized concretely. Despite the influence of Feuerbach, which will become all the more apparent in the *1844 Manuscripts* written just after, the proletariat is not described in the "Introduction" in terms of an anthropological substance. Instead, in attempting to grasp what historical agent will achieve human emancipation, Marx turns his attention to "a class of civil society which is not a class of civil society, an estate which is the dissolution of all estates, a sphere which has

---

[17] Florence Gauthier, "The French Revolution: Revolution of the Rights of Man and the Citizen," in *History and Revolution: Refuting Revisionism*, ed. Mike Haynes and Jim Wolfreys (New York: Verso, 2007), 91.
[18] Wendy Brown, *States of Injury* (Princeton: Princeton University Press, 1995), 134.
[19] Marx and Engels, *Collected Works*, 3:168.

a universal character by its universal suffering."[20] The proletariat is the class which in its very lack of substance is the negation of the whole society, and thus cannot emancipate itself without emancipating the whole society.

The tension I identify in the young Marx is that between the proletariat as negation and the proletariat as foundation, the latter formulated as species-being within the theory of alienation, which we must read not so much as a theory of the labor process as a philosophy of history. In the *1844 Manuscripts*, the political principle is that raising or equalizing wages, as previous socialists had demanded, would do nothing to eliminate the underlying problem with the labor process itself, since it alienates human species-being. Here Marx clearly elaborates the principle that "the emancipation of the workers contains universal human emancipation" by guaranteeing emancipation with the theory of alienation, which shows that "the whole of human servitude is involved in the relation of the worker to production, and all relations of servitude are but modifications and consequences of this relation."[21]

But the elaboration of this emancipatory perspective runs up against critical problems. This conception of the "human," or species-being, derived from the critique of religion, does not clearly justify itself as a foundation for real emancipation. The division between political and real emancipation is resolved into a progressive development by instituting man as the subject and goal of the historical process. As a consequence, there is a conflation of the human subject with the political subject. The human functions as the origin and end of history, providing a purportedly material content to Hegel's idealism, and it is for this reason that the human is a limit for the young Marx.

This is the enduring relevance of Louis Althusser's argument that Feuerbach's anthropological conception of history lost sight of Hegel's major contribution to Marx's thought, which is the conception of history as a process, and indeed a process without a subject, since for Hegel history is the alienation not of man, but of spirit, and it is a process which has always already begun. In other words, in Hegel the subject of history "is the very *teleology* of the *process*, it is the *Idea*, in the process of self-alienation which constitutes it as the Idea... The only *subject* of the process of alienation is *the process itself in its teleology*." To abstract from the teleology of Hegel's dialectic is to conceive of history as a process without a subject, and indeed, therefore, without an origin or goal.[22]

The significance of this reading, labeled, for better or worse, "theoretical anti-humanism," is not that it is a skeptical critique of human nature, though

---

[20] Marx and Engels, *Collected Works*, 3:86.
[21] Marx and Engels, *Collected Works*, 3:280.
[22] Louis Althusser, *Politics and History: Montesquieu, Rousseau, Hegel and Marx*, trans. Ben Brewster (London: New Left Books, 1972), 183–84.

it may also be that. It is rather the putting into question of the philosophy of history which has man as its subject. This is important because an implication of theoretical anti-humanism is that the posthumanist categories of Marx after his break with the Feuerbachian problematic sometimes reassert the general teleological structure. In *The German Ideology*, the language of human essence is displaced by that of the "concrete individual," a seemingly even more materialist category which largely begs the question and essentially erects the productive forces as the subject of history, their development expressed in particular social relations of production which proceed through progressive stages.[23]

Later, with the *Grundrisse*, Marx criticizes even this supposedly materialist perspective, beginning with the critique of ideology, the ideology of political economy: it too revolves around individuals, which it conceives of as the starting point rather than the *result* of a process of individuation initiated by the dissolution of feudalism. In precapitalist societies, the individual is subordinated to the community, while political economy writes stories of Robinson Crusoe, in which the capitalist relations of production are generated spontaneously in supposedly natural conditions—the projection of characteristics of bourgeois society onto a mythical past. Marx turns here to a principle of historical specificity, fully realized in *Capital*, which sees the origin of capitalism in the primitive accumulation which produces capitalist social relations, a historical rupture rather than the expression of a transhistorical progression.

This new conception of the historical process leads, then, to a thoroughgoing critique of the category of the subject, which Étienne Balibar clearly elaborated in his contribution to *Reading Capital*:

> Marx formulated the very concept of the dependence of the forms of individuality with respect to the structure of the process or the "mode" of production. His terminology itself is marked by the epistemological fact that in the analysis of the "combination" we are not dealing with concrete men, but only with men insofar as they fulfill certain determinate functions in the structure.

That is, so-called men are divided into the "bearers of labor power" and the "representatives of capital," in an exposition which does not revolve around categories like "man" or "subject" but rather "activity which conforms to the norms of the mode of production," and designates individuals as "supports." "Men," writes Balibar, "do not appear in the theory except in the form of

---

[23] Louis Althusser, *For Marx*, trans. Ben Brewster (London: Verso, 1977), 108.

supports for the connections implied by the structure, and the forms of their individuality as determinate effects of the structure."[24]

However, we now arrive at a vexing puzzle which this critique leaves in its wake. Without the subject of man and its teleology, the character of emancipation becomes unclear. As a consequence of the critique of the category of the human subject and the subject of history, the political subject has all but disappeared. Without a foundation, it is not clear how emancipation can be thought. If the late Marx is a thinker who undermines the subject, what is left of the subject of emancipation?

Even in *Capital*, which presents a non-teleological account of the origins of capitalism, the revolution is presented as automatic. While the problematic of species-being and its philosophy of history could not sustain emancipation, in its absence, emancipation appears to be miraculous.

This is not to say that there is no language of emancipation. Throughout this period, there is a thinking of emancipation, summed up in the phrase of rules of the International, penned by Marx in 1864: "the emancipation of the working classes must be conquered by the working classes themselves."[25] Yet the problem to explain is that Marx's explicit thought of emancipation in his earlier problematics—not only the humanist, but also the materialist ontology which characterizes the early stages of the shifts in his thought—makes it part of a transhistorical sequence, from the realization of human species-being to the sequence of class hegemonies and the development of the productive forces. When, in the *Grundrisse* and *Capital*, Marx presents a historically specific account of the origins of capitalism, he does not present a philosophical account of emancipation.

What Marx gives us instead is the rudiments of a theory of the organization of emancipation. This is clear when he writes of the Paris Commune: "It was essentially a working-class government, the produce of the struggle of the producing against the appropriating class, the political form at last discovered under which to work out the economical emancipation of Labour."[26] The realization that the emancipation of labor would take the form of the destruction of the state machine recalls Marx's earlier argument about real emancipation as the reabsorption of the separate powers of the state into the human community. However, the question is not posed here in terms of a subject of history or the realization of a transhistorical process. The organization of emancipation is not the automatic result of the concentration of the

---

[24] Louis Althusser and Étienne Balibar, *Reading Capital*, trans. Ben Brewster (New York: Verso, 2006), 252.
[25] Karl Marx and Frederick Engels, *Collected Works*, vol. 20 (London: Lawrence and Wishart, 1985), 14.
[26] Karl Marx and Frederick Engels, *Collected Works*, vol. 22 (London: Lawrence and Wishart, 1986), 334.

proletariat in factories, its constitution as a cooperative productive force, the contradiction between the socialization of production and capitalist property relations. Rather, a subject composed of a complex heterogeneity of social groups elaborates new forms of life within an aleatory situation. It is organization which constitutes this subject, a subject which does not exist prior to its organization, and which mobilizes for the production of new political forms.

But we are nevertheless left unable to account for this emancipation philosophically in Marx's new theoretical problematic. What remains, then, is a serious problem: how can there be a subject which is not an effect of the structure? How can the proletariat, now carefully theorized in terms of its position in the mode of production, work out a political form, and act as a political subject which emancipates itself?

Here I will consider some suggestive indications of Alain Badiou, who emerges as a thinker of subjectivity who has absorbed, rather than disavowed, the theoretical anti-humanist critique. In *Theory of the Subject*, Badiou argues that theoretical anti-humanism presented a necessary critique of the idealism of man, which in itself had criticized the idealism of God, but it ended up producing an idealism of language, with "a decentred subject, a subjugated subject."[27] Marx too had provided a "theory of the self, a critique of the illusions of consciousness." After this critique, it is clearly established that it is necessary to "exclude all attempts to put the subject back into the saddle as simple centre, as point of origin, as constitutive of experience. The theory of the subject is diametrically opposed to all elucidating transparency."[28] And yet the central task after theoretical anti-humanism becomes "a materialism centred upon a theory of the subject."[29] This will not be a psychological or phenomenological theory of the subject, but a political subject in which the question of its organization is primary, as Marx's fleeting notes on the Commune suggest.

Within this framework we can reconsider the character of the class subject, the emancipatory subject of the proletariat. I refer to an extremely dense sentence from *Theory of the Subject*:

> the proletariat as political class—as force—is linked to the bourgeoisie in a wholly historical unity-of-struggle, which cannot be distributed into the domains of the social whole and which structures the same being—the people—without prohibiting, but actually requiring, that we orient the class position in its placed groundedness, that is, in the social relations of production.[30]

---

[27] Alain Badiou, *Theory of the Subject*, trans. Bruno Bosteels (New York: Continuum, 2009), 188.
[28] Badiou, *Theory of the Subject*, 180.
[29] Badiou, *Theory of the Subject*, 189.
[30] Badiou, *Theory of the Subject*, 36.

The proletariat as a category—and this is the case for any objective category—is not already given and does not represent a community prior to its placement, in its link to the principal aspect of the contradiction, the bourgeoisie. In the unity of struggle which structures what we call "the people," the proletariat as a *political* class is divided between the *force* of its historical disruption and its grounding in the structured assignment of places. This is a dialectic of scission rather than synthesis. The proletariat is, Badiou argues, a "notorious element" of the "bourgeois world," or "imperialist society," which, rather than the bourgeoisie as a class, is the true contrary of the proletariat. The opposition is not between the proletariat and the bourgeoisie, but between imperialist society and the proletariat which is simultaneously its "principal productive force" and "the antagonistic political pole."[31]

What's more, the proletariat is not the expression of a prior foundation, anthropological or technological, which would then be realized in its overcoming. This was already a potentiality of the logic of self-abolition proposed by Marx and Engels in *The Holy Family*: "the proletariat can and must emancipate itself. But it cannot emancipate itself without abolishing the conditions of its own life."[32] As Badiou argues, this is not the automatic accomplishment of a historical goal, but an active organizational process: "the project of the proletariat, its internal being, is not to contradict the bourgeoisie, or to cut its feet from under it." It is rather "the abolition of any place in which something like a proletariat can be installed. The political project of the proletariat is the disappearance of the space of the placement of classes."[33]

This account of the groundedness of class position returns us to a language with which we began, that of the *situation*. In *Being and Event*, Badiou develops the groundedness of class position into the theory of the situation, which demonstrates that subjects only exist in situations, which are organized into a particular state. Yet the subject is in excess of the state of the situation.[34] The theory of the situation allows us to rigorously distinguish between a theory of the social or historical totality which would determine a subject, and a theory of subjects as consequences of the specificity of situations. Crucially, the site of the subject is an element which is specific to the situation; it does not *precede* the situation in the sense of a subject of history or a social foundation. It is rather the consequence of the "generic": that which has no identity or particular property, which is part of a situation yet indiscernible within it.[35]

---

[31] Badiou, *Theory of the Subject*, 7.
[32] Karl Marx and Frederick Engels, *Collected Works*, vol. 4 (London: Lawrence and Wishart, 1975), 37.
[33] Badiou, *Theory of the Subject*, 7.
[34] Alain Badiou, *Being and Event*, trans. Oliver Feltham (London: Continuum, 2006), 392.
[35] Badiou, *Being and Event*, 338.

The proletariat represents the status of the generic precisely because it is the "void" of the capitalist situation, as the young Marx described.[36]

We can reconceive of the political role of the human in the young Marx in terms of the generic. As I have tried to argue, the young Marx remains locked in a theoretical problematic which cannot think the subject independently of the historical teleology, yet it is only at this stage that Marx theoretically poses the question of the emancipatory subject. In *Metapolitics*, Badiou suggests that the human functions in the young Marx as an index of the generic rather than as a substantial property. The reason the young Marx turns toward humanism, besides the theoretical utility of its critique of Hegelian idealism, is its correspondence to the generic, which provides a philosophical foundation for communism. From this vantage point there are two senses of the generic in the young Marx. First, Badiou writes of Marx's vision in the *1844 Manuscripts* of "generic communism": "an egalitarian society of free association between polymorphous labourers," in which "the State as an authority separate from public coercion is dissolved," and thus "politics, which is the expression of the interests of social groups, and whose aim is the conquest of power, is itself dissolved."[37]

Badiou goes on to juxtapose the vision of generic communism with the classical political-philosophical vision of the "good State," both of which foreclose politics. These are foundations which cannot be compatible with politics, which "can be defined sequentially as that which attempts to create the impossibility of non-egalitarian statements relative to a situation."[38] In this latter sense, equality is "an axiom and not a goal."[39] In other words, "universal equality is not an objective state to be accomplished or approximated, but the guiding principle of a purely subjective mobilization."[40]

Yet while even generic communism cannot function as a foundation of politics, the generic status of the proletariat is fundamental in constituting it as a political subject. This is the second sense of the generic, which corresponds to the principle of purely subjective mobilization. The proletariat is not the political subject because of its substantial content, its being as community. To fill the proletariat with a substance converts the void discovered by the young Marx into a foundation, a risk which Marx himself did not entirely escape. What nevertheless contributes in Marxism to a theory of the subject is that the proletariat is considered the agent of emancipation—and thus its program is self-emancipation—because it is the name of the generic, and not because its

---

[36] Alain Badiou, *Ethics: An Essay on the Understanding of Evil*, trans. Peter Hallward (New York: Verso, 2013), 69.
[37] Alain Badiou, *Metapolitics*, trans. Jason Barker (New York: Verso, 2012), 80.
[38] Badiou, *Metapolitics*, 94.
[39] Badiou, *Metapolitics*, 112.
[40] Peter Hallward, *Badiou: A Subject To Truth* (Minneapolis: University of Minnesota Press, 2003), 45.

substance makes it a foundation of the political. The language of the human, while caught up in the anthropological conception of history, divides into two and points to the genericity of the emancipatory subject.

Our problem, then, is whether it is possible to think emancipation without a foundation. This is the crucial question that is presented in Marx's overall development. As I have argued, Marx's critique of rights constitutes not primarily the suspicion of rights as a bourgeois illusion, but the division of emancipation from the foundation of natural right. He subsequently discovers the emancipatory political subject in the proletariat as the void of bourgeois society, but ends up establishing a new foundation through the philosophy of history of the theory of alienation. This foundationalist teleology is undermined by the method of historical specificity that appears in the late Marx, but he presents no systematic theory of emancipation within the new problematic. The juxtaposition of the language of emancipation in late political texts with the new analysis of the capitalist mode of production suggests that emancipation must be understood strictly in terms of the historical specificity of the organized proletarian revolt against the capitalist mode of production, rather than in terms of the transhistorical process of the realization of the subject of man.

Yet how, then, are we to understand the persistence of emancipation across time and across worlds? Marx, who loved Spartacus, also referred regularly to the rebellions of slaves. If the proletariat is the historical agent of emancipation, then what of the slave revolts of the ancient world, or indeed of the many slaves incorporated into the capitalist world market?

These were central questions for Marx in his political life. In an 1860 letter to Engels, Marx wrote that "the most momentous thing happening in the world today is the slave movement."[41] The following year, in another letter to Engels, he would turn from modern to ancient slavery, describing Spartacus as "a real representative of the proletariat of ancient times."[42] In a noteworthy late reference to the category of emancipation, Marx would famously write in *Capital*: "In the United States of America, every independent workers' movement was paralysed as long as slavery disfigured a part of the republic. Labour in a white skin cannot emancipate itself where it is branded in a black skin."[43] In the same volume, Marx would also allude to the role of slavery in primitive accumulation:

> The discovery of gold and silver in America, the extirpation, enslavement and entombment in mines of the indigenous population of that continent, the

---

[41] Karl Marx and Frederick Engels, *Collected Works*, vol. 41 (London: Lawrence and Wishart, 1985), 4.
[42] Marx and Engels, *Collected Works*, 41:265.
[43] Karl Marx, *Capital: A Critique of Political Economy*, vol. 1, trans. Ben Fowkes (New York: Penguin, 1992), 414.

beginnings of the conquest and plunder of India, and the conversion of Africa into a preserve for the commercial hunting of blackskins, are all things which characterize the dawn of the era of capitalist production.[44]

However, these political and descriptive comments do not lead to a theoretical elaboration. What made precapitalist struggles against domination relevant to the class struggles of the modern capitalist world? What was the concrete relation between the emancipatory projects of black and white laborers? What role did slavery play in capitalist production once the latter had been established, and what were the implications of this role for the political content of struggles against slavery in the capitalist world?

If we were to engage in theoretical elaboration on Marx's behalf, we might be tempted to literalize the remark on the proletarian character of slaves in the ancient world, or to emphasize the centrality of modern slavery to global capitalist development. In the first case, we would lose the specificity of the capitalist mode of production, and in the second case, by guaranteeing the emancipatory character of slave revolts with social analysis, we would subordinate the political subject to objective conditions.

What if, instead, we begin with the theory of the emancipatory subject? In *Logics of Worlds*, Badiou identifies the "subjective form" of the "mass rebel" in Spartacus himself, and the slaves who form a body around him determined by the principle that "it is possible, for a slave, no longer to be a slave, and to do so *in the present*."[45] That is, "the revolt of Spartacus is the event which originates for the ancient world a maxim of emancipation in the present tense."[46] The defeat of such a revolt does not mean, however, that the principle is extinguished—instead, there is the figure of the "black Spartacus," a phrase introduced by Enlightenment abolitionism and extended to Toussaint-Louverture, the leader, Badiou writes, of

> the first victorious slave revolt . . . the revolt which made the principle of the abolition of slavery real . . . and which, in the exhilarating context of the French Revolution, created the first state led by former black slaves. In sum, the revolution that fully freed the black slaves of Santo Domingo constitutes a new present for the maxim of emancipation.[47]

---

[44] Marx, *Capital*, 915.
[45] Alain Badiou, *Logics of Worlds*, trans. Alberto Toscano (London: Continuum, 2009), 51.
[46] Badiou, *Logics of Worlds*, 63.
[47] Badiou, *Logics of Worlds*, 64. The "Black Spartacus" trope has been subjected to critical scrutiny in Marlene L. Daut, *Tropics of Haiti: Race and the Literary History of the Haitian Revolution in the Atlantic World, 1789–1865* (Liverpool: Liverpool University Press, 2015) and Grégory Pierrot, *The Black Avenger in Atlantic Culture* (Athens: University of Georgia Press, 2019). Badiou's use of the trope is criticized in Nick Nesbitt, *Caribbean Critique: Antillean Critical Theory from Toussaint to Glissant* (Liverpool: Liverpool University Press, 2013) and defended in Maurya

We have to pause here to consider the challenge that is posed by the Haitian Revolution to the classical conceptions of political emancipation, returning us to the problems posed by slavery as a whole within modernity. Alongside Marx's critique of rights and their declarations, a study of the historical situations within which they were advanced requires us to be attentive to another critique: the theoretical problem of the French Revolution is not only that its revolt against domination is waged in the name of natural right, but also that this coexists with colonial slavery.

In response to this seeming paradox, we might seek to demonstrate that the universal declarations of rights were not completely universal, since they rested on the exclusion of those in the colonies; it thus took the anti-colonial revolts to complete the universalism which was initiated in Europe by the Enlightenment and the modern revolutions. This argument has the great merit of decentering Europe in a historical narrative of universality. And it is indeed remarkable that the French revolutionary sequence is followed immediately by the Haitian sequence, in which the exclusion of slaves from the rights of man was challenged. But such an argument nevertheless grants primacy to Europe, which sets the agenda that is then carried out in the colonies; the world outside Europe merely realizes European achievements. We might then instead, as Adom Getachew proposes, consider the universality of the Haitian Revolution in terms of its radical specificity, which advances an entirely different set of norms than those of natural rights: the principles of the individual autonomy of peasants and their control of the land, and the collective autonomy of the nation of Haiti. The paradox of modernity, from this perspective, should not be understood in terms of the *exclusion* of slaves from the rights of man, but rather in terms of colonial *domination*.[48]

However, when the critique of Eurocentrism is extended to the suspicion of universality itself, we run up against an important limit. We cannot conceive of a revolt against domination which does not refer to that domination itself, unless we formulate a set of norms which are held to be independent of the situation, as the language of natural rights is usually interpreted. If a non-European universalism is articulated independent of the situation of European domination, we are now confronted with two sets of universal norms, and thus the peculiarity of a universalist relativism. Perhaps worse, we also have

---

Wickstrom, *Fiery Temporalities in Theatre and Performance: The Initiation of History* (London: Bloomsbury, 2018). If we have understood the complex relation Badiou presents between singularity and resurrection, we are no longer dealing with empirical questions of the influence of European philosophy on the Haitian Revolution or the critique of Eurocentrism which inverts its hierarchy. There is no question of events outside Europe—this "outside" which is both a Eurocentrist and inverted Eurocentrist characterization—being derivative of events in Europe. These political events are simultaneously singular and universal.

[48] Adom Getachew, "Universalism After the Post-Colonial Turn: Interpreting the Haitian Revolution," *Political Theory* 44, no. 6 (December 2016): 821–45.

the mirror of Eurocentrism which sees events in Europe as general and events outside Europe as specific. And finally, we veer dangerously close to the romantic ideal of a return to a prelapsarian condition before the corruption and decline induced by the introduction of power relations.

In fact, if we are to follow the principle of specificity to its fullest conclusion, we must recognize the specificity of *both* the French and Haitian cases. While the question of the Haitian Revolution is constantly debated in terms of universalism, I believe we have to begin first and foremost within the question of emancipation. To begin with the notion of the universalism of principles effaces the specificity of situations, as well as the character of the political subjectivities which are active in them. The fact that emancipation refers to domination is not specific to Haiti but is the case with every situation of emancipation—it always refers to an external power, even though it is self-emancipation and therefore must be sufficient in itself. This is the general conceptual problem which is played out in the debate about Haiti and Eurocentrism.

If we cannot refer emancipation to norms or foundations, and cannot predict its historical trajectory in advance, we must refer instead to concrete situations, and my claim is that in fact this is true even of moments of emancipatory struggle which conceive of themselves in terms of norms and foundations. The declarations of the rights of man are founded on the abstract and transhistorical universality of a unity of human nature. Yet we are justified in asking if what declares itself to be a foundation is actually operative as a foundation in its declaration, if it is actually a mutable declaration, which is repeated throughout revolutionary history and antagonistically adopted and adapted. There are multiple declarations, as Sophie Wahnich has pointed out, which are themselves "political and cultural—and hence not natural—objects… This natural right only exists if it is culturally declared."[49] In other words, natural right can be understood as the site of an antagonism. Marx's critique of the language of the rights of man as the expression of the atomized individual of civil society does not change the fact that natural right represented the struggle against the possessing classes, just as much as the latter claimed the rights of liberty as the rights of property.

Natural right can be conceived as a mobilization against either feudal privilege or colonialism. But we now exclude from the outset the question as to whether the revolt from the periphery only completes a project of universal emancipation which originates in Europe. Conceptually, we already know that this is not the case, because there is no world of abstraction in which rights enjoy a natural existence, there are only situations in which declarations can

---

[49] Sophie Wahnich, "Has Universality Ever Been Abstract? An FAQ," trans. Patrick King, *Viewpoint Magazine*, July 14, 2015, https://viewpointmag.com/2015/07/14/has-universality-ever-been-abstract-an-faq/.

be mobilized in politics. When natural right is the regulating category of a political sequence, it must be constantly reiterated, because its character is cultural and historical; the culturally and historically specific declarations of natural rights are historically contingent forms taken by emancipation, which exists only in historically contingent forms.

For these reasons, I will invoke a peculiar term Badiou introduces to frame the enduring character of universal emancipation: resurrection. Its full meaning is drawn out by Badiou's third example of the insurrectionary figure:

> More than a century later, when in 1919 the communist insurgents of Berlin, led by Karl Liebknecht and Rosa Luxemburg, brandished the name of "Spartakus" and called themselves "Spartakists," they too made it so that the "forgetting" (or failure) of the slave insurrection was itself forgotten and its maxim restored.[50]

Our problem now is that emancipation is understood in terms of the singularity of politics, and yet it resonates across times and worlds. This resonance, however, is irreducible to any foundation, which forecloses emancipation. It thus becomes necessary to study specific situations, and how emancipation emerges within them. To identify a foundation as the basis of the universality of emancipation does not respect its singularity. On the other hand, thinking the state of the situation means thinking its necessity, rather than the exception that is the emancipatory subject. The theory of emancipation, then, begins with the study of situations, but only insofar as it is oriented toward encountering the subjectivities that exceed them.

BIBLIOGRAPHY

Althusser, Louis. *For Marx.* Translated by Ben Brewster. London: Verso, 1977.
Althusser, Louis. *Politics and History: Montesquieu, Rousseau, Hegel and Marx.* Translated by Ben Brewster. London: New Left Books, 1972.
Althusser, Louis, and Étienne Balibar. *Reading Capital.* Translated by Ben Brewster. New York: Verso, 2006.
Badiou, Alain. *Being and Event.* Translated by Oliver Feltham. London: Continuum, 2006.
Badiou, Alain. *Ethics: An Essay on the Understanding of Evil.* Translated by Peter Hallward. New York: Verso, 2013.
Badiou, Alain. *Logics of Worlds.* Translated by Alberto Toscano. London: Continuum, 2009.
Badiou, Alain. *Metapolitics.* Translated by Jason Barker. New York: Verso, 2012.

---

[50] Badiou, *Logics of Worlds*, 64–65.

Badiou, Alain. *Theory of the Subject.* Translated by Bruno Bosteels. New York: Continuum, 2009.

Brown, Wendy. *States of Injury.* Princeton: Princeton University Press, 1995.

Daut, Marlene L. *Tropics of Haiti: Race and the Literary History of the Haitian Revolution in the Atlantic World, 1789–1865.* Liverpool: Liverpool University Press, 2015.

Gauthier, Florence. "The French Revolution: Revolution of the Rights of Man and the Citizen." In *History and Revolution: Refuting Revisionism*, edited by Mike Haynes and Jim Wolfreys, 71–92. New York: Verso, 2007.

Getachew, Adom. "Universalism After the Post-Colonial Turn: Interpreting the Haitian Revolution." *Political Theory* 44, no. 6 (December 2016): 821–45.

Hallward, Peter. *Badiou: A Subject to Truth.* Minneapolis: University of Minnesota Press, 2003.

Hartman, Saidiya V. *Scenes of Subjection: Terror, Slavery, and Self-Making in Nineteenth-Century America.* New York: Oxford University Press, 1997.

King, Jr., Martin Luther. *The Radical King.* Edited by Cornel West. Boston: Beacon Press, 2016.

Koselleck, Reinhart. *The Practice of Conceptual History: Timing History, Spacing Concepts.* Stanford: Stanford University Press, 2002.

Lazarus, Sylvain. *Anthropology of the Name.* Translated by Gila Walker. New York: Seagull Books, 2015.

Long, George. "Emancipatio." In *A Dictionary of Greek and Roman Antiquities*, edited by William Smith. London: John Murray, 1875.

Marx, Karl. *Capital: A Critique of Political Economy.* Vol. 1. Translated by Ben Fowkes. New York: Penguin, 1992.

Marx, Karl, and Frederick Engels. *Collected Works.* 50 Vols. London: Lawrence and Wishart, 1975–2004.

Neocosmos, Michael. *Thinking Freedom in Africa.* Johannesburg: Wits University Press, 2016.

Nesbitt, Nick. *Caribbean Critique: Antillean Critical Theory from Toussaint to Glissant.* Liverpool: Liverpool University Press, 2013.

Pierrot, Grégory. *The Black Avenger in Atlantic Culture.* Athens: University of Georgia Press, 2019.

Scott, Joan Wallach. "The Vexed Relationship of Emancipation and Equality." *History of the Present* 2, no. 2 (Fall 2012): 148–68.

Tomba, Massimiliano. "Emancipation as Therapy: Bauer and Marx on the Jewish Question." In *Die linken Hegelianer*, edited by Michael Quante and Amir Mohseni, 161–75. Paderborn, Germany: Wilhelm Fink, 2015.

Tomba, Massimiliano. "Exclusiveness and Political Universalism in Bruno Bauer." In *The New Hegelians*, edited by Douglas Moggach, 91–113. Cambridge: Cambridge University Press, 2006.

Wahnich, Sophie. "Has Universality Ever Been Abstract? An FAQ." Translated by Patrick King. *Viewpoint Magazine*, July 14, 2015, https://viewpointmag.com/2015/07/14/has-universality-ever-been-abstract-an-faq/.

Wickstrom, Maurya. *Fiery Temporalities in Theatre and Performance: The Initiation of History.* London: Bloomsbury, 2018.

Chapter 4

On a Critical Realist Theory of Identity[1]

Rosaura Sánchez

The ongoing work of post-positivist realists[2] interested in reclaiming reality and identity as epistemological sites has generated much discussion in recent conferences and publications. While agreeing in general with the positions of post-positive realists, in this essay I would like to contribute to the discussion by turning to several fundamental issues and categories that often get misconstrued or subsumed in discussions of identity politics. I have considered it important to begin disarticulating the process of identity formation by focusing on the salient features of some basic categories. There is without a doubt a need to formulate a theory that posits a materialist grounding of knowledge and analyzes the always political nature of the production of that knowledge. I would like therefore to suggest that we engage in a critical realist analysis of identity formation. This requires, in my opinion, attention to three major points: (a) what is at stake in positing a reclaiming of reality, (b) what is involved in rethinking or refashioning identity in the current context, and (c) the need for a recentering of class and a reconsideration of the role of the state in any discussion of identity formation.

In the preface to *Literary Theory and the Claims of History*, Mohanty calls for exploring and developing a theoretical alternative to the notion of objectivity, one that could be called "realist."[3] This desire for what I am calling a

---

[1] My thanks to Satya Mohanty, Linda Alcoff, and Paula Moya for the opportunity to address these issues, and to Beatrice Pita for all her generous suggestions and comments on this paper.

[2] Satya P. Mohanty, *Literary Theory and the Claims of History* (Ithaca: Cornell University Press, 1997). Paula Moya and Michael R. Hames-García, ed. *Reclaiming Identity* (Berkeley: University of California Press, 2000). See also Paula Moya, *Learning from Experience* (Berkeley: University of California Press, 2002).

[3] Mohanty, *Literary Theory*, xii.

"critical realist" alternative, a term I am borrowing from Bhaskar,[4] and for reclaiming reality is linked to epistemological as well as concrete political objectives. For, if the ultimate struggle is against forms of domination (material and ideological), then what is indispensable is a politics of agency, that is, political action within the many domains of capitalist society. Concretely, then, one of our main concerns needs to be exploring the role that a politics of identity can play in generating agency and in creating critical spaces from which to resist and contest hegemonic shaping and defining of "reality." At one level, this implies a conscious search for commonalities, for identities-in-difference[5] that can serve to unite individuals and collectivities alike around common interests in order to produce political alliances and solidarity for social struggle. At another, it implies a conscious awareness of differences that are not only discursive but also social and economic, and definitely divisive.

It goes without saying that in the last two decades identity issues and identity politics have been the object around which not only theorizing but social and political organizing have revolved. Since at least the beginning of the post-civil rights period, identity politics have generated a great deal of discussion and been subject to appropriation, attacks, and dismissal from various quarters.[6] The most facile attack has been to accuse proponents of identity politics (the so-called identitarians) of essentialism. Some on the right are arguing that in what is construed as a race-blind society identity politics is now irrelevant.[7] Others have argued that advocates of identity politics have given up the struggle against capitalism and, in foregrounding culture, identity, and performativity, have in good measure relinquished interest in political economy and in differential structural positioning and access to resources. Finding that capitalism has penetrated to nearly every corner of the world, it is argued, these identity culturalists tend to naturalize it, leaving aside to a large extent the fact that it is exploitative and oppressive, subjecting workers to the requirements of profit maximization and capital accumulation throughout the world. This critique of the culturalists' shortcomings is valid to some extent and for that reason I see a need for a politics of identity that is less focused on recognition and representation and more interested in the constitution of political agents involved in global/local struggles for social transformation.

While not all proponents of identity politics have gone beyond critiques grounded in the economic disparities that characterize capitalism, there are

---

[4] Roy Bhaskar, *Philosophy and the Idea of Freedom* (Cambridge: Blackwell, 1991), 139.
[5] Roy Bhaskar, *Dialectic. The Pulse of Freedom* (London: Verso, 1993), 10.
[6] Bill Albertini et al., "Introduction," to "Is There Life After Identity Politics," *New Literary History* 31, no. 4 (2000): 621–25.
[7] In California, Ward Connerly and his allies, through their Racial Privacy Initiative, sought to eliminate all classifications on the basis of race, ethnicity, color, or national origin within public employment, public contracting, and public education. See Evan McLaughlin, "Connerly, Moores Team up on Racial Initiative," *The UCSD Guardian*, February 4, 2002, https://ucsdguardian.org/2002/02/04/connerly-moores-team-up-on-racial-initiative/.

undoubtedly those who find that the ideological/economic is no longer a productive site for social transformation. I would disagree on this point, not only because all social sites are in some way also economic and ideological, but because the very elements of negativity, always necessary for change and agential action, are generated by class differences. In fact, I would argue that the tendency to focus on cultural differences as practices or performances delinked from those social relations and contradictions that are the causal grounding of these differences is fetishistic. A critical realist politics of identity, I would offer, rejects all types of idealisms and provides a materialist account of identity formation that meets explanatory adequacy by examining identity in direct relation to social structures, noting how social structures configure, condition, limit, and constrain agency and never forgetting that agency has the potential to transform social structures. Identity, unlike identification, is agentially formed, and for this reason generating a critical and self-reflexive critique of identity in relation to non-identity, contradiction, absence, negation, and change is especially important.

In our search for the constitution of radical subjects that can organize to challenge the hegemonic order and eliminate structural constraints, bringing about social—especially radical or revolutionary—change, it is important to bear in mind that meaningful political organizing is seldom, if ever, spontaneous but rather deliberate and painstakingly achieved; moreover it is always marked by immediate goals or short-term objectives as well as long-term goals. Surely there can be no major global/national struggle for substantive transformation without prior political organizing at the local level; but the opposite has also been the case historically, as local struggles often recall previous sites of national struggle (as is clear in the case of the Zapatistas in Chiapas). Organizing around issues of cultural identity can create sites of common political interests and political agency, that is, the constitution of political subjects willing to struggle. The fact that identity struggles are not necessarily transformative but rather reformist in nature at given historical conjunctures should not deter us, as it will instigate political subjects with accrued prior political activist experience (political "capital" so to speak) to take additional transformative steps. At the same time, a critical analysis requires that one recognize the shortcomings and limitations of particular struggles, but without necessarily dismissing them as peripheral or of little consequence, as some of my colleagues on the left, who have argued that social change will not come from "voices on the margin."[8]

While I harbor no illusions about transgressive "identity politics," insofar as ultimately effecting transformative social change, and while I recognize

---

[8] David Harvey, *Justice, Nature, and the Geography of Difference* (Cambridge: Blackwell Publishers, 1996), 101.

that "identity politics" can be manipulated by hegemonic forces, I will argue that a critical politics of identity can play a part in political organizing and in challenging hegemonic discourses, even if structural transformation is not the issue at hand in the short term. Political agency, after all, can always simply lead to the perpetuation of existing structures.[9] Yet, without agency there can be no emancipation. Structural social transformation will require, then, reflexivity and entail many battles along the way, of different types and at different levels, that can prepare us for larger struggles. In today's stratified and divided context, I believe, retaining a critical politics of identity makes political sense and is strategically practical.

There is, then, a strategic rationale for a politics of identity and that is: developing critical political agency. For this reason, we need to go beyond issues of inclusion/exclusion and an exaltation of difference as difference to engage in an exploration of events, relations, and structures that have a constitutive role in identity formation. Identity, though discursive in nature, is ultimately grounded in social reality, that is, social structures and relations; unfortunately in recent times, we have in many instances boxed ourselves into a discursive corner, positing discourse as itself constitutive over and above social structures.[10] Is "the word the medium in which power works" as Stuart Hall affirms?[11] I think that we need to look at this formulation closely and say that it is *a* medium but not the only one, for power works at all levels of our social structures, including, but not exclusively, within the cultural terrain. By contrast, reality is most definitely not limited to the discursive domain. Let us not incur, then, in the linguistic fallacy, confusing reality with our discourses about reality. Nor should we define reality in terms of knowledge—the epistemic fallacy.[12] Thus, while recognizing that discourses mediate our knowledge and intuition about the world, it is also important to bear in mind that reality is not reducible to our discourses—or to our knowledge of it—nor can any transformational social struggle be reduced to a negotiation over meaning.[13] Reality is not, then, limited to the way we construct it or theorize it. We, although cognizant and sentient beings, are not the litmus test of reality. What we call reality, as noted by Prigogine, is nevertheless "revealed to us only through the active construction in which we participate."[14] And, yet, clearly

---

[9] Bhaskar, *Dialectic*, 279.
[10] Stuart Hall, "New Ethnicities," *Stuart Hall: Critical Dialogues in Cultural Studies*, ed. David Morley and Kuan-Hsisng Chen (London: Routledge, 1996), 443.
[11] Stuart Hall, "Subjects in History. Making Diasporic Identities," *The House that Race Built*, ed. Wahneema Lubiano (New York: Pantheon Books, 1997), 299.
[12] Bhaskar, *Philosophy*, 33.
[13] Timothy Brennan, "Black Theorists and Left Antagonists," *The Minnesota Review* 37 (1991): 89–113.
[14] Ilya Prigogine and Isabelle Stengers, *Order Out of Chaos* (New York: Bantam Books, 1984), 293.

we don't all participate in this process of construction on an equal footing, an issue that, though crucial, is all but avoided by some knowledge theorists.

Let us recall, furthermore, that our knowledge of reality is itself constantly changing; knowledge itself is productive and transformative and conditions the emergence of new social identities, that, by virtue of being constituted in tension with other identities—that is, as non-identities, as differentiations—always are already political. Identity formation, then, takes place at a conjuncture of external and internal, contingent and necessary, processes that interconnect and emerge within specific historical conditions that are in good measure not of our own making. It would be foolhardy, then, to explore identity formation outside the complex web of social structural relations. What is needed is a critical theory that is grounded in a fuller recognition of how particular social structures and relations condition a diversity of social and historical experiences and generate concrete social spaces that give rise to social, political, and cultural identities. In turn, these social spaces are themselves productive sites, enabling the construction of new and potentially radical/transformative political subjects.

Acknowledging the risk of stating the obvious, I think it bears repeating that we are all born into a multiply determined and contradictory world that preexists us, and is situated within specific social structures (be they economic, political, or cultural). As social agents, however, we are not reduced to one social location as we are constantly in the process not only of reproducing but also of transforming these very same social sites.[15] The desire to transform the material world is a product of reflexivity, a conscious, though contingent, awareness on our part of gaps, absences, discontinuities, and inconsistencies between our social world and the discourses available to us with which to apprehend it. The transformation of social structures will, however, have to go beyond discursive change or redescriptions of reality, although revolutionary structural changes will undoubtedly involve the development of new explanatory discourses and critiques of particular practices.[16] While seemingly an obvious point, it carries within it key implications for the construction of a reality-based critique, as I will develop below.

Broadly speaking, these are a few of the elements of a critical realist theoretical framework that I find promising for a fuller exploration of identity formation. And because, as I have sketched out above, social actors' knowledge is conditioned by social structures—the very structures that human agency can transform—I want to first look more closely into two useful categories for exploring identity: positioning and positionality.

---

[15] Bhaskar, *Philosophy*, 71.
[16] Bhaskar, *Philosophy*, 72.

POSITIONING AND POSITIONALITY

Identity, as Harvey notes in *Spaces of Hope*, "cannot be understood outside of the forces that swirl around it and construct it."[17] Identity formation is itself a process shaped by political, economic, and cultural forces that come together and mutually constitute one another in distinctive and dynamic ways. Key among these forces, although often backgrounded when not omitted, is the labor process, which positions one within a given class structure. The very fact that in the last three decades it has not been fashionable to talk about class, that, often, any mention of class is immediately labeled reductionist, should already raise a flag: we are facing denial and/or displacement of a central fact of social life. This retreat from class, as noted by Meiksins Wood,[18] is prevalent particularly among postmodernist/poststructuralist proponents of a "politics of difference," who have no problem leveling off all differences and precisely because of this often fail to link particular differences with social location. A critical realist theory of identity formation, on the other hand, necessarily implies viewing class/structural positioning as part and parcel of *all* social conjunctures and inseparably connected to every distinctive conflictual difference. Identity, of course, cannot be reduced to social location or positioning, but it also cannot be analyzed in any meaningful way without taking it into account. In fact, I would argue, social location and identity could be said to be distinct but inseparable.

If social positioning is one's location within a set or conjuncture of economic, political, and cultural structures, it follows necessarily that class cannot be the *only* positioning that matters; one is always also situated within interconnected and interrelated gender, racial/ethnic, and sexual social structures as well and subject to a network of social relations linking these various structures. Political structures situate us as citizens (first-class or second-class) or non-citizens, residents, etc., of a particular nation-state, with various rights and obligations. Through its coercive powers and authority and through its underpinning of the capitalist system, the state also constrains us in multiple ways. The state has the power to curb our actions and to subject us to unwarranted searches and imprisonment; it, in fact, defines for us what our social status will be: legal/illegal, dependent, spouse, draftee, and so on. There are multiple means available to the state to restrict political action against the state and history teaches us that the state has, in the past, taken action not only against its "enemies" but against its citizens, as in cases where

---

[17] David Harvey, *Spaces of Hope* (Berkeley: University of California Press, 2000), 16.
[18] Ellen Meiksins Wood, *The Retreat From Class. A New "True" Socialism* (London: Verso, 1986). See also her "Modernity, Postmodernity, or Capitalism?" *Monthly Review* 48, no. 3 (1996): 21–39, and "Labor, the State and Class Struggle," *Monthly Review* 49, no. 3 (1997): 1–17.

troop action has been used against demonstrators or strikers, or in cases where state-funded researchers have conducted chemical and nuclear experimentation with patients, soldiers, and other citizens. The state's multiple powers position us in many ways; the arm of the law is indeed long. Aside from the coercive reach of the state, perhaps the most powerful area in which the state operates is in exerting its power of identification, not only through its census-taking, as the most obvious example, but through a variety of apparatuses that institute systems of labels that categorize and classify us. This labeling is no mean thing as we know all too well; at its most malign it is linked to its coercive powers to criminalize entire segments of the population on the basis of social location as determined by race, ethnicity, and economic standing, as is evident in police profiling, or to order and implement wholesale "relocations" of populations.

While the state may base particular cases of discrimination and oppression on social positioning, it is also fast to manipulate particular positionings, if it finds these expedient. The United States' false allegation of weapons of mass destruction in Iraq to justify an invasion and occupation is a clear example of the state's ability to manipulate positionings for the profit of oil companies and the war machine. U.S. action in Afghanistan has likewise been explained in terms of police action against terrorists and against nations that support and shelter terrorists. During the period of intensive bombing of this area, interestingly, the state and mass media chose to foreground the need to improve conditions for Muslim women in Afghanistan, in the process implicitly legitimating military action there. This ostensible concern for positioning within sexist gender structures is, however, not evident at home, where women continue to be the objects of sexist practices, abuse, rape, and domestic violence. Women die every day in the United States at the hands of violent husbands and partners, much as children too die every day at the hands of parents, guardians, and sitters. Of course, it is quite understandable that those positioned in oppressive or exploitative locations should seek to improve their situation by whatever means are available. But those of us observing events from afar, who have not been consulted about military policies that we do not support, can see the astute way in which fashionable discourses can be manipulated by the state for its own agenda.

Gender positioning, like subordinate status by virtue of age or legal status, cannot, of course, be considered in isolation as it is always part of a conjuncture in which various factors are simultaneously implicated. Yet, the complexity of the conjuncture is often ignored as is clear in the many discussions dominating cultural criticism today and that focus almost exclusively—after paying lip service to the notion of the intersection of race, class, and gender—on single issues or positionings. For this reason, and because it has been key in the positioning of Chicanas and Chicanos, I see the need to stress the intersectedness of positionings and to include class positioning in any conjunctural analysis, even when class is not the dominant issue. Unlike some that wish to envision the United States as a classless society, I see a thoroughly and even increasingly class-based social structure that conditions agency and shapes social relations, enabling or constraining possibilities.

Class, then, is not merely a "discourse" or a "narrative" but a concrete social positioning. For me the key term linked to class positioning is exploitation, but I recognize that today economists and other theorists are wary about defining class, lest it fall into essentialism.[19] That danger can be avoided in a theory that posits social positioning, of any type, as not fixed, but rather as relational and, like reality itself, always in flux, always changing. Various theorists wishing to avoid static class definitions based on what sound like fixed relations of production have offered other conceptualizations. Harvey, for example, prefers to define class as a "situatedness or positionality in relation to processes of capital accumulation."[20] This definition is meant to be more inclusive since all of us are positioned in relation to capital accumulation, by selling our labor power and consuming commodities, if not actively involved in exploiting labor or investing, and the like. We all relate, then, in various ways to different circuits of capital, and often in more than one way at any given time. What is important to note here is that class positioning situates us in relation to and within capitalist structures and thus locates us (and dislocates us) socially in highly complex and significant ways.

Discussions of class structures are too often skirted or avoided outright by focusing on issues of income, access to consumption, poverty, or socioeconomic inequality. In effect, discussions of poverty—the "poor," the "underclass," "the underprivileged," according to the source—serve to displace attention away from social contradictions that are structural in nature. One cannot deny that inequality is a global problem that not only divides the rich North from the poor south, but also the very rich from the poor within individual countries, even in advanced economies, as noted by Callinicos,[21] among others. Poverty, however, is only the most overt manifestation of structural contradictions that can be traced to capitalist relations of production, and the formulation is one that reduces the problem to one of distribution rather than to the class stratification inherent in society. While it is useful to contrast conditions in the affluent first world with those in much of the third

---

[19] J. K. Gibson-Graham, Stephen A. Resnick, and Richard D. Wolff, "Introduction: Class in a Poststructuralist Frame," *Class and its Others*, ed. J. K. Gibson-Graham, Stephen A. Resnick, and Richard D. Wolff (Minneapolis: University of Minnesota Press, 2000), 10.

[20] Harvey, *Justice*, 359.

[21] Alex Callinicos, *Equality* (Malden, MA: Polity Press, 2000), 2–3. Citing Robert Brenner, Callinicos points to the fact that real wages and salaries have fallen since 1979 and that the United States "is evolving into a two-tier society, and the upper tier is shrinking."

world, or consider the discrepancies between conditions in wealthy communities and those in ghettos and barrios, it does not necessarily call into account the role that national and multinational capitalist enterprises as well as the policies of international agencies like the IMF (International Monetary Fund), World Bank, and trade agreements like NAFTA (North American Free Trade Agreement) have in creating conditions of unemployment, underemployment, and low-wage employment, at both the national and global level. What should be increasingly clear is that we are all positioned structurally not only within national but also international contexts, as much economically as politically. And however much we seek to ignore this positioning, the social situation is as close as the very blouse or shirt on our backs or the shoes on our feet, more likely than not the product of super-exploited cheap labor, mostly female labor, in maquiladoras or sweatshops, often owned by U.S.-based companies.

Gender, class, and race are always part of the social conjuncture. The question is why one should stress class location if the conjuncture is, in fact, constituted by several positionings? In response, one should recall that class considerations do not disallow other positions, but rather require an analysis of positioning in terms of antagonistic social relations and contradictions, which themselves are structural and geo-historically specific. Issues of gender, racial/ethnic, and sexual orientation are, as previously mentioned, too often contained within a framework of difference that masks the structural grounding of these relations. Class, on the other hand, is first and foremost a structural positioning; class relations are, moreover, implicitly problematic and not easily naturalized. Class can function, then, as a heuristic construct that invites the exploration of varied social problems on the basis of social positioning and social structures. Structural analyses also allow for a grasp of commonalities shared across different social positionings. In other words, an analysis of antagonistic relations within class, gender, racial/ethnic, and/or heterosexual structures is also an analysis of equivalencies among non-equivalent positionings, or, to employ Bhaskar's formulation, "identities-in-difference."[22]

Before moving on to "positionality," let me sum up by reiterating that "positioning" refers to one's location within a given social reality. Positioning, as previously noted, is structurally determined but it goes without saying that it is unavoidably discursively mediated. It is also relational; in other words, one is always situated with respect to other locations, enabling individuals to become aware of differences between and commonalities among positionings. Positioning also implies standing in opposition to other locations; certain positionings are not merely different, but antagonistic. It

---

[22] Bhaskar, *Dialectic*, 122.

is one's awareness of positioning within a conjuncture, one's awareness of disjuncture, that is, of social contradictions, of the lack or absence of certain powers, goods, opportunities, or privileges, that is politically critical and productive. Reflexivity with respect to one's positioning is contingent on a series of factors. It may lead to complicity or a conciliatory compromise with given social structures and perhaps to a desire to maintain the status quo, or it may lead to transformative practices. This reflexivity vis-à-vis a particular conjuncture is what I would like to term positionality to draw attention to and differentiate from social positioning.

I would like to distinguish, then, between one's social location or positioning and positionality, that is, one's imagined relation or standpoint relative to that positioning. This reflexivity, understanding of, or subjective relation with regard to social location is ideological. While positioning is extra-discursive (i.e., structural), although conceptually mediated, positionality is discursive and may be contingent upon other factors, other complementary or competing discourses, not specifically implicated by one's social location. Positionality is a useful diagnostic construct as it enables one to better examine and understand why individuals sharing a similar or even the same positioning do not *live* their situation in the same way. A working-class Chicano, for example, may see the structural location of people living in his barrio variously: from a bourgeois perspective (disdain in the face of what he considers lack of individual effort or merit on the part of those he considers lazy and incompetent), a religious perspective (resignation before the will of God who determined their condition of poverty), or a progressive perspective (resentment against capitalist enterprises in collusion with the state to keep his segregated community polluted by industries, fragmented by freeways, underemployed, ill-served by poor schools that lead to a high dropout rate, and faced with conditions that generate violence and drug dealing). One's positionality is thus conditioned, but not strictly determined, by one's social positioning; moreover, positionality is always at variance with other positionalities, including one's own on other issues, as one's perspectives are always multiple, contradictory, and, again, constantly in a state of flux, renegotiating themselves in the face of changing realities.

What we generally intend to capture by the term "experience" is constituted by an aggregate of dialectically contradictory positionings and positionalities. In experience, positionings and positionalities are distinct but inseparable, connected yet contradictory. It is this interconnection between positioning and positionality that determines one's lived experience, that is, how one lives one's situation (actual and perceived) in the world. And in this regard, I consider the "post-positive realist project's" rejection of an "empiricist notion of experience" to be a key theorizing move. With recognition that experience is mediated, that a series of positional discourses intervene and mediate one's way of perceiving positionings, comes as well an awareness that one's experience may be mediated as much by hegemonic discourses as by critical anti-hegemonic discourses. It is then not surprising to find conservative Chicanos like Richard Rodríguez or African-Americans like Clarence Thomas, both of whom assume hegemonic positionalities vis-à-vis the experiences of those with whom they at some point have shared social positioning.

Of course, the cognitive dissonance, asymmetry, or lack of sync between one's positioning and one's positionality can also, as previously noted, be politically productive. The moment positionality is mediated by counter-discourses and one experiences alienation and becomes aware of disjunctures, social inequities, lacks, the non-parity of citizens, the social constraints, and inconsistencies in society, then, one has reached the space of critical questioning, which can give rise to a critical assessment of hegemonic ideologies. Awareness of disjunctures between hegemonic discourses and one's reality may also be brought home by violence (e.g. police brutality, state violence against its citizens, class or racial discrimination, gender abuse, etc.). While a lack of sync between positioning and positionality can be a catalyst for reassessing the explanatory adequacy of hegemonic discourses, the "ill-fit" between hegemonic discourses of equality and opportunity and a reality of racist, sexist, and classist practices may also lead to disidentification, not only—or necessarily—with the forces of domination but also with those sharing one's positioning, that is, with one's own group. This brings us to consider a second set of key issues: identification and identity, as these mesh in an often problematic fashion with social position and positionality. Clearly, one needs to consider not only positioning and positionality, but also identification, non-identification, disidentification, and misidentification in analyzing the broader process of identity formation.

IDENTIFICATION AND IDENTITIES

To try to chart what I consider the important differences between these sets of terms, let me begin the discussion by noting that unlike positioning, which is extra-discursive although discursively mediated, identification is a relational and discursive process that is always linked to a group or collectivity that is contained within a particular social space. That space is the product of social location. Not only are social spaces themselves productive of other spaces, but one is always necessarily situated in several spaces. Multiple socio-spatial positioning also implies by definition being linked to a variety of social groupings that are spatially distributed. It is this particular socio-spatial distribution of collectivities that creates conditions for identification on the basis of distinctive groupings. To simplify, identification, then, is relationalist rather than individualist; it always designates individuals as part of a whole; the implication is thus always collective and socio-spatial in nature. It is the socio-spatial and structural positioning of collectivities of social actors that gives rise to discourses of identification.

The process itself of identification, of "ascription," presupposes awareness of relations between socio-spatial positionings. Identification not only refers to a designation of ties or connections between groups and socio-spatial-structural positionings but also revolves around a contradiction, a negation, a concomitant non-identification, with particular social spaces and actors. Identification always implies a non-identification, or even a concretized disidentification with one or more social groups and social spaces. The fact that one can be linked to more than one collectivity points to the contingent nature of identification processes, which are always partial and in flux. Yet, one cannot deny that some identifications are more enduring, more critical, if not dominant, than others. To belabor the point, given a dominant Eurocentric worldview, identification as a person of color has been highly significant for the past 500 years; being of the female persuasion in male-dominant contexts, on the other hand, has been critical for an even longer period of time.

As a discursive process, identification can be imposed from outside or it can be assumed as a matter of choice; it can emerge from outside or from within a social space or group. It can be forced upon a community or collectivity from beyond its confines, as in the case of the derogatory designation of people of Mexican origin as "greasers." Identification can be imposed by the state, as in census reports that designate Latinos as "Hispanics" or "white" or as in its targeting of particular segments of minority populations under the rubric of criminal or terroristic. Schools are an important state agency that often identifies entire segments of its minority student population as unfit for higher education or suited only for vocational training. Identification can also be generated from within in relation to the outside, as in the case of our self-identification as "Chicanos." Identification is, then, a discursive process that can serve to signal a group's isolation, uniqueness, segregation, rejection, subordination, domination, or difference vis-à-vis others; it can involve a defensive or exclusionary mechanism, but, as noted earlier, it can also serve as a rallying call for recognition and redress of grievances. What is clear is that identification arises from and serves to account for distinctions or conflictual differences coming out of relationships of power involving exploitation, domination, and subordination, and stemming not simply from "non-identity."

As social processes, identifications are also generative and serve as catalysts to new and varied identifications. Consider, for example, the misidentification of the native population of the Americas as "indios," as Indians. As Mariátegui recalled, the Quechua-speaking population of Perú, dispossessed, super-exploited, abused, and culturally oppressed, resolved to make the people's misidentification/ identification as "Indians" into a revolutionary identity by stating that if "Indian" was the name under which they had been oppressed, "Indian" would also be the name under which they would rebel.[23] Thus, new identifications, even those arising out of misidentification, colonialism, and subordinate social positioning as in the case above, can serve as rallying strategies, but they can also be deployed to stigmatize and censure particular groups, as is still the case in the pejorative use of "indio" to designate an uneducated and/or uncouth person throughout Latin America today.

As opposed to identification processes, individual identity, on the other hand, emerges precisely out of individuation from a collectivity. While identification can be imposed from the outside, as we have noted above, identity is always agential; it involves an awareness of identification as a containment process and entails a conscious acceptance of a designation, that is, of a discourse, whether it be imposed from the outside or generated from within a group. Identity implies reflexivity, a willing connection to a collectivity, and a recognition of being bound to a group. By default, identity also implies non-identity, that is, an acknowledgment of difference, of being one thing and not another (the "not-I"). In the absence of reflexivity, identification is not problematic and identity is a non-issue, as is often the case for Latinos/as who have been isolated in white communities of the Midwest, for example. Often it is when they migrate to the southwest or to a large metropolis and they are stopped by the police or are discriminated at work or at a coffee shop as people of color that they become suddenly acutely aware of the identification process and of their designation as members of a particular group. At that point, their positionality, the way they view their positioning, is forced to undergo a major shift. In the process of becoming aware of social contradictions and difference (non-identity or alterity), the individual may opt for a particular designation or identity linking him to a group. Of course, the individual may just as well want to get as far away from being associated with any given group as he/she can. In either case, the response will be identity or non-identity, but the issue cannot be skirted, although it may be displaced. Identity, then, implies an agential act of affirmation or negation and action, a coming to terms with the fact of identification processes at work.

---

[23] From "Manifiesto del Movimiento Indio Pedro Vilca Apaza, Perú": ("Si "indio ha sido el nombre con el que fuimos sometidos, indio será el nombre con el que nos sublevaremos." Cited in Marie-Chantal Barre, *Ideologías indigenistas y movimientos indios* (México: Siglo Veintiuno, 1983), 18.

Given the varied socio-spatial-structural location of individuals, and their links to a variety of groupings (family, community, gender grouping, etc.), identities are necessarily also multiple. One can then posit constellations of identities that are themselves distinct but connected, all grounded in historically specific social spaces but always open and in flux. Logically, it also stands to reason that not all identities can be foregrounded at any one time. There is, however, a tactical value to be gained in foregrounding—or backgrounding—particular identities at given times, precisely because identity equips one discursively to relate to the world, to make sense of one's social positioning, or to further a given agenda at a particular moment. Identity, then, is a discourse that serves to mediate between the individual and the world.

The issue for critical realists is not only to link identity to social positioning and positionality but, in view of our desire for social transformation, to examine how the deployment of identities plays out. It should be expected that mapping social interaction, that is, the various recombinations of identities, and accounting for identities-in-difference, should be no less complicated than mapping the human genome.

THE EPISTEMIC VALUE OF EXPERIENCE

Both identification and identity are discursive processes that cannot be examined outside of experience, that is, outside of the varied social positionings and positionalities that situate individuals. Positioning, as previously noted, does not produce one experience, this in view of the fact that individuals often interpret and live their social location in a variety of ways. Similarly, positioning will trigger particular identifications, but there is no rule ensuring willing acceptance of that identity by individuals. Non-identity or disidentification from an ascribed collectivity, however, does not eliminate identification that is externally imposed, as any person of color trying to pass for white can attest. The dialectical connection between positioning and positionality is however crucial for an understanding of agency and experience. Further complicating this contradictory connection is the fact that one is positioned within multiple overlapping sites. Experience is thus variable as one is never situated only within one social site. Often this variability is ignored by a universalizing move that blurs particularity, resulting in the reification of experience, as in the phrase "barrio experience," as if there were one universally shared, homogenous experience in the barrio. A woman in the barrio does not have or live the same experience as a man, nor will any two men necessarily experience the barrio in like fashion. The space of gender as it overlaps with the space of class, for example, produces an entirely different social space, an entirely different experience. Experience, then, can only be considered within a constellation of positionings that interconnect in multiple ways, never only in one way, as there are always social boundaries and limits that impact particular interconnections and overlappings that are open or closed, that is, available or unavailable, to us, depending on our positioning.

What about the epistemic value of experience? Do positioning and positionality offer a particular—or privileged—vantage point regarding reality, and a particular understanding or knowledge of the world? It's a vexed question. One could argue that positioning and positionality enable a partial view of the world, an understanding grounded in the social spaces within which one is situated and in the discourses with which one is conversant. That would be true for every human being on Earth, as each and every one of us is socially and discursively located. If experience, however, enables only a partial view (and isn't all knowledge partial?), this vantage point can also serve as the basis for either a distorted or enlightened view of reality. What becomes important, then, is reflexivity, that is, an acute awareness (however contingent) of contradictions between positioning and positionality that prepare us, make us ready so to speak, to seek new understandings and explanations that can point the way to emancipatory practices and, by the same token, unmask false antagonisms. The important distinction to remember is that experience is concrete and knowledge is theoretically based. At bottom, it seems to me that, in formulating a "critical realist" framework, what one seeks is a theoretical explanation or account of the concrete, both past and present. We need, however, to distinguish between descriptive and explanatory adequacy. The practical wisdom that any given experience affords may meet descriptive rather than explanatory adequacy, for it is the case that particular positionings may place constraints on the types of theoretical discourses accessible to one and result in "explaining" matters by merely describing them, or couching them in accessible discourses. For example, in the barrio, as noted before, one may have access to religious discourses or hegemonic discourses acquired at school to explain social reality. An awareness of contradictions, that is, the ill-fit between one's reality and the explanatory discourses available to one, on the other hand, can give rise to a questioning of both one's reality and hegemonic discourses. It is this explanatory inadequacy—what I want to term "discursive insufficiency"—as it were, that can lead to epistemic questioning and a search for discourses that provide more satisfactory accounts of "reality."

We can of course, as Mohanty notes, be right or wrong "about the way our social locations enable or inhibit certain kinds of understanding."[24] What

---

[24] Mohanty, *Literary Theory*, 148.

is crucial here, I think, is the language or theory available to the individual and by extension to the collective; with theoretical discourses as with other resources often it is a matter of differential access. The acquisition of particular discourses is not automatic and often a marker of privilege. And yet, especially when contradictions between positioning and positionality become acute, particular social locations can trigger an awareness of cognitive dissonance and generate questioning, resentment, resignation, accommodation, complicity, or disillusionment as a response to this explanatory insufficiency. The choice of questions we raise, the contradictions and processes we become aware of, and the causal factors we identify, on the other hand, will be very much linked to the particular language or theory that we deploy. A critical theory of reality that allows for new epistemologies, critical alternative cognitive frameworks born out of incongruent lived experience, has a great deal to offer both at the level of theorizing and of concrete political practice, particularly now.

Being a literature person, I want to look now at how a number of these notions about positioning/positionality, identification/identity, and the epistemic value of experience play out, are revealed, and problematized, in a splendid short story, "The Salamanders" by Tomás Rivera.[25] In this short allegorical realist narrative, we find a young boy positioned as part of a Texas Chicano migrant family working in Minnesota and Iowa in the late 1940s or early 1950s. The family, on a yearly migrant farm-labor circuit, is forced to leave a Minnesota farmer's chicken coop, where they have been living, after three-week rains stop the harvest of beets. Faced with the prospect of having to feed or tend to the migrant family on his land, the farmer prefers to send it on its way, suggesting the family head south to Iowa, where work might be available. Unable to return home, driving an old car, with almost no money for gas and none for food, the family indeed heads south, searching for work along the way. The family's social positioning is painfully clear, but the positionality of the family members begins to waver along the way, as they, facing continual rejection on the part of the farmers, desperately attempt to find work. The potential employers do not even allow them to come out of the car; they merely shake their heads from inside their homes, as a way of sending them on their way and off their land.

In Crystal Lake, Iowa, their car battery runs down, and they stop in town to look for work, while they have the battery charged at a garage, but a policeman runs them out of town, saying the town is off limits to "Gypsies." The family's futile explanations are readily dismissed and their identification as unwanted "foreigners" takes them out of town and into the night. Here, what

---

[25] Tomás Rivera, "The Salamanders," *Tomás Rivera. The Complete Works*, ed. Julián Olivares (Houston: Arte Público Press, 1992), 159–61.

seems a misidentification of the family as gypsies is really an interpellation of the migrant family as unwelcome, racially marked "outsiders." The family is made to feel "different" and rejected. They are not like "them," that is, the white and local townspeople. Positioning as unemployed farm workers and as members of an ethnic/racial group is what triggers their identification as unwelcome foreigners and what in turn begins to trigger a shift in the positionality of the narrator—a boy, around twelve years old.

The family's situation becomes increasingly desperate. Hungry and tired, with nowhere to go, they stop the car on the side of the highway, hoping to sleep and rest up for the next day's search. As dawn approaches, the boy awakens to see his sleeping parents and brothers as waxen dead bodies; this reification of family members makes evident his distancing and sense of disconnection from the family. The boy's reaction of increasing defamiliarization—literally—continues for three nights; the more he faces up to the family's desperate situation, the more he reifies family members, disidentifies with them, and begins to want to leave them. Finally, days later, an Iowa farmer grudgingly allows them to set up their tent near the edge of his field, where, if they're willing, they can wait to see if, once the rains stop, there is anything left to be harvested. This stop affords the family some respite, a temporary space of their own, and they are finally able to stretch out to rest after many days of sleeping cramped up in the car. Late at night the family awakens, however, to another dispossession and literal displacement by an invasion of salamanders, ironically also seeking a dry spot. Horrified, the family engages in a collective act of stomping them to death, channeling in the process a whole series of pent-up frustrations onto the battle against another—encroaching—species. In the collective act, they also recuperate their family solidarity. The now-grown narrator recalls his childhood and in particular this episode, saying that after that collective act of rage he again felt like part of the family.

Parenthetically, it always proves interesting to me that students, when we read this story, always assume that the migrants are immigrants—that is, foreigners—and, moreover, undocumented. I repeatedly explain that these are native-born Texans, following the migrant stream to the Midwest to pick crops in the 1940s and 1950s. These are U.S. citizens, acutely aware of their dislocation and forced to come to terms with the disjuncture between positioning and hegemonic discourses. The parents are presented as anguished, but ultimately resigned. The boy, on the other hand, is desperate to distance himself from the situation and from the collectivity; that is why he begins to think of leaving them. The rejection of the farmers and the distrust and disdain of the townspeople are too much to take. At one level, Rivera's story is all about second-class citizenship, class location, racial discrimination, and police coercion, but it is also very much about the ways in which social location produces insecurity and self-blame, giving rise to disidentification. At the same time, the story is about the dynamics and potential that collectivities under duress have for solidarity and collective struggle. And it is here, to my mind, that Rivera's story speaks directly to issues revolving around the politics of identity.

Identification as unwelcome foreigners points to the family's non-white identity or perhaps one should say, its non-identity with the Anglo population, but the family is further identified in terms of its positioning, as poor migrant workers. Internalization of social rejection leads not only to the parents' quiet desperation, but to the young boy's growing rebelliousness, silent though it is, in the face of their plight, revealing an awareness of dissonance between what he expects and what he is experiencing that takes the form of disidentification with the family. Unable to change their social location vis-à-vis the white-dominant population, the family does however assume an agential positionality when family members resolve to take a stand at the edge of the field, on ground that they are calling theirs for the night, in the process affirming themselves as human agents. Their resistance against this final act of dislocation is embodied in the very material struggle against the salamanders. This fight is thus allegorical; it is a socially symbolic act suggesting that the collectivity, now not merely that of migrant families but of the broader Mexican origin population, can, in the process of suffering alienation and reification, find a way to reposition and reidentify itself in struggle. It is the conscious self-identification of the family as united in struggle that leads the boy to his individuation and his forging of an identity as a part of the larger collectivity.

There is, however, another narrative dimension in the story that weakens the ethnic identification that the story constructs so well. It is a secondary discourse that appears only in a couple of sentences in the narrative and suggests a motif that is existentialist in nature, that is, that alienation is species-specific. The narrator recalls both at the beginning and at the end of the story that he was particularly struck by the salamanders' alterity and death, projecting, a-la-Cortázar in "Axolotl," a consciousness of death in the salamanders as he squeezed the life out of them. Here, the story suggests that social dislocation is not limited to those positioned structurally as economically exploited and racially oppressed by positing a displaced existential condition and angst of which both species partake. Rivera's brief attempt at naturalizing the family's plight by having both the family and the salamanders share in the struggle for space and survival is undercut ultimately by the story's demonstration that the family's circumstances have a clear material base.

In a sense, Rivera's existential twist in "The Salamanders" is a positionality at variance with the positionings constructed in the story. In another Rivera story, the young narrator, seeing that his father is ill from working in unbearable heat in the fields and finding that his parent's prayers go unanswered, becomes furious at an uncaring God who forsakes them. The boy reflects on his social location and realizes that his father may die of sunstroke, while also recalling that his aunt and uncle have recently died of tuberculosis. Things come to a head when the narrator's younger brothers faint in the heat as they try to work in the field. Feeling a total lack of fit between the family's social positioning and the religious discourses at his disposal to explain their situation, the boy begins to question the sense of life and challenges the existence and righteousness of God by doing the unthinkable: cursing God. As the title of the story indicates, the boy has a poignant but transformative epiphany when "the Earth did not part."[26] His understanding does not however lead to a search for other causes or other explanatory analyses of their suffering, but rather to a certain calm and even comfort allowing him to go on working without fear of being struck down by a metaphysical power. Here when the "truth value" of one explanatory framework is put to the test, it does not automatically generate an alternative knowledge set, although it may lead to it ultimately.

The site of identification in several of Rivera stories is with the family and the migrant worker collectivity. The importance of self-identification as a way to counter external identification is nowhere more poignantly stressed than in the story "Zoo Island," where three young boys set about carrying out their own mini-census of the several extended migrant families living in chicken coops on a farm where they work.[27] To people from the small town nearby who drive by to stare at their shacks and at them, as if they were monkeys in a zoo—as one of the boys' father complains—they are merely "dirty Mexicans." This identification as "Other," imposed upon them from the outside, leads to a conscious non-identification with the Gringos and in turn this non-identity generates a desire for an identity of their own, especially among the young, who come up with the idea of the mini-census. The women and men at the camp soon find themselves involved in an impromptu survey for the first time in their lives, and rather than gripe about the questions, one woman remarks that being counted, that having one's name written down, is significant. As she puts it, the simple act of having their names written down not only makes clear that each and every one of them counts but it also makes her acutely aware of their numbers and their circumstances. Thus, despite being superior in numbers to the townspeople, the farm workers

---

[26] Tomás Rivera, "...And the Earth Did Not Part," *Tomás Rivera: The Complete Works*, ed. Julián Olivares (Houston: Arte Público Press, 1992), 88 (translated here as "...And the Earth Did Not Devour Him").

[27] Tomás Rivera, "Zoo Island," in *Tomás Rivera. The Complete Works*, ed. Julián Olivares (Houston: Arte Público Press, 1992), 177–81.

have nothing, no services, no amenities, nothing to call their own, while the townspeople, who do "count" as people with needs to be met, have a church, a dance hall, a filling station, a grocery store, and even a little school. Here too another character gives the revelation an existential spin, noting that the survey and more precisely the process of counting, makes them conscious of their existence: "by counting yourself, you begin everything. That way you know you're not only here but that you're alive."[28] When the survey is over, the boys significantly move to "incorporate" as a collectivity by putting up a sign naming their site "Zoo Island" and specifying the number of people at the camp; the youths along with the rest of the migrant camp workers derive an ironic pleasure and shared sense of collective pride in the act of naming themselves and for once "counting" for something. The migrants, who even have their picture taken next to the sign, have taken a negative practice and given it their own spin; they now have an identity, a self-designated identity; they belong to a collectivity and to a social space that they themselves have carved out in this world, or more specifically, for now, at least, in Iowa. For the first time, those positioned as cheap migrant laborers count, not merely as field hands but as individuals that are part of a concrete and named collectivity. The story ends by telling that the young boy who had organized the census felt like whooping and hollering whenever he saw the sign they had put up at the farm gate, and, importantly, that the boy's reaction was something the employing farmer "never managed to understand."[29]

In all of these stories, positioning and positionality enable a particular network of social relations and lead to a sense of identification or disidentification; in every case, the process is linked to the affirmation or assertiveness of the individual, the family, or the ethnic group. The workers are aware of their structural positioning, their class location vis-à-vis the farmers, the owners of the land who hire and fire them, but they do not curse the farmers as the labor relation is "denaturalized" or dare I say "white-washed?" One of the fathers does curse the looky-loos who stare at them when they drive by, and the young boy does curse God, but their anger and resentment are not directed at the social structure. None of the characters express a desire to be part of a larger struggle, nor do they allow themselves to conceive of ways of transforming society or removing constraints on their ability to satisfy their needs. And, it should be noted, if only in passing, that in none of the Rivera stories are women more than abject victims (as in the case of Maria, the agoraphobic mother in "The Night Before Christmas"), murderous villainesses (as in the case of Doña Bone in "Hand in His Pocket"), or sexual commodities (as in

---

[28] Rivera, "Zoo Island," 181.
[29] Rivera, "Zoo Island," 181.

the case of "La Chata" in "On the Road to Texas: Pete Fonseca"). We have to go to literature by Chicanas to find non-stereotypical portrayals of women.

In Helena María Viramontes' novel, *Under the Feet of Jesus*, we have a social location similar to that of Rivera's constructed in the text; only here the migrant farm workers are in California and the main character is a young woman.[30] The eldest of five children, Estrella has had to be strong for her mother, Petra, a single head of household, whose husband has run off to Mexico, leaving the family without money, lodging, or food, and forced to live in labor camps. When Perfecto, an older man, a handyman who with his toolbox can fix anything, takes up with Petra, Estrella begins acquiring skills that only boys are generally taught. The use of tools, the wood saw, the sledgehammer, the ax, screwdrivers, and the like, signal new skills that reposition her as his apprentice and free her from certain gender constraints without eliminating them entirely. She is "naturally" still expected to be the nurturer and mother's helper as well as breadwinner. When her boyfriend Alejo becomes hopelessly ill from the insecticide sprayed on the orchards, it is Estrella who is aggressive in her demands for medical attention for him. By contrast, the senior male figure Perfecto seems immobilized and unable to "fix" matters. Faced with the possibility of being arrested for Estrella's action at the clinic, anxious over his failing health, particularly when confronted by the fact that Petra is pregnant by him, Perfecto stands frozen by his old station wagon that night with only four dollars to his name, nowhere to go and seemingly unable to decide what to do. By contrast, it is Estrella's determination to face up to the challenges that leaves the narrative open to new possibilities. Social positioning, especially class location, here marks the constraints that she and the other migrant farm workers face, but positionality born of countering social constraints allows Estrella to make use of new "tools," to think and do the previously unthinkable; she imagines herself as able to resist. It is positionality that affords her the wherewithal to climb to the roof of the empty barn in the novel's defining scene, raising herself on the chain to the loft and once there lifting the boarded opening to the roof. Once on the roof, Estrella feels enabled, sure of herself and from that positioning, goes on to take in the majesty of the stars, the trees, and the birds flying about her from a different standpoint.

Identification here, as in the Rivera stories, is both externally imposed, on the one hand, by the whites who see Estrella and her family as undocumented workers, even though they are native-born Californians, and, on the other, internally determined on the basis of their work: "piscadores" (farm workers). But Estrella overrides gender- and class-based identification to

---

[30] Helena María Viramontes, *Under the Feet of Jesus* (New York: Penguin Group/Dutton, 1995).

become a warrior of sorts, a woman that will make herself heard and demand respect, even if it takes the swing of a crowbar at the clinic where Alejo is refused care. Her individualized action, her wielding of "tools" unbecoming a woman, does not at this stage go beyond local and immediate goals, nor is she even certain of having saved Alejo's life, but what goes without saying is that she is transformed. Both the past and class positioning weigh heavily on all of Viramontes' characters in this novel and both at the same time constrain them from acting and compel them to action. A few agential possibilities are open to them and agency comes not automatically for subjects whose social and gender location entails more constraints than entitlements, but only after questioning and rebelling against norms.

IDENTITIES, THEIR IMPLICATIONS, AND SOCIAL MOVEMENTS

The relational character of social identities as played out in Viramontes' novel offers us a place from which to comment on the futility of individualized action outside of a social context of collective struggle, and I want to end the paper by addressing some of the implications of identity politics in recent social struggles. Removing social constraints and gaining power and knowledge have been at the forefront of what Touraine has termed "new social movements" that emerged principally in the first world during the latter half of the twentieth century.[31] Unlike more traditional social movements that were concerned with labor and social needs or with armed struggle against colonial domination or authoritarian governments, these new social movements emerged in highly developed areas, primarily Europe and the United States, with a focus on issues of recognition and representation, giving rise to their being called "culturalist movements" or identity politics. In Latin America, social movements have dominated the political scene as well, especially after the failure of armed struggles in Central America and the Southern Cone, but they have not always fit the description of "new social movements." In the last three decades, most Latin American social movements have been grassroots movements involved in struggles for basic needs and democratization. In the case of indigenous movements, the struggle has gone far beyond issues of identity, of recognition and representation, focusing on redressing structural inequities faced by these populations. In the case of *feminist movements*, on the other hand, issues of recognition and representation—often in relation to the state and centered on citizenship—have been central to these struggles,

---

[31] Alain Touraine, *Actores sociales y sistemas políticos en América Latina* (Geneva: PREALC, 1987).

to the point that feminist groups[32] have often been at odds and clashed with *women's movements*, more concerned with demands for basic social needs and material grievances.

The differences in political analyses and objectives within Latin American women's movements are in effect quite similar to those dividing collective struggles in other parts of the world. In her work, Nancy Fraser makes a similar distinction between two types of struggles in the United States: those against injustices of distribution and those against injustices of recognition.[33] The first, Fraser argues, derives from a distributive inequity and implicates the structural underpinnings of capitalist society, while the second is the product of misrecognition and is more identitarian in focus. Citing an example, in her debate with Butler,[34] for example, over whether struggles over sexuality are economic by definition or function,[35] Fraser provocatively argues that "It is highly implausible that gay and lesbian struggles threaten capitalism in its actually existing historical form."[36] She goes on to say that to remedy the problems caused by the effects of heterosexism, "we do not need to overthrow capitalism in order to remedy those disabilities."[37] In a subsequent article, Fraser further laments what she sees as the decline in movements for redistributive justice and an increase in claims for the recognition of difference.[38] What I would like to suggest is that *neither* type of movement necessarily poses a threat to the structures that underpin the capitalist system.

Both of these types of struggles can be circumscribed to non-transformational strategies. While I am not as willing to concede that heterosexism can be disabled without dismantling patriarchy, I agree that identity struggles focusing strictly on recognition and inclusion are not inherently at odds with capitalist society. On the other hand, redistribution, as the term points out, calls for redistributive policies and social provisions to ameliorate social problems, but not for an overhaul of the organizational basis of society. Redistribution involves what Meiksins Wood calls "protective strategies" that make provisions for certain basic necessities.[39] These measures can also go beyond redistribution to include labor organizing and struggles over the

---

[32] Of course, these feminist groups have also been divided by politics, with more militant and leftist feminists choosing to struggle at the side of working-class women. See Maxine Molyneux, "Género y ciudadanía en América Latina: cuestiones históricas y contemporáneas," *Debate Feminista* 12, no. 23 (2001): 3–66.

[33] Nancy Fraser, "Heterosexism, Misrecognition, and Capitalism: A Response to Judith Butler," *Social Text*, no. 52/53 (1997): 280.

[34] Judith Butler, "Merely Cultural," *Social Text*, no. 52/53 (1997): 265–77.

[35] Fraser, "Heterosexism," 284–85.

[36] Fraser, "Heterosexism," 285.

[37] Fraser, "Heterosexism," 285.

[38] Nancy Fraser, "Rethinking Recognition," *New Left Review* 3 (2000): 107–8.

[39] Ellen Meiksins Wood, "The Politics of Capitalism," *Monthly Review* 51, no. 4 (1999): 19.

terms and conditions of labor. Social protection and workplace advances are of course part of the class-based struggle but tend to be of a reformist nature. All of these non-transformational or short-term struggles are nevertheless important, not only because they can achieve immediate reforms and improve the conditions of life and work, but also because they can enhance consciousness of what I earlier termed the "explanatory insufficiency" of hegemonic epistemologies, and in that, allow for the articulation and organization of struggle for long-term transformational change.[40]

The importance of theorizing, of mapping, of finding a way to connect particular struggles to more general struggles is of course the overriding but difficult goal. But as Harvey notes, it is often difficult to make these wider connections since these movements often "rest on the perpetuation of patterns of social relations and community solidarities,"[41] that is, they are invested in buttressing already existing identities and epistemological frameworks, and less so in forging new ones. Nevertheless, I think that under the present circumstances, social movements for recognition and redistribution *can* play a role in maintaining people politically active and connected, and in finding equivalencies in the non-equivalent,[42] that is, in constructing identities-in-difference. By seeing that despite differences, there are shared commonalities, shared structural constraints at work across communities, local struggles may connect in movements involved in what Harvey, borrowing from Raymond Williams, calls "militant particularisms."[43]

The Zapatista Rebellion in Chiapas in 1994 provides a good example of how a local indigenous insurrection based on both economic and ethnic/cultural demands has become linked not only to urban worker struggles throughout Mexico but to national protests against neoliberalism and the institution of NAFTA. Within Mexico, the Zapatistas have also used the national spotlight to call for political reform and democratization more broadly. Spurred on by events in Chiapas, the same year, 1994, tens of thousands of Mexican workers took to the streets in various cities.[44] This militant particularism, evident in a ferment in labor struggles and the resurgence of armed struggle, has demonstrated two things: (a) that local struggles can transcend particularities and have both national and global dimensions, and (b) that politics of identity can be an intrinsic and key part of the politics of social change. The figure of subcomandante Marcos that emerged from the EZLN (Zapatista National Liberation Army) struggle makes for a useful case to demonstrate the power

---

[40] Meiksins Wood, "Capitalism," 25.
[41] Harvey, *Justice*, 40.
[42] Bhaskar, *Dialectic*, 122.
[43] Harvey, *Justice*, 35.
[44] Richard Roman and Edur Velasco Arregui, "Zapatismo and the Workers Movement in Mexico at the End of the Century," *Monthly Review* 49, no. 3 (1997): 105.

of the politicization of identity. Recall that the very identity of the *guerrillero* Marcos was deconstructed at the same time that it was deployed and cloned with the slogan "Todos somos Marcos" (we are all Marcos). Thus, while it is true that many social movements of the last three or four decades have been largely reformist, often seeking basic needs or recognition or redress for injustices, still, it is important to note that these movements and the inequities they point out may at some point come together and serve as necessary stepping stones for future and more broadly based struggles. In the Zapatista case, their very social positioning as subordinated, exploited, and dispossessed indigenous peoples became linked not only with redress of grievances cultural in nature, but with a positionality of revolutionary struggle. Their identification as "indios," as part of a non-Western culture, has become not a derogatory term, but a call to action and to a new identity as Zapatistas, building in the process on a national revolutionary past that unites not only these indigenous groups but others in the nation-state—like peasants, workers, and the like—who seek social changes that are unlikely to be met under existing economic and political regimes.

If the task is not only to understand the world but to change it, then it is important to explore, again quoting Harvey, "different forms of alliances that can reconstitute and renew class politics,"[45] and, I would add, that seek to transform capitalist forms of domination and exploitation in their various incarnations. Transformational agency, as underscored by Bhaskar, is informed by explanatory critique and entails a participatory-emancipatory politics.[46] To bring collectivities marked by difference to join in larger social struggles will involve an analysis and rethinking of the politics of identity and for that, a critical realist theory will be indispensable.

BIBLIOGRAPHY

Albertini, Bill, Ben Lee, Heather Love, Mike Millner, Ken Parille, Alice Rutkowski, and Bryan Wagner. "Introduction." *New Literary History* 31, no. 4 (2000): 621–26.
Barre, Marie-Chanta. *Ideologías indigenistas y movimientos indios*. México: Siglo Veintiuno, 1983.
Bhaskar, Roy. *Dialectic. The Pulse of Freedom*. London: Verso, 1993.
Bhaskar, Roy. *Philosophy and the Idea of Freedom*. Cambridge: Blackwell, 1991.
Brennan, Timothy. "Black Theorists and Left Antagonists." *The Minnesota Review* 37 (1991): 89–113.
Butler, Judith. "Merely Cultural." *Social Text*, no. 52/53 (1997): 265–77.

---

[45] Harvey, *Justice*, 41.
[46] Bhaskar refers to "transformationist" agency (*Dialectic*, 120).

Callinicos, Alex. *Equality*. Malden, MA: Polity Press, 2000.
Fraser, Nancy. "Heterosexism, Misrecognition, and Capitalism: A Response to Judith Butler." *Social Text*, no. 52/53 (1997): 279–89.
Fraser, Nancy. "Rethinking Recognition." *New Left Review* 3 (2000): 107–20.
Gibson-Graham, J. K., Stephen A. Resnick, and Richard D. Wolff, eds. *Class and its Others*. Minneapolis: University of Minnesota Press, 2000.
Hall, Stuart. "New Ethnicities." In *Stuart Hall: Critical Dialogues in Cultural Studies*, edited by David Morley and Kuan-Hsisng Chen, 442–51. London: Routledge, 1996.
Hall, Stuart. "Subjects in History. Making Diasporic Identities." In *The House that Race Built*, edited by Wahneema Lubiano, 289–99. New York: Pantheon Books, 1997.
Harvey, David. *Justice, Nature, and the Geography of Difference*. Cambridge: Blackwell Publishers, 1996.
Harvey, David. *Spaces of Hope*. Berkeley: University of California Press, 2000.
McLaughlin, Evan. "Connerly, Moores team up on racial initiative." *The UCSD Guardian*, February 4, 2002, https://ucsdguardian.org/2002/02/04/connerly-moores-team-up-on-racial-initiative/.
Mohanty, Satya P. *Literary Theory and the Claims of History*. Ithaca: Cornell University Press, 1997.
Molyneux, Maxine. "Género y ciudadanía en América Latina: cuestiones históricas y contemporáneas." *Debate Feminista* 12, no. 23 (2001): 3–66.
Moya, Paula. *Learning from Experience*. Berkeley: University of California Press, 2002.
Moya, Paula, and Michael R. Hames-García, ed. *Reclaiming Identity*. Berkeley: University of California Press, 2000.
Prigogine, Ilya, and Isabelle Stengers. *Order Out of Chaos*. New York: Bantam Books, 1984.
Rivera, Tomás. *Tomás Rivera. The Complete Works*. Edited by Julián Olivares. Houston: Arte Público Press, 1992.
Roman, Richard, and Edur Velasco Arregui. "Zapatismo and the Workers Movement in Mexico at the End of the Century." *Monthly Review* 49, no. 3 (1997): 98–116.
Touraine, Alain. *Actores sociales y sistemas políticos en América Latina*. Geneva: PREALC, 1987.
Viramontes, Helena María. *Under the Feet of Jesus*. New York: Penguin Group/ Dutton, 1995.
Wood, Ellen Meiksins. "Labor, the State and Class Struggle." *Monthly Review* 49, no. 3 (1997): 1–17.
Wood, Ellen Meiksins. "Modernity, Postmodernity, or Capitalism?" *Monthly Review* 48, no. 3 (1996): 21–39.
Wood, Ellen Meiksins. "The Politics of Capitalism." *Monthly Review* 51, no. 4 (1999): 12–26.
Wood, Ellen Meiksins. *The Retreat from Class. A New "True" Socialism*. London: Verso, 1986.

Part III

COUNTER-HISTORIES

Chapter 5

Critical and Revolutionary Theory
For the Reinvention of Critique in the Age of Ideological Realignment[1]

Gabriel Rockhill

> The bourgeoisie and the opportunists in the labor movement concur in this "revision" of Marxism. They omit, obliterate and distort the revolutionary side of its doctrine, its revolutionary soul. They push to the foreground and extol what is or seems acceptable to the bourgeoisie.
>
> —V.I. Lenin

The tradition that presents itself as "critical theory" is woefully lacking in critique. Having retreated from the project of developing a systemic and radical analysis of capitalism as a socio-economic system of exploitation, oppression, and repression—which is simultaneously the primary motor behind the unprecedented environmental catastrophe—it gives pride of place to discursive communication, inclusive recognition, and mild reformism over and against revolutionary contestation and the concrete struggle to build a world beyond capitalism. Turning its back on the Marxist tradition out of which it originally emerged, contemporary critical theory affiliated with the Frankfurt School has attempted to corral critique within the liberal fold. One of its primary social functions is to recuperate potential radicals within the

---

[1] I would like to express my gratitude to readers of earlier drafts of this essay, who provided valuable feedback, including Daniel Benson, Larry Busk, Derek Ford, John Harfouch, Andrews Little, and Jennifer Ponce de León. I would also like to thank Jared Bly for his helpful assistance with some of the research.

ideological consensus that a world beyond capitalism and pseudo-democracy is not only impossible but undesirable.[2]

This chapter elucidates the reasons behind the retreat from Marxism in contemporary critical theory, and it offers an account of the revolutionary theory that is born of emancipatory struggles as an antidote to this retreat. It begins by briefly elucidating the explanatory power and transformative force of revolutionary theory, as it has been developed in the Marxist tradition, in order to shake it loose from the straw-person depictions, gormless mantras, anti-communist dogmas, historical tommyrot, and vulgarly reductive accounts that petty-bourgeois intellectuals and many others have used to try and discredit it. After clarifying how historical materialism is a collectively produced, transdisciplinary, systemic, radical, and fallibilistic science of history rooted in collective struggle, it deploys this framework of analysis to develop a counter-history of critical theory. In this sense, the critique of the Frankfurt School that it advances is not simply an internal or immanent critique but is rather a materialist analysis of its social and historical function in the international political economy of ideas. As we shall see, the type of research promoted under the label "critical" by the global theory industry—which is driven by capitalist interests and policed by their hegemonic enforcers—is work whose critical appearance belies a conformist core.

REVOLUTIONARY THEORY

> The very least that can be said about Marxism is that it has one inestimable advantage over all other systems of economic and social theory that have claimed to supersede it, namely that it subjects to critical scrutiny not only capitalism itself but also the analytic categories associated with it.
>
> —Ellen Meiksins Wood

---

[2] Stanislas Kouvélakis writes: "The paradox that is currently operative—according to which 'critical theories' [*pensées critiques*] flourish in the shelter of a university world that has become their last refuge following the collapse of the revolutionary movements of the last century—is largely apparent. For what characterizes these 'critical theories' [*pensées critiques*]—with the exception of certain very minor, anti-capitalist figures, who are almost always of Marxist and/or libertarian inspiration—is precisely their absence of a general questioning [*mise en cause*] of the current social and political order, in other words the emptying of their critical dimension, unless that term henceforth designates something completely different than in the days of Kant or of Marx". *La Critique défaite: Émergence et domestication de la Théorie critique* (Paris: Éditions Amsterdam, 2019), 22 (my translation).

Karl Marx and Friedrich Engels developed a materialist science of history that proposed a systemic and radical analysis of society in the sense that it seeks to provide a holistic account of every aspect of social life, while going to the root causes behind them in order to identify how they can be transformed. Historical materialism eschews empiricism as the thoughtless "collection of dead facts" and idealism as the reduction of history to "an imagined activity of imagined subjects."[3] Founded on the ontological great divide between "world" and "mind," both orientations overlook the fact that "human beings" historically emerge in a material world that they then strive to understand, and that their experience of the world has already been forged by the deep history of material social relations. "The sensuous world," Marx and Engels explain,

> is not a thing given direct from all eternity, remaining ever the same, but the product of industry and of the state of society; and, indeed [a product] in the sense that it is a historical product, the result of the activity of a whole succession of generations.[4]

In this regard, historical materialism examines real-life activity, as it has developed over time, and it attempts to forge the most coherent, systemic, and self-reflexive account of it, which requires concrete analysis, conceptualization, and self-critical reflection on one's own material conditions of experience:

> In direct contrast to German philosophy which descends from heaven to earth, here it is a matter of ascending from earth to heaven. That is to say, not of setting out from what men say, imagine, conceive, nor from men as narrated, thought of, imagined, conceived, in order to arrive at men in the flesh; but setting out from real, active men, and on the basis of their real life-process demonstrating the development of the ideological reflexes and echoes of this life-process.[5]

It necessarily follows that historical materialism is fallibilistic and that its truths are based on an ongoing, collective process of verification and adjustment. Rather than being a dogmatic doctrine that could potentially be true for all time, it understands itself to be a historical product through and through. Self-critique and adaptation to new and different situations are thus built into

---

[3] Karl Marx and Friedrich Engels, *Collected Works*, vol. 5, *Marx and Engels: 1845-47* (New York: International Publishers, 1976), 37.
[4] Marx and Engels, *Collected Works*, vol. 5, 39.
[5] Marx and Engels, *Collected Works*, vol. 5, 36.

its very logic.⁶ In other words, historical materialism is *both* a materialist account of history *and* a historically evolving framework of explanation.⁷

To take but one very clear example, Vladimir Lenin explained how Marx significantly modified his understanding of the state based on his analysis of the Paris Commune, which led him to revise "The Communist Manifesto" and add the following "vital correction": "the working class cannot simply lay hold of the ready-made state machinery and wield it for its own purposes"—it needs to smash it.⁸ According to Kristin Ross, it was around the same time that Marx, through his discussions with Elisabeth Dmitrieff, and his immersion in the writings of Nikolay Chernyshevsky, openly accepted "the possibility of multiple paths to socialism—a turn that would only come to full fruition several years later in the form of his correspondence with another young Russian woman, Vera Zasulich."⁹ As a matter of fact, he emphatically rejected, in "A Letter to *Otechestvennye Zapiski*," one of the most widespread mischaracterizations of his thought, viz. that he imposed a single, determinist, and teleological model onto the totality of history. Responding to one of his critics, he wrote:

> He absolutely insists on transforming my historical sketch of the genesis of capitalism in Western Europe into a historico-philosophical theory of the general course fatally imposed on all peoples, whatever the historical circumstances in which they find themselves placed.... But I beg his pardon. That is to do me both too much honor and too much discredit.... Events of striking similarity, taking place in different historical contexts, [have] led to totally disparate results. By studying each of these developments separately, and then comparing

---

[6] "There can be nothing dogmatic about revolutionary theory," wrote George Jackson: "It is to be born out of each popular struggle." *Blood in My Eye* (Baltimore: Black Classic Press, 1990), 13.

[7] As Samir Amin explained with incisive clarity: "To be a 'Marxist' is to continue the work that Marx merely began, even though that beginning was of an unequaled power. It is not to stop at Marx, but to start from him. For Marx is not a prophet whose conclusions, drawn from a critique of both reality and how it has been read, are all necessarily 'correct' or 'final.' His opus is not a closed theory. Marx is boundless, because the radical critique that he initiated is itself boundless, always incomplete, and must always be the object of its own critique ("Marxism as formulated at a particular moment has to undergo a Marxist critique"), must unceasingly enrich itself through radical critique, treating whatever novelties the real system produces as newly opened fields of knowledge." *Modern Imperialism, Monopoly Finance Capital, and Marx's Law of Value* (New York: Monthly Review Press, 2018), 9–10.

[8] Henry M. Christman, ed., *Essential Works of Lenin* (New York: Dover Publications, 1987), 297. Lenin went on to explain that "there is no trace of utopianism in Marx, in the sense that he invented or imagined a 'new society.' No, he studied the *birth* of the new society *from* the old, the forms of transition from the latter to the former as a natural historical process ... He 'learned' from the Commune, like all the great revolutionary thinkers who were not afraid to learn from the experience of the great movements of the oppressed classes, and who never preached pedantic 'sermons.'" Christman, *Lenin*, 306.

[9] Kristin Ross, *Communal Luxury: The Political Imaginary of the Paris Commune* (London: Verso, 2015), 26–27.

them, one may easily discover the key to this phenomenon. But success will never come with the master-key of a historico-philosophical theory, whose supreme virtue consists in being supra-historical.[10]

Moreover, Marx and Engels regularly insisted on the role of agency in history, which leads us to a third aspect of historical materialism.[11] It not only develops a materialist account of history that dialectically adapts itself to changing times and circumstances, but it also seeks to provide the theoretical coordinates necessary for effectively intervening in history and changing the world. In other words, it is a science with real use-value because it takes its bearings from the project of collective emancipation. It is revolutionary theory simpliciter.

FROM MARXIAN ORIGINS TO THE WASHINGTON SCHOOL

> At Horkheimer's with Eisler for lunch. Afterwards Eisler suggests a plot for the *Tui-Novel*: the story of the Frankfurt Sociological Institute. A rich old man (Weil, the speculator in wheat) dies, disturbed at the poverty in the world. In his will he leaves a large sum to set up an institute which will do research on the source of this poverty. Which is, of course, himself.
>
> —Bertolt Brecht

The Frankfurt School was originally founded as an interdisciplinary Marxist think tank dedicated to elucidating the reasons why revolution had failed in early twentieth-century Germany and how it might potentially succeed in the future. Its founders considered naming it the *Institut für Marxismus* (Institute for Marxism), but then settled on the less provocative and more neutral *Institut für Sozialforschung* (Institute for Social Research). Nevertheless, its first director, Carl Grünberg, asserted that the Institute was going to be Marxist and adhere to Marxism as a scientific methodology. The research agenda that he outlined included questions of political economy,

---

[10] Teodor Shanin, ed., *Late Marx and the Russian Road: Marx and 'the Peripheries of Capitalism'* (New York: Monthly Review Press, 1983), 136.
[11] In *Socialism: Utopian and Scientific*, Friedrich Engels defined historical materialism as the "view of the course of history which seeks the ultimate cause and the great moving power of all important historic events in the economic development of society, in the changes in the modes of production and exchange, in the consequent division of society into distinct classes, and *in the struggles of these classes against one another.*" *Essential Writings of Friedrich Engels* (St Petersburg, FL: Red and Black Publishers, 2011), 13 (my emphasis).

labor struggles, and revolutionary politics. While it is true that the Institute was plagued by certain contradictions—it was bankrolled by a capitalist, for instance, and it was generally not invested in direct political mobilization[12]—it nonetheless explicitly claimed to be founded on Marxist science.

When Friedrich Pollock and then Max Horkheimer took over the directorship of the Institute in the late 1920s, there was a decisive shift toward more speculative reflections and academic research that was increasingly distant from historical materialism and labor politics.[13] According to Gillian Rose:

> By the early thirties, it [the Institute] had dropped its orientation towards the workers' movement, a process which was capped by the replacement of Carl Grünberg by Max Horkheimer as director of the Institute, and by the substitution of the Zeitschrift für Sozialforschung (Journal for Social Research) edited by Horkheimer for Grünberg's Archiv für die Geschichte des Sozialismus und der Arbeiterbewegung (Archive for the History of Socialism and the Workers' Movement). It even dropped its interest in class analysis and increasingly turned its attention to the analysis of culture and authority. Instead of politicizing academia, it academized politics.[14]

One telling sign of the degree and intensity of this academization of politics is the lack of any sustained engagement with the work of a Marxist intellectual who is sometimes embraced in academic circles: Leon Trotsky.[15] This is particularly remarkable because Trotsky shared some of the Frankfurt School's criticisms of actually existing socialism, as well as its preoccupation with the question of the failure of the revolution in Germany and the subsequent rise of European fascism. Although there

---

[12] There were a few exceptions to this general tendency, like Henryk Grossman, a "street-fighting revolutionary turned academic," who "developed a Leninist-inspired economic theory of capitalism's demise." Stuart Jeffries, *Grand Hotel Abyss: The Lives of the Frankfurt School* (London: Verso, 2017), 77.

[13] "The constant policy of the Institute under Horkheimer's direction," writes Rolf Wiggershaus, "continued to be abstinence, not only from every activity which was even remotely political, but also from any collective or organized effort to publicize the situation in Germany or to support émigrés." Rolf Wiggershaus, *The Frankfurt School: Its History, Theories, and Political Significance*, trans. Michael Robertson (Cambridge, MA: The MIT Press, 1995), 133.

[14] Gillian Rose, *The Melancholy Science: An Introduction to the Thought of Theodor W. Adorno* (New York: Columbia University Press, 1978), 2. "Horkheimer," as Ingar Solty explained, did not conduct empirical research on capitalism and its crises, on capital/labor relations and the creation and distribution of surplus value, on the expanded reproduction of the system, the hierarchical nature of the international division of labor, the organization of internationalizing capitalism in a system of nation-states, the origins of imperialism and inter-imperial rivalries, or such. Ingar Solty, "Max Horkheimer, a Teacher without a Class," *Jacobin*, February 15, 2020, https://www.jacobinmag.com/2020/02/max-horkheimer-frankfurt-school-adorno-working-class-marxism.

[15] See Leon Trotsky, *The Struggle Against Fascism in Germany* (New York: Pathfinder Press, 1971).

are some passing references in the writings of the critical theory cognoscenti to Trotsky, they generally ignored or avoided engaging with the group known as the "Left Opposition" and then the Fourth International, which ran the journal *Bulletin of the Opposition*. Trotsky's secretary Walter Held (Heinz Epe) did know the Frankfurt School, however, and he wrote a review of Horkheimer's journal under a revealing title: "Critical Theory without Political Practice?" For the most part, then, the members of the Frankfurt School close to Horkheimer were not Trotskyists, which is arguably the most acceptable form of Marxism in the Western academy, due in no small part to its contributions to anti-Sovietism and, more generally, the intellectual repudiation of actually existing socialism. What is more, some of them were not even social democrats, in the sense of reformist second-International Marxists (whom Trotsky himself vociferously criticized for their responsibility in crushing the Spartacus League and contributing to the rise of fascism).[16] While loath to take concrete positions on a number of topics, Horkheimer situated his work with Adorno to the right of the social democrats. "We don't want people to say that our writings are so terribly radical," he wrote: "Whoever does not work should not be allowed to eat—that's the point at which we must attack the Social Democrats."[17]

When the Institute was relocated to the United States in the early 1930s due to the rise of Nazism in Germany, it "gravitated steadily toward adaptation to the local bourgeois order, censoring its own past and present work to suit local academic or corporate susceptibilities."[18] Marcuse later explained that Horkheimer strictly forbade "any type of political activity."[19] "Throughout its exile years in the United States," writes Stuart Jeffries, "Horkheimer insisted that the M word and the R word (Marxism and Revolution) be excised from

---

[16] "In Germany, as early as 1918," writes Michael Parenti, "the Social Democratic leader Ebert entered an alliance with Field Marshal von Hindenburg 'in order to fight Bolshevism.'" Michael Parenti, *Dirty Truths: Reflections on Politics, Media, Ideology, Conspiracy, Ethnic Life and Class Power* (San Francisco: City Lights Books, 1996), 39–40.
[17] Theodor Adorno and Max Horkheimer, "Towards a New Manifesto?" *New Left Review* 65 (September-October 2010): 47.
[18] Perry Anderson, *Considerations on Western Marxism* (London: Verso, 1989), 33. According to Thomas Wheatland, the Horkheimer circle in New York chose to "remain silent about the major political questions of the day and . . . [concealed] its Marxism almost completely . . . Horkheimer remained unwilling to risk the possible repercussions of political activism or even political engagement with the major topics of the era." Thomas Wheatland, *The Frankfurt School in Exile* (Minneapolis: University of Minnesota Press, 2009), 99.
[19] Wheatland, *The Frankfurt School in Exile*, 72 (also see 141).

its papers so as not to scare the Institute's American sponsors."[20] What is more, as Thomas Wheatland has explained in detail, the Institute went out of its way to incorporate the "politically neutral" forms of Anglo-American techno-scientific sociology into their research program in order to secure funding from organizations like the Jewish Labor Committee, the American Jewish Committee (whose journal, *Commentary*, had links to CIA), and later the Rockefeller Foundation, the German Defense Ministry, and the High Commissioner of Germany.[21] The Institute was also closely involved with Paul Lazarsfeld's Office of Radio Research, which later evolved into the Bureau of Applied Social Research (BASR). This center for communication studies, which hired members of the Horkheimer circle like Adorno (whom it was able to bring to the United States) was one of the "de facto adjuncts of government psychological warfare programs" according to Christopher Simpson.[22] In addition to receiving "a very considerable grant of $67,000 from the Rockefeller Foundation," which worked very closely with the U.S. national security state, it had numerous military, intelligence, and propaganda

---

[20] Jeffries, *Grand Hotel Abyss*, 72. In a telling example, when the Institute published Walter Benjamin's well-known article on "The Work of Art in the Age of Mechanical Reproduction," it changed the final sentence: "Benjamin had written: 'This is the situation which Fascism is rendering aesthetic. Communism responds by politicizing art.' In the *Zeitschrift* version, though, 'the totalitarian doctrine' was substituted for 'Fascism' and 'the constructive forces of mankind' for 'communism.'" Jeffries, *Grand Hotel Abyss*, 197. Some might see this approach as justified due to the fact that FBI files demonstrate that U.S. officialdom was concerned that the Institute was a potential communist front. Although the records released by my FOIA request for Theodor Adorno—which are now available online (https://vault.fbi.gov/theodor-adorno/theodor-adorno-part-01-of-01/view)—are sparse and slightly redacted, a general pattern emerges that appears more or less reliable. A detailed FBI report was prepared on January 21, 1944, which provided a history of the Institute and a summary of some of its research. It claimed that there was evidence that the Institute was "a communist organization of intellectuals operating under the cloak of social and economic research." The Bureau mobilized its expansive network of informants—including university professors like Karl Wittfogel, professional associates, and neighbors—to monitor and spy on the scholars during the coming decade or so, but it appears to have found little to no evidence of suspicious activity. FBI files indicate that officers appear to have been reassured when informants, who knew the Frankfurt scholars personally, told them that, "they believe there is no difference between Hitler and Stalin as to purpose and tactics."

[21] See Wheatland, *The Frankfurt School in Exile* (particularly chapters 5 and 6) and Steven Müller-Doohm, *Adorno: A Biography*, trans. Rodney Livingstone (Cambridge: Polity Press, 2005), 414. Regarding *Commentary*, Irving Kristol became "assistant editor of *Commentary* and executive secretary of the ACCF in 1952-3." Giles Scott-Smith, *The Politics of Apolitical Culture: The Congress for Cultural Freedom, the CIA and Post-War American Hegemony* (New York: Routledge, 2002), 129. The ACCF was a CIA front organization. Finally, it should be noted that the Institute's self-censorship continued after the war. For instance, according to Wiggershaus, a remarkable series of changes were made to the 1947 publication of *Dialectic of Enlightenment* (see *The Frankfurt School*, 401), and Horkheimer stopped mentioning capitalism when he returned to Germany: "This was primarily for tactical reasons. If one criticized capitalism, one would have no chance of gaining the goodwill and support of the American authorities which permitted his activities as an American citizen in Germany, and which would possibly allow an Institute to be founded." *The Frankfurt School*, 401.

[22] Christopher Simpson, *Science of Coercion: Communication Research and Psychological Warfare 1945-1960* (Oxford: Oxford University Press, 1996), 4.

contracts, including with the CIA, and government money made up over 75 percent of its annual budget.²³

During the Great Depression, the Institute's endowment allowed Horkheimer's inner circle to work in very comfortable conditions, which included renovated headquarters on 117th street in Manhattan, a multilingual secretarial staff, almost no teaching or administrative duties and "salaries sufficiently ample to hire domestic help" and take regular vacations.²⁴ This situation changed drastically in 1937, however, when investment mistakes led to a substantial decrease in the Institute's endowment. Pollock was the group's economic specialist tasked with solving this problem, and his office "gradually took on the characteristics of a Wall Street analyst, and outside financial advisers were consulted to assist Pollock with a number of investment strategies (including residential real estate in upstate New York)."²⁵ Horkheimer cut salaries and personnel, while making a concerted effort to assimilate the Institute's research to American standards in order to obtain the grants mentioned in the preceding paragraph.²⁶ In the late 1930s,

> in spite of the fact that the Institute's social critique had begun to shift toward mass culture and the theory of the racket society, Horkheimer hired the Phoenix News Publicity Bureau as the group's public relations firm . . . to promote the

---

²³ Wiggershaus, *The Frankfurt School*, 239. Daniel Lerner, who had served as the "chief editor of the Intelligence Section of the Psychological Warfare Division of the U.S. Army during the Second World War," was a member of BASR's supervisory staff. Rohan Samarajiwa, "The Murky Beginnings of the Communication and Development Field: Voice of America and The Passing of Traditional Society," in *Rethinking Development Communication*, ed. Neville Jayaweera and Sarath Amumugama (Singapore: The Asian Mass Communication Research and Information Centre, 1987), 6. Samarajiwa criticized Lerner's research project and book, *The Passing of Traditional Society*, for having served as the basis for finding target audiences for the government propaganda outlet Voice of America. Regarding the connections between the BASR and the CIA, the *Columbia Daily Spectator* reported on April 17, 1980 that the CIA had directed numerous research projects at Columbia University in the 1950s and 1960s, including Columbia's War Documentation Project, which was administered by the BASR. One of the two directors of the Princeton Radio Research Project, where Adorno headed the music section, was Frank Stanton, the research director of CBS, as well as its future president (from 1946 to 1971) and chairman of the Rand Corporation (1961–1967). CBS had such deep ties to the U.S. national security state that its directors later established a private phone line that "bypassed the CBS switchboard" to communicate regularly with the CIA, provided cover for CIA agents as reporters or staff, used the William S. Paley Foundation to launder CIA funds, and "CBS correspondents joined the CIA hierarchy once a year for private dinners and briefings." Hugh Wilford, *The Mighty Wurlitzer: How the CIA Played America* (Cambridge, MA: Harvard University Press, 2008), 227; Frances Stonor Saunders, *The Cultural Cold War: The CIA and the World of Arts and Letters* (New York: The New Press, 1999), 221. The other director of the Princeton Radio Research Project was Hadley Cantril, who became a consultant for Nelson Rockefeller's Office of the Coordinator of Inter-American Affairs, the propaganda and intelligence agency overseeing Latin America.

²⁴ Wheatland, *The Frankfurt School in Exile*, 215.

²⁵ Wheatland, *The Frankfurt School in Exile*, 215–16.

²⁶ See Wheatland, *The Frankfurt School in Exile*, 214 and following.

reputation and the accomplishments of the Institute for Social Research in the United States.[27]

With the Institute doing nearly everything it could to master the market and secure corporate funding, while hiring a PR firm to promote its writings in the U.S. press, it is not surprising that Marxist intellectuals like Bertolt Brecht came to regard the Frankfurt scholars as—in the words of Stuart Jeffries—"prostitutes in their quest for foundation support during their American exile, selling their skills and opinions as commodities in order to support the dominant ideology of oppressive U.S. society."[28]

Due in large part to Horkheimer's drastic financial cuts, five of the eight members of his circle eventually found work in Washington, where they were employed by the U.S. government and national security state.[29] Leo Löwenthal was hired by the Office of War Information (OWI), which ran large-scale propaganda campaigns both domestically and abroad, and Friedrich Pollock worked at the Anti-Trust Division of the Department of Justice. Herbert Marcuse, Franz Neumann, and Otto Kirchheimer were all employed by the OWI before being recruited to the Research and Analysis Branch of the Office of Strategic Services (OSS), the predecessor organization to the CIA.[30]

---

[27] Wheatland, *The Frankfurt School in Exile*, 221.

[28] Jeffries, *Grand Hotel Abyss*, 136. Brecht maintained that "the Frankfurt School perpetrated a bourgeois sleight of hand by posturing as a Marxist institute while at the same time insisting that revolution could no longer depend on insurrection by the working class, and declining to take part in the overthrow of capitalism." Jeffries, *Grand Hotel Abyss*, 77. He would later bring together his notes on the "Tuis"—a neologism he used to refer to "intellectuals of this age of markets and commodities"—in his masterful play *Turandot or The Whitewashers' Congress*. Bertolt Brecht, *Collected Plays: Six*, ed. John Willett and Ralph Manheim (London: Random House, 1998), 248. As his journal makes clear, this was a Marxist satirical critique of the Frankfurt School and, more generally, of the social function of intellectuals (*Intellektuellen*) in the failure of the Weimar Republic and the rise of Nazism. In the words of Barry Katz, "Brecht mercilessly lampooned those intellectuals 'who always get everything backwards' (hence *Tellekt-uellen-in*)." Barry M. Katz, *Herbert Marcuse and the Art of Liberation: An Intellectual Biography* (London: Verso, 1982), 106.

[29] The body of literature on the history of American intelligence organizations and propaganda outlets, as well as their relationships with the professional intellectual class, is much too expansive to be summarized here, but a few works that provide useful overviews are: Saunders, *The Cultural Cold War*; Barry M. Katz, *Foreign Intelligence: Research and Analysis in the Office of Strategic Services 1942-1945* (Cambridge, MA: Harvard University Press, 1989); Robin W. Winks, *Cloak and Gown: Scholars in the Secret War, 1939-1961* (New Haven: Yale University Press, 1987); Ray S. Cline, *Secrets, Spies and Scholars: Blueprint of the Essential CIA* (Washington, DC: Acropolis Books, 1976); Nicholas J. Cull, *The Cold War and the United States Information Agency: American Propaganda and Public Diplomacy, 1945-1989* (Cambridge: Cambridge University Press, 2008).

[30] Arkady Gurland, another associate of the Institute, also worked at the OSS. Wiggershaus summarizes the situation as follows: "In 1943 six more or less full associates of the Institute were in full-or part-time government service, and were in this way visibly contributing to the war effort: Neumann as deputy chief of the Central European Section of the Office of Strategic Services (OSS), and consultant at the Board of Economic Warfare; Marcuse as senior analyst at the OSS; Kirchheimer and Gurland, also as members of staff at the OSS; Lowenthal as a consultant at the Office of War Information; and Pollock as consultant at the Department of Justice's Anti-Trust Division. The

At the OSS, they prepared reports on Germany regarding such issues as the rise and spread of Nazism, the consequences of the defeat of the Third Reich, oppositional politics and communism within Germany, and the process of so-called denazification.[31] All five of them remained in Washington after the war, before eventually moving on to university positions. Neumann, who was later discovered to have been a double agent working for Moscow, was the first to leave.[32] He became a professor of political science at Columbia University in 1948. Löwenthal was the last because he served for a number of years as the research director of the U.S. propaganda outlet Voice of America. He began teaching at the University of California at Berkeley in 1956. Since only three members of the Horkheimer circle—Horkheimer, Adorno, and Fromm—settled in New York (before the first two moved on to California), the standard historical narrative regarding their American exile should be corrected. Numerically, their primary site of resettlement during the war and immediate postwar was Washington, where they were welcomed with open arms by the U.S. national security state as left-leaning specialists of German culture and society. The Frankfurt School would thus be better described, at that time, as the Washington School: the majority of its intellectuals were doing research, analysis, and propaganda for the American government.

DEFENDING THE WESTERN STATUS QUO

> In the long run things cannot change . . . . That means we have to reject both Marxism and ontology.... We can expect nothing more from mankind than a more or less worn-out version of the American system.
>
> —Max Horkheimer

When the Institute decided to return to Frankfurt after the war, the young Jürgen Habermas

> feared that Horkheimer . . . had become too allied with the Federal Republic. "His public demeanor and his policy for the institute seemed to us to be almost

---

only ones who were spared were Horkheimer and Adorno, the two principal theoreticians." *The Frankfurt School*, 301.
[31] See Raffaele Laudani, ed., *Secret Reports on Nazi Germany: The Frankfurt School Contribution to the War Effort* (Princeton: Princeton University Press, 2013).
[32] On Neumann, see Allen Weinstein and Alexander Vassiliev, *The Haunted Wood: Soviet Espionage in America—the Stalin Era* (New York: Random House, 1999). KGB files indicate that the Soviet intelligence service had taken an interest in Neumann's close friend, Marcuse, and might have considered recruiting him. It is not clear, however, if they ever initiated contact.

the expression of an opportunist conformity which was at odds with the critical tradition which, after all, he embodied."[33]

Contextually, it is worth recalling that Horkheimer had sidelined and censored Habermas due to his relative political radicality in the 1950s, and he had even recommended removing him from the Institute on the same grounds.[34] He had refused to publish two of Habermas' articles because one was critical of liberal democracy and another spoke of "revolution" and referenced the possibility of a liberation from "the shackles of bourgeois society." In his correspondence with Adorno, Horkheimer intoned: "It is simply not possible to have admissions of this sort in the research report of an Institute that exists on the public funds of this shackling society" (including financing from John McCloy, the U.S. High Commissioner of Germany, who worked closely with the CIA on a number of projects and oversaw its collaborations with the Ford Foundation).[35] Horkheimer had aligned himself with the Christian Democratic Union, the anti-communist center-right party funded and backed by the CIA, and he defended U.S. foreign policy in expressing his public support for the war in Vietnam, which he claimed was necessary to stop the Chinese.[36] "In America," he announced in 1967 to an audience at one of the *Amerika-Häuser* set up by the United States after the war as outposts in its anti-communist *Kulturkampf*, "when it is necessary to conduct a war,—and now listen to me… it is not so much a question of the defense of the homeland, but it is essentially a matter of the defense of the constitution, the defense of the rights of man."[37] When Horkheimer had first returned to Germany in April 1948 to take up a guest professorship at Frankfurt University, it was as an American citizen, we should recall, and with a grant from the Rockefeller Foundation, the very institution that "by his own standards"—in the words of Wiggershaus—"was investing the merest

---

[33] Jeffries, *Grand Hotel Abyss*, 297.
[34] See Wiggershaus, *The Frankfurt School*, 554–56.
[35] Quoted in Wiggershaus, *The Frankfurt School*, 554. "In 1950," Wiggershaus writes, "the US High Commissioner, John McCloy, put DM 200,000 at the Institute's disposal, with a further DM 235,000 for rebuilding" (*The Frankfurt School*, 434). The city of Frankfurt also contributed funds, as well as the Society of Social Research and private donors (see *The Frankfurt School*, 435). In 1954, the Institute signed a research contract with the Mannesmann corporation—which "had been a founding member of the Anti-Bolshevik League and had financed the Nazi Party"—in order to undertake a sociological study of worker's opinions, with the implicit implication that such knowledge would help management stall or prevent socialist stirrings and Bolshevik-style organizing. *The Frankfurt School*, 479.
[36] According to Wiggershaus: "Horkheimer did not, like Paul Tillich, defend socialism or, like Hugo Sinzheimer or Hermann Heller, belong to the committed democrats and declared opponents of Nazism." *The Frankfurt School*, 112.
[37] Quoted in Wolfgang Kraushaar, ed., *Frankfurter Schule und Studentenbewegung: Von der Flaschenpost zum Molotowcocktail 1946-1995*, vol. I, *Chronik* (Hamburg: Rogner & Bernhard GmbH & Co. Verlags KG, 1998), 252–53.

fraction of the surplus from the oldest and largest capitalist conglomerates in the USA in the corruption of intellectual activity and culture."[38]

In 1956, Horkheimer and Adorno wrote to the magazine *Der Spiegel* to defend the tripartite aggression of Israel, Britain, and France, who invaded Egypt to regain Western control of the Suez Canal (an act condemned by the United Nations). "No one even ventures to point out," they wrote in a rare but clear affirmation of political commitment for Adorno, "that these Arab robber states have been on the lookout for years for an opportunity to fall upon Israel and to slaughter the Jews who have found refuge there."[39] The same year, they published one of their most overtly political texts, with a view to actually composing a contemporary version of *The Communist Manifesto*. It was a dialogue in which they celebrated—with a few minor exceptions—the superiority of the Western world and repeatedly maligned the Soviet Union and China by relying on stock racist descriptions of the "barbarians" in the East, whom they described as "beasts," "hordes," and "fascists" that had chosen "slavery."[40] "I believe," Horkheimer flatly proclaimed, "that Europe and America are probably the best civilizations that history has produced up to now as far as prosperity and justice are concerned. The key point now is to ensure the preservation of these gains."[41]

If Habermas occasionally outflanked Horkheimer and Adorno to the left on specific issues in the early years, he was far from being a revolutionary, as his later record of endorsing the Persian Gulf War and NATO's intervention in Yugoslavia would prove.[42] It is worth recalling that he had been a member of the Hitler Youth and served as an auxiliary at the front during the war, and that he went on to study for four years under an intellectual whom he later called a "Nazi philosopher" (Horkheimer had also studied under Heidegger,

---

[38] Wiggershaus, *The Frankfurt School*, 397.
[39] Quoted in Jeffries, *Grand Hotel Abyss*, 297.
[40] The racialization of communists has been an important part of anti-communist ideology, as Domenico Losurdo explained in *War and Revolution*, trans. Gregory Elliott (London: Verso, 2015).
[41] Adorno and Horkheimer, "Towards a New Manifesto?" 41. Horkheimer takes a similar position in his 1968 preface to a collection of his essays: "An open declaration that even a dubious democracy, for all its defects, is always better than the dictatorship which would inevitably result from a revolution today, seems to me necessary for the sake of truth." Max Horkheimer, *Critical Theory: Selected Essays*, trans. Matthew J. O'Connell et al. (New York: Continuum, 2002), viii.
[42] James L. Marsh notes that "Habermas somewhat reluctantly endorsed the Persian Gulf War, and more recently and more enthusiastically supported NATO's intervention in Yugoslavia." "Toward a New Critical Theory," in *New Critical Theory: Essays on Liberation*, ed. William S. Wilkerson and Jeffrey Paris (Lanham, Maryland: Rowman & Littlefield Publishers, 2001, 50. For Habermas' attempt to justify these positions, see for instance Danny Postel. "Letter to America" (an interview with Jürgen Habermas), *The Nation*, December 16, 2002, https://archive.globalpolicy.org/security/issues/iraq/attack/2002/1216jurgen.htm.

as well as Marcuse).⁴³ Although Habermas was initially somewhat receptive to the anti-imperialist and anti-capitalist student activism of the 1960s, he ultimately took the side of his colleagues at the Institute by condemning the movement as a form of "Left fascism."

Adorno proudly repeated this pithy formulation by the spokesperson for discourse ethics and mobilized a carnivalesque form of dialectics to defend this *contradictio in adjecto* against the following reproach by Marcuse: "the (authentic) left is not able to transform itself into the Right 'by the force of its immanent antinomies,' without decisively changing its social basis and objectives."⁴⁴ Adorno took to defending West Germany by disdainfully explaining to the student activists, who had sunk into irrationalism and thoughtless violence according to him, that West Germany was a democracy rather than a fascist state to be criticized (Habermas would later claim that "the *Bundesrepublik* was one of the six or seven most liberal countries in the world").⁴⁵ Adorno also added that the university was not an operational base for changing society and that attempts to introduce radical changes would simply fan resentment against intellectuals. To theoretically justify his support of West Germany and his position that the war in Vietnam should not make us lose sleep at night because "the Vietcong… use Chinese methods of torture," he published "Marginalia on Theory and Practice."⁴⁶ In this article, he used a self-serving form of dialectical pyrotechnics to try and demonstrate that inaction was the best kind of action ("the goal of real praxis would be its own abolition"), and that theory was the most arduous and necessary "practice."⁴⁷ He even went so far as to defend what he himself calls a "petit bourgeois truism," namely "that fascism and communism are the same."⁴⁸ To hammer his point home with an example, he added that the *ApO*

---

⁴³ On Habermas' involvement with the Nazi Youth, see Steven Müller-Doohm, *Habermas: A Biography*, trans. Daniel Steuer (Cambridge: Polity Press, 2016), 17–19. According to Stuart Jeffries, "there's no sense in his writings" that Habermas felt "guilt or shame for his adolescent role in fighting for Hitler." Jeffries, *Grand Hotel Abyss*, 357.

⁴⁴ Theodor Adorno and Herbert Marcuse, "Correspondence on the German Student Movement," *New Left Review* 233 (January–February 1999): 129.

⁴⁵ Peter Dews, ed., *Autonomy and Solidarity: Interviews with Jürgen Habermas* (London: Verso, 1992), 231.

⁴⁶ Theodor Adorno, *Critical Models: Inventions and Catchwords*, trans. Henry W. Pickford (New York: Columbia University Press, 2005), 274.

⁴⁷ Adorno, *Critical Models*, 267. Adorno's "dialectical" praise of inaction as the best form of action is reiterated in his correspondence with Marcuse regarding the student protests: "We withstood in our time, you no less than me, a much more dreadful situation—that of the murder of the Jews, without proceeding to praxis; simply because it was blocked to us . . . To put it bluntly: I think that you are deluding yourself in being unable to go on without participating in the student stunts, because of what is occurring in Vietnam or Biafra. If that really is your reaction, then you should not only protest against the horror of napalm bombs but also against the unspeakable Chinese-style tortures that the Vietcong carry out permanently." Adorno and Marcuse, "Correspondence," 127.

⁴⁸ Adorno, *Critical Models*, 268.

(*Ausserparlamentarische Opposition*, a New Left movement) carried water for the *NPD* (*Nationaldemokratische Partei Deutschlands*, an extreme right, ultra-nationalist neo-Nazi party). He also made a similar assertion elsewhere: "They [Germans] think the Russians stand for socialism. The people are as yet unaware that the Russians are fascists, especially ordinary people. The industrialists and bankers are well aware of it."[49] Since the Soviet Union had fought and won a world war in which some 27 million Russians gave their lives *fighting fascism*, it is not surprising that the "ordinary people" would assume that the USSR is anti-fascist. It is also not shocking to learn that industrialists and bankers —or professional intellectuals like Adorno, whose father was a "wealthy wine merchant"—would mischaracterize communists as "fascists" because they were a threat to their propertied interests.[50] One of the student leaflets in the late 1960s summed up a widespread sentiment by activists that the Frankfurt scholars were "left idiots of the authoritarian state" who were "critical in theory, conformist in practice."[51] When Adorno famously called the police on his doctoral student Hans-Jürgen Krahl and other SDS protesters occupying a room at the Institute for Social Research, Krahl gave voice to their collective discontent by declaring Adorno and the other professors "*scheißkritische Theoretiker* [shit-critical theorists]!"[52] The author of *Minima Moralia* pressed charges against Krahl, as he had done in 1964 against the student group *Subversive Aktion*, and he refused to drop them in spite of pressure to do so.

It is important to point out that the Institute's defense of West Germany's purported democracy over and against the supposed fascism of the student activists wildly misrepresents material reality. To begin with, the Adenauer government in West Germany was financially supported and controlled by the CIA, as former agent Philip Agee and others have explained in detail.[53] The OSS/CIA also put "some four thousand agents," of which at least a hundred "had clear ties to Nazi atrocities," under the control of a well-connected

---

[49] Adorno and Horkheimer, "Towards a New Manifesto?," 49.
[50] Wheatland, *The Frankfurt School in Exile*, 24. It is worth noting that Horkheimer's father has been described as a "millionaire" who "owned several textile factories." Solty, "Horkheimer," and Wheatland, *The Frankfurt School in Exile*, 13. Pollock "also came from a prosperous family (his father owned some leather-goods factories)," and Marcuse's father ran a successful textile business and then got into real estate. Wheatland, *The Frankfurt School in Exile*, 22.
[51] Quoted in Esther Leslie, "Introduction to Adorno/Marcuse Correspondence on the German Student Movement," *New Left Review* 233 (January-February 1999), 119 and Kraushaar, *Frankfurter Schule*, 374.
[52] Kraushaar, *Frankfurter Schule*, 398.
[53] Philip Agee and Louis Wolf, eds., *Dirty Work: The CIA in Western Europe* (New York: Dorset Press, 1978), 186. Gustav Hilger, the former Nazi Foreign Office executive who was integrated into the upper echelons of the U.S. imperial elite, had lobbied his handlers in support of Adenauer's ascension to power and then became an unofficial ambassador to the United States for his Christian Democratic party. See Christopher Simpson, *Blowback: America's Recruitment of Nazis and Its Effects on the Cold War* (New York: Weidenfeld & Nicolson, 1988), 112–18.

ex-Nazi brigadier general named Reinhard Gehlen, who collaborated directly with Adenauer and was put at the helm of the CIA-controlled postwar German intelligence service.[54] Additionally, the U.S. national security state financed, trained, and equipped right-wing subversives to run a vast terror and destabilization campaign against East Germany.[55] Finally, the OSS/CIA recruited Nazis to establish secret fascist stay-behind armies tasked with sabotage missions and anti-communist terrorism.[56] While the extent of CIA activity in West Germany was not as well known in the immediate postwar era as it is today (although the pattern was clear, including too many of the student activists at the time), there is no reason why the Institute's leaders should have been ignorant of the fascist stay-behind armies because there were articles on them in *Der Spiegel*, *Frankfurter Allgemeine Zeitung*, *Frankfurter Rundeschau*, *New York Times*, *Times* of London, and *Newsweek* in October 1952.[57] In fact, it was in Frankfurt that former SS officer Hans Otto had turned himself in at the police station and declared that he was the member of a branch of a secret fascist army, the *Technischer Dienst* (TD), which included some 2,000 extreme right-wing militants. During the investigation that followed, which led to heated public debates in Frankfurt and beyond, it was discovered that this terrorist network—composed primarily of Nazis that were trained, armed, and overseen by the CIA—had a long list of communists and forty top social democratic functionaries to be eliminated "in case of X" (it could not be established if "X" referred to the moment of a potential Soviet invasion, mass protests, or an electoral victory by the left).[58] If Germany was not openly fascist at the time, then, it is simply because it was concealing its fascism under the thin cover of a centrist puppet government. The students saw through this, as did astute intellectuals like Daniel Guérin.[59] Adorno and his closest colleagues obviously did not.[60]

---

[54] Eric Lichtblau, *The Nazis Next Door: How America Became a Safe Haven for Hitler's Men* (New York: Mariner Books, 2015), 33.
[55] See William Blum, *Killing Hope: US Military and CIA Interventions since World War II* (London: Zed Books, 2014), 61–64.
[56] See Danielle Ganser, *Nato's Secret Armies: Operation Gladio and Terrorism in Western Europe* (New York: Routledge, 2005).
[57] Ganser, *Nato's Secret Armies*, 193. The *Newsweek* article was entitled "Germany Rocked by Scandal of U.S. Arming Storm Troops," *Newsweek*, October 20, 1952, 42–47.
[58] Ganser, *Nato's Secret Armies*, 196.
[59] "The 'democratic' state that succeeded it [fascism] is still entirely infected with the fascist virus (just as the 'democratic' state that had preceded it was already entirely infected with the fascist virus." Daniel Guérin, *Fascisme et grand capital* (Paris: Libertalia, 2014).
[60] "Post-war West Germany," writes Perry Anderson regarding the return of the Institute for Social Research to Frankfurt in 1949–1950," was now politically and culturally the most reactionary major capitalist country in Europe—its Marxist traditions excised by Nazi chauvinism and Anglo-American repression, its proletariat temporarily passive and quiescent. In this milieu, in which the KPD was to be banned and the SPD formally abandoned any connection with Marxism, the depoliticization of the Institute was completed: whereas it had been an isolated enclave in the academic

Although the history of the debates internal to the Frankfurt School is complex, with shifting allegiances and different positions staked out over time, it is safe to say that—with the exception of Marcuse at a certain point in time—the leading members of the Frankfurt School were generally either indifferent to or critical of the student movement, while being skeptical of the New Left and dismissive of the Old Left.[61] Horkheimer was never "an overt member of any working-class party," and Adorno "had no personal ties at all to socialist political life."[62] In fact, as Rolf Wiggershaus notes regarding the figures involved in the early years of the Frankfurt School, "none of those belonging to the Horkheimer circle was politically active; none of them had his origins either in the labor movement or in Marxism."[63] The expression *critical theory*, as it was established as an intellectual tradition in the academy, is a form of *theory* that is overwhelmingly *critical* of the praxis of radical social movements.[64] Critique is understood as an intellectual endeavor of self-clarification that draws on the spirit of Marxism at the expense of its substance. In this way, the Frankfurt theorists have diluted Marx's revolutionary theory into a speculative tradition of critique, in the discursive and abstract sense of the term, which included idealist liberals and reactionaries. "They remained," Wheatland observes,

> radical naysayers (as Löwenthal liked to put it, "I never wanted to play along") committed to humanism and the ideal of critical reason, and their inspirations for all of these values originated from classical German thought—the heritage of Kant, the Romantics, Hegel, Marx, Schopenhauer, Nietzsche, Freud, and Weber.[65]

---

world in the USA, it was officially fêted and patronized in West Germany. The 'critical theory' advocated by Horkheimer in the thirties now explicitly renounced any link with socialist practice. Horkheimer himself ultimately collapsed into ignominious apologies for capitalism itself, in his retirement." Anderson, *Considerations on Western Marxism*, 34.

[61] Since it is impossible to provide a concise summary, see works such as the following: Martin Jay, *The Dialectical Imagination: A History of the Frankfurt School and the Institute of Social Research, 1923-1950* (Berkeley: University of California Press, 1996); Wiggershaus, *The Frankfurt School*; Wheatland, *The Frankfurt School in Exile*; Jeffries, *Grand Hotel Abyss*; and Simone Chambers, "The Politics of Critical Theory," in *The Cambridge Companion to Critical Theory*, ed. Fred Rush (Cambridge: Cambridge University Press, 2004), 219–47. The artist Hito Steyerl's project, *Adorno's Grey* (2012), is an interesting revisitation of some of these issues.

[62] Anderson, *Considerations on Western Marxism*, 33.

[63] Wiggershaus, *The Frankfurt School*, 104.

[64] Erich Fromm, according to Kieran Durkin, was "highly suspicious" of the label "critical theory," which he described as "a 'hoax' to keep the Institute's work from being labeled Marxist." Kieran Durkin, "Erich Fromm and Theodor W. Adorno Reconsidered: A Case Study in Intellectual History," *New German Critique* 46, no. 1 (February 2019): 112.

[65] Wheatland, *The Frankfurt School in Exile*, 272.

What Louis Althusser referred to as class struggle in theory, meaning the very real ideological battle between materialism and idealism, simply disappears due to the partial or total victory of the latter. "In essence," Ingar Solty concludes:

> Horkheimer and Adorno considered historic fascism as a final defeat of the socialist project and withdrew to a position of an abstract anti-capitalism and theoretical non-conformism . . . With that position, however, they essentially fell behind Marx's own "critique of critical critique" in the "German ideology." Like Bruno Bauer and Max Stirner, they effectively lamented, "if only people saw, like we do, through the universal connection of deception (*universelle Ver blendungszusammenhang*)!"[66]

So much ink has been spilled over the Frankfurt scholars' strategy of putting a "message in a bottle" for future generations, as if they were simply *too radical* for their immediate "non-revolutionary" context, that a few people have raised the question of the precise content of that message, and whose purpose it actually served as it drifted away in a speculative sea as a distraction from terrestrial struggles in the here and now.[67]

It is not at all surprising, in this regard, that the leading members of the Frankfurt School had ties to the Congress for Cultural Freedom (CCF), which was revealed to be a CIA front organization in 1966. The CCF was one of the most important weapons in the CIA's intellectual world war against the very idea of egalitarian politics, and it financed and promoted the non-communist

---

[66] Solty, "Horkheimer."
[67] In addressing the idea that the Frankfurt scholars were trapped in a "non-revolutionary" situation, it is important to foreground at least two issues. The first is that, from an internationalist perspective, they lived through some of the most intense revolutionary struggles of the twentieth century—which some of them openly rejected—including the Cuban Revolution, the Chinese Cultural Revolution, the Vietnamese Resistance War against America, etc. Secondly, if we were to restrict their "context" to Western Europe and the Unites States, we would be well served to revisit the words and deeds of Lenin: "It is far more difficult—and of far greater value—to be a revolutionary when the conditions for direct, open, really mass and really revolutionary struggle *do not yet exist*, to be able to champion the interests of the revolution (by propaganda, agitation and organization) in non-revolutionary bodies and often enough in downright reactionary bodies, in a non-revolutionary situation, among masses who are incapable of immediately appreciating the need for revolutionary methods of action. To be able to find, to probe for, to correctly determine the specific path or the particular turn of events that will *lead* the masses to the real, last, decisive, and great revolutionary struggle—such is the main task of Communism in Western Europe and America today." V.I. Lenin, *"Left-Wing" Communism an Infantile Disorder* (New York: Red Star Publishers, 2016), 83. George Jackson wrote from the heart of the imperial beast: "Conditions will never be altogether right for a broadly based revolutionary war unless the fascists are stricken by an uncharacteristic fit of total madness. Should we wait for something that is not likely to occur at least for decades? The conditions that are not present must be manufactured." *Blood in My Eye*, 16.

left.⁶⁸ Horkheimer participated in one of its conferences in Hamburg, and Adorno published in its journal *Der Monat*. One of his articles also appeared in *Encounter*, and another in *Tempo presente* (both of which were funded by the CIA).⁶⁹ The U.S. reception of the Frankfurt School and their mounting fame in the postwar era was greatly aided by journals like *Partisan Review* and *Commentary*.⁷⁰ The former was a CIA asset, and the latter's assistant editor, Irving Kristol, was the executive secretary of the American Congress for Cultural Freedom or the ACCF (the American chapter of the CCF).⁷¹ *Commentary* was, like the Institute, funded by the American Jewish Committee and its editor in chief, Elliot Cohen, was a friend of the Institute (a CIA document released in 2006 reveals that Cohen was also a consultant to the President's Foreign Intelligence Advisory Board).⁷² Wheatland describes *Commentary*, which was effectively one of the ACCF's journals, as "among the most significant in terms of promoting the work and the reputations of the figures affiliated with the Institute for Social Research."⁷³ In addition to Cohen, other close collaborators with the Institute also had ties to the national security state. One of Horkheimer's first correspondents in the United States, the philosophy professor Sidney Hook, was an ardent cold warrior in the front lines of the CIA's cultural Cold War. He was deeply involved in the ACCF and the CCF, and he was also a consultant to the director of the CIA from 1950 to 1953, as well as an advisor to the Psychological Strategy Board (an agency established in 1951 to oversee and coordinate anti-communist

---

[68] See Gabriel Rockhill, "The CIA Reads French Theory: On the Intellectual Labor of Dismantling the Cultural Left," *The Philosophical Salon*, February 28, 2017, http://thephilosophicalsalon.com/the-cia-reads-french-theory-on-the-intellectual-labor-of-dismantling-the-cultural-left/ and Gabriel Rockhill, *Radical History and the Politics of Art* (New York: Columbia University Press, 2014), 191–217.

[69] Although I was unable to track down the exact reference, which I believe was Pierre Grémion's *Intelligence de l'anticommunisme*, I remember reading that Adorno was one of Hans Schwab-Felisch's most important interlocutors as he set about building CCF groups in West Germany, even after it was revealed that it was a CIA front organization.

[70] "Even the most casual perusal of *Partisan Review*, *Politics*, *Commentary*, and *Dissent*," writes Wheatland, "discloses a continuous fascination with the basic set of interrelated topics that the Horkheimer Circle helped many of the New York writers to comprehend and interconnect. In fact, the emerging importance and stature of the Institute among the New York Intellectuals is also demonstrated by the large number of articles that members of the Horkheimer Circle published in the main journals of New York's intellectual community during the late 1940s and 1950s." Wheatland, *The Frankfurt School in Exile*, 186–87. The New York Intellectuals, whose circles overlapped significantly with those of the Frankfurt School, had a very intimate relationship to the U.S. national security state. See, for instance, Hugh Wilford, *The New York Intellectuals: From Vanguard to Institution* (Manchester: Manchester University Press, 1995); Wilford, *The Mighty Wurlitzer*; Saunders, *The Cultural Cold War*.

[71] See Scott-Smith, *The Politics of Apolitical Culture*, 129.

[72] See "Letter to Robert Gates from Roy Godson," October 20, 1987, FOIA CIA-RDP89G01321R000700330003-7, https://www.cia.gov/library/readingroom/document/cia-rdp89g00720r000700890016-0.

[73] Wheatland, *The Frankfurt School in Exile*, 153.

propaganda efforts). The Institute's "longtime collaborator" Edward Shils was a dedicated cold warrior working for the CCF, and he admitted knowing it was a CIA front organization as early as 1955.[74]

While one could argue that the material support and promotion provided by this network of intellectuals with ties to the national security state do not prove that Horkheimer's inner circle was a witting agent of deep state propaganda, this is missing the point. What his group of anti-communist left intellectuals had to offer was precisely the kind of work that Thomas Braden and other CIA officers involved in the cultural Cold War wanted to promote, on a strictly "need-to-know" basis (meaning that only those who absolutely needed to know about the clandestine operations were informed): "in much of Europe in the 1950s, socialists, people who called themselves 'left'—the very people whom many Americans thought no better than communists—were the only people who gave a damn about fighting Communism."[75] These were the intellectuals who were supported and promoted, often unwittingly, by the CIA and their vast network of collaborators (governmental agencies, private foundations, universities, publishers, the press, etc.), many of whom continued this work well beyond the direct reach of the agency and up to the present. In the case of the Institute for Social Research, not only was it part of the "non-communist left," but its members vociferously criticized actually existing socialism, as we have seen, and they argued at great length that capitalism was inescapable. "If Marcuse and the Horkheimer Circle had contributed anything to the American Left and Western Marxism," Wheatland reminds us, "it was the idea that 'late capitalism' was far more stable and entrenched than traditional Marxists had ever thought. Nearly all of the Institute's postemigration thought was devoted to this single thesis, which it attempted to demonstrate in many fields of social research."[76] It is interesting to note, moreover, that none of the leading figures of the Frankfurt School—as far as I know—ever spoke out publicly against the CIA's role in promoting the non-communist left and the ideological realignment of the Western intelligentsia.

Georg Lukács, who had participated in the preliminary research seminar—the *Erste Marxistische Arbeitswoche*—out of which the Institute grew, suggested that the Frankfurt scholars' pessimistic resignation and imperial complicity were the price paid for their exquisite lifestyle as leading Western intellectuals. In his 1962 preface to *Theory of the Novel*, he extended his earlier critique of Schopenhauer to "a considerable part of the leading German

---

[74] See Wheatland, *The Frankfurt School in Exile*, 251 and Saunders, *The Cultural Cold War*, 395.
[75] Thomas W. Braden, "I'm Glad the CIA Is 'Immoral,'" *Saturday Evening Post*, May 20, 1967, 10.
[76] Wheatland, *The Frankfurt School in Exile*, 327.

intelligentsia, including Adorno."⁷⁷ This critique, which he had developed in *The Destruction of Reason*, described how Schopenhauer—and thus, by extension, Adorno and Co.—had taken up residence in the "Grand Hotel Abyss": "a beautiful hotel, equipped with every comfort, on the edge of an abyss, of nothingness, of absurdity. And the daily contemplation of the abyss between excellent meals or artistic entertainments, can only heighten the enjoyment of the subtle comforts offered."⁷⁸

POLICING THE LEFT BORDER OF CRITIQUE

> The appeal to class won't work any more, since today you are really all proletarians.
>
> —Theodor Adorno
>
> If those who have plenty were to hand some over to the needy, they would ultimately find themselves overwhelmed by them.
>
> —Max Horkheimer

Frankfurt School critical theory has primarily been preoccupied with the history of Western culture and civilization. Although it has provided some insightful accounts of social life under consumer capitalism and its culture industries, it has generally maintained significant distance from workers' struggles, anti-colonial wars of liberation, materialist feminism, and other revolutionary movements. Edward Said has cogently summed up some of this missed encounter with international leftist politics by reminding us of the myopic blindness to imperialism on the part of many Western Marxian intellectuals:

> Frankfurt School critical theory, despite its seminal insights into the relationships between domination, modern society, and the opportunities for redemption through art and critique, is stunningly silent on racist theory, anti-imperialist resistance, and oppositional practice in the empire. And lest that silence be interpreted as an oversight, we have today's leading Frankfurt theorist, Jürgen Habermas, explaining in an interview (originally published in *The New Left Review*) that the silence is deliberate abstention: no, he says, we have nothing to

---

⁷⁷ Georg Lukács, *The Theory of the Novel*, trans. Anna Bostock (Cambridge, MA: The MIT Press, 1999), 22.
⁷⁸ Lukács, *The Theory of the Novel*, 22.

say to "anti-imperialist and anti-capitalist struggles in the Third World," even if, he adds, "I am aware of the fact that this is a eurocentrically limited view."[79]

To his credit, Herbert Marcuse is one of the only leading figures affiliated with the Frankfurt School to have evolved to the point of lending his support in the late 1960s and early 1970s to radical social movements, so much so that he came to be identified—in spite of his rejection of the term—as a kind of "grandfather" of the New Left.[80] This was, however, the exception, and Andrew Feenberg has depicted the Marcusian orientation, at least after 1968, in terms of a more resolute dedication to historical materialism and the risks of praxis: "Where Horkheimer and Adorno ultimately rejected the New Left, Marcuse took the Hegelian-Marxian-Lukácsian plunge back into history."[81] Indeed, on June 2, 1969, in the heat of major anti-capitalist movements on the part of students and workers, the magazine *Konkret* lauded Marcuse as "the only representative of the 'Frankfurt School' who supports those who wish to realize the claims of Critical Theory: the students, young workers, persecuted minorities in the metropolises, and the oppressed in the Third World."[82]

It is important to note, in this regard, that the social reputation of Marcuse in the academy, as well as the dominant historiography used to frame the developments of the Frankfurt School, is directly related to his overt political commitments. Marcuse is often dismissed or sidelined as an anachronistic simpleton, or even the obsolescent icon of the bygone world of 1960s counter-culture. As his former student, Angela Davis, remarked in 2004, "the most well-known and widely read thinker associated with the Frankfurt School thirty years ago became the least studied in the 1980s and 1990s, while Theodor Adorno, Max Horkheimer, and Walter Benjamin are extensively studied in the contemporary era."[83] Horkheimer himself was partially responsible for Marcuse's reputation since he publicly accused him of "simplifying and coarsening Adorno's and my thought."[84] Marcuse responded,

---

[79] Edward W. Said, *Culture and Imperialism* (New York: Vintage Books, 1993), 278. In his famous essay, "Traditional and Critical Theory," Horkheimer frames his entire argument in terms of the European tradition of theory, and one of his unstated premises is that this tradition simply is *the* tradition of thought itself. Moreover, he at no point explicitly acknowledges that the critical theoretical task of establishing the "right form of society" means overcoming the oppression and exploitation of non-whites, women, or non-Westerners.

[80] For Marcuse's rejection of this label see, for instance, "Interview with Marcuse," *Australian Left Review* 1, no. 22 (1969): 36, https://ro.uow.edu.au/alr/vol1/iss22/6.

[81] Andrew Feenberg, "Waiting for History: Horkheimer and Adorno's Theatre of the Absurd," *The Platypus Review*, Supplement to Issue 37 (July 2011): 4.

[82] Cited in Leslie, "Adorno-Marcuse Correspondence," 121.

[83] Angela Y. Davis, "Marcuse's Legacies," in *Herbert Marcuse: A Critical Reader*, ed. John Abromeit and W. Mark Cobb (New York: Routledge, 2004), 43. "It was the reception of Marcuse during the 1960s, 1970s, and 1980s," Wheatland writes, "that established the academic reputation of the Frankfurt School in the United States." Wheatland, *The Frankfurt School in Exile*, 297.

[84] Leslie, "Adorno-Marcuse Correspondence," 122.

in his correspondence with Adorno, by explaining that simplification is an effective tactic because it maximizes the use-value of ideas for social change:

> It seems extraordinary to me that, in his attack, Max [Horkheimer] reclaims as private property ideas that were worked out in communal discussions; I gladly accept that these thoughts got "cruder and simpler" in my work. I believe crudeness and simplification have made the barely recognizable radical substance of these thoughts visible again.[85]

Regarding Davis herself, she has all but vanished from the standard accounts of the critical theory tradition, which faithfully orbit around Habermas and the neo-Habermasians. Rolf Wiggershaus does not so much as mention her in his 788-page study, which bears a promising subtitle: *The Frankfurt School: Its History, Theories, and Political Significance.* Martin Jay, in his well-known book on the same topic, only mentions her in the preface to the 1996 edition (the book was originally published in 1973) in a revealing statement that describes her in dismissive terms as Marcuse's "controversial former student and Communist Party leader."[86] Early on, Adorno had discouraged Davis from seeking to discover ways of linking her "seemingly discrepant interests in philosophy and social activism."[87] "He suggested," Davis later explained, "that my desire to work directly in the radical movements of that period was akin to a media studies scholar deciding to become a radio technician."[88]

Adorno's unstated premise was, of course, that the true scholar does not engage in the practices he or she might study. According to this petty-bourgeois ideology, the scientific value and relevance of scholarly work diminish in direct proportion to its political engagements and real use-value to parties and movements on the ground. What is presented as politically neutral, and therefore truly "scientific," is work whose political orientation is more or less invisible because it seamlessly coalesces with the dominant ideology. Oppositional politics cannot be "scientific" precisely because it calls out the political ideology undergirding bourgeois science.

The standard accounts of the history of the Frankfurt School are thus themselves the vehicles for politicized, racialized, and gendered narratives. In the forking path separating the revolutionary activism of a certain Marcusian heritage—particularly as it manifested itself in the work of a communist black woman with ties to the revolutionary Black Panther Party—from the relative conservativism of the Horkheimer–Habermas lineage, academic

---

[85] Adorno and Marcuse, "Correspondence," 134.
[86] Martin Jay, *The Dialectical Imagination*, xii.
[87] Davis, "Marcuse's Legacies," 46.
[88] Davis, "Marcuse's Legacies," 47.

historiography has made a very clear choice. This is, of course, not the only forking path in this tradition, nor does it mean that this Marcusian heritage is itself beyond critique, but it nonetheless provides a helpful insight into the political history of the Frankfurt School.[89]

EXORCISING THE SPECTER OF MARX

> The utopian accents have moved from the concept of labor to the concept of communication.
>
> —Jürgen Habermas

If the substance was lacking, there was still a certain Marxian spirit to what would later become known as the first generation of the Frankfurt School. In subsequent generations—if it be the second generation in the work of Habermas, or the third with the likes of Seyla Benhabib, Axel Honneth, Nancy Fraser, Rainer Forst, and others—this spirit has all but disappeared. Habermas set the agenda by explicitly arguing for a recuperation of socialism *within* the capitalist system and its purportedly democratic institutions. In a revealing article in which he reacted to the fall of the Berlin Wall, he wrote:

> It might well be the case that many East German intellectuals will have to adapt to a situation that the West European Left has been in for decades—that of transforming socialist ideas into the radically reformist self-criticism of a capitalist society, which, in the form of a constitutional democracy with universal suffrage and a welfare state, has developed not only weaknesses but also strengths. With the bankruptcy of state socialism, this is the eye of the needle through which everything must pass.... The hope that humanity can emancipate itself from self-imposed tutelage and degrading living conditions has not lost its power, but it is filtered by a fallibilist consciousness, and an awareness of the historical lesson that one would already have achieved a considerable amount if the balance

---

[89] In fact, the high road of the established lineage has cut its swath through history by persistently overrunning or cutting off important offshoots and alternative paths. Although there are too many examples to cite, it is worth noting the case of Erich Fromm. Although he was by far one of the most prominent representatives of the Frankfurt School in the early years of its exile, after the rift with Horkheimer "the Horkheimer Circle went to great lengths to de-emphasize Fromm's role in the development of Critical Theory." Wheatland, *The Frankfurt School in Exile*, 224. Regarding Marcuse and Davis, there are a number of important critiques, particularly of some of Marcuse's early work. Joy James has provided one of the most incisive criticisms of Davis' work in recent lectures, some of which are available on YouTube, and in "Airbrushing Revolution for the Sake of Abolition," *Black Agenda Report*, July 29, 2020, https://blackagendareport.com/airbrushing-revolution-sake-abolition.

of a tolerable existence could be preserved for the fortunate few—and, most of all, if it could be established on the other, ravaged continents.[90]

By threading the eye of this reformist needle, Habermas sought to redirect the critical pinprick of radical theory by seamlessly weaving it into the systems in place. In order to do so, his entire recuperative agenda is dependent upon reworking material history in order to present the European Enlightenment project as one of trying to spread the intersubjective light of communicative reason. He thereby downplays, sidelines, excludes, or renders accidental the extent to which the development of what was later called modern democracy and capitalism has gone hand in hand with the global repression, exploitation, and oppression of imperialism, colonialism, slavery, and the genocide of indigenous people.

As Domenico Losurdo and others—including myself—have argued by marshaling extensive historical evidence, these were not somehow two separate projects, and the history of modern "democratic" Europe can nowise be separated from the global catastrophe of capitalist expansion.[91] The so-called Enlightenment ideals were deeply rooted in oligarchic social structures and repressive class, gender, and race relations. They were, indeed, only for the few, and that was precisely their purpose: to put the many of the world population in service of the few Enlightened white, male, property-owning Europeans who formed the ruling class of global capitalism (and who sought to justify or conceal their status by buying the creative labor power of intellectuals willing to work as professional whitewashers). The mythological story of progressive inclusion has been a constitutive feature of this very project, and it allows for its perpetuation by claiming unjustified credit for the successes of past struggles from below, while reiterating promises for a brighter future when these struggles have failed.

In the case of Habermas' work, such promises do not imply material changes since the "utopian idea of a society based on social labor has lost its persuasive power" and has been replaced by the concept of communication, whose "utopian content" as a grounding for society is limited to "the

---

[90] Jürgen Habermas, "What Does Socialism Mean Today? The Revolutions of Recuperation and the Need for New Thinking," in *After the Fall: The Failure of Communism and the Future of Socialism,* ed. Robin Blackburn (London: Verso, 1991), 45. "Since 1989–90," Habermas proclaims elsewhere, "it has become impossible to break out of the universe of capitalism; the only remaining option is to civilize or tame the capitalist dynamic from within." Jürgen Habermas, *The Crisis of the European Union: A Response,* trans. Ciaran Cronin (Cambridge: Polity Books, 2012), 106.

[91] See Domenico Losurdo, *Liberalism: A Counter-*History, trans. Gregory Elliott (London: Verso, 2014) and Gabriel Rockhill, *Counter-History of the Present* (Durham, NC: Duke University Press, 2017).

formal aspects of an undamaged intersubjectivity."[92] This is the reformist future aspired to by contemporary critical theory, which is one in which there is space *inside* of capitalism and administered "democracy" for rational communication and a purportedly inclusive "procedure of discursive will formation."[93]

LIBERAL IDEOLOGY AS THE GRAMMAR OF CRITIQUE

The praise of inherited diversities proposed in place of the necessary effort to transcend the limits of bourgeois universalism . . . functions in perfect accord with the requirements of contemporary imperialism's project of globalization.

—Samir Amin

The moral infrastructure of modern, liberal-capitalist societies can be regarded as the legitimate starting point for a political ethic.

—Axel Honneth

Habermas' work remains the tuning fork for the well-organized orchestra that is third-generation critical theory. In their writings and lectures, even when they are critical of him or bring in issues outside of his purview, third-generation critical theorists draw extensively on his reformist political orientation and bankrupt historiography. In fact, it might make more sense to speak of two generations of the Frankfurt School, separated by the watershed moment that is Habermas, as Tom Rockmore has argued:

The relation of Habermas to critical social theory, aka as critical theory, has had a crucial effect on the declining fortunes of this form of neo-Marxism.... Habermas... is the central figure of the second generation of critical social theorists who, whatever his intentions, decisively stultified its further development. He may even have brought critical social theory to an early end by reintegrating it into traditional theory, from which it emerged, and which, as understood from

---

[92] Jürgen Habermas, *The New Conservatism: Cultural Criticism and the Historians' Debate*, ed. and trans. Shierry Weber Nicholsen (Cambridge, MA: The MIT Press, 1990), 53 and 69. "In advanced capitalist countries," Habermas proclaims, "the standard of living has [...] risen to such an extent, at least among broad strata of the population, that the interest in the emancipation of society can no longer be articulated directly in economic terms. "Alienation" has been deprived of its palpable economic form as misery." Jürgen Habermas, *Theory and Practice*, trans. John Viertel (Boston: Beacon Press, 1973), 195.

[93] Habermas, *The New Conservatism*, 69.

Habermas' perspective, is finally just another form of traditional theory, but crucially without an emancipatory potential.[94]

Although this is not the place for an extensive assessment of the neo-Habermasians, I would like to briefly discuss the two figures who—according to Nancy Fraser—have purportedly pursued the broad tradition of a totalizing critique of society: Axel Honneth and Fraser herself.[95] In their co-authored book, *Redistribution or Recognition?* (2003), Honneth squarely inscribes his research within Habermas' recuperative revolution by flatly asserting the collapse of Marxism and explicitly valorizing liberal, capitalist societies of the Western world as morally—and therefore politically—superior:

> In my overview of the recognition relations of liberal-capitalist societies, I already had to make a number of implicit assumptions about the moral direction of social development. For only on the assumption that the new order involves a morally superior form of social integration can its internal principles be considered a legitimate, justified starting point for outlining a political ethic ... I had to first presume the moral superiority of modernity by assuming that its normative constitution is the result of past directed development.[96]

In order to arrive at this Eurocentric conclusion, he begins by claiming that the formal expectation of "social recognition" "represents an anthropological constant," even though the precise content of this expectation changes based on the society in question.[97] He then appeals to what we might call, echoing the term *scientism*, *social-scientism*: by drawing on a select number of "empirical" studies that he as a petty-bourgeois intellectual from Europe has read, he claims to have arrived at a universal conclusion regarding the

---

[94] Tom Rockmore, "Habermas, Critical Theory, and Political Economy," in *Radical Intellectuals and the Subversion of Progressive Politics: Political Philosophy and Public Purpose*, ed. G. Smulewicz-Zucker and M.J. Thompson (New York: Palgrave Macmillan, 2015), 191–92. Michael J. Thompson has arrived at a similar conclusion: "Today a new paradigm of critical theory has risen from the ashes of the old. What I am calling here the 'domestication' of critical theory therefore refers to the ways that the linguistic, procedural, and recognitive turn in critical theory that was initiated in the 1970s and 1980s by figures such as Jürgen Habermas, Axel Honneth, and others has receded from the confrontation with the primary source of social domination and the disfiguration of human culture: capitalist market society. In essence, the domestication of critical theory implies that it has been effectively emptied of radical political content." Michael J. Thompson, *The Domestication of Critical Theory* (London: Rowman & Littlefield International, 2016), 2.
[95] See Nancy Fraser, "Global Justice and the Renewal of the Critical Theory Tradition: Dialogue with Alfredo Gomez-Muller and Gabriel Rockhill," in *Politics of Culture and the Spirit of Critique: Dialogues*, ed. Alfredo Gomez-Muller and Gabriel Rockhill (New York: Columbia University Press, 2011), 69.
[96] Nancy Fraser and Axel Honneth, *Redistribution or Recognition? A Political-Philosophical Exchange* (London: Verso, 2003), 184 (on the purported collapse of Marxism see 126).
[97] Fraser and Honneth, *Redistribution or Recognition?*, 174.

"human" experience of injustice *in general*. The "core of all experiences of injustice," he unflinchingly asserts, is the "withdrawal of social recognition."[98] The "material plight" of the oppressed, we learn, is less important to them than the fact that their "ways of life and achievements" are not deemed worthy of respect by the rest of society.[99] In fact, he has elsewhere stated that social classes themselves do not "have any common, objective interest," and that "it is with good reason that we have abandoned the notion that emancipatory interests or experiences can be attributed to a group of people [i.e. a class] who have nothing but socio-economic circumstances in common."[100] Exeunt class struggles.

This position is more or less identical to that of R.P. Tempels, the Belgian missionary to the Congo who explained in *Bantu Philosophy*, that what the Bantus really want is recognition and respect, whereas their material conditions of existence are secondary. The work of Aimé Césaire, which was not included in what Honneth unabashedly calls "all of the empirical evidence," sums up Tempels' position while articulating a fundamental critique of the nostrum of the bourgeois politics of recognition. Césaire explains that Tempels' patronizing respect for the spiritual nature of Bantu philosophy provides scant cover for material oppression and exploitation. The scene begins with Césaire paraphrasing Tempels' response to the Bantu's material demands, then he quotes him directly:

> Decent wages! Comfortable housing! Food! These Bantu are pure spirits, I tell you: "What they desire first of all and above all is not the improvement of their economic or material situation, but the white man's recognition of and respect for their dignity as men, their full human value."

---

[98] Fraser and Honneth, *Redistribution or Recognition?*, 134.

[99] Fraser and Honneth, *Redistribution or Recognition?* 131. "The experience of social injustice," which includes "economic disadvantage" for him, "*always* corresponds to the withholding of what is taken to be legitimate recognition." Fraser and Honneth, *Redistribution or Recognition?*, 170 (my emphasis).

[100] Axel Honneth, *Disrespect: The Normative Foundations of Critical Theory* (Cambridge: Polity Press, 2007), 69. Very much like Honneth, Hartmut Rosa has combined Habermasian historiographical myths regarding European modernity's purported promise of autonomy with the dissolution of critique into a liberal diagnosis of social pathologies. He not only abandons the critique of capitalism, but he openly indulges in the blackmail of the gulag: "there can be little doubt that any attempt for a political and cultural elimination of alienation leads to totalitarian forms of philosophy, culture and politics, and to authoritarian forms of personality." *Alienation and Acceleration: Towards a Critical Theory of Late-Modern Temporality* (Malmö, Sweden: NSU Press, 2010), 98–99.

Césaire then draws out the ultimate consequences of this position: "In short, tip your hat to Bantu vital force, wink at the Bantu immortal soul, and you are done! You have to admit that it's a good deal!"[101]

Honneth has cashed in on this deal, building a highly successful academic career on the basis of a "critical theory" grounded in the politics of recognition. After naturalizing and universalizing a purportedly human need for the type of individual recognition that emerged in bourgeois society in Europe, he unsurprisingly claims—in ways more than reminiscent of the civilizing mission of colonialism—that the best form of intersubjective recognition is to be found in modern capitalist societies. Indeed, he understands the latter as having been truly "subversive" and "revolutionary" by establishing three new spheres of recognition in the moral order of society: love, law, and achievement.[102] These spheres, along with their guiding principles, are "institutionally anchored in modern capitalist societies" and constitute the moral grammar of our times.[103] They form what we might call the *bourgeois order of individual recognition*. It is superior, for him, precisely because it allows for a greater realization of "personal identity formation"[104]:

> It [seems] justified to understand the breakthrough to the modern, liberal-capitalist social order as moral progress, since the differentiation of the three recognition spheres of love, legal equality, and the achievement principle went along with an increase in the social possibilities for individualization as well as a rise in social inclusion.[105]

It is not only that this order is superior to all others, by better satisfying the anthropological constant that is the individual's need for inclusive social recognition, it is that it provides the normative order for evaluating all contemporary moral and political claims. The task of critique thus consists for Honneth in pointing out areas where there is still more recognition to be had: "in order to be up to the task of critique, the theory of justice outlined here can wield the recognition principles' surplus validity against the facticity of their social interpretation."[106] This is one of the reasons why he explicitly defines his project as a "teleological liberalism" that seeks to spell out "a normative idea of the goals for whose sake the establishment and realization of social

---

[101] Aimé Césaire, *Discourse on Colonialism*, trans. Joan Pinkham (New York: Monthly Review Press, 2000), 58–59.
[102] Fraser and Honneth, *Redistribution or Recognition?*, 140.
[103] Fraser and Honneth, *Redistribution or Recognition?*, 160.
[104] Fraser and Honneth, *Redistribution or Recognition?*, 176.
[105] Fraser and Honneth, *Redistribution or Recognition?*, 185.
[106] Fraser and Honneth, *Redistribution or Recognition?*, 186.

justice represent a political task that we consider ethically well-grounded."[107] The criterion of progress in this domain is directly dependent upon the bourgeois morality of the era of imperial capitalism:

> Only demands that potentially contribute to the expansion of social relations of recognition can be considered normatively grounded, since they point in the direction of a rise in the moral level of social integration. The two measures of individualization and inclusion... represent the criteria by means of which this weighing can be accomplished.[108]

The liberal-capitalist order, at the hands of Honneth, is not only legitimated as such, but it becomes the *summum bonum* of human existence, the moral arbiter for the totality of political activities, and the unquestionable given of the world order.

If we were to assess Honneth's assertions from a Marxist perspective, we would be forced to recognize that the cunning of dialectical history has done unprecedented work, transforming the critique of bourgeois society into the embourgeoisement of critique. The ideology of bourgeois individualism, which Marx clearly demonstrated to be a product of capitalist social relations, becomes the guiding framework for all normative claims. Rather than ideology critique, Honneth delivers ideology itself—in ways strongly reminiscent of Habermas—as the normative framework and foundation for critique. He then universalizes this, making the modern, European, bourgeois order of individual recognition into *the* moral and political model for humanity in general. Critical theory is thereby fully integrated into its supposed object of critique, and it comes to function as the philosophical handmaiden of colonial capitalism and pseudo-democracy. Bourgeois ideology becomes the very grammar of "emancipation."[109]

---

[107] Fraser and Honneth, *Redistribution or Recognition?*, 178.
[108] Fraser and Honneth, *Redistribution or Recognition?*, 187.
[109] Honneth has reacted to the relatively recent uptick in discussions of socialism within the Western intelligentsia by publishing a book with the revealing title *The Idea of Socialism* (2015). In it, he puts forth what he admits is an account of socialism "that would make its main purpose and theoretical impulse unrecognizable to the majority of its previous followers." Axel Honneth, *The Idea of Socialism*, trans. Joseph Ganahl (Cambridge: Polity Press, 2017), 106. Indeed, he lambasts those who cling to "their illusions" that a world beyond capitalism might be possible, or even desirable: "There no longer seems to be any hope that capitalism will eventually bring about its own demise, nor that the working class bears within itself the seed of the new society." Honneth, *The Idea of Socialism*, 106. Socialism, we learn, would thus best be redefined *within* the parameters of "liberal-democratic capitalism." Honneth, *The Idea of Socialism*, 106.

LEFT ANTICOMMUNISM

In the academy, it has become a kind of intellectual common sense to dismiss Marxism and its methods *in toto* as "totalizing,". . . "reductive," . . . or "universalizing.". . . A main feminist critique has been that women and female labor were excluded from analysis.... The charge of reductivism might be leveled more accurately against anti-Marxist feminism.

—Carol A. Stabile

Nancy Fraser arguably occupies the left wing of the contemporary institution of critical theory. She is a self-proclaimed "socialist," and she is well known for her mantra "no recognition without redistribution!"[110] To her credit, she has certainly been one of the most outspoken supporters, within the critical theory tradition, of certain types of redistributive measures, and she has recently been advocating for a "return" to the question of capitalism that numerous practitioners of critique "abandoned in previous decades."[111] She has also developed a rhetoric of external critique and transformation, provided an important condemnation of corporate feminism, and highlighted the need to connect feminism to anti-capitalist struggles.[112]

However, her project is largely dependent upon a problematic Habermasian historiography regarding the march of democracy and the supposed failure of Marxism (which is largely dissolved into the standard image of Stalinism that has been conjured by the Western bourgeois intelligentsia). Citing, in support of her claims, Habermas' thesis on the exhaustion of utopian energies and the supposed turn of social movements away from economic issues, she makes the blanket assertion that "Marxism is no longer a force to be reckoned with, having been supplanted by culturalist paradigms, both in politics and in the academy."[113] She also avers that contemporary critical theorists find themselves in a new historical context: "Unlike earlier Frankfurt School thinkers, they cannot assume a political culture in which emancipatory hopes find focus in socialism, labor holds pride of place among social movements,

---

[110] In addition to *Justice Interruptus*, see for instance the interview with Nancy A. Naples entitled "To Interpret the World and to Change It: An Interview with Nancy Fraser," *Signs: Journal of Women in Culture and Society* 29, no. 4 (2004): 1122.

[111] Luc Boltanski and Nancy Fraser, "Domination and Emancipation: For a Revival of Social Critique," chapter 1 of this volume, 27.

[112] Boltanski and Fraser, "Domination and Emancipation," 20.

[113] Fraser and Honneth, *Redistribution or Recognition?*, 212. "In 1915," Michael Parenti reminds us, "Lenin wrote that '[bourgeois] science will not even hear of Marxism, declaring that it has been refuted and annihilated.'" Michael Parenti, *Blackshirts & Reds: Rational Fascism & the Overthrow of Communism* (San Francisco: City Lights Books, 1997), 121.

and social egalitarianism enjoys broad support."[114] As Honneth himself has pointed out, she relies on the parochial perspective of the American academy in claiming that there has been a shift from the politics of redistribution to the politics of recognition. More fundamentally, she does not adequately account for the material forces driving the development and spread of the ideology of identitarian politics, in myriad forms, during the ascendancy and then hegemony of neoliberal capitalism. As Marxist critics have consistently pointed out, identitarian politics *is a class project* that deceptively transforms the struggle for social justice into an innocuous symbolic politics of representation and inclusion at the precise moment at which a radical analysis of global capitalism was the most necessary.[115] "It is no wonder," writes William I. Robinson,

> that the transnational elite embraced as its own the politics of "diversity" and "multiculturalism" as a strategy to channel the struggle for social justice and anti-capitalist transformation into non-threatening demands for inclusion if not outright cooptation. The strategy served to eclipse the language of the working and popular classes and of anti-capitalism.[116]

Furthermore, Fraser's simplistic, sequential historiography sidelines or misrepresents the deeply intertwined relationship between class, race, and gender in modern history, and it downplays or ignores many of the revolutionary political movements of the contemporary world, from the Cuban Revolution and the Black Panthers to the Young Lords, the Democratic and Popular Revolution in Burkina Faso, the Zapatistas, the Sandinistas, the Bolivarian Revolution, and beyond. As Domenico Losurdo has argued with his signature acumen, the Habermasian and neo-Habermasian preoccupation with the "disappearance" and potential "return" of the working poor or class struggle demonstrates a profound ignorance of the fact that class struggle never disappeared in the first place (even if it was phased out of the consciousness of significant sectors of the Western intelligentsia).[117]

---

[114] Fraser and Honneth, *Redistribution or Recognition?*, 198.
[115] See, for instance, Adolph Reed Jr., *Class Notes: Posing as Politics and Other Thoughts on the American Scene* (New York: The New Press, 2001).
[116] William I. Robinson, "The Betrayal of the Intellectuals," *Great Transition Initiative*, April 2020, https://greattransition.org/images/Planetize-Movement-Robinson.pdf?fbclid=IwAR0gnGW4WsO8QXh9tJ9ZJk417VgtIoD35dVoA9R3zjE6rUT6R7SvcZVxVJQ.
[117] Domenico Losurdo, *Class Struggle: A Political and Philosophical History*, trans. Gregory Elliott (New York: Palgrave Macmillan, 2016), 2–3. Unsurprisingly, Fraser and Rahel Jaeggi have historically framed their recent co-authored book, *Capitalism*, in precisely these terms. Demonstrating their ignorance of the breadth and depth of the Marxist tradition, as well as of the incessant forms of anti-capitalist class struggle going on around the globe, they pretentiously claim that the notion of capitalism as "an overarching form of life" is "making a comeback." Nancy Fraser and Rahel Jaeggi, *Capitalism: A Conversation in Critical Theory* (Cambridge: Polity, 2018), 2. As the

Moreover, as Losurdo explains, "the thesis that income redistribution represented the dominant paradigm for '150 years,' until the 'demise of communism,' proves extremely reductive."[118] By working through the writings and political activism of Marx, Engels, Lenin, Mao, and others—at a level of detail and historical precision nowhere to be found in the writings of Habermas and the neo-Habermasians on the Marxist tradition—he demonstrates how the communist understanding of class struggle has always included the fight for recognition (*Anerkennung*):

> What is at stake in class struggle? Subjugated peoples, the proletariat and subaltern classes, women enduring domestic slavery—these very different subjects can advance the most varied demands: national liberation; abolition of slavery proper and the conquest of the most basic forms of freedom; better living and working conditions; the transformation of property and production relations; an end to domestic segregation.... On the economic-political level, it comprises the objective of altering the division of labor (internationally, inside the factory or family); on the politico-moral level, that of overcoming the dehumanizing and reifying processes which characterize capitalist society—the objective of achieving recognition.[119]

As he points out, it is not the Marxist heritage that is reductively economistic. It is the liberal tradition that "interprets class struggle in reductionist and vulgarly economistic terms."[120]

This same tradition has constructed a mythological progress narrative according to which questions of racial, gender, and sexual equality were outside the purview of Marxist analysis, and that the latter was disproportionately preoccupied with economic questions affecting primarily white, male working-class subjects. For instance, in a self-described manifesto that

---

book unfolds, it becomes increasingly clear why they consider this to be a new development: the idea of capitalism is beginning to seep into their intellectual circles for nearly the first time. They identify Habermas' *Theory of Communicative Action* as "the last attempt to ground critical theory in a large-scale social theory," and they recognize that subsequent critical theorists followed Habermas in effectively removing "the economic sphere from the realm of criticism." Fraser and Jaeggi, *Capitalism*, 5. The "return" of capitalism, is thus, strictly speaking, its reappearance within the tiny academic circles of an intellectual tradition that had abandoned it.

[118] Losurdo, *Class Struggle*, 73.
[119] Losurdo, *Class Struggle*, 83.
[120] Losurdo, *Class Struggle*, 75. "What distinguishes his [Marx's] analysis so radically from classical political economy," Ellen Meiksins Wood explains, "is that it creates no sharp discontinuities between economic and political spheres; and he is able to trace the continuities because he treats the economy itself not as a network of disembodied forces but, like the political sphere, as a set of social relations." Ellen Meiksins Wood, *Democracy Against Capitalism: Renewing Historical Materialism* (London: Verso, 2016), 21.

Nancy Fraser co-authored with Cinzia Arruzza and Tithi Bhattacharya in 2019, we read:

> Marx's followers have not always grasped that neither the working class nor humanity is an undifferentiated, homogenous entity and that universality cannot be achieved by ignoring their internal differences. We are still paying the price today for these political and intellectual lapses . . . too many sections of the left still fall back on the old formula holding that what unites us is an abstract and homogenous notion of class, and that feminism and anti-racism can only divide us. What is becoming increasingly clear, however, is that the standard portrait of the militant worker as white and male is badly out of sync with the times—indeed, it was never accurate in the first place. As we argued in our *Manifesto*, today's global working class also comprises billions of women, immigrants, and people of color.[121]

Who, we must ask, are the followers of Marx that they have in mind? Was it Rosa Luxemburg in her critique of the ways in which "the toil of the proletarian women and mothers in the four walls of their homes is considered unproductive" under capitalism?[122] Was it Clara Zetkin, one of the founding leaders of the Communist Women's International, who debated the "women's question" with Lenin and penned the following lines in her text tellingly entitled "What the Women Owe to Karl Marx": "he created the most irreplaceable and important weapons for the women's fight to obtain all of their rights"?[123] Was it Lenin writing books whose titles presage their contents, like *The Right of Nations to Self-Determination* and *The Emancipation of Women*, or leading a revolution that—in the words of Valentine Moghadam—was "more audacious in its approach to gender than any revolution before or since"?[124]

---

[121] Cinzia Arruzza, Nancy Fraser and Tithi Bhattacharya, *Feminism for the 99%: A Manifesto* (London: Verso, 2019), 83–84.
[122] Peter Hudis and Kevin B. Anderson, eds., *The Rosa Luxemburg Reader* (New York: Monthly Review Press, 2004), 241.
[123] Philip S. Foner, ed., *Clara Zetkin: Selected Writings* (Chicago: Haymarket Books, 2015), 93.
[124] Valentine M. Moghadam, *Modernizing Women: Gender and Social Change in the Middle East* (Boulder: Lynne Rienner Publishers, 1993), 77. "Under Alexandra Kollantai, people's commissar for social welfare," Moghadam explains, "labor legislation was passed to give women an eight-hour day, social insurance, pregnancy leave for two months before and after childbirth, and time at work to breast-feed. It also prohibited child labor and night work for women. The early months of the revolution also saw legislation to establish equality between husband and wife, civil registration of marriage, easy divorce, abolition of illegitimacy, and the wife's right not to take her husband's name or share his domicile... The Bolsheviks also stressed the need for political participation of women . . . The Bolsheviks strongly supported 'free union' and therefore legalized divorce." Moghadam, *Modernizing Women*, 78–79. See also, Tatiana Cozzarelli, "Socialist Revolution, Women's Liberation, and the Withering Away of the Family," *Left Voice*, May 19, 2020, https://www.leftvoice.org/socialist-revolution-womens-liberation-and-the-withering-away-of-the-family?fbclid=IwAR0ab1MPCxR0ISKhW2ILpQEFQxevixOuBx2CDM2ol8sWbnNj2TkUb190Jho.

Were Mao Zedong, Ho Chi Minh, Thomas Sankara, George Jackson, Huey Newton, Fidel Castro, and Ernesto "Che" Guevara—not to mention the millions of communists working under their leadership—the ones who ignored anti-racism and assumed that the militant worker was white? Are the 3.8 million members of the Federation of Cuban Women—who have helped achieve for women such things as paid maternity leave, free medical care, expanded educational opportunities, access to every sector of the workforce, equal pay, and the 1975 Family Code, which "made it the legal obligation of men to share in the housework and childrearing responsibilities"—an old school clique of reductive Marxists whose ignorant dogmatism could be overcome by reading this manifesto?[125] Were Alexandra Kollantai, Claudia Jones, Celia Sánchez, Vilma Espín, Haydee Santamaría, Kathleen Cleaver, Assata Shakur, Denise Oliver-Velez, and Comandanta Ramona not thinking about race and gender because they were too tainted by "white male" Marxism? Is it the Marxists who have been reductionist or their radical liberal detractors?

The "manifesto" that Fraser co-authored makes regular references to "old school" approaches and the "class reductionist" left, which it affiliates with the Marxist tradition, without giving concrete examples.[126] This allows them to present their project as novel and proclaim, for instance, that there is now "the possibility of a new, unprecedented phase of class struggle: feminist, internationalist, environmentalist, and anti-racist."[127] What they neglect to mention is that the Marxist tradition has understood class struggle to be feminist, internationalist, environmentalist, and anti-racist. In a passage that is in perfect harmony with Marx's view, Engels showered praise on what he described as Jean-Baptiste Joseph Fourier's masterly "criticism of the bourgeois form of the relations between the sexes, and the position of woman in bourgeois society."[128] "He [Fourier] was the first to declare," Engels writes in

---

[125] Malena Hinze, "The Revolutionary Role of Women in Cuba," *Liberation School*, March 1, 2007, https://liberationschool.org/07-03-01-the-revolutionary-role-women-in-html/ Also see the documentary film by María Torrellas entitled *Cubanas, Mujeres en Revolución*, 2018, https://vimeo.com/277301522 (accessed on January 21, 2021).

[126] This is not to deny, of course, that there have been, and continue to be, certain forms of vulgar and reductionist "Marxism," in spite of the fact that the Marxist tradition is overflowing with critiques of such approaches. To take but two examples, Clara Zetkin wrote in 1923: "In contrast to the Second International, the Comintern is not an International for the elite of white proletarians of Europe and America. It is an International for the exploited of all races." Clara Zetkin, *Fighting Fascism: How to Struggle and How to Win*, ed. Mike Taber and John Riddell (Chicago: Haymarket Books, 2017), 61. Thomas Sankara, in his speech "The Revolution Cannot Triumph without the Emancipation of Women," drew attention to the fact that the revolution he had spearheaded had helped liberate men, but that "the authenticity and future of… [the] revolution depend[ed] on women." Thomas Sankara, *Women's Liberation and the African Freedom Struggle* (Atlanta, GA: Pathfinder Press, 2010), 22.

[127] Arruzza et al., *Feminism for the 99%*, 9.

[128] Karl Marx and Friedrich Engels, *Collected Works*, vol. 25, *Frederick Engels: Anti-Dühring, Dialectics of Nature* (New York: International Publishers, 1987), 248.

order to express his agreement, "that in any given society *the degree of woman's emancipation is the natural measure of the general emancipation.*"[129] As Domenico Losurdo has explained:

> The liberal tradition interprets class struggle in reductionist and vulgarly economistic terms. Relying on the conceptual couple liberty/equality, it has assigned itself jealous, disinterested love of liberty and branded its opponents as vulgar, envious souls, motivated solely by material interest and pursuit of economic equality... Concrete commitment to the emancipation of women and oppressed nations [Marx's position]; readiness (during the American Civil War) to support the heaviest material sacrifices to help break the chains imposed on African-Americans [Marx's position]; determination to abolish "modern wage slavery" along with slavery proper [Marx's position]; the daily struggle against the bosses' "despotism" in the factory and Bismarck's legislation suppressing freedoms—all this is forgotten in an interpretation notable more for political and ideological passion (these were the years of the Cold War) than philological and philosophical rigor.[130]

It is likely this historiography that brings Fraser to her formal definition of emancipation in her debate with Luc Boltanski: "emancipation means overcoming domination."[131] She does not stipulate the content of emancipation but instead asserts that new forms of domination might become visible in the future so we cannot know for sure what it will look like. However, she nevertheless digs in her heels to defend the need for a constitutional state, markets, and consumer products:

> I wanted to propose a new synthesis, a new alliance between emancipation and social protection. Social protection implies reinforcing institutions, rules, and the logic of the constitutional state....
>
> We also can't do without markets. I can't imagine a desirable society in which markets and consumer goods were abolished . . . There are at least three domains in which consumer products must have a market: the environment, social protection, and finance. These are areas in which robust markets are required, heavily regulated and restricted, markets that impose rules.[132]

---

[129] Marx and Engels, *Collected Works*, vol. 25, 248 (my emphasis).
[130] Losurdo, *Class Struggle*, 75.
[131] Boltanski and Fraser, "Domination and Emancipation," 28.
[132] Boltanski and Fraser, "Domination and Emancipation," 21. Minqi Li has convincingly argued that capitalism or any other market-based economy cannot solve the problem of ecological collapse: "Only with a combination of zero economic growth and rapid reduction of emission intensity (which in turn requires massive infrastructure transformation), does humanity have a realistic chance to achieve a level of climate stabilization consistent with the preservation of civilization. [. . .] The requirement of zero economic growth rules out not only capitalism, but any other

Rosaura Sánchez has argued in this regard that neither the politics of redistribution nor the politics of recognition, as Fraser understands them, necessarily pose a "threat to the structures that underpin the capitalist system."[133] On the contrary, they are aimed at inclusive and reformist measures that can shore it up, as Andrea D'Atri and Celeste Murillo have pointed out in their critique of Fraser's reliance—in her co-authored "manifesto"—on the social movement and reform model.[134] It makes perfect sense, in this regard, that William I. Robinson would describe Fordism-Keynesianism, the economic policy in the Western world for much of the twentieth century, as "redistributive capitalism":

> His [Keynes] demand-side economic strategy emphasized such measures as state intervention through credit and employment creation, progressive taxation, and government spending on public works and social programs to generate demand, along with other mechanisms for regulating (and therefore stabilizing) accumulation. In this way governments could overcome crises, assure long-term growth and employment, and *stabilize capitalist society.*[135]

While it is true that Fraser, in works like *Justice Interruptus* (1997), has claimed to be an advocate for the "transformative remedy" of "socialism" over and against the "affirmative remedy" of the liberal welfare state, she clearly demarcates her understanding of the former from the revolutionary tradition and actually existing socialism.[136] In a 2016 interview, she describes herself as a social democrat but admits that she doesn't really know what that means because "we have a hard time defining a positive program."[137] The negative program, however, is clear: "We know that it [democratic socialism] doesn't mean anything like the authoritarian command economy, single-party

---

conceivable market-based economic system as a viable historical option in the 21st century." Minqi Li, "The 21st Century: Is There an Alternative (to Socialism)?" *Science & Society* 77, no. 1 (January 2013): 38–39.

[133] Rosaura Sánchez, "On a Critical Realist Theory of Identity," see chapter 4 of the present volume, 111.

[134] D'Atri and Murillo write: "We believe that any feminism that claims to be anti-capitalist needs to fight the sectoral, bureaucratic leaderships of the workers' movement that maintain an arbitrary separation between the economic demands of wage earners and the democratic demands of the broader masses—this separation is beneficial to capitalism. But it also means fighting the (equally bureaucratic and sectoral) leaderships of the social movements that, denying the social power of the concentrated sectors of the working class in the struggle against capitalism, try to subjugate these democratic struggles to a limited reformist perspective, which in the context of the crisis is becoming increasingly utopian." "Feminism for the 99%: A Debate on Strategy," *Left Voice*, August 20, 2019, https://www.leftvoice.org/feminism-for-the-99-a-debate-about-strategy?fbclid=IwAR2vF9A8ZU2X2LQCpxjUk0MCmkrMSpsVPQbo-yMH5uu4gVPPrxa7tYU_1NE).

[135] William I. Robinson, *Global Capitalism and the Crisis of Humanity* (Cambridge: Cambridge University Press, 2014), 54 (my emphasis).

[136] See Nancy Fraser, *Justice Interruptus: Critical Reflections on the "Postsocialist" Condition* (New York: Routledge, 1997), 37, note 33.

[137] Nancy Fraser, "Capitalism's Crisis of Care," *Dissent* 63, no. 4 (fall 2016): 35.

model of Communism."[138] If we remove the derogatory epithets, which are a poor ersatz for concrete analysis, then we see that democratic socialism is simply nothing like communism. In fact, it doesn't seem to have much of anything to do with socialism in the real world. If we carefully read the footnotes in *Justice Interruptus*, we learn that Fraser begins from the purportedly obvious assumption that many features of actually existing socialism are "problematic," and she sets forth what amounts to an ideal theory of the "socialist idea," which is not only distinct from "socialism" but explicitly avoids assigning to it "a precise content."[139] This idealist approach leads her to "deliberately" sketch "a picture that is ambiguous between socialism and robust social democracy."[140] Indeed, in her description of her idea of transformative remedies, she provides a list of features that overlap significantly with those of redistributive capitalism: "Transformative remedies typically combine universalist social-welfare programs, steeply progressive taxation, macroeconomic policies aimed at creating full employment, a large non-market public sector, significant public and/or collective ownership, and democratic decision making about basic socioeconomic priorities."[141] It is worth recalling, in this regard, that Ernest Mandel argued that certain forms of redistribution are actually imposed on the backs of workers. Citing some of the most important experiences with social security—in France and Great Britain—he explained that they were financed largely by "taxing the workers themselves."[142] "That is why," he wrote, "we have never seen a genuine and radical redistribution of the national income by taxation in the capitalist

---

[138] Fraser, "Crisis of Care," 35.

[139] Fraser, *Justice Interruptus*, 37. For those interested in examining the real content of actually existing socialism, see sources such as the following: Minqi Li, "The 21st Century: Is There an Alternative (to Socialism)?"; Vicente Navarro, "Has Socialism Failed? An Analysis of Health Indicators under Capitalism and Socialism," *Science & Society* 57, no. 1 (spring 1993): 6–30; Michael Parenti, "Reflections on the Overthrow of Communism" (recorded lecture): https://archive.org/details/ReflectionOnTheOverthrowOfCommunismNLSubtitlesDutch (accessed on January 20, 2021). Parenti has provided perhaps the best summary of the scientific research on actually existing socialism: "To say that 'socialism doesn't work' is to overlook the fact that it did. In Eastern Europe, Russia, China, Mongolia, North Korea, and Cuba, revolutionary communism created a life for the mass of people that was far better than the wretched existence they had endured under feudal lords, military bosses, foreign colonizers, and Western capitalists. The end result was a dramatic improvement in living conditions for hundreds of millions of people on a scale never before or since witnessed in history." Michael Parenti, *Blackshirts & Reds: Rational Fascism and the Overthrow of Communism* (San Francisco: City Lights Publishers, 1997), 85.

[140] Fraser, *Justice Interruptus*, 38. Fraser has taken some more concrete positions, such as expressing her support for Bernie Sanders—not, for instance, for Gloria La Riva—as "the true feminist choice." See Nancy Fraser and Liza Featherstone, "Why Bernie Is the True Feminist Choice," *Jacobin*, February 10, 2020, https://www.jacobinmag.com/2020/02/bernie-sanders-feminism-2020-democratic-race-women.

[141] Fraser, *Justice Interruptus*, 25–26. Moreover, Fraser advocates for combining this form of "socialism" with deconstruction, an academic tradition that has made no contribution to collective revolutionary social change, and whose luminaries include Nazis (Martin Heidegger and Paul De Man) and woolly anti-communist liberals (Jacques Derrida).

[142] Ernest Mandel, *An Introduction to Marxist Economic Theory* (New York: Pathfinder Press, 1973), 88.

system; it remains one of the great 'myths' of reformism."¹⁴³ If Fraser is closer to the reformist position of social democrats than some of the other critical theorists, she is a self-described "radical democrat" who is far from being a Marxist, or even providing a reliable account of Marxism.¹⁴⁴

REVOLUTIONARY THEORY

> If the designing of the future and the proclamation of ready-made solutions for all time is not our affair, then we realize all the more clearly what we have to accomplish in the present—I am speaking of a *ruthless criticism of everything existing*, ruthless in two senses: The criticism must not be afraid of its own conclusions, nor of conflict with the powers that be.
>
> —Karl Marx

The Frankfurt School heritage, at least in certain circles, has exercised a monopoly over the expression *critical theory*, portraying itself as the modern theoretical instantiation of the Marxian intellectual tradition. This is one of the reasons why it is important to confront this heritage and undertake a diligent, systemic, and unswerving analysis of its role in the global theory industry, as well as of the forces driving this industry. Given its contribution to the withdrawal from revolutionary politics in a historical conjuncture marked by the expansion of U.S. imperialism, the increase in global inequality, and the unprecedented capitalist-driven decimation of the biosphere, so-called critical theory needs to be held accountable for the type of world that it explicitly or implicitly condones and supports.¹⁴⁵ The question of legitimation should be formulated at precisely this level, meaning in terms of its social legitimacy for working people as a political and intellectual project (rather than its purported ability to ground itself through a Euro-provincial appeal to purified forms of reason, communication, or recognition).¹⁴⁶

---

¹⁴³ Mandel, *Marxist Economic Theory*, 89.
¹⁴⁴ See Fraser, *Justice Interruptus*, 173–88.
¹⁴⁵ "The figures compiled by the international development agency Oxfam are now well known: the richest 1 percent of humanity in 2017 controlled more than half of the world's wealth; the top 30 percent of the population controlled more than 95 percent of global wealth, while the remaining 70 percent of the population had to make do with less than 5 percent of the world's resources." William I. Robinson, "Introduction: Who Rules the World?," in *Giants: The Global Power Elite*, ed. Peter Phillips (New York: Seven Stories Press, 2018), 15.
¹⁴⁶ For a critique of critical theory's Eurocentrism, see Amy Allen, *The End of Progress: Decolonizing the Normative Foundations of Critical Theory* (New York: Columbia University Press, 2017).

If critical theory is indeed self-reflexive and vigilantly aware of its internal and external power dynamics, including the economic factors driving its own promotion as the only "critical theory" worthy of the name, it would indeed invite and call for a radicalization of critique by questioning its own self-assurance as a theoretical tradition and by reexamining its material relevance to the current world order. Moreover, it would embrace the need to resituate subjects such as petty-bourgeois academics in objective relations of power by identifying how the intelligentsia plays a crucial role in the consolidation and perpetuation of ideology.

Revolutionary theory not only provides us with the tools necessary for this task, namely a historical materialist methodology that situates intellectual practice within the social totality of global class struggle, but it also cultivates a form of critique that is dialectical through and through. It is never simply intellectual, nor is it only rooted in individual reflection or grounded in a purely negative project. Revolutionary theory constantly tests itself in practice, and it continues to refine and develop itself through its engagements with actual social and political struggles. This is a collective process, meaning that the true power of revolutionary theory is to connect with the masses because it provides a trustworthy compass for coordinated action. One of the reasons for this is that revolutionary theory always tethers the negative aspect of critique to the positive task of emancipation insofar as the very purpose of criticism is to advance the egalitarian and ecological project of collectively building a better world.

BIBLIOGRAPHY

Adorno, Theodor. *Critical Models: Inventions and Catchwords.* Translated by Henry W. Pickford. New York: Columbia University Press, 2005.

Adorno, Theodor, and Max Horkheimer. "Towards a New Manifesto?" *New Left Review* 65 (September-October 2010): 33–61.

Adorno, Theodor, and Herbert Marcuse. "Correspondence on the German Student Movement." *New Left Review* 233 (January-February 1999): 123–36.

Agee, Philip, and Louis Wolf, eds. *Dirty Work: The CIA in Western Europe.* New York: Dorset Press, 1978.

Allen, Amy. *The End of Progress: Decolonizing the Normative Foundations of Critical Theory.* New York: Columbia University Press, 2017.

Amin, Samir. *Modern Imperialism, Monopoly Finance Capital, and Marx's Law of Value.* New York: Monthly Review Press, 2018.

Anderson, Perry. *Considerations on Western Marxism.* London: Verso, 1989.

Arruzza, Cinzia, Nancy Fraser, and Tithi Bhattacharya. *Feminism for the 99%: A Manifesto.* London: Verso, 2019.

Blum, William. *Killing Hope: US Military and CIA Interventions since World War II.* London: Zed Books, 2014.

Braden, Thomas W. "I'm Glad the CIA Is 'Immoral.'" *Saturday Evening Post*, May 20, 1967.

Brecht, Bertolt. *Collected Plays: Six.* Edited by John Willett and Ralph Manheim. London: Random House, 1998.

Césaire, Aimé. *Discourse on Colonialism.* Translated by Joan Pinkham. New York: Monthly Review Press, 2000.

Chambers, Simone. "The Politics of Critical Theory." In *The Cambridge Companion to Critical Theory*, edited by Fred Rush, 219–47. Cambridge: Cambridge University Press, 2004.

Christman, Henry M., ed. *Essential Works of Lenin.* New York: Dover Publications, 1987.

Cozzarelli, Tatiana. "Socialist Revolution, Women's Liberation, and the Withering Away of the Family." *Left Voice,* May 19, 2020. https://www.leftvoice.org/socialist-revolution-womens-liberation-and-the-withering-away-of-the-family?fbclid=IwAR0ab1MPCxR0ISKhW2ILpQEFQxevixOuBx2CDM2ol8sWbnNj2TkUb190Jho.

Cline, Ray S. *Secrets, Spies and Scholars: Blueprint of the Essential CIA.* Washington, DC: Acropolis Books, 1976.

Cull, Nicholas J. *The Cold War and the United States Information Agency: American Propaganda and Public Diplomacy, 1945-1989.* Cambridge: Cambridge University Press, 2008.

D'Atri, Andrea, and Celeste Murillo. "Feminism for the 99%: A Debate on Strategy." *Left Voice,* August 20, 2019. https://www.leftvoice.org/feminism-for-the-99-a-debate-about-strategy?fbclid=IwAR2vF9A8ZU2X2LQCpxjUk0MCmkrMSpsVPQbo-yMH5uu4gVPPrxa7tYU_1NE).

Davis, Angela Y. "Marcuse's Legacies." In *Herbert Marcuse: A Critical Reader*, edited by John Abromeit and W. Mark Cobb, 43–50. New York: Routledge, 2004.

Dews, Peter, ed. *Autonomy and Solidarity: Interviews with Jürgen Habermas.* London: Verso, 1992.

Durkin, Kieran. "Erich Fromm and Theodor W. Adorno Reconsidered: A Case Study in Intellectual History." *New German Critique* 46, no. 1 (February 2019): 103–26.

Engels, Friedrich. *Essential Writings of Friedrich Engels.* St Petersburg, Florida: Red and Black Publishers, 2011.

Feenberg, Andrew. "Waiting for History: Horkheimer and Adorno's Theatre of the Absurd." *The Platypus Review*, Supplement to Issue 37 (July 2011): 1–5.

Foner, Philip S., ed. *Clara Zetkin: Selected Writings.* Chicago: Haymarket Books, 2015.

Fraser, Nancy. "Capitalism's Crisis of Care." *Dissent* 63, no. 4 (fall 2016): 30–37.

Fraser, Nancy. "Global Justice and the Renewal of the Critical Theory Tradition: Dialogue with Alfredo Gomez-Muller and Gabriel Rockhill." In *Politics of Culture and the Spirit of Critique: Dialogues*, edited by Alfredo Gomez-Muller and Gabriel Rockhill, 66–80. New York: Columbia University Press, 2011.

Fraser, Nancy. *Justice Interruptus: Critical Reflections on the "Postsocialist" Condition.* New York: Routledge, 1997.

Fraser, Nancy, and Axel Honneth. *Redistribution or Recognition? A Political-Philosophical Exchange.* London: Verso, 2003.

Fraser, Nancy, and Liza Featherstone. "Why Bernie Is the True Feminist Choice." *Jacobin,* February 10, 2020. https://www.jacobinmag.com/2020/02/bernie-sanders-feminism-2020-democratic-race-women.

Fraser, Nancy, and Rahel Jaeggi. *Capitalism: A Conversation in Critical Theory.* Cambridge: Polity, 2018.
Fraser, Nancy, and Nancy A. Naples. "To Interpret the World and to Change It: An Interview with Nancy Fraser." *Signs: Journal of Women in Culture and Society* 29, no. 4 (2004): 1103–24.
Ganser, Danielle. *Nato's Secret Armies: Operation Gladio and Terrorism in Western Europe.* New York: Routledge, 2005.
Guérin, Daniel. *Fascisme et grand capital.* Paris: Libertalia, 2014.
Habermas, Jürgen. *The Crisis of the European Union: A Response.* Translated by Ciaran Cronin. Cambridge: Polity Books, 2012.
Habermas, Jürgen. *The New Conservativism: Cultural Criticism and the Historians' Debate.* Edited and translated by Shierry Weber Nicholsen. Cambridge, MA: The MIT Press, 1990.
Habermas, Jürgen. *Theory and Practice.* Translated by John Viertel. Boston: Beacon Press, 1973.
Habermas, Jürgen. "What Does Socialism Mean Today? The Revolutions of Recuperation and the Need for New Thinking." In *After the Fall: The Failure of Communism and the Future of Socialism,* edited by Robin Blackburn, 25–46. London: Verso, 1991.
Hinze, Malena. "The Revolutionary Role of Women in Cuba." *Liberation School,* March 1, 2007, https://liberationschool.org/07-03-01-the-revolutionary-role-women-in-html/
Honneth, Axel. *Disrespect: The Normative Foundations of Critical Theory.* Cambridge: Polity Press, 2007.
Honneth, Axel. *The Idea of Socialism.* Translated by Joseph Ganahl. Cambridge: Polity Press, 2017.
Horkheimer, Max. *Critical Theory: Selected Essays,* translated by Matthew J. O'Connel et al. New York: Continuum, 2002.
Hudis, Peter, and Kevin B. Anderson, eds. *The Rosa Luxemburg Reader.* New York: Monthly Review Press, 2004.
"Interview with Marcuse." *Australian Left Review* 1, no. 22 (1969): 36–39-42–47. https://ro.uow.edu.au/alr/vol1/iss22/6.
Jackson, George. *Blood in My Eye.* Baltimore: Black Classic Press, 1990.
James, Joy. "Airbrushing Revolution for the Sake of Abolition." *Black Agenda Report,* July 29, 2020. https://blackagendareport.com/airbrushing-revolution-sake-abolition.
Jay, Martin. *The Dialectical Imagination: A History of the Frankfurt School and the Institute of Social Research, 1923-1950.* Berkeley: University of California Press, 1996.
Jeffries, Stuart. *Grand Hotel Abyss: The Lives of the Frankfurt School.* London: Verso, 2017.
Katz, Barry M. *Foreign Intelligence: Research and Analysis in the Office of Strategic Services 1942-1945.* Cambridge, MA: Harvard University Press, 1989.
Katz, Barry M. *Herbert Marcuse and the Art of Liberation: An Intellectual Biography.* London: Verso, 1982.

Kouvelakis, Stathis. *La Critique défaite: Émergence et domestication de la théorie critique*. Paris: Édions Amsterdam, 2019.

Kraushaar, Wolfgang, ed. *Frankfurter Schule und Studentenbewegung: Von der Flaschenpost zum Molotowcocktail 1946-1995*. Vol. I, *Chronik*. Hamburg: Rogner & Bernhard GmbH & Co. Verlags KG, 1998.

Laudani, Raffaele, ed. *Secret Reports on Nazi Germany: The Frankfurt School Contribution to the War Effort*. Princeton: Princeton University Press, 2013.

Lenin, Vladimir Ilyich. *"Left-Wing" Communism an Infantile Disorder*. New York: Red Star Publishers, 2016.

Leslie, Esther. "Introduction to Adorno/Marcuse Correspondence on the German Student Movement." *New Left Review* 233 (January-February 1999): 118–23.

"Letter to Robert Gates from Roy Godson." October 20, 1987, FOIA CIA-RDP89G01321R000700330003-7. https://www.cia.gov/library/readingroom/document/cia-rdp89g00720r000700890016-0.

Li, Minqi. "The 21st Century: Is There an Alternative (to Socialism)?" *Science & Society* 77, no. 1 (January 2013): 10–43.

Lichtblau, Eric. *The Nazis Next Door: How America Became a Safe Haven for Hitler's Men*. New York: Mariner Books, 2015.

Losurdo, Domenico. *Class Struggle: A Political and Philosophical History*. Translated by Gregory Elliott. New York: Palgrave Macmillan, 2016.

Losurdo, Domenico. *Liberalism: A Counter-History*. Translated by Gregory Elliott. London: Verso, 2014.

Losurdo, Domenico. *War and Revolution*. Translated by Gregory Elliott. London: Verso, 2015.

Lukács, Georg. *The Theory of the Novel*. Translated by Anna Bostock. Cambridge, Massachusetts: The MIT Press, 1999.

Mandel, Ernest. *An Introduction to Marxist Economic Theory*. New York: Pathfinder Press, 1973.

Marsh, James L. "Toward a New Critical Theory." In *New Critical Theory: Essays on Liberation*, edited by William S. Wilkerson and Jeffrey Paris, 49–64. Lanham, MD: Rowman & Littlefield Publishers, 2001.

Marx, Karl, and Friedrich Engels. *Collected Works*. Vol. 5, *Marx and Engels: 1845-47*. New York: International Publishers, 1976.

Marx, Karl, and Friedrich Engels. *Collected Works*. Vol. 25, *Frederick Engels: Anti-Dühring, Dialectics of Nature*. New York: International Publishers, 1987.

Moghadam, Valentine M. *Modernizing Women: Gender and Social Change in the Middle East*. Boulder: Lynne Rienner Publishers, 1993.

Müller-Doohm, Steven. *Adorno: A Biography*. Translated by Rodney Livingstone. Cambridge: Polity Press, 2005.

Müller-Doohm, Steven. *Habermas: A Biography*. Translated by Daniel Steuer. Cambridge: Polity Press, 2016.

Navarro, Vicente. "Has Socialism Failed? An Analysis of Health Indicators under Capitalism and Socialism." *Science & Society* 57, no. 1 (spring 1993): 6–30.

Parenti, Michael. *Blackshirts & Reds: Rational Fascism and the Overthrow of Communism*. San Francisco: City Lights Publishers, 1997.

Parenti, Michael. *Dirty Truths: Reflections on Politics, Media, Ideology, Conspiracy, Ethnic Life and Class Power.* San Francisco: City Lights Books, 1996.
Parenti, Michael. "Reflections on the Overthrow of Communism." Recorded lecture, accessed on January 20, 2021. https://archive.org/details/ReflectionOnTheOverthrowOfCommunismNLSubtitlesDutch.
Phillips, Peter. *Giants: The Global Power Elite.* New York: Seven Stories Press, 2018.
Postel, Danny. "Letter to America." *The Nation,* December 16, 2002. https://archive.globalpolicy.org/security/issues/iraq/attack/2002/1216jurgen.htm.
Reed, Jr., Adolph. *Class Notes: Posing as Politics and Other Thoughts on the American Scene.* New York: The New Press, 2001.
Robinson, William I. "The Betrayal of the Intellectuals." *Great Transition Initiative,* April 2020, https://greattransition.org/images/Planetize-Movement-Robinson.pdf?fbclid=IwAR0gnGW4WsO8QXh9tJ9ZJk417VgtIoD35dVoA9R3zjE6rUT6R7SvcZVxVJQ.
Robinson, William I. *Global Capitalism and the Crisis of Humanity.* Cambridge: Cambridge University Press, 2014.
Rockhill, Gabriel. "The CIA Reads French Theory: On the Intellectual Labor of Dismantling the Cultural Left." *The Philosophical Salon,* February 28, 2017. http://thephilosophicalsalon.com/the-cia-reads-french-theory-on-the-intellectual-labor-of-dismantling-the-cultural-left/.
Rockhill, Gabriel. *Counter-History of the Present.* Durham, NC: Duke University Press, 2017.
Rockhill, Gabriel. *Radical History and the Politics of Art.* New York: Columbia University Press, 2014.
Rockmore, Tom. "Habermas, Critical Theory, and Political Economy." In *Radical Intellectuals and the Subversion of Progressive Politics: Political Philosophy and Public Purpose,* edited by G. Smulewicz-Zucker and M.J. Thompson, 191–210. New York: Palgrave Macmillan, 2015.
Rosa, Hartmut. *Alienation and Acceleration: Towards a Critical Theory of Late-Modern Temporality.* Malmö, Sweden: NSU Press, 2010.
Rose, Gillian. *The Melancholy Science: An Introduction to the Thought of Theodor W. Adorno.* New York: Columbia University Press, 1978.
Ross, Kristin. *Communal Luxury: The Political Imaginary of the Paris Commune.* London: Verso, 2015.
Said, Edward W. *Culture and Imperialism.* New York: Vintage Books, 1993.
Samarajiwa, Rohan. "The Murky Beginnings of the Communication and Development Field: Voice of America and The Passing of Traditional Society." In *Rethinking Development Communication,* edited by Neville Jayaweera and Sarath Amumugama, 3–19. Singapore: The Asian Mass Communication Research and Information Centre, 1987.
Sankara, Thomas. *Women's Liberation and the African Freedom Struggle.* Atlanta, GA: Pathfinder Press, 2010.

Scott-Smith, Giles. *The Politics of Apolitical Culture: The Congress for Cultural Freedom, the CIA and Post-War American Hegemony.* New York: Routledge, 2002.

Shanin, Teodor, ed. *Late Marx and the Russian Road: Marx and 'the Peripheries of Capitalism.'* New York: Monthly Review Press, 1983.

Simpson, Christopher. *Blowback: America's Recruitment of Nazis and Its Effects on the Cold War.* New York: Weidenfeld & Nicolson, 1988.

Simpson, Christopher. *Science of Coercion: Communication Research and Psychological Warfare 1945-1960.* Oxford: Oxford University Press, 1996.

Solty, Ingar. "Max Horkheimer, a Teacher without a Class." *Jacobin*, February 15, 2020. https://www.jacobinmag.com/2020/02/max-horkheimer-frankfurt-school-adorno-working-class-marxism.

Saunders, Frances Stonor. *The Cultural Cold War: The CIA and the World of Arts and Letters.* New York: The New Press, 1999.

Thompson, Michael J. *The Domestication of Critical Theory.* London: Rowman & Littlefield International, 2016.

Torrellas, María. *Cubanas, Mujeres en Revolución.* Documentary, 2018. https://vimeo.com/277301522.

Trotsky, Leon. *The Struggle Against Fascism in Germany.* New York: Pathfinder Press, 1971.

Weinstein, Allen, and Alexander Vassiliev. *The Haunted Wood: Soviet Espionage in America—the Stalin Era.* New York: Random House, 1999.

Wheatland, Thomas. *The Frankfurt School in Exile.* Minneapolis: University of Minnesota Press, 2009.

Wiggershaus, Rolf. *The Frankfurt School: Its History, Theories, and Political Significance.* Translated by Michael Robertson. Cambridge, MA: The MIT Press, 1995.

Wilford, Hugh. *The Mighty Wurlitzer: How the CIA Played America.* Cambridge, MA: Harvard University Press, 2008.

Wilford, Hugh. *The New York Intellectuals: From Vanguard to Institution.* Manchester: Manchester University Press, 1995.

Winks, Robin W. *Cloak and Gown: Scholars in the Secret War, 1939-1961.* New Haven: Yale University Press, 1987.

Wood, Ellen Meiksins. *Democracy Against Capitalism: Renewing Historical Materialism.* London: Verso, 2016.

Zetkin, Clara. *Fighting Fascism: How to Struggle and How to Win.* Edited by Mike Taber and John Riddell. Chicago: Haymarket Books, 2017.

Chapter 6

Like a Riot

The Politics of Forgetfulness, Relearning the South, and the Island of Dr. Moreau

Françoise Vergès

> The learning process is something you can incite, literally incite, like a riot.
>
> —Audre Lorde[1]

The mechanism of forgetfulness has ramifications far beyond the importance it has played in psychoanalysis. Sigmund Freud notes that forgetfulness is not "left to psychic arbitrariness, but that it follows lawful and rational paths." Forgetting, he writes, moreover, has "proved to be founded on a motive of displeasure." Considering the infamous "return of the repressed," Freud provides evidence of the capacity of the repressed to express itself.[2] If we apply this theory to the fabrication of forgetfulness in imperialism and capitalism, colonial and capitalist crimes certainly represent a source of unpleasant memories that explain the fabrication of forgetfulness by empire the world over. But forgetfulness is not just a psychological mechanism; it is the result of economic and political choices. In its logic, there is no need to do away with inequalities and precariousness. They are, in fact, structural to neoliberal logic. What is important in this system is to negotiate and renegotiate the threshold of "bearable" precariousness, to avoid revolts and insurrections by shifting the blame onto individuals (if their lives are precarious, it's because they are lazy), by systematic displacement and dispossession.

---

[1] Audre Lorde, *Sister Outsider: Essays and Speeches* (New York: Ten Speed Press, 2007), 98.
[2] Sigmund Freud, *The Psychopathology of Everyday Life*, chap. I and VII, trans. A. A. Brill (New York: The Macmillan Company, 1914), https://www.bartleby.com/284/.

On a global scale, following the mapping and remapping of what matters—and what does not—means following the routes of racial capitalism, the transformation of land into spaces for the working of capital. Consider those glass towers all over the globe that constitute safe deposit boxes for the wealthy, the privatization of the commons. See how it leads to a competition between territories: better to be on the map of what matters, one reasons, than to be forgotten, even if that means the destruction of environment, of community, of life. Frantz Fanon's analysis of the condition of *The Wretched of the Earth*[3] can be understood as the "forgetfulness of damnation,"[4] the process whereby a state of amnesia has led to murder, destruction, and the epistemic will to power—with a European good conscience. For Fanon, any opposition to Western modernity and its racism must address this amnesia and the invisibility of the damned; he wanted to bring into view what had remained invisible for centuries. Following Fanon, decolonial thinkers have spoken of the "forgetfulness of coloniality"[5] in both Western philosophy and contemporary social theory. A counter-strategy has been to excavate forgotten maps, imagining new ones or valorizing those that have been marginalized.

But historical and political cartographies mix with personal cartographies, building a multidimensional space of memories. Where and how I grew up gave me a cartography of global resistance to power, colonialism, and imperialism. From the Greek χάρτης, or "map," and γράφειν, "write," cartography is, of course, the art and science of drawing maps. My first geography of resistance was drawn by the Réunion Island anti-colonial movement. It was from this small island in the Indian Ocean that I read the world. To the local cartography of cultural and political resistance, I added the millenary world of exchanges between Africa and Asia; the world of solidarity routes among anti-imperialist movements of the various Souths; the Southern world of music, literature, and images. Europe was geographically and culturally on the periphery.

It was a solid cartography. I knew its contours, I could name its leaders, its movements, its authors. On my teenage bedroom walls there were no posters of bands but rather of the Black Panther Party, of the Vietnam National Front of Liberation, and of the Cuban Revolution. On this small island, where the French state deployed from the 1960s until the 1980s a politics of repression mixed with false promises of assimilation—using censorship, mass incarceration of anti-colonialists, armed police against peasants and workers, and

---

[3] Frantz Fanon, *The Wretched of the Earth*, trans. Constance Farrington (New York: Penguin Books, 1990).
[4] Nelson Maldonado-Torres, "The Topology of Being and the Geopolitics of Knowledge: Modernity, Empire, Coloniality," *City* 8, no. 1 (2004): 29–56, doi: 10.1080/1360481042000199787.
[5] Maldonado-Terres, "The Topology of Being," 40.

mandated cultural norms that denied vernacular practices and expression—
the South was the promise of other things to come. It was the world of *The
Wretched of the Earth*, of those who "invented neither powder nor compass/
those who explored neither the sea nor the sky/but those without whom the
earth would never be the earth,"[6] as Aimé Césaire wrote. It was a map of
third-world feminism, of national liberation movements, of the promise of
Bandung.

I was sustained by this cartography. I knew where the South was and
what it was about. There was comfort in it. It helped me counter the French
colonial cartography that was taught at school and imposed in the media.
This Southern map gave me dreams, the capacity to imagine change, a
world greater than the narrow postcolonial French world. It also gave me a
vocabulary, a language of feminism, anti-racism, anti-imperialism, and anti-
capitalism. Feminism was not yet simply about equality but about fighting
the patriarchal and capitalist system; development was not about increased
dependence on Western technology and the banking system, but about
respecting vernacular knowledge and inventing disparate ways of living in
the world and with the world. It supported a process of unlearning and learning: unlearning Eurocentric education, learning the vernacular, the intangible. Our house in Réunion was instructive in this process, being filled with
books from across the world, the result of the failure of one of my mother's
enterprises, a bookstore of world literature. But her loss was our gain. All
the books she had bought came home, and thus we had novels from South
America, Russia, Africa, and Europe at our disposal. My communist and
feminist parents made sure we grew up listening to popular songs, speaking
Creole, witnessing popular rituals, discussing the anti-apartheid struggle, the
Vietnam War, the wars of liberation in Algeria, Mozambique, and Angola. At
the dinner table, we could listen to Malagasy, Mauritians, and other anti-colonial activists debating *their* South. Because of the state brutality I witnessed
as a child on Réunion Island—the denial of basic rights, people being beaten
to death, my parents harassed and jailed—early on I became interested in the
fabrication by the powerful of people *who do not matter*, as well as by the
process of fabricating consent to that fact, this silent conformity to hegemonic
norms. And yet I was equally impressed by the capacity to build resistance, to
laugh at power, to find ways of imagining alternatives. The singular history
of Réunion Island added to the geography of the South a space of imagination and emancipation. True, the island was intimately connected to the history of French colonialism. There was no native population when Réunion
became a French colony in the seventeenth century, and yet, because it was

---

[6] Aimé Césaire, *Notebook of a Return to My Native Land*, trans. Clayton Eshleman and Annette Smith (Middletown, CT: Wesleyan University Press, 2001), 38.

in the Indian Ocean, it was inscribed in a complex temporality and spatiality of routes of exchanges and encounters in which Europe was a late actor, and then just one among others.

From Réunion, a series of intertwined geographies emerged: an Africa–Asia axis independent of Europe; the geography of an eighteenth-century shift when slavery in the Americas and the Caribbean gave European powers economic hegemony, all thanks to the silver extracted in colonial mines and to the production by slaves of coffee, sugar, and cotton, which overcame Asian production. On the island, slavery and postslavery colonialism inscribed Réunion in a regional and global history, on which colonial power imposed a long silence or forgetfulness. Though I never learned this history at school, at home I was told stories of the maroons who had established communities in the Réunion mountains in the eighteenth century, defying the rules and laws of enslavement. Punishment against marooning was brutal and public; the maroons had to bear on their face and bodies the punition of their transgression. The infamous *Code noir* listed the punishments: authorities punished the first attempt of marooning by branding the person's face with the *fleur de lys* or cutting an ear; the second by cutting the hollow of the knee; the third by death. When communities of maroons were discovered, women and men were publicly tortured and massacred. In Réunion, the French colonial power armed troops to hunt maroons. The war waged against these communities lasted almost a hundred years, eliminating them by the end of the eighteenth century. Yet the spirit of the maroons was stronger than the erasure of their history by colonial power. They had traced a geography of resistance by giving Malagasy names to mountains and rivers, and these names survived the attempted erasure of their world. They divided the island into two worlds, making visible the border between the world of servitude and bonded labor and the world of freedom and sovereignty. And this border was both oral and textual, as the coast was writ with a litany of Christian names: Saint-Denis, Saint-Pierre, Sainte-Marie, Saint-Leu, Sainte-Suzanne, Saint-Louis, Saint-Benoît, Saint-Joseph. In the interior, meanwhile, Malagasy names were spoken, either the names of maroon leaders like Cimendef, Dimitile, and Anchaing, or of mountains including Cilaos and Salazie.

The cartography drawn from Réunion evoked a time and space that was not European but of the Indian Ocean, a millenary site of exchanges and encounters between the Muslim world and other worlds, a maritime cultural space with its multiple geographies and multidirectional memories,[7] its cartography of servitude and resistance. Yet I had not finished high school when I decided to leave the island. Finding Réunion's patriarchal conformism too stifling, I decided to go to Algeria for my last year in high school, a country that had

---

[7] Michael Rothberg, *Multidirectional Memories: Remembering the Holocaust in the Age of Decolonization* (Redwood City, CA: Stanford University Press, 2009).

mobilized my childhood imagination. In Réunion, colonial power had sought to censor opposition to the war against the Algerian people. But my uncle had been an attorney for Algerian nationalists and a founding member of a group of lawyers who challenged the legitimacy of French tribunals to try Algerians; he had defended and later married Djamila Bouhired, a heroine of the Battle of Algiers. Thus, I arrived in a country I had long idealized, and my experience there enriched my multidimensional cartography. Algiers was still *the* capital of the third world: it was home to members of the Black Panther Party, of the liberation movement of Angola and Mozambique, of the ANC (African National Congress), and of political refugees from the military dictatorship of Brazil. The Cinémathèque of Algiers, first under the direction of Ahmed Hocine and then of Boudjemaâ Karèche, was still the legendary site for third-world cinema. There I perfected my cinematography, which had started in Réunion, where my mother took me to the only existing *ciné-club* on the island. Yet there were already fissures in my idealized South. Patriarchy in Algeria was strong. The postcolonial regime repressed minority rights, adopted the model of export industry, and was led by army generals. The lesson? The South should not be idealized; it was a reality and reality is always full of contradictions.

If in Réunion the world had seemed cut in two, in Algeria I began to see what Fanon had analyzed in his work on national bourgeoisies. Here was the limitless greed of which he had written, the unleashed consumerism and contempt for the vernacular, the endless search for profit. Algeria was rushing to imitate Western rules of consumption and exhibition of wealth; soon they would find arrangements with racial capitalism. The West remained hegemonic: U.S. imperialism dominated the world, the American army was still playing the international *gendarme*, its soft power dictating tastes, its companies among the most powerful. While the World Bank and the IMF were unleashing the violence of structural adjustment programs upon the South, the West supported military dictatorships while developing its ideology of "humanitarian intervention." By the 1990s, the Western imperial project went hand in hand with unleashed consumerism. By the beginning of the twenty-first century, it was a global phenomenon. Identities that had been spontaneously associated with counter-hegemonic practices— feminists, the colonized, gays, etc.—could now be easily transformed into commodities. Borrowing from the emancipatory discourse of the 1970s, consumerism and new technologies promised individual emancipation, a limitless extension of the self, free from all social, cultural, and religious constraints. Emancipation was no longer exclusively collective. You could emancipate yourself without the fear of prison, torture, exile, death. It was seductive and it found an echo all over the world.[8] Where was the South now?

To find my South again as the site of decolonial politics, I was required to think about the extent to which freedom had become more important than equality; about new forms of exploitation and colonization coexisting with old forms; about the fabrication of precariousness and disposability; about new politics of dispossession and privatization; and about science, technology, and what some scientists call the "Anthropocene." Averse to utopias and their false consciousness, and after an era of genocide and global warfare, the West proposed a choice between postmodern gloom and phony happiness. The intensity once situated in revolutions moved to sex. Capitalism was able to endlessly multiply differentiation. Further, though white males still dominated the international institutions and multinationals, their logic of accumulation of wealth based on dispossession and depletion of resources was contaminating all regimes. True, a new multipolarity of power was threatening Western domination, and new formations were emerging, but the model of development that had been shown to be unsustainable had become global. Without falling into catastrophism, the new challenges were real.

In the South, a reflection on political defeat was needed, the lesson being that struggle is long and difficult and that enemies cannot be underestimated (or overestimated). The proliferation of protective walls, the militarization of borders, and the criminalization of migrants went along with the ethos of mobility. All these mutations transformed the cartography of the South as a coordinated site of resistance. If difference as difference could no longer by itself constitute the terrain upon which emancipation was imagined, what kind of memories, histories, and cartographies would disrupt the capitalist logic of coding/decoding and differing? What to do with what Melinda Cooper calls "life as surplus"? As she has written, "Where industrial production depends on finite reserves available on planet earth, life, like contemporary debt production, needs to be understood as a process of continuous autopoiesis, a self-engendering of life from life, without conceivable beginning or end."[9] Life could now be produced in labs. Science, technology, militarism, and capitalism had created a powerful nexus to reshape the techniques of discipline and punishment. Had the South as a promise of another world disappeared, defeated by racial capitalism and the pursuit of power? Where was it now located?

---

[8] On this topic, see, for instance Rosi Braidotti, "The Posthuman Predicament," in *The Scientific Imaginary in Visual Culture*, ed. Anneke Smelik (Göttingen: V&R Unipress, 2010), 69–89; "Meta(l)flesh," in *The Future of Flesh: Bodily Mutation and Change*, ed. Zoe Detsi-Diamanti, Katerina Kitsi-Mitakou, and Effie Yiannopoulou (New York: Palgrave Macmillan, 2009), 241–61.
[9] Melinda Cooper, *Life as Surplus: Biotechnology and Capitalism in the Neoliberal Era* (Seattle: University of Washington Press, 2008), 38.

I have still a South. I look for its emergence in the resistance to the constant process of territorialization and deterritorialization operated by racial capital. I observe and analyze the sites produced by the process of "southification," fabricating new racialized territories where the lives that do not matter are dumped, the toxic waste and chemicals, all the refuse of global capitalism. The "there is no alternative" doctrine, as Margaret Thatcher so famously pronounced, with its clearly translated capitalist logic, works as well with *There is a future for a few and no future for the many*. Europe was built upon the Promethean ideal that affirms the limitless power of "Man" to master the world, all living things, and technology. It is an ideology of progress and individual emancipation resting on the dualism of spirit/matter.[10] In this logic, the world is *offered* to exploration and exploitation, and the individual is indebted neither to its social nor its natural environment. The Promethean ideal as a masculinist ideology of forgetfulness is intimately connected with the current search to free the individual of all constraints, human and natural.

The racialized politics of dispossession, displacement, and discrimination; the fabrication of disposable peoples and forgotten territories; the exploitation of resources, of female reproductive labor; masculinity itself: all constitute the nexus through which "southification" is produced. During colonial times, mountains were displaced, rivers rerouted, forests destroyed, and plants, animals, and humans moved around. Postcolonial ideology of development followed the same logic: nothing would stop human desire to shape its environment and remake it in its own image. Today, the stem-cell industry, biotechnology, patenting seeds (the politics of research and distribution of Monsanto, DuPont, and Syngenta),[11] and the control of biodiversity show that the politics of dispossession continue to fuel racial capitalism. "And the original appropriation—the monopolization of the earth by a few, the exclusion of the rest from that which is the condition of their life—yields nothing in immorality to the subsequent huckstering of the earth," as Engels wrote. The "monopolization of the Earth by a few"[12] is now reaching incredible proportions. By 2020, a mere 250,000 individuals will control $40 trillion of global assets. But before looking at how the new politics of dispossession are being countered, I want to look at past connections among a global, mobile, gendered, and racialized workforce, of technologies of control. And for this, I go back to Réunion Island.

---

[10] See François Flahault, "Entre émancipation et destruction. Les fondements de l'idéal prométhéen," *Communications* 78 (2005): 5–49, doi: 10.3406/comm.2005.2272.

[11] Ken Roseboro, "The GMO Seed Cartel," *The Organic & Non-GMO Report*, February 1, 2013, https://non-gmoreport.com/articles/february2013/the-gmo-seed-cartel.php.

[12] The expression is from Friedrich Engels, *Outlines of a Critique of Political Economy* (1844). It is cited by John Bellamy Foster in *Marx's Ecology: Materialism and Nature* (New York: Monthly Review Press, 2000), 106.

In June 1970, a doctor was called to the bedside of a seventeen-year-old woman in a small, poor village of Réunion Island. She was bleeding profusely, the result of a botched abortion. For more than a year, the newspapers of the local communist party and of the Catholic Church had reported rumors about a clinic owned by a powerful white man where thousands of illegal abortions were supposedly performed. The reported rumors were met with official silence. This time, though, since the doctor had called the police, an inquiry was ordered. The police learned that every year since 1966, in a clinic owned by Dr. Moreau, 6,000 to 8,000 women had been given abortions without their consent. They entered Dr. Moreau's clinic three to seven months pregnant; they left after their abortions commenced, many also sterilized. They were sent to the clinic by colonial government institutions in charge of birth control and prenatal care. In France, meanwhile, at exactly the same time, abortion and contraception remained illegal and criminalized; doctors who performed abortions, as well as the women who aborted, could receive long prison terms.

Moreau, who was born a *blanc sale*, had become a member of the local white elite thanks to his marriage to the daughter of a wealthy owner of a dozen sugarcane factories on the island. Soon he would himself preside over many of the island's stores, resorts, and clinics, and he became an active member of the local anti-communist and pro-colonial parties. In 1952, Moreau was elected mayor of the same city in which he operated his clinic, with 98 percent of the vote. He was a supporter of Michel Debré, a former prime minister of the Fifth Republic fiercely opposed to Algerian independence and women's rights, who had come to Réunion Island to "save" the island from communism and decolonization. The postcolonial powers did not want to indict Moreau. He was a powerful white businessman, a pillar of the local conservative party. In August, the police made two arrests: a doctor of Moroccan origin (and there was a constant reminder in the media of his origins) and a nurse descended from Indian indentured workers. Both were sent to prison and forbidden to exercise their trade. Moreau himself was never investigated, and his political career continued unblemished. At the end of 1970, he was unanimously elected to the island's general council, where he remained as vice president for twenty-three years. The victims of Dr. Moreau received no reparations.

I cannot help but invoke H. G. Wells' 1896 novel, *The Island of Doctor Moreau*.[13] In the book, the fictional Doctor Moreau has fled England under the suspicion of his non-ethical use of dissection. He has found refuge on

---

[13] H. G. Wells, *The Island of Doctor Moreau* (Oxford: Oxford University Press, 2017).

an isolated tropical island where, with the help of two other white men, he performs cruel and painful surgical procedures on the "Beast People," a half-animal, half-human species he has created and whose description echoes descriptions of colonized non-white peoples: intellectually inferior, obeying only the whip, speaking gibberish. Wells' novel was a metaphor for colonialism, imperialism, and racism published in a year full of important events in the history of racial imperialism. Among them, consider the defeat of the Ashanti Kingdom in West Africa by British troops, the first Italo-Ethiopian war, and the "separate but equal" decision of *Plessy v. Ferguson* in the United States, which upheld the constitutionality of institutional racial segregation in the American South.

In Wells' novel, Moreau's victims call his laboratory the "house of pain." In their prayer, the Beast People repeat endlessly a series of sentences that end with the refrain, "Are we not Men?" "Not to go on all-Fours; that is the Law. Are we not Men? Not to suck up Drink; that is the Law. Are we not Men?" Their recitation has echoes of the abolitionist maxim: "Am I not a Man and your Brother?" The politics of forgetfulness also play a pivotal role in the novel. The book's narrator, Edward Prendick, who is shipwrecked on the island and exposes Doctor Moreau's violence there, finally escapes to England and tells the story of what he has seen. His narrative is met with accusations of madness, so he eventually pretends to have amnesia. Nevertheless, the real Dr. Moreau had more luck than the fictitious one, who was finally killed by his creatures. It appears that justice in real postcolonial society was more difficult to obtain than in nineteenth-century fiction.

In addition to the thousands of pregnancies aborted without the mothers' consent in Réunion, other policies were developed in French overseas territories to control the birth rate. In 1962, a law authorized the use of contraceptives in overseas departments with special regulations: free distribution of contraceptives included IUDs imposed on teenagers without parental consent, and Depo-Provera was also largely used. Meanwhile, offices of birth control opened everywhere. The story of French state policies of abortion and contraception in its overseas colonial territories is a corrective to the French feminist history of abortion and contraception that goes thus: a courageous struggle of French feminists against patriarchy and misogyny. Let us recall some of this latter struggle's landmarks. A year after Réunion's abortion-clinic scandal, on April 5, 1971, the "Manifesto of the 343" (also known as the "Manifesto of the 343 Sluts") was published in the French magazine *Le Nouvel Observateur*. In it, 343 French women declared publicly that they had had an abortion, signing a text written by Simone de Beauvoir. In October and November of 1972, the "Bobigny affair" became a landmark case for the right to an abortion. A minor who had been raped and had aborted was on trial with her mother. Feminist demonstrations were held in France, testimonies were published, abortions were performed in public defying the law. This led to the law, enacted in January 1975, that decriminalized abortion in France. In this story, the situation of poor and non-white women in French overseas territories was ignored; it did not fit the dominant narrative of exclusion and patriarchy. The struggles of feminist movements in the colonies were also ignored; they too did not fit the narrative of white European women's emancipation. Neither the logic of exclusion nor patriarchy could fully explain the kind of social subjection operated by the French state on impoverished and non-white women, who were made an object of public policy.

But the politics of birth control must be understood by crossing the local with the national, the local with the global. On the local level, one found a racialized politics of contraception contemporary with a new division of labor and a new politics of migration. On the national level, home birth and large families were encouraged, while simultaneously contraception and abortion were encouraged in overseas territories. Non-white children were not desired. On the global level, one encountered politics that, in the second half of the twentieth century, saw international institutions pay close attention to female fertility in developing countries, where it became (and remains) the most studied aspect of women's lives. The link made between poverty and birth rate was central to national and global policies that did not address the woman's right to exercise control over her sexuality but rather sought to enforce the power of the state or international institutions to impose programs of birth control.

Behind this history stands another forgotten site: female reproductive work in racial capitalism. Historians have told us that among the 15 million Africans shipped into slavery in the Americas, the Caribbean, and the European colonies of the Indian Ocean, nearly 5 million were women. If in the United States plantation owners chose to organize an internal trade and the social reproduction of the workforce after abolition, this was not the case in all colonies. Most plantation owners counted on the constant arrival of slaves to compensate for the high mortality rate on their land (the rate of survival among slaves was initially eight to ten years). In other words, there was a need for a constant supply of African bodies. For the supply to be guaranteed, slave traders had to steal African boys and girls from their mothers. Though female reproductive work was not directly organized by a state, the burden of reproducing a mobile, gendered, and racialized workforce fell on African women, *in Africa*. The source of "production" of a bonded workforce was there. Yet the African women who bore and nurtured the more than 15 million Africans (and this number represents the number of those *who arrived*—it does not take into account those who died en route) are totally forgotten. Forgotten because despite the long struggle of feminists to have women's reproductive work recognized, this history is either ignored or commodified.[14]

If the law of slavery recognized the role of the enslaved woman in producing future slaves, yet fully denied her rights as mother, slave trade was pure predatory politics. During the rise of racial capitalism, the most important part of the social reproduction of a racialized and gendered workforce was located in Africa, and the legitimate focus on the situation of enslaved mothers on the plantation has obscured that predation. As Karl Marx wrote,

> the discovery of gold and silver in America, the extirpation, enslavement, and entombment in mines of the aboriginal population, the beginning of the conquest and looting of the East Indies, the turning of Africa into a warren for the commercial hunting of black-skins, signal[ed] the rosy dawn of the era of capitalist production.[15]

The unacknowledged "delegation" of the social reproduction of a bonded workforce division on non-European women did not end with abolition, however. Following the end of slavery in European colonies in the mid-nineteenth century, European powers organized a massive displacement of Indians, Chinese, Southeast Asians, Malagasy, and Africans across the world to work in its mines, railways, and plantations. Nearly 30 million Indians and 50 million Chinese were moved from one colony to another, a vast south–south movement of racialized bodies. The ratio was again two-thirds men and one-third women. Women were often shared as "wives" by four or five indentured men, though their working conditions were as harsh. In the meantime, 60 million Europeans left their continent fleeing famine, pogroms, and poverty, leading to the creation of "countries of white and free men" in Australia, New Zealand, Canada, the United States, and Argentina. They settled in countries whose native populations had been decimated and dispossessed. Europeans used the notion of *terra nullius* to justify the appropriation of lands; the systematic politics of land dispossession were inseparable from the denial of rights and the reconfiguration of masculinity and femininity in these territories.

The historians Marilyn Lake and Henry Reynolds have shown evidence of how during this time Western states, in spite of their divergent interests, found common ground in the racialization of the workforce throughout the world, and in a new reordering of the globe between consumers and producers, fit

---

[14] On the relation between enclosures, the persecution of witches, the repression of women and their knowledge in Europe, and the slave trade, see Silvia Federici, *Caliban and the Witch: Women, the Body and Primitive Accumulation* (Brooklyn, NY: Autonomedia, 2004).

[15] Karl Marx, "Genesis of the Industrial Capitalist," in *Capital*, vol. 1, chap. 31, ed. Friedrich Engels, trans. Samuel Moore and Edward Aveling (Moscow: Progress Publishers, 1887), transcribed at *Marx and Engels Internet Archive*, www.marxists.org/archive/marx/works/1867-c1/ch31.htm.

and unfit peoples.[16] Moving a racialized workforce across continents with the aim of preserving and enhancing European economic interests and its need for new resources and goods followed the steps of the slave trade: conventions between European powers, use of the national maritime industry, gendering and racializing sexualities and work. Further, transport conditions, as well as living and working conditions, were barely different from those of colonial slavery.[17] In the meantime, however, Western workers in France, the United States, and England were winning important labor victories. The importation of indentured peoples in European colonies changed forever the cartography of trade, labor, and race. While the enslaved had to fight against the silence imposed by the West and to find their own voice, the mother of the captive had no voice. In the Western tradition, the enslaved was heard only if she or he spoke through the vocabulary of Western human rights. The freedom and dignity of the enslaved remained framed by the vocabulary of pity. The voice of the enslaved could not be angry or loud, full of insults and shouts. But the sorrow and rage of the slave's mother was even more silenced. We still need to unearth her muted voice, because her mourning sounds what is at the heart of predatory economy, the will to power.

But if "colonial societies work[ed] through race," so did the metropole.[18] Following decolonization and the return of the colonizers to the metropolis, the discourse of racial whiteness was brought back to European countries. It became clear that memories of colonial history "do not simply vanish from social landscape, but appear—unasked—at unexpected moments. They can be discerned too in other stories, which on the surface might seem to have little to do with the imperial past."[19] In the post-WWII reorganization of capital and the international division of labor, however, female reproduction by non-white women was no longer needed. Third-world women's fertility was said to be responsible for poverty, an obstacle to development and modernization. It became a source of concern, a threat to global well-being, debated in World Population Conferences where, in the early 1950s, the United States was able to impose its views that third-world women were having too many children, which was a threat to world security, a potential menace of revolts and insurrection.[20] The West would save women of color from a millenary servitude; the wombs of African, Indian, and Chinese women were no longer

---

[16] Marilyn Lake and Henry Reynolds, *Drawing the Global Colour Line: White Men's Countries and the International Challenge to Racial Equality* (Cambridge: Cambridge University Press, 2008).

[17] David Northrup, *Indentured Labor in the Age of Imperialism, 1834–1922* (Cambridge: Cambridge University Press, 1995).

[18] Bill Schwarz, *The White Man's World* (Oxford: Oxford University Press, 2011).

[19] Schwarz, *The White Man's World*, 54.

[20] See the successive resolutions of United Nations Conferences on Population since 1974 at https://www.un.org/en/development/desa/population/events/conference/index.asp.

needed. And women who had been deported to the colonies were said to have too many children too. They were the cause of their own poverty; they had the wrong kind of families. Consequently, non-white women constitute the majority of precarious workers in the world today, and they are the first victims of new forms of colonization. They constitute 55 percent of trafficked people, and they play an increasing role in new medical industries such as stem-cell production, which requires high volumes of human embryos, fetal tissue, and umbilical-cord blood. Thus, do poor and non-white women's bodies still constitute a site of exploitation for racial capitalism?

*

Proposed in 2000 by the atmospheric chemist and Nobel laureate Paul Crutzen, the term "Anthropocene" describes a turning point in human history. In 2011, the Royal Swedish Academy of Sciences argued that "the scale and speed of change have become incredible. Humankind has caused mass extinctions of plant and animal species, polluted the oceans and altered the atmosphere."[21] A majority of scientists agree that we are at a turning point: for the first time in the history of humanity, human action is having geological consequences, and there is a *negative planetary impact* of human activities. There has been debate about when this age started, and it is an important debate. Simon Lewis and Mark Maslin have suggested that we take 1610 as the starting date of the Anthropocene. There was a sharp shift, they say, in carbon deposits because of the death of more than 50 million indigenous residents of the Americas in the first century after European contact, the result of genocide, famine, and enslavement. As species were moved around the world, new plants sucked up CO_2 from the atmosphere. The long European sixteenth century led to the greatest exchange of humans, diseases, plants, and animals across the globe. Sylvia Wynter has also looked at the conquest of the Americas to mark the beginning of the "Age of Man." The environmental historian Joachim Radkau, meanwhile, has argued that the slave trade was a turning point in the global history of the environment. All these remarks are important because they connect geological human impact with colonial slavery and imperialism.

The global historian Jason Moore, meanwhile, has argued that the "Anthropocene argument—in its Two Century Model of modernity—is poor history," and that we must see the modern world system as a "*capitalist world-ecology*: a civilization that joins the accumulation of capital, the

---

[21] See Will Steffen et al., "The Anthropocene: From Global Change to Planetary Stewardship," *Ambio* 40, no. 7 (November 2011): 739–61, doi: 10.1007/s13280-011-0185-x.

pursuit of power, and the production of nature as an organic whole."[22] He has given the name "Capitalocene" to this long historical period that began in the sixteenth century with the colonial expansion of European powers. Thus, the notion of the Anthropocene is problematic because it explains our age

> with a longstanding environmentalist argument about the Industrial Revolution as *the* turning point in human affairs.
>
> This, however, denies a longer history of capitalism that begins in the era of Columbus.... While there is no question that environmental change accelerated sharply after 1850, and especially after 1945, it seems equally fruitless to explain these transformations without identifying how they fit into patterns of power, capital, and nature established some four centuries earlier.
>
> From this standpoint, we may ask, Are we really living in the Anthropocene—the "age of man"—with its Eurocentric and techno-determinist vistas? Or are we living in the Capitalocene—the "age of capital"—the historical era shaped by the endless accumulation of capital?[23]

To the French historians Christophe Bonneuil and Jean-Baptiste Fressoz, though, the Anthropocene is also the result of a political defeat, of the victory of a kind of environmental thought that favors a sustainable management of the Earth by science, of the Promethean belief that science and technology will save the Earth. The thesis of the end of nature as we know it is, in fact, they argue, a thesis about total control over nature.[24]

The concern for the Earth and the future of humanity has become the subject of intense international lobbying and negotiation. Multinationals have entered the field, concerned both by the control of as many resources as possible *and* by the threat of losing access to water, sugar, or other commodities. Businesses and states are investing large amounts in green research, which Bonneuil and Fressoz understand as another way of avoiding the question at the root of the matter, in its denial of the otherness of nature. But it seems that no term can fully grasp what we are witnessing, nor the plurality of forms of dispossession and displacement. Considering this, Jussi Parikka suggests that we have entered the age of the "Anthrobscene."[25] Though smartphones, tablets, laptops and e-readers once held the promise of ending deforestation, a world less dependent on paper, Parikka argues that the result

---

[22] Jason W. Moore, "Anthropocene or Capitalocene? On World-Ecology and the Nature of Our Crisis, Part III," May 19, 2013, on Jason W. Moore's website, https://jasonwmoore.wordpress.com/2013/05/19/anthropocene-or-capitalocene-part-iii/.

[23] Jason W. Moore "The Capitalocene, Part I: On the Nature and Origins of Our Ecological Crisis," *The Journal of Peasant Studies* 44, no. 3 (2017): 596, doi: 10.1080/03066150.2016.1235036.

[24] Christophe Bonneuil and Jean-Baptiste Fressoz, *L'Événement anthropocène* (Paris: Seuil, 2014).

[25] Jussi Parikka, *The Anthrobscene* (Minneapolis: University of Minnesota Press, 2014).

is quite the opposite: an environmental wasteland where media never die, and a colonization of the self. Racial capitalism has thus entered a new era, in which new sites of forgetfulness are created, new Souths. There are new liquid cemeteries: if the Atlantic is a vast African cemetery of the past, today the Mediterranean, the Pacific, and the Indian Ocean are the new cemeteries of disposable and racialized peoples. As structural adjustment programs are now applied to southern Western countries after having brought devastation to countries in South America, Africa, and Asia, a new cartography is emerging, a cartography of forgotten territories where the basic needs of people are neglected, toxic wastes dumped, and chemical plants installed, but also of new counter-hegemonic practices.

One old strategy has been to force the state and its powers to recognize the existence of a group, a community, a people. Enslaved, colonized, women, workers, peasants, refugees, and displaced people claim: "Our lives matter! We will not allow you to forget!" This has been essential to the expansion of rights and democratization. The struggle for recognition (or memory) has been about giving an ethical dimension to Western democracy, in its call for the full application of universal rights. It is concerned with the constant re-evaluation of what it is to be human, but it is also about the acknowledgment that justice is not applied equally, that the politics of lives that matter means recognizing the structural discriminations and injustice at work and the disparities that each marginalized group faces. But if the movement of decolonization in the 1960s contributed to the fight against the global politics of forgetfulness, postcolonial states have since deployed their own fabrication of forgetfulness. And the adoption of the logic of neoliberalism has accentuated this production. It is not enough, then, to fill the ethical gaps of Western democracy with our memory. Instead, we need to renew the ethics of emancipation itself.

Whatever is produced as non-existent, Boaventura de Sousa Santos has argued, vanishes as reality. Hence, the need to challenge an "abyssal gap."[26] Not only does humanity's future depend on rejecting the European model at present, but we must rethink the long history of dispossession. In his conclusion to *The Wretched of the Earth*, Fanon wrote that we must forget Europe. "If we want humanity to advance a step farther, if we want to bring it up to a different level than that which Europe has shown it, then we must invent and we must make discoveries," he notes.[27] Fanon suggests that we articulate a position where forgetfulness would be a starting point of knowledge,

---

[26] Boaventura de Sousa Santos, João Arriscado Nunes, and Maria Paula Meneses, "Opening Up the Canon of Knowledge and Recognition of Difference," in *Another Knowledge Is Possible: Beyond Northern Epistemologies*, ed. Boaventura de Sousa Santos (New York: Verso, 2007), xix–lxii.
[27] Fanon, *The Wretched of the Earth*, 254.

thinking, and action. In this, he traced the road from the forgetfulness of damnation to post-European humanism.

The culture of the vanquished is rarely embodied in pure material objects; it is about manual work and intangible culture, about rituals and festivals. The vanquished bequeath words rather than palaces, hope rather than private property, texts and music rather than monuments. However, we are working from a mutilated and mutilating cartography. The notions of palimpsest and of cumulative palimpsests can be useful here to draw a cartography that might show both roots and routes. A palimpsest is, of course, a parchment or other writing surface on which the original text has been effaced or partially erased, and then overwritten by another. In other words, a palimpsest is a multilayered record. The nature of the palimpsest is twofold: it preserves the distinctness of individual texts, while exposing the contamination of one by the other. Therefore, even though the process of layering which creates a palimpsest was born out of the need to erase and destroy previous texts, the re-emergence of those destroyed texts renders a structure that privileges heterogeneity and diversity.

Roland Barthes' description of the slippery nature of an "ideal textuality" matches that of the palimpsest:

> In this ideal text, the networks are many and interact, without any one of them being able to surpass the rest; this text is a galaxy of signifiers, not a structure of signifieds; it has no beginning; it is reversible; we gain access to it by several entrances, none of which can be authoritatively declared to be the main one; the codes it mobilizes extend as far as the eye can reach, they are indeterminable ... the systems of meaning can take over this absolutely plural text, but their number is never closed, based as it is on the infinity of language.[28]

Archaeologists have proposed the notion of "cumulative palimpsest" to describe monuments in which "the successive episodes of deposition, or layers of activity, remain superimposed one upon the other without loss of evidence, but are so re-worked and mixed together that it is difficult or impossible to separate them out into their original constituents."[29] Instead of providing a narrative of origin or evolution, these palimpsests trace the inscriptions and erasures of different cultures, which in turn compete and struggle with each other. These ideas point to Foucault's assertion that what genealogy finds "at the beginning of things is not the inviolable identity of their origins;

---

[28] Roland Barthes, *S/Z*, trans. Richard Miller (New York: Farrar, Straus & Giroux, 1991), 5.
[29] See Geoff Bailey, "Time Perspectives, Palimpsests and the Archaeology of Time," *Journal of Anthropological Archaeology* 22, no. 2 (June 2007): 198–223.

it is the dissension of other things. It is disparity."[30] Therefore, while on the surface the cumulative archaeological palimpsest tries to present a multitemporal and utopian intermingling of cultures, an attempt at unraveling the palimpsest reveals its violent and disruptive impulses. This multifarious vision projected by the palimpsest, despite being the product of an attempt of erasure, demands a revision of conceptual systems based on the notions of fixity, linearity, center, and hierarchy. It impels us to replace these systems with new foundations that privilege the conceptions of "multilinearity, nodes, links, and networks."[31] Also, palimpsests tend to have visual manifestations (think Angkor Wat or Timbuktu).

The notion of the cumulative palimpsest can help develop other strategies of remembrance, where the ghosts are evoked, but the goal is not to fill a gap or to mask a disappearance, but rather to make the absence visible, to show it as a symptom of an economy that requires forgetfulness. This was the strategy I adopted when I organized guided visits in the Louvre for the 2012 Paris Triennial, entitled "The Slave in Le Louvre: An Invisible Humanity." The visits were not about searching for the representation of enslaved Africans in Western art history. Rather, they were about evidencing the ways in which the goods produced by the slaves in the European colonies—coffee, cotton, tobacco, sugar, tea—had contaminated social and cultural European life to such an extent that they had become integrated in its pictorial representation. It was a way to evoke the ghosts of slavery, their presence/absence. To that end, the collection of the Louvre is framed between two important dates in the history of the anti-slavery struggle: 1793, date of the first abolition of slavery in a French colony, Saint-Domingue; and 1848, the date of the second and final abolition of slavery in the French colonies. Saint-Domingue was the most important French colony, producing more than half of the sugar consumed in Europe in the late eighteenth century. The August 1791 uprising of its slaves shook the world and launched the Haitian Revolution, the only anti-colonial and anti-slavery revolution of that century. The 1793 decree to abolish slavery in Saint-Domingue was taken in the hope that it would stop the revolution, but it was too late. On November 18, 1803, at the Battle of Vertières, the Haitians finally defeated French expeditionary forces sent by Napoléon. Nearly half a century later, 1848 finally ended slavery, which had been re-established by Napoléon in May 1802.

Though these dates have no meaning for art historians, they inscribe the history of the Louvre in the long history of the anti-slavery struggle. The

---

[30] Michel Foucault, "Nietzsche, Genealogy, History," in *The Foucault Reader*, ed. Paul Rabinow (New York: Pantheon Books, 1984), 79.

[31] George P. Landow, *Hypertext 3.0: Critical theory and new media in an era of globalization* (Baltimore: Johns Hopkins University Press, 2006), 1.

museum is thus a perfect site to explore how the figure of the enslaved was both forgotten and could be remembered. For the "Slave in Le Louvre" project, and with the museum's curators, I identified the first paintings representing a man smoking a pipe, aristocratic women wearing cotton, and still lifes with sugar bowls or coffee pots. In political life, as in art history, consumption requires the construction of an abyssal gap between the presence and availability of these goods and the conditions of their production. The project creates a space of self-reflection: if consent to an abyssal gap was then fabricated in Europe, what gaps are being fabricated today? What are the mechanisms of the current imperial politics of forgetfulness?

The notion of cumulative palimpsests can help to draw a cartography of the many Souths, reinscribing the routes of solidarity that have accumulated in multilayered levels of signification; instead of foreclosing the present and the future, these palimpsests might allow new futures to be imagined. In the current process of decolonization, memories of itineraries of the enslaved, migrants, and refugees are reactivated against new politics of forgetfulness. Memory here is not the realm of subjective fleeting thought but a source of images, texts, and songs that constitute a counter-hegemonic library for present battles. Past defeats are reexamined and analyzed. Patience is remembered as a political strategy. The indomitable wish for freedom and social justice of the ancestors the world over remains the power that fuels the struggle. The politics of lives that matter means imagining a politics with "those without whom the Earth would never be the Earth."[32]

BIBLIOGRAPHY

Bailey, Geoff. "Time Perspectives, Palimpsests and the Archaeology of Time." *Journal of Anthropological Archaeology* 22, no. 2 (June 2007): 198–223.

Barthes, Roland. *S/Z*. Translated by Richard Miller. New York: Farrar, Straus & Giroux, 1991.

Bonneuil, Christophe, and Jean-Baptiste Fressoz. *L'Événement anthropocène*. Paris: Seuil, 2014.

Braidotti, Rosi. "Meta(l)flesh." In *The Future of Flesh: Bodily Mutation and Change*, edited by Zoe Detsi-Diamanti, Katerina Kitsi-Mitakou, and Effie Yiannopoulou, 241–61. New York: Palgrave Macmillan, 2009.

Braidotti, Rosi. "The Posthuman Predicament." In *The Scientific Imaginary in Visual Culture*, edited by Anneke Smelik, 69–89. Göttingen: V&R Unipress, 2010.

Césaire, Aimé. *Notebook of a Return to My Native Land*. Translated by Clayton Eshleman and Annette Smith. Middletown, CT: Wesleyan University Press, 2001.

---

[32] Césaire, *Notebook of a Return to My Native Land*, 38.

Cooper, Melinda. *Life as Surplus: Biotechnology and Capitalism in the Neoliberal Era*. Seattle: University of Washington Press, 2008.
Fanon, Frantz. *The Wretched of the Earth*. Translated by Constance Farrington. New York: Penguin Books, 1990.
Federici, Silvia. *Caliban and the Witch: Women, the Body and Primitive Accumulation.* Brooklyn, NY: Autonomedia, 2004.
Flahault, François. "Entre émancipation et destruction. Les fondements de l'idéal prométhéen." *Communications* 78 (2005): 5–49. doi: 10.3406/comm.2005.2272.
Foster, John Bellamy. *Marx's Ecology: Materialism and Nature*. New York: Monthly Review Press, 2000.
Freud, Sigmund. *The Psychopathology of Everyday Life*. New York: The Macmillan Company, 1914. https://www.bartleby.com/284/.
Foucault, Michel. "Nietzsche, Genealogy, History." In *The Foucault Reader*, edited by Paul Rabinow, 76–100. New York: Pantheon Books, 1984.
Lake, Marilyn, and Henry Reynolds. *Drawing the Global Colour Line: White Men's Countries and the International Challenge to Racial Equality*. Cambridge: Cambridge University Press, 2008.
Landow, George P. *Hypertext 3.0: Critical Theory and New Media in an Era of Globalization*. Baltimore: Johns Hopkins University Press, 2006.
Lorde, Audre. *Sister Outsider: Essays and Speeches*. New York: Ten Speed Press, 2007.
Maldonado-Torres, Nelson. "The Topology of Being and the Geopolitics of Knowledge: Modernity, Empire, Coloniality." *City* 8, no. 1 (2004): 29–56. doi: 10.1080/1360481042000199787.
Marx, Karl. *Capital*. Vol. 1. Edited by Friedrich Engels, translated by Samuel Moore and Edward Aveling. Moscow: Progress Publishers, 1887. www.marxists.org/archive/marx/works/1867-c1/ch31.htm.
Moore, Jason W. "Anthropocene or Capitalocene? On World-Ecology and the Nature of Our Crisis, Part III." Personal Website, May 19, 2013, https://jasonwmoore.wordpress.com/2013/05/19/anthropocene-or-capitalocene-part-iii/.
Moore, Jason W. "The Capitalocene, Part I: On the Nature and Origins of Our Ecological Crisis." *The Journal of Peasant Studies* 44, no. 3 (2017): 594–630. doi: 10.1080/03066150.2016.1235036.
Northrup, David. *Indentured Labor in the Age of Imperialism, 1834–1922*. Cambridge: Cambridge University Press, 1995.
Parikka, Jussi. *The Anthrobscene*. Minneapolis: University of Minnesota Press, 2014.
Roseboro, Ken. "The GMO Seed Cartel." *The Organic & Non-GMO Report*, February 1, 2013, https://non-gmoreport.com/articles/february2013/the-gmo-seed-cartel.php.
Rothberg, Michael. *Multidirectional Memories: Remembering the Holocaust in the Age of Decolonization*. Redwood City, CA: Stanford University Press, 2009.
Santos, Boaventura de Sousa, João Arriscado Nunes, and Maria Paula Meneses. "Opening Up the Canon of Knowledge and Recognition of Difference." In *Another

Knowledge Is Possible: Beyond Northern Epistemologies, edited by Boaventura de Sousa Santos, xix–lxii. New York: Verso, 2007.

Schwarz, Bill. *The White Man's World*. Oxford: Oxford University Press, 2011.

Steffen, Will, Åsa Persson, Lisa Deutsch, Jan Zalasiewicz, Mark Williams, Katherine Richardson, Carole Crumley et al., "The Anthropocene: From Global Change to Planetary Stewardship." *Ambio* 40, no. 7 (November 2011): 739–61. doi: 10.1007/s13280-011-0185-x.

Wells, H. G. *The Island of Doctor Moreau*. Oxford: Oxford University Press, 2017.

Part IV

CRITICAL TENSIONS

Chapter 7

Emancipation, Domination, and Critical Theory in the Anthropocene

Ajay Singh Chaudhary

The true politician reckons only in dates. And if the abolition of the bourgeoisie is not completed by an almost calculable moment in economic and technical development (a moment signaled by inflation and poison-gas warfare) all is lost. Before the spark reaches the dynamite, the lighted fuse must be cut.[1]

One is tempted in the twenty-first century to want to replace "inflation" with "profitability" and "poison-gas warfare" with "atmospheric carbon concentration." When Walter Benjamin was writing these lines in the mid-1920s, the question was whether a catastrophe even more far-reaching than the First World War—one that was already apparent to thinkers like Benjamin—could be forestalled. Far from being a historical event that was over, the war was characteristic of the modern capitalist world. The rationalized barbarity of mechanized warfare was not isolated to the battlefield; it was in operation in the increasingly Taylorized factory, in the design of capitalist cities, and through a commodified cultural system and overall life predicated on "shock" and "phantasmagoria." While blind liberal observers might observe a sudden shock to their system by particular symptoms followed by an exasperated sigh that "things can't go on like this,"[2] the reality is they can and will as part of the ordinary functioning of capitalism. Long before Benjamin would codify these arguments in his last known work, the "Theses on the Philosophy of History," he had already noticed that this attitude—although characteristic of the bourgeoisie in that moment—had its corollaries within Marxism itself. Instead of a *faith* (in the most Christian theological definition of the word)

---

[1] Walter Benjamin, *One-Way Street*, ed. Michael W. Jennings, trans. Edmund Jephcott (Cambridge, MA: Belknap Press, 2005), 66.
[2] Benjamin, *One-Way Street*, 33—famously recapitulated and expanded in Benjamin's last work, "Theses on the Philosophy of History."

in an idea of necessary and often mechanistic progress—whether through automatic reform or revolution—historical materialism ought to orient itself differently. As Benjamin would suggest in 1930: "Marx says that revolutions are the locomotive of history. But perhaps it is quite otherwise. Perhaps revolutions are an attempt by the passengers on the train—namely, the human race—to activate the emergency break."[3]

It doesn't take much to reformulate Benjamin on twenty-first-century ecological terms. As I write, atmospheric carbon concentration hovers around 418 ppm.[4] Pre-industrial levels stood at 280 ppm; 350 ppm is an oft-cited guideline within the climate sciences for what might be considered "a safe operating space for humanity."[5] Nearly 56 percent of added atmospheric carbon has been generated since 1980. 2020 tied 2016 as the warmest year on record. Rates of species extinction are estimated at between 100 and 1,000 times Holocene levels.[6] As I write, it is approximately a year into the COVID-19 pandemic. Not only can the pandemic be directly linked with the ongoing process of anthropogenic climate change; pandemics and disease more broadly are expected to proliferate just as once-a-century "superstorms" are now a regular occurrence. The last few years have seen bushfires rage across Australia, unprecedented floods and mudslides in South Asia, wildfires crisscross California—lighting the sky an eerie orange glow—and water shortages (and cut-offs) from southern Africa to Jackson, Mississippi. Separating an economic migrant, from a political migrant, from a climate migrant is an exercise in futility as it is increasingly clear that capitalism, as an "ensemble of social relations" as Marx would put it, or as "the dominant global socio-economic system"[7] as a recent climate study more delicately approached the question, is the principal driver of anthropogenic climate change. Consider the following paragraph:

> the earth system requires much more than small tweaks and incremental changes. Instead, it will require radical departures from the status quo where the complex system of intertwined sustainability challenges are confronted in order to shift multiple unsustainable trajectories toward "good" Anthropocenes where normative goals for sustainability are achieved and political and economic power structures deliver the common good.... The tendency to focus on biophysical or economic quantification of the couplings between society and

---

[3] Walter Benjamin, *Selected Writings, Volume 4: 1938–1940*, ed. Howard Eiland and Michael W. Jennings (Cambridge, MA: Belknap Press, 2006), 402.
[4] As measured by the Mauna Loa Observatory in Hawaii, March 3, 2021.
[5] Johan Rockström et al., "A Safe Operating Space for Humanity," *Nature* 461 (2009): 472–75.
[6] Rockström et al., "Operating Space."
[7] Will Steffen et al., "Trajectories of the Earth System in the Anthropocene," *PNAS* 115, no. 33 (2018): 8252–59.

technology or society and ecological systems can overlook a critical element of radical thinking—the necessity to consider underlying social drivers such as capitalist competition and unequal power relations in ways that do not reproduce dominant growth and efficiency logics.[8]

This is *not* a critical theory. It is not a Marxian, ecosocialist, or deeply radically informed analysis. This is a quote from a recent literature review article in *Nature Sustainability* by a team of natural and social scientists, reflecting what is increasingly a consensus *empirical* case about capitalism and climate change.[9] The facts, as Theodor Adorno would put it, do not speak for themselves. The desire for scientistic politics—notably rarely embraced in actual climate science—is liberal fantasy for emancipation from a transcendental outside, emancipation without politics.

Indeed, there is something we might call an "intuitive critical theory" at least partially at work in recent climate research. Unlike the model laid out in Max Horkheimer's "Traditional and Critical Theory," "traditional" studies of this kind smuggle in a quasi-emancipatory and at least implicit normative assumption—"the good Anthropocene," "common good," etc. Because of the very nature (no pun intended) of ecosystem complexity and climate change, systemic theories which focus on one single question or variable are often eschewed in favor of trying to understand an overall, interconnected system, in terms of natural ecosystems as well as the intercourse between the natural and the social. Scientific inquiry in this mode presents "brutal facts" but not "as something eternally immune to intervention."[10] The facts do not merely speak, *pace* Adorno, they scream. The catastrophe, as Benjamin put it, is not some punctum or rupture. The catastrophe is that things go on like this. Climate change is not over some tipping point or on the horizon; it is already here and experience of it—although of course mediated—is palpable in everyday life across the world.

Frankfurt School critical theory is well known for engendering a kind of political paralysis. But far from the caricature as detached or inattentive to historical conditions and empirical realities, critical theory was in many ways prompted by an open engagement with empirical realities and new phenomena that did not accord well with Marxist "orthodoxy" as it was construed at the time. It was a product of the crisis of Marxism in the early 1920s and

---

[8] Timon McPhearson et al., "Radical Changes Are Needed for Transformations to a Good Anthropocene," *npj Urban Sustain* 1, no. 5 (2021).

[9] See my recent article "Sustaining What? Capitalism, Socialism, and Climate Change," in *Capital, Democracy, Socialism: Critical Debates*, ed. Albena Azmanova and James Chamberlain (Cham: Springer, forthcoming).

[10] Theodor Adorno and Max Horkheimer, *Dialectic of Enlightenment*, ed. Gunzelin Schmid Noerr, trans. Edmund Jephcott (Stanford: Stanford University Press, 2002), 11.

was concerned analytically with a *more* materialist account. Capitalism didn't merely exploit or dominate. It produced, as Adorno commented, "people . . . down to the innermost fibre of their being."[11] The political thrust of critical theory, as we will see, is far more complicated in texts like *Dialectic of Enlightenment*. It fell back on a political idealism which eschewed practical politics (revolutionary or reformist), a stance considered as "resistance" to the integrative patterns of modern capitalist societies; or it sought to overcome political arguments based on power with instead something closer to neo-Kantian reason. This amounted to a "ruthless" critique on the one hand but a praxiological vacuum on the other.

This however may be a feature of critical theory, not a bug, as we reconsider it in light of the socio-ecological crises that are illustrated so well by some of its most well-known arguments. It is not an accident that so much ecosocialist and other radical climate writing is covered with ideas and frameworks from classical critical theory, but this moment prompts circumspection, not hasty congratulation. Some elements of its initial formulation have long ceased to be operative while some of its principle claims are even more pertinent. It still has much to offer in understanding the domination of nature but also in opening theoretical space for comprehending a multiplicity of dominations that are *integral* to the overall functioning of capital in the twenty-first century. Reconstituted (and knocking some claims down a peg or two), it provides an ideal methodology for the kind of interdisciplinary critical synthesis required to understand the material conditions of today.[12] While it must jettison its allergy to positive political programs, it likely *shouldn't* produce that program. By looking at a comparison of Angela Davis and Theodor Adorno, we can see just how such a reformulation might operate. I'll then consider how ideology critique and the unique category of *Flaschenposten* are differently operative as partner to the emancipatory climate politics, or left-wing realism, needed for our time. A reconstituted critical theory is perhaps the ideal mode for thinking the utopian—but lateral—challenges that climate change poses and for understanding the continuing role of critique in the liberation of the negative.

---

[11] Theodor Adorno and Max Horkheimer, *Towards a New Manifesto,* trans. Rodney Livingstone (New York/London: Verso, 2011), 112.

[12] For an excellent recent summation of critical theory methodology, see Albena Azmanova, *Capitalism on Edge* (New York: Columbia University Press, 2020), 27–37.

THE CRISIS OF MARXISM, THE CLIMATE CRISIS, AND THE CRITIQUE OF PROGRESS

Critical theory never set out to dismiss the facts. To dismiss the facts is to descend into irrationalism, to in turn reify or even sanctify nature instead of understanding the social relation of society and nature. As Benjamin writes: "No historical category without its natural substance, no natural category without its historical filtration." What Benjamin was already outlining as early as the 1920s would become some of the central arguments of critical theory, especially in its early efflorescence beginning in the 1930s.[13] This famously included some of the first systematic attempts by Marxian research to understand capitalism as a system which was fundamentally predicated on the domination of nature.[14] The productive capacities for a free society already existed but they lay fettered within a society that did not clearly have the mechanical motion or particular political agency that some Marxist theories posited. These were "corrupted" by an understanding of nature as "ex gratis" which complemented the exploitation of labor power.[15] Progress and regress were dialectical counterparts; technology, which could have underwritten Marx's "realm of freedom," was instead shaped, transformed, and funneled into the colossal war machines of WWI.[16] As Theodor Adorno and Max Horkheimer argued later, capitalism had engendered an ever-narrowing understanding of the Enlightenment as instrumental rationality, purely technical reason constituted through the "mastery of nature" which was fundamentally "patriarchal" and fed into further logics of social and racial exclusion and ultimately self-annihilation. "Enlightenment, understood in the widest sense as the advance of thought, has always aimed at liberating human beings from fear and installing them as masters. Yet the wholly enlightened Earth is radiant with triumphant calamity."[17] This brief treatment hardly scratches the surface of resonant and pertinent arguments from the first generation of critical theorists as considered in the light of the already existing catastrophic

---

[13] See Miriam Hansen, *Cinema and Experience: Siegfried Kracauer, Walter Benjamin and Theodor W. Adorno* (Berkeley: University of California Press, 2011) and Douglas Kellner, *Critical Theory, Marxism, and Modernity* (Baltimore: Johns Hopkins University Press, 1989), among others.
[14] See Andreas Malm, "Ecology & Marxism," Reading guide, *Historical Materialism*, https://www.historicalmaterialism.org/reading-guides/ecology-marxism-andreas-malm; as recent scholarship like Kohei Saito's *Karl Marx's Ecosocialism* (New York: Monthly Review Press, 2017) has shown, Marx himself had a rather sophisticated understanding of and engagement with the biological sciences of his day. What Benjamin and then critical theory were addressing was the more moribund and dogmatic nature of what Marxism had become, particularly as regards empirical phenomena that were discomfiting to the kind of Marxist orthodoxy that had developed around figures like Karl Kautsky and the German Social Democratic Party more broadly.
[15] Benjamin, *Selected Writings, Volume 4*, 394.
[16] Benjamin, *One-Way Street*, 94–95.
[17] Adorno and Horkheimer, *Dialectic of Enlightenment*, 1.

(although not apocalyptic, at least in the Christian eschatological sense of the word) conditions of anthropogenic climate change for the vast majority of people, but it is easy to see why theorists like Benjamin, Adorno, and others have become such critical touch points for so many contemporary reflections on a world in socio-ecological crisis, quite literally radiant with triumphant calamity.

Although there is more than just this question of the domination of nature or the dialectical critique of progress that makes critical theory in some of its initial arguments, as well as more broadly in its methodology, well suited for thinking about what emancipation might mean in this era; but this should hardly be understood as some kind of unequivocal vindication. In the present moment, the facts enable a certain kind of articulation—that of the immanent contradictions between prevalent ideals like "sustainability"[18] and liberal equity and the brute force of reality. Ideology is still omnipresent but it has less purchase. Changing historical realities underwrote the original Critical Theoretical project: and the Critical Theoretical project must change alongside conditions—of which we have better knowledge, but which also have just fundamentally changed.

However, the question at hand is not only about understanding theory today. Benjamin's argument from *One-Way Street* is not about the *theorist;* it is about the *politician*. Capitalism in the twenty-first century is a perfected machine (an "extractive circuit"[19]) that can be understood as a quintessential expression of instrumental rationality. The circuit not only runs on "fossil capital"[20]; it draws from social and ecological inputs and modes of domination that stretch long into the past and globally in a world of tiered powers, characterized not—as some fear—by some kind of nascent global sovereign, nor by the eclipse of empire, but by a suprasovereign world of frictionless capital flows, "ungovernable" multinational corporations, and the near-total orientation of global social life toward maintaining *flagging* global growth rates. The extractive circuit finds added value through classic exploitation, from extraction in "hidden abodes," gendered and racialized, in the ecological niche as much as in a global, neocolonial system in which capital increasingly relates to even the developed core as space for colonization and extraction, all

---

[18] On the fuzziness of this concept overall and its tensions in contemporary practice, see Chaudhary, "Sustaining What?..." and Christian Fuchs, "M. N. Roy and the Frankfurt School: Socialist Humanism and the Critical Analysis of Communication, Culture, Technology, Fascism and Nationalism," *tripleC* 17, no. 2 (2019): 249–86.

[19] Ajay Singh Chaudhary, "It's Already Here," *n+1*, October 10, 2018; "The Climate of Socialism," *Socialist Forum* (Winter 2019); "Sustaining What?"

[20] Andreas Malm, *Fossil Capital: The Rise of Steam Power and the Roots of Global Warming* (New York: Verso, 2016).

the while accelerating dispossession, enclosure, and expropriation.[21] It is, as I have argued elsewhere, fundamentally predicated on exhaustion—ecological and social—in every sense except one: that of automatic collapse.

The *politics* of climate change, however, require an almost precise inversion of what Adorno and Horkheimer reject so vehemently in a work like *Dialectic of Enlightenment*. Adorno and Horkheimer at one point argue that "bourgeois" consciousness is the expression of Spinoza's *conatus*—the desire for any given body to persist in the world. It is self-preservation run amok. Although this interpretation of Spinoza is a touch tendentious, one can see its logic *immanently* within the ever-narrowing reason of the self-preservation of capital itself. All of the above socio-ecological conditions facilitate the persistence of capital, the persistence of social surplus through "the insatiable and destructive expansive principle" of capitalism.[22]

But the dialectic of Enlightenment in the Anthropocene cuts both ways. It is not technological instrumentality per se that is the question, but rather *political instrumentality* from the same conative, self-preserving impulse that is the beginning of politics (but far from the end) for the vast majority of people who have an immediate interest in an emancipatory climate politics. There are many places in which we can see critical theory in desperate need of rethinking under contemporary conditions—but it is here that it begins to come apart at the seams.

What has been absent in so much green thought is theorizing the interests, the feelings, the positions, and the power (in an ordinary sense[23]) that could constitute a successful, even flourishing, adaptation and mitigation scenario for the vast majority. This certainly speaks to the question of political subjectivity that critical theory posed but to which it had no answer.

---

[21] See Nancy Fraser, "Behind Marx's Hidden Abode," *New Left Review* 86 (Mar/Apr 2014): 55–72; Nancy Fraser, "Expropriation and Exploitation in Racialized Capitalism: A Reply to Michael Dawson." *Critical Historical Studies* 3, no. 1 (2016): 163–78; Chaudhary "The Climate of Socialism" and "Sustaining What?..."; and also Jason Moore, *Capitalism in the Web of Life: Ecology and the Accumulation of Capital* (New York/London: Verso, 2015); Anna Tsing, *The Mushroom at the End of the World: On the Possibility of Life in Capitalist Ruins* (Princeton: Princeton University Press, 2017); Kathryn Yusoff, *A Billion Black Anthropocenes or None* (Minneapolis: University of Minnesota Press, 2019); Alyssa Battistoni, "Ways of Making a Living: Revaluing the Work of Social and Ecological Reproduction," *Socialist Register* 56 (Oct 2019): 182–98; Mike Davis, *Late Victorian HolocaustsL El Niño Famines and the Making of the Third World* (New York/London: Verso, 2017) to name just a few of the critical studies.

[22] Theodor Adorno, *Hegel: Three Studies*, trans. Shierry Weber Nicholson (Cambridge, MA/London: MIT Press, 1993), 28.

[23] See Raymond Geuss, *Philosophy and Real Politics* (Princeton: Princeton University Press, 2008), 21–30. "Although Lenin's formula is basically correct . . . it needs to be extended twice. First of all the formula should not read 'who whom?' but rather 'who <does> what to whom for whose benefit?' with four distinct variables to be filled in, i.e. (1) Who?; (2) What? (3) To Whom?; (4) for whose benefit? To think politically is to think about agency, power, and interests, and the relations among these." Guess, *Philosophy,* 25.

In the fine-tuning of human subjectivity as human capital, as marketable skillsets, as infinitely flexible and fungible units, but also of intra-human, microbiological optimization and pharmaceutical maintenance to the acceleration of the extractive circuit,[24] we can see just how much the neoliberal world—which should be understood as a primary governing force and cultural logic in the totality of the extractive circuit—*was* characterized perhaps even more than Adorno's era by the kinds of phenomena of integration he describes.

My use of the past tense here is to pose the question of integration—not that it does not still exist, nor that these phenomena are not *more* intense today than ten years ago or in the mid-twentieth century, but rather to notice how threadbare the nature of ideology is in contemporary socio-ecological realities, to ask where integration is and where it isn't. What has been characterized as "Zombie Neoliberalism"[25] has a difficult task today—even though, as Mark Fisher quipped: "it is sometimes harder to kill a zombie than a living person."[26] Part of a *political theory* of climate change looks to where such integration is weakest, where neoliberalism, vital to the return to profitability for capitalism as a whole, has lost purchase. Good critical theory—that is, good historical materialism—must take account of the recent global upsurge in social mobilization and politicization, as well as inchoate phenomena, particularly in the wake of such a long period of depoliticization. Whether this takes the form of the George Floyd uprisings in the United States, the successful pushback of American-backed coup forces by the socialist indigenous movement in Bolivia, popular protests in Chile against neoliberalism, or, more comfortable for some Marxists, the largest general strike in human history this past year in India. And these alongside general political destabilization and transformation, such as the re-emergence of neofascist movements, the turn to the authoritarian liberalism of "Macronism," and inchoate

---

[24] Arguments like these are often thought to reflect purely first-world conditions, but in fact these are global realities. As I have written in an unpublished chapter: "Multinational companies ('big pharma') . . . already report massively expanding sales of their products in what they graspingly call 'pharmerging countries' in Asia and Latin America." There are also "local entrepreneurs ('little pharma') who trade on the generic leftovers of the branded blockbusters," a semi-formal market reflecting the manufacturing of pharmaceuticals in places like India and Brazil. And: One is justified in speaking of the commercial globalization of psychiatry through the medium of the pill, or "psychopharmaceutical globalization." Amphetamines aren't alone; a whole panoply of pharmacology—from the opioids that are now the most prescribed medication in the United States, to SSRIs, benzodiazepines, and beyond—is part of an affective maintenance and survival network for those both in and around the extractive circuit.

[25] See for instance Sarah Jaffe, "Zombie Neoliberalism: How 'There Is No Alternative' gave us Donald Trump," *Dissent,* Fall 2017, or Mark Fisher, "How to kill a zombie: strategizing the end of neoliberalism," openDemocracy, July 18, 2013.

[26] Fisher, "How to kill a zombie."

phenomena like the Yellow Vests in France. Gramsci's poetic phrase about "interregnum" is much abused but rarely placed in full context:

> If the ruling class has lost its consensus, i.e., it is no longer "leading" but only "dominant," exercising coercive force alone, this means precisely that the great masses have become detached from their traditional ideologies, and no longer believe what they used to believe previously, etc. The crisis consists precisely in the fact that the old is dying and the new cannot be born; in this interregnum a great variety of morbid symptoms appear.[27]

Marx had claimed that capitalism would produce its own gravediggers in *The Communist Manifesto* but spends many chapters of *Capital* devoted to just how damaging production is to proletarians, the proposed gravediggers. Critical theorists broadly took this question of "damage" seriously. The Frankfurt School was hardly one "school" when it came to politics, but the question of a new subject was always being posed, as the theoretical understanding of the revolutionary proletariat seemed ill-matched to actual history. This does not call for some kind of return to left-liberalism (as the later Habermas would more or less endorse in critiquing earlier thinkers) but rather asks how such "damage" or "dehumanization" might still allow for revolutionary subjectivity, for a mass political subject.

As Adam Przeworski demonstrated in *Capitalism and Social Democracy*, one key aspect of Marx and Engels' predictions in terms of class theory, which "was viewed as a necessary feature of capitalist development," certainly did not play out: in no society ever (save Belgium in 1912 which reached 50.1 percent) did the urban industrial proletariat become a simple majority.[28] All socialist politics—whether reformist or revolutionary—was cross-class in the formal Marxist sense, and coalitional. Furthermore, successful class struggle—particularly through a labor movement and electoral activity, in the absence of a broader revolutionary or radical movement—resulted in the "embourgeoisement" of the proletariat.[29] Such a phenomenon, argues Przeworski, can be understood in pure economic terms—such well-placed workers in fact acquire similar wealth and earnings as "middle-class" professionals, petit-bourgeois business owners, and lower-level managers—as well as ideological ones—the likelihood to identify with hegemonic bourgeois

---

[27] Antonio Gramsci, *Selections from the Prison Notebooks*, ed. and trans. Quintin Hoare and Geoffrey Nowell Smith (New York: International Publishers, 1971), 276.
[28] Adam Przeworski, *Capitalism and Social Democracy* (Cambridge, UK: Cambridge University Press, 1985), 18, 23.
[29] Przeworski, *Capitalism and Social Democracy*, 14.

norms or with other categories of identity within liberal society, such as the nation.

In thinking through the conditions of the post-WWII era—as Adorno and Horkheimer were—what "orthodox" (read Kautskyite) Marxism posited as the sine-qua-non agent had little reason to want to break with capitalism. Bereft of a more radical social and cultural movement, capital could offer in the immediate term simply a better deal than even the smoothest transition to socialism. It was on these terms—although long before this data was all known—that Benjamin excoriated social democrats whose faith in technological progress under capital was matched only by their faith in "scientific socialism" (supposedly demonstrating "natural" laws of society). Even closer to Przeworski, Adorno would argue in 1942 that "the proletariat does have more to lose than its chains."[30] Against the "orthodox" doctrine "all the statistics could be marshalled ... their standard of living has not deteriorated but improved."[31] Even if compelled "at the start, by the pressure of the masses," this process of integration ultimately is brought to serve the stabilization of capitalism and the nation-state.[32] "Colonial profits" and monopolistic rents facilitated the rechanneling of once radical demands into overall systemic reproduction, binding the (implicitly Global North) proletarian to the firm, the nation, and ultimately, war. Immiseration of the proletariat is unexpectedly halted in this way, "economic pauperization" in the form of the persistence of poverty walked hand in hand with the "extra-economic improvement of the standard of living."[33] Class society in such a situation is "dominated by monopolies" and "tends toward fascism."[34] There is no rational basis for solidarity with either the locally impoverished or the colonized since the Global North proletarian, in what some social democrats regard as the Golden Age[35]

---

[30] Theodor Adorno, "Reflections on Class Theory," in *Can One Live After Auschwitz?* ed. Rolf Tiedemann, trans. Rodney Livingstone (Stanford: Stanford University Press, 2003), 103; see also Raymond Geuss, "Dialectics and the Revolutionary Impulse," in *The Cambridge Companion to Critical Theory*, ed. Fred Rush (Cambridge, UK: Cambridge University Press, 2004), 113: "What if capitalism came to be capable of raising the standard of living of the workers rather than further depressing it? A trade union consciousness could then establish itself that was not inherently and irrevocably revolutionary, one that was itself, as Lenin claimed, a form of bourgeois ideology, that is, a form of consciousness that was itself a means through which the bourgeoisie could extend and solidify its domination over the working class".

[31] Adorno, *After Auschwitz?*, 103.

[32] Compare with Aaron Benanav, *Automation and the Future of Work* (New York/London: Verso, 2020), 50: "In [European and wealthy Asian countries], postwar labor market institutions were mostly designed not by left-wing governments but by right-wing politicians who emphasized the importance of national-imperial identities, the formation of male breadwinner households, and the maintenance of relatively fixed workplace hierarchies."

[33] Adorno, *After Auschwitz?*, 105.

[34] Adorno, *After Auschwitz?*, 96.

[35] Please see this lecture by my colleague Rebecca Ariel Porte for thinking "The Golden Age" as a category of critique: https://www.youtube.com/watch?v=52hA6ZSf_TY.

of capitalism, profits off the latter and can "take liberties" with the former. Although class society can be said to persist, it was difficult in light of both empirical and theoretical challenges to make any kind of case for the proletariat as an exclusive, unique bearer of universal emancipation.

Although posing the question of who or what an alternative mass or class subject might be is often considered one of the principle "heresies" of critical theory, questioning the model of class struggle developed by European social democratic thinkers of the period was actually quite common everywhere *but* within these circles over the course of the twentieth century. When Adorno says that capitalism "produced people . . . down to the innermost fibre of their being," in the obscure and ultimately abortive 1956 attempt by an increasingly conservative Horkheimer and himself to write a new manifesto, he adds: "Lenin was the first to articulate such a theory."[36]

As with Przeworski, Adorno, or Benjamin, Lenin connected the economism of the social democrats to a pernicious "trade union consciousness" all too eager to conform and integrate with capital.[37] Adding to this propensity, Lenin's understanding of imperialism also called into question the immiseration thesis as far as proletarians in the developed world were concerned. As my colleague Barnaby Raine has put it:

> On the dissenting left flank, of which Lenin was a key member, it was denied that imperialism would improve either the subjugated periphery or the metropolitan core. Instead—displacing optimistic teleologies of progress leading neatly from feudalism to capitalism to socialism—an arresting thing about Lenin's writing is the place of catastrophe as a terrifying specter looming on the horizon. Wars induced by imperialism—as Lenin and his comrades read the slaughter of 1914—constituted an urgent catastrophe to be avoided by way of revolutions. This was revolution as "an emergency brake," as Walter Benjamin later had it—though nuclear annihilation and now climate disaster have functioned in the same role for later radical thinking.[38]

Benjamin openly linked his own historical materialism with Lenin's, for example demanding the "welding" of revolutionary aesthetic experience with "the constructive, dictatorial side of revolution."[39] Long before right-wing (and left-wing) conspiracy theories developed around the Frankfurt

---

[36] Adorno and Horkheimer, *Towards a New Manifesto*, 112.
[37] Geuss, "Dialectics and the Revolutionary Impulse," 115.
[38] Barnaby Raine, "The Anti-Colonial Revolt Was Key to Lenin's Vision of Revolution," *Jacobin*, March 1, 2021.
[39] Walter Benjamin, *Selected Writings, Volume 2: Part 1: 1927–1930* (Cambridge, MA: Belknap Press, 2005), 215.

School, Benjamin was happy to proclaim to Adorno that their work was that of "Cultural Bolshevism."[40] As Raine continues:

> peasant and anti-colonial struggles could be objectively anti-capitalist if they could break the food supply on which the hydra relied. At Baku in 1920, delegates echoed Lenin at the Second Congress of the Comintern and deliberately expanded Marx's invocation "Workers of the world unite!" to include "oppressed peoples" beyond the proletariat. Rather than the stuff of total voluntarism—as is often assumed by critics and admirers alike—this was a model of situated political theory, whose prescriptions were rooted in a critical social theory of contemporary capitalist society and the possible political subjects it generated.[41]

The first claim can be directly transposed to capital in the twenty-first century in socio-ecological terms. As I've argued elsewhere, Global South peasant movements and anti-colonial struggles for self-determination are as much of a climate policy as renewable energy or decreasing material resource use.[42] This is today not a question of food supply per se but rather of placing immediate breakers and resistors on the *speed* of contemporary capital, in terms of financial flows and "unbundled production" alike. When Lenin observes— and learns—from the Chinese Revolution, and extols an "advanced Asia" as against a "backward Europe," he is also performing a critique of the concept of progress and one well suited to the practicalities of climate politics. In light of contemporary realities, one should look to cases like Cuba's successful and sustainable transition to agroecology for the period immediately following the fall of the Soviet Union, or to Kerala's spectacular achievements in human and cultural development over the course of the second half of the twentieth century with little to no formal economic growth. Similarly, Lenin's recasting of a potential political subject as broadened or stretched far beyond the theoretical proletariat finds echoes in Benjamin's constant slippage to "the masses," Marcuse's later embrace of the New Left in its multiplicity, and even Adorno's more tenuous speculations about "those who have been left behind,"[43] and, perhaps ironically, in one of his final lectures in 1969, "among

---

[40] See, e.g., letter to Adorno, February 23, 1939, in Walter Benjamin, *The Correspondence of Walter Benjamin,* ed. Gershom Scholem, Theodor W. Adorno et al. (Chicago: University of Chicago Press, 1994), 599. In a letter to Scholem in 1924, Benjamin remarks again: "at the various points of contact I have with radical Bolshevist theory...," *The Correspondence,* 258.
[41] Raine, "Anti-Colonial Revolt."
[42] See Chaudhary, "Sustaining What?..."; Chaudhary, "The Climate of Socialism."
[43] Adorno and Horkheimer, *Dialectic of Enlightenment,* 28; Lenin's invocation of *jihad* might appear simply canny rhetoric, but seen in this light, it seems far closer to Benjamin's secularization of Judaic theological concepts. I have long argued that such theoretical interventions (with *deep* practical implications) are *materialist* correctives to the vestiges of Hegel's Christian providentialism

various sections of the younger generation" who exhibit "resistance to blind conformism, the freedom to choose rational goals, revulsion from the world's deceptions and illusions, the recollection of the possibility of change."[44]

This is not only a question of Leninism and critical theory. Franz Fanon would propose a radically different formation in what he calls a "stretched Marxism" in *The Wretched of the Earth;* C. L. R. James broke with Trotsky over Trotsky's dogmatic insistence that it was the European proletariat who would lead and the colonized world which would follow. The history of the Haitian Revolution—"the first slave society to achieve the permanent destruction of the slave system" as Cedric Robinson argues in *Black Marxism*—led James to see, similarly, different possibilities in political subjectivity, subjectification, and agency that were of necessity historically specific in their relationship to the conditions which produced them and were simultaneously incongruous with class theory in its "orthodox" sense. Perhaps nowhere more than in socialist-feminist theory was the question of a new political subject, or many new subjects, taken up, from *Feminist Contentions* to Donna Haraway's "Cyborg Manifesto" or Kathi Weeks' *Constituting Feminist Subjects*, among many others.

But the world of the mid-century is no more. It was not only critical theorists who mistook its exceptionality for generality; this was also the era that prompted the now invalidated Kuznet's curve predicting the long-term trends on different time scales *against* inequality. It also prompted the later, even more erroneous environmental Kuznet's curve which similarly argued that after a period of increasing environmental degradation, all geographies would eventually become "unpolluted." Most of the original generation of critical theorists died before the eventual neoliberal turn, and even before the earliest moments of the crises of profitability in the 1970s. What I have been calling the extractive circuit was not fully assembled. Although some later critical theorists like Nancy Fraser, Angela Davis, Susan Buck-Morss, Seyla Benhabib, or Jürgen Habermas in his early work, did reformulate and adapt the initial Critical Theoretical project for this changing time, many arguments and foundations of critical theory remain suspended between WWI and an unending mid-century. Critical theory, as a mode of historical materialism, even if it will not be generative of the actual *politics* of an emancipatory climate realism, must internalize the vast transformations in global society and in what we know of the full ecological portrait of capitalist "social totality" and its imbrication in various Earth systems.

---

that remained unexamined within Marxism. See also Chaudhary, "Religions of Doubt: Religion, Critique, and Modernity in Jalal Al-e Ahmad and Walter Benjamin" (PhD diss., Columbia University, 2013).

[44] Adorno, *After Auschwitz?*, 123–24.

Even in the Global North, the immiseration thesis is back on the table. But while the kinds of fully integrated workers described from the mid-century may play an outsize role in contemporary socialist imaginaries, they constitute a tiny fraction of the overall workforce. In fact, far from integrating, more and more are thrown out of regular capitalist function.[45] Almost all Marxists thought the proletariat would proliferate numerically as a percentage of the population. In reality, it is the exact opposite that has happened. Attempts to account for world demography in terms of class and "relative surplus population" result in stunning numbers. Out of the global working age population of just under 5 billion, under 2 billion could be considered "workers" even under the loosest standards.[46] Overall, the relative surplus population is some 2.47 times the "active army" (including the actively unemployed).[47] Broken into developmental categories, the least developed countries have a surplus ratio of 8.9 to 1, middle income 2.4 to 1, and the developed world 1.37 to 1. And these ratios are only increasing across the board, if unevenly. As the authors of one study grimly note:

> The empirical evidence presented in this paper demonstrates that a clear majority of the world's labouring population is now relatively surplus to the functioning of capitalism. Of particular concern is that engineering increasing demand to stimulate the redeployment tendency is no longer a solution because it implies the escalating consumption and destabilisation of an already materially depleted and ecologically destabilised planet.[48]

The case is actually far *worse* than this rather dire conclusion. Not only is green growth not possible,[49] we are entering a post-growth era no matter what. The only real question is what kind. Today's culture industry is more omnipresent and more penetrating than at any time in the twentieth century, but it also seems far less successful in its integrative nature. If anything, it is far closer to the therapeutic models of culture Adorno outlined as well: functional "entertainment" to prepare oneself for another bout of exhaustive hyperwork or equally exhaustive underwork. Or worse, not ideological integration, but extractive value maximization through continual participation in productive economic activity. One might be able to justify an indefinite

---

[45] Although such people can still serve as sources of value for extraction, whether in informal economies, in data mining, or as geopolitical chips. See Chaudhary "Sustaining What?..."

[46] David Neilson and Thomas Stubbs, "Relative Surplus Population and Uneven Development in the Neoliberal Era: Theory and Empirical Application," *Capital and Class* 35, no. 3 (2011): 444.

[47] Neilson and Stubbs, "Relative Surplus Population," 450.

[48] Neilson and Stubbs, "Relative Surplus Population," 450; this paragraph adapted from Chaudhary, *The Exhausted of the Earth*, unpublished manuscript.

[49] See also Jason Hickel and Giorgios Kallis, "Is Green Growth Possible?," *New Political Economy* 25, no. 4 (2020): 469–86; Chaudhary, "Sustaining What?..."

suspension or caution toward praxis in favor of exclusively seeking out semi-autonomous spaces for critical reason, when one imagines that the catastrophe is likely to be nuclear annihilation between superpowers. But when the domination of nature is so intense, so exhaustive that it threatens to foreclose the very latent possibilities for an emancipated society that critical theory predicated itself on, it is impossible to avoid embracing a *political* reversal of the dialectic of Enlightenment. Even Marcuse's more optimistic embrace of the New Left reflected a relation to a politics that is different from the organic crises (in the Gramscian sense) produced through the intertwined global economic slowdown and anthropogenic climate change and the legitimation crises (in the Habermasian, as corrected by Fraser, sense) that crisscross the world. As Przeworski concludes:

> Socialism may perhaps become possible but only on the condition that the movement for socialism regains the integral scope that characterized several of its currents outside the dogma of the Internationals, only on the condition that this movement ceases to make the socialist project conditional upon the continual improvement of material conditions of the working class. It may become possible when socialism once again becomes a social movement and not solely an economic one, when it learns from the women's movement, when it reassimilates cultural issues.[50]

As a host of theorists on the left—from Fraser to Mark Fisher—have argued, the failure to construct this broader social movement is one of the most recent, great historical missed opportunities. Although a left-wing climate realism may fall short of what some imagine socialism to be, it faces this challenge no less. Marxists risk making the same error that was made during this last major phase of capitalist *social* crisis in the Global North in the late 1960s and early 1970s, during the end of the so-called thirty glorious years in the developed Global North. Much of the "traditional" Marxist left were wary of new social movements and a historical opportunity was missed. But as we will examine more closely in looking at the case of Davis and Adorno, critical theory engendered a space within Marxian theory for not only the domination of nature but for different modes of social domination in capitalism understood as an "ensemble of social relations"—a space that proved *popular* and attractive to the very same social movements held at best at arm's length by Marxist "orthodoxy." It additionally provoked and prompted a much needed further critical analysis.

---

[50] Przeworski, *Capitalism and Social Democracy*, 248. It is clear these outside currents refer to Lenin and Marcuse—once again suggesting, as I will explore, a radical remapping of how we understand developments in historical materialism.

At the same time, the precise kind of political project abjured by the most famous theorists of the Frankfurt School is now unavoidable. It is not the political project, though, that is the question at hand here. Rather, whither critical theory? In order to answer this, we must push further into the methodology of critical theory—itself an extension of Marx's own method understood as an "open science"—in general and in the particular context of ecology. Above all we must reconsider critical theory in the era of ecological crisis, destabilizing political orders, *global* movement resurgence, inequality, and immiseration. These were not the conditions for the formulation of Marxism or for early Frankfurt School arguments. How do these conditions inform new directions for critique, challenge previous theoretical assumptions, and open up new possibilities—new not only for theory, but indeed for how we understand domination and imagine emancipation itself? In the next two sections, I will outline the methodological foundations of a renewed critical theory and its particular relevance for elaborating a historically situated emancipation in a moment of ongoing and accelerating ecological catastrophe.

POLITICAL TIME, ECOLOGY, AND CRITICAL THEORY

There has probably never been a political time that simultaneously underscores many of the most important (and most controversial) arguments of critical theory while at the same time calling the entire project into question. Progress today is ecological crisis, the proliferation of means of coercion, a world perfectly attuned to the needs of an "always-on" capitalism; progress in a world in which capital and empire can deliver a predator drone or a cruise missile in mere minutes but whose public health infrastructures leave literally millions on death's door as if 1918 were *really* just yesterday. Patriarchy, racialized violence, intra- and international caste systems, and the domination of nature are the order of the day.[51] The critique of instrumental reason has proved catastrophically true. Progress and regress are dialectical partners with no particular vector. As even critics of Frankfurt School theory concede, arguments, aphorisms, and theoretical concepts from classical critical theory are quite literally unavoidable in ecosocialist writing and others engaged with climate crisis.

The ecological poses a particularly acute challenge. It is unsurprising when a leading ecological Marxist like Andreas Malm cites Benjamin or Theodor Adorno as key points of theoretical reference in explicating a Marxist

---

[51] Ajay Singh Chaudhary, "Not in This."

ecology.⁵² Not only are Frankfurt School thinkers often noted for an early focus on the domination and destruction of nature as paradigmatic of capitalist modernity; all ecological social thought has to contend with classic critical theoretical propositions like the critiques of progress, questions regarding agency, and how to understand technology.

Climate change does not pose "the apocalypse" in the sense of extinction.⁵³ For all but the most ideologically blinkered, it does mean calling into question the sweeping idea of progress in its liberal Hegelian or Marxian modes. It means a window is rapidly closing that critical theorists (and most Marxists among others) always thought remained open—that a more reasonable society predicated on mass flourishing was possible. Critical theoretical challenges to the "who" of political thought are *sharpened* by climate change. As Malm notes, the idea of predicating climate politics on the exact same revolutionary horizon as that of traditional Marxism is just as insane as liberal apologetics for capitalism as we know it. The idea that the world revolution will come, will come *now*, and will come *before* climate politics, completely misunderstands both the history of socialist struggle⁵⁴ and the temporal implications of even the most filtered and mollified contemporary climate science consensus. Technology can neither be forsworn nor upheld as a utopian foundation. "No universal history leads from savagery to humanitarianism, but there is one leading from the slingshot to the atom bomb."⁵⁵ Capitalism has furnished the world not with the technological capacity to *finally* achieve socialism but with an ecological niche technologically adapted to its own needs.

I am interested here in considering critical theory as a methodology well suited for understanding the full scope of the contemporary conditions of climate change, and for providing a critical and scientifically literate account that is the basis for a *politics* of climate change. Indeed, as I have argued elsewhere, within both natural and social sciences that are *not* critical theories or built around any notion of radical politics at all, there is something which I will call here a kind of intuitive critical theory.⁵⁶ One finds this particularly in the climate sciences, ecological economics, and some forms of interdisciplinary sustainability studies. The realities of ecology and climate change tend to pull these inquires toward broadly systemic analyses, to models of

---

⁵² See Malm, *Fossil Capital*, last chapter, as well as Andreas Malm, *The Progress of This Storm: Nature and Society in a Warming World* (New York/London: Verso, 2020) and *Corona, Climate, Chronic Emergency: War Communism in the Twenty-First Century* (New York/London: Verso, 2020).
⁵³ This is commonly acknowledged in the natural scientific literature. See Rockström et al., "operating space" for just one example.
⁵⁴ See Przeworski, *Capitalism and Social Democracy*.
⁵⁵ Theodor Adorno, *Negative Dialectics*, trans. E.B. Ashton (New York/London: Continuum, 2007), 320.
⁵⁶ Chaudhary, "Sustaining What?..."

social-natural interaction, and, indeed, to models of the domination of the Earth system by social and specifically socio-economic activity. Although certainly not across the board, many also, because of the very subject matter, smuggle in some approximate "emancipatory" notion, although most commonly a kind of straightforward maximizing utilitarianism.

Elsewhere I have looked at some of these studies in more technical depth,[57] but the question at hand here is one of methodology and interdisciplinary practice. I don't call these intuitive critical theories because they already have all the answers or that there is nothing to critique (indeed, many of these studies contain questions and assumptions drawn over from hegemonic *non-scientific* liberal culture). Quite often climate scientists will solicit some sort of interdisciplinary assistance in developing more comprehensively the necessarily social aspects of ecology, particularly as regards climate change. To this urgent need, I want instead to highlight the complementary nature of a reconstituted or reconsidered critical theory.

One of the most cited interdisciplinary papers in serious work on climate adaptation and mitigation, "A Good Life for All within Planetary Boundaries,"[58] is an example of what I am calling an intuitive critical theory, now understood in even *more* materialist terms. In it, the authors demonstrate that meeting "basic needs"—"nutrition, sanitation, access to energy, and elimination of poverty"—can be achieved within planetary boundaries, but that "more qualitative goals (that is, life satisfaction, healthy life expectancy, secondary education, democratic quality, social support, and equality)" exceed planetary boundaries per capita by two to six times.[59] There is nothing wrong with the science the paper works with; it need not be grounded in some way in "dialectical materialism," as some Marxists claim. Furthermore, there is nothing wrong with its social scientific statistical methods: the authors try to account for the way wealthy countries almost certainly skew the data; they remove statistical outliers; they use the lowest level of biophysical resource use for each social indicator, in an attempt to balance the calculations, and so on. The authors seem to understand—without explicitly saying it—that the "improvements in social provisioning" they propone are almost certainly at odds with capitalism, at least in any recognizable form.

Many of the studies *already* acknowledge the limitations of a scientistic approach and even a broader epistemic humility about natural science

---

[57] Chaudhary "Sustaining What?..." and "It's Already Here"; see also Ajay Singh Chaudhary, "The Extractive Circuit," in *The Exhausted of the Earth* (unpublished manuscript).
[58] Daniel O'Neill et al., "A Good Life for All within Planetary Boundaries," *Nature Sustainability* 1 (2018); see also already mentioned McPhearson et al., "Radical Changes," Steffen et al., "Trajectories," Rockström et al., "Operating Space" for other examples within climate science alone. For a fuller discussion, see Chaudhary "Sustaining What?..."
[59] O'Neill et al., "A Good Life."

altogether. Many already evince the material conditions which limit their own production and question the suppositions of positivistic *social* science that seem at odds with the intuitive critical theory nascent within this mode of natural scientific inquiry. A reconstituted critical theoretical approach would have to take all of this into account, and go further: what such a critical theory suggests is the active formulation and direction of new areas of inquiry, new questions, and new interpretative frameworks for the further production of natural scientific research, especially as arise out of contradictions within the data already produced. It would point to the dialectical nature of the "metabolism" Marx notes between society and nature, as well as give an account of "social totality" based in Marxian political economy though understood as necessarily involving multiple modes of domination. What is at stake is neither an answer nor a complete picture, but the recognition of the methodological need for synthesizing further understandings and experiences of social domination far beyond the initial Critical Theoretical project, and integrating multiple formal disciplines.[60]

In more specific terms, taking "A Good Life..." as an example, such a methodology might entail thinking how, even after removing outliers, Vietnam stands out as meeting several social goals at costs out of line with the medians calculated. Other historical instances might be suggested to create a set for study. Indeed, history overall, as understood in historical materialist terms, is an invaluable resource for further natural scientific research. One such case: the Indian state of Kerala (which I have discussed elsewhere[61]) for most of the second half of the twentieth century achieved *all* (and more) of the social goals discussed by the authors of "A Good Life..."—and it did so at resource use nowhere near the median rates and with extremely low to no growth rates, such that it was once touted as a wholly alternative development model. Another: the case of Cuba after the fall of the Soviet Union (much discussed in agroecological literature[62]), and so on.[63] How can we understand this variance? Researchers might consider how to assess resource costs that are clearly historically dynamic where they only appear static—*not* because

---

[60] I have already discussed later feminist work but am thinking here also of, say, World-Systems Theory, Eco-Marxism, or anthropologies of technology, critical race theory, and so on.

[61] See Chaudhary, "Climate of Socialism"; Chaudhary, *The Exhausted of the Earth*.

[62] See for example, Miguel Altieri and Peter Rosset, *Agroecology: Science and Politics* (Winnipeg: Fernwood, 2017) or Max Ajl, "The Hypertrophic City versus The Planet of Fields," in *Implosions/Explosions: Towards a Study of Planetary Urbanization*, ed. Neil Brenner (Berlin: JOVIS, 2014), 533–50.

[63] See Patrick Heller, *The Labour of Development: Workers and the Transformations of Capitalism in Kerala, India* (Ithaca: Cornell University Press, 1999) and some of the classic works of Amartya Sen and Jean Dreze. It is notable that in practical political terms, the ecological Black radical communism of an organization like Cooperation Jackson looks to this as one of their models. See also Kali Akuno and Ajamu Nangwaya, eds., *Jackson Rising: The Struggle for Economic Democracy and Black Self-Determination in Jackson, Mississippi* (Cantley, QC: Daraja Press, 2017).

of natural forces independent of society (planetary boundaries themselves, overshoots, the fundamental ecological characteristics of the Anthropocene, etc. are not in need of "dialectical" intervention) but because society, and its metabolic relation with nature, conceived within the broader model as having "natural laws," has been reified. A grounding in Marxian political economy is explicitly about denaturalizing the supposedly "natural laws" of human society. In addition, it brings the question of power within the frame explicitly. To use two frequently cited examples: it is not just that climate change leads to environmental racism, or that climate change, filtered through existing international inequality, impacts geographies which had the least to do with it. It is *also* that radical domination and an unequal world system are *drivers* of climate change. Ecological economics—one of the disciplines represented in "A Good Life…"—has already done pathbreaking work in thinking through energy across nature and society. Critical theory should encourage a systemization of this approach—"for it regards all such abuses as necessarily connected with the way in which the social structure is organized"[64]—but with particular attention to the many related dominations in today's "ensemble of social relations." Put more simply, this is a question of the incompatibility of capitalism as we know it with necessary climate mitigation and adaptation measures, but more fundamentally, this is actually about how capitalism is a system which *needs* exploitation, expropriation, extraction, and exhaustion (and in the vicious cycle of the extractive circuit creates greater such need in social and ecological terms). In simpler cases, critical theory can help research move away from questions that produce paradoxes (already often identified in the literatures) and toward questions in concord with what the already implicit emancipatory interest within these intuitive critical theories might demand.

The goal is to understand the potential roles of a reconstituted critical theory in an era in which the critique of progress itself *demands* unflinching political action. One of the co-authors of "A Good Life…," Julia Steinberger, also co-authored the recent interdisciplinary paper "Scientists' Warning on Affluence," which argues that the consumption of the global affluent accounts for most environmental degradation.[65] Steinberger also co-authored "Roots, Riots, and Radical Change,"[66] which explicitly calls for Marxian political economy as the best unifying methodology for ecological economics. While the former article contains equivocation and even a review of multiple

---

[64] Max Horkheimer, *Critical Theory: Selected Essays* (New York: Continuum, 2002), 207.
[65] Thomas Wiedmann et al., "Scientists' Warning on Affluence," *Nature Communications* 11, no. 3107 (2020): 1–10. Again a common argument in climate science work. See the extremely influential studies of Kevin Anderson and Alice Bowes for another example.
[66] Elke Pirgmaier and Julia K. Steinberger, "Roots, Riots, and Radical Change—A Road Less Travelled for Ecological Economics," *Sustainability* 11, no. 7 (2019): 1–18.

mainstream and radical approaches (and is authored by both natural and social scientists), the latter is unequivocal but exclusively about ecological economics. In this case, an intuitive critical theory has, at the very least, some non-intuitive roots in Marx's critical theory. Critical theory *needs* natural scientific inquiry, ecological economics, and other interdisciplinary studies—and *needs* as well precisely the kind of work that Steinberger argues for. Likewise, it can *assist* or at least be in conversation with research in wholly different methodologies.

One clear model for this kind of approach is in *The Authoritarian Personality* and the *Studies in Prejudice* in general, particularly in the way that Eric Oberle describes it as prompting the successful further development of a critical theory enriched by American empirical methods and "transforming"—at least for a time—key theoretical concepts for American social science.[67] Another example is actually Marx's *Capital* itself, which drew extensively on the "bourgeois" sciences of its day. Another is Andreas Malm's work, which not only openly draws on classic critical theory—Benjamin's arguments are frequent reference points and frameworks, while Malm at one point calls Adorno "the greatest thinker of the twentieth century"—but displays this mode of ecumenicism in bringing together different methodological approaches, from the natural sciences, to eco-Marxism, ecological economics, history of science, etc.[68] Critical theory reconstituted cannot supply every answer, and other approaches (from *buen vivir* to ecofeminism) offer key components of an analysis (and of a political project). Critical theory can serve, beyond its own analytic frames, this kind of methodological suture. This is about praxis, albeit not of a political kind. As McKenzie Wark puts it, praxis implies creating "the space within which very

---

[67] Eric Oberle, *Theodor Adorno and the Century of Negative Identity* (Stanford: Stanford University Press, 2018), 109; Oberle points out it was in not only the phenomenon and experience of nationalist chauvinism and then Nazi anti-semitism and "race science" that pushed critical theorists to engage with the question of racial domination. The more sophisticated critiques that one finds in post-1944 work—take, for example, the "Elements of Anti-Semitism" section in the *Dialectic of Enlightenment*, the "Melange" essay from *Minima Moralia* and perhaps most importantly the whole *Studies in Prejudice* series as well as *The Authoritarian Personality*—were the results of theoretical limitations but also the encounter with American racism and catching up with "African American theorists' discovery of the political importance of negating negative identity." Oberle, *Theodor Adorno*, 66–67.

[68] As I will return to later, I don't think it a small matter that particularly compelling imagery, crafted *precisely* to provoke critical thought in early critical theory, appears, for example, in the title to Malm's *The Progress of the Storm* and as calling cards throughout. Or, similarly, when Malm's frequent writing partner, the anthropologist Alf Hornburg, ends his framing for *The Power of the Machine* with a programmatic reference to *The Dialectic of Enlightenment*. Malm's critiques of object-oriented ontology and so-called radical ecology are biting but almost certainly warranted. But, in a case like the debate with Jason Moore, one can in fact usefully pry Moore's arguments about for example "Cheap Food" from within his larger philosophical framework.

different kinds of knowledge and practice might meet."[69] A critical theory reconstituted as I have been describing it takes as it were a "comradely" approach to the natural sciences (and natural scientists!).

While eco-Marxism continues to produce vital concepts, analyses, and interventions—for example, John Bellamy Foster's elaborations on "metabolic rift" or Richard York's engagement with Jevon's Paradox—as a school it has rejected critical theory on several grounds. Without engaging in a long philosophical excursus, the eco-Marxist critique of critical theory boils down to several claims. The first is Marxological; critical theorists misunderstood Marx's initial engagements with the natural sciences of his day. This is broadly correct, although it should be noted that their principle case—Alfred Schmidt—actually wrote quite extensively on this engagement and in fact was one of the first to highlight Marx's concept of metabolism. However, Marxology is mostly irrelevant here.[70] Second is the philosophical claim that there should be a properly dialectical science. If such a claim truly means dialectics inhere in nature across the board and that a dialectical science can negate principle natural scientific claims, then Foster et al. actually run afoul of the very definition of Lysenkoism that some of their preferred natural scientific models—biologists Richard Lewontin and Richard Levins—propose.[71] Since this is almost certainly not the case, then, as various scholars like Deborah Cook and Carl Cassegård argue, the methodology being called for is *actually* already the "critical materialism" of the Frankfurt School. As Cook puts it, Foster "seems to ally Marx much more closely with Adorno than even Adorno thinks."[72] Third is the claim that it contains no explicit ecological science. Again, this is clearly true, but the goal of a reconstituted critical theory would be to cultivate a critical mode that faces empirical realities without reifying them. When we think about the necessary engagement with already existing climate science—already "intuitively" emancipatory—this is a feature, not a bug. As Cassegård notes, in the present conjuncture,

---

[69] Wark, *Molecular Red: Theory for the Anthropocene* (New York/London: Verso, 2015), xv. Wark doesn't have in mind the classic mode of critical theory but perhaps that's the point—this is about a reconstituted critical theory.

[70] Kohei Saito's *Karl Marx's Ecosocialism* is probably the best work of this nature as it not only is the most thorough in its engagement with Marx and his natural scientific influences but also in connecting them to live questions.

[71] Richard Lewontin and Richard Levins, "The Problem of Lysenkoism," in *The Radicalisation of Science* (London: Macmillan, 1976), 60: "dialectical materialism is not, and has never been, a programmatic method for the solution of particular physical problems. Rather, dialectical analysis provides us with an overview and a set of warning signs against particular forms of dogmatism and narrowness of thought . . . . 'Remember to pay attention to real objects in space and time and not lose them utterly in idealised abstractions'; 'Remember that qualitative effects of context and interaction may be lost when phenomena are isolated'; and above all else; 'Remember that all the other caveats are only reminders and warning signs whose application to different circumstances of the real world is contingent.' To attempt to do more and to try to distinguish competing theories of physical events, or to discredit a physical theory by contradiction, is a hopeless task".

[72] Deborah Cook, *Adorno on Nature* (New York/London: Routledge, 2011).

Foster's arguments amount to a call for confrontation with the already existing sciences.[73]

Finally, eco-Marxists contend that critical theory alienates scientists. This is an empirical question, and brings us back to debates over the New Left. In fact, much of the initial environmentalist social movements *were* informed by critical theory. Donna Haraway writing in 1975 notes that "fundamental to the development of the new scientific left" have been the theoretical ideas of "contemporary critics of the ideology of scientific rationality"—namely Marcuse, the early Habermas, and Marcuse-influenced Theodore Roszak.[74] One of the specific organizations she examines is Science for the People:

> Scientists and Engineers for Social and Political Action (SESPA) grew out of the failure of the approaches of groups like UCS in the physics community to persuade the professional scientific societies to take overt political stands on the Vietnam War. The founders of SESPA were largely physicists; they began organizing in early 1969, and by late 1969 the magazine Science for the People began to appear bimonthly. Membership came to include many biologists and engineers.[75]

Science for the People, first as magazine and then organization, quite literally nurtured the very scientists like Lewontin and Levins that eco-Marxists cite as examples of dialectical materialist science. References to Adorno, Marcuse, Horkheimer are all found in its archives.[76] Comparing—cautiously—Old and New Left formations, Haraway argues that SEPSA and then Science for the

---

[73] Cassegård, Carl. "Eco-Marxism and the Critical Theory of Nature: Two Perspectives on Ecology and Dialectics," *Distinktion: Journal of Social Theory* 18, no. 3 (2017): 314–32.

[74] Donna Haraway, "The Transformation of the Left in Science: Radical Associations in Britain in the 30s and the U.S.A. in the 60s," *Surroundings: An Interdisciplinary Journal* 58, no. 4 (Winter 1975): 449; just a few years later, in 1978, E.O. Wilson would lament the influence of critical theory (and scientists like Steven Jay Gould) as having a pernicious influence in garnering pushback against his right-wing, deterministic sociobiology which continues to promote eugenicist, patriarchal, and racist influence to this day. See Wilson, "The Attempt to Suppress Human Behavioral Genetics," *J Gen Educ* 29, no. 4 (Winter 1980): 277–87.

[75] Haraway, "The Transformation of the Left," 453–54.

[76] Similarly, Foster cites the ecofeminism of Ariel Sallah as among the only other proper approaches to ecological critique (Foser, *Marx's Ecology: Materialism and Nature*. New York: Monthly Review Press, 2000). But Sallah argues of her own approach: "My own ecofeminist understanding of instrumental reason crystallised while reading the neo-Marxist analysis of the Frankfurt School. The 'perpetual internal conquest of the lower faculties' which had marked eurocentric culture since classical Greece was a preoccupation of Max Horkheimer, Theodor Adorno, and Herbert Marcuse. They saw the Enlightenment image of science as command of disenchanted nature paving the way for detached rational manipulation of matter. The Industrial Revolution, by providing a sophisticated machinery for the exploitation of natural and human resources, soon propelled the dream of mastery forward under the banner of 'development.'" Sallah, *Ecofeminism as Politics: Nature, Marx and the Postmodern* (London: Zed Books, 1997), 58.

People were an explicitly Marxist organization, "replete with participatory democracy, feminism," and showing constant concern with "militarism, sexism, racism, and imperialism." In contrast to the hippies-vs-hardhats myth that plagues contemporary ecological critique, this New Left formation was committed, Haraway notes, to being an anti-imperialist organization based on a class analysis of all workers, but comprised of scientific workers, and coordinating activities with worker organizations.[77] Organizations like Science for the People proved far more open not only to engaging other modes of domination but also to arguing scientific cases using social and political remedies rather than technical ones. It turned a theoretically informed critical scientific gaze at supposed technological progress, and saw the damage it was doing in ecological, political economic, gendered, racialized, and imperialist terms.[78]

Haraway's caution is predicated on how critique can be subsumed, whether in the Old or New Left.[79] She argues, nevertheless, that the latter is generally more fruitful in developing a total analysis and in popularizing radical ideals. More to the point: the strange idea that critical theory is somehow anti-science and alienating to scientists is belied in Haraway's mostly forgotten early analysis. Foster et al. posit that critical theory lacks the ability to address climate crisis. What we see here is, rather, that critical theory is called for, at least in terms of methodology. One of the papers discussed earlier, "Scientists' Warning on Affluence," ends with a series of open-ended questions: about alternative visions for sustainable life within planetary boundaries; about social change; about institutions and cultural barriers; and about learning from societies that were not predicated on economic growth.[80]

This opens a different way in which a reconstituted critical theory has precisely what is needed for a socio-ecological critique of capital in the twenty-first century. These are questions about mediation, culture, power, and a kind of negative utopia—they reflect precisely the lateral move of an emancipatory climate politics, a left-wing climate realism. It involves the

---

[77] Haraway, "The Transformation of the Left," 454.
[78] Haraway, "The Transformation of the Left," 454; as my colleague Alyssa Battistoni has suggested, there is an oversimplification in the political theory of contemporary ecological Marxism, particularly when we take ecological and social reproductive questions seriously: "We should see workers performing the work of social and ecological reproduction, whether for wages or not, as workers who can form part of the political force for left climate programs. Yet the disjuncture between the sites of militant labour struggle and the sites of capital accumulation that I have just described is likely to produce new contradictions as the former build power." "Making a Living," 193–194. In Battistoni's analysis, we see another example of the limitations of dogmatic Marxist axioms as they run into the twin problems of radically changed historical conditions and new concepts—in this case, not only a socio-ecological critique but also an accounting for how such critique is predicated on more contemporary historical materialist analyses of social reproduction.
[79] Perhaps prefiguring her later work on subjectivity as in the *Cyborg Manifesto*, she is correctly insisting on a necessary political continuity between these formations—not a rejection of New Left perspectives to "recover" some kind of lost Marxist truth.
[80] Wiedmann et al., "Scientists' Warning on Affluence."

determinate negation of present conditions as they are actually constituted, in favor of the enabling conditions for a sustainable global ecological niche so that some 7–9 billion people may flourish. As Malm puts it, comparing the place of climate change today to Auschwitz in Adorno's thought: "The warming condition spells the death of affirmative politics."[81] Invoking Benjamin's destructive character, "whose deepest emotion is an insuperable mistrust in the course of things,"[82] and reflecting on Adorno's claim that "progress in controlling nature may increasingly help to weave the very calamity it is supposed to protect us from," Malm concludes another work (while quoting Horkheimer): "Likewise, every concrete measure proposed here and by many others for coming to terms with nature and ending the 'boundless imperialism' against it may well be brushed aside as utopian. They are exactly as utopian as survival."[83]

It is the critique of the concept of progress that makes emancipatory socio-ecological analysis possible. It helps produce the methodological possibilities discussed here, the social openness discussed before, and enables a mode of utopianism we are currently observing and will return to in the conclusion. The critique of the concept of progress reorients us toward the past geologically, including in human history, to search for elements which can constitute an ecologically sound notion of freedom today, an emancipation in which "human beings become conscious of their own naturalness and call a halt to their domination of nature, a domination by means of which nature's own domination is perpetuated. In this sense, we might say that progress occurs where it comes to an end."[84] It is the particular relation to progress, history, and domination that gives a reconstituted critical theory abilities to answer the questions posed above.

It can, in newer and *more* critical hands, elaborate a critique open to multiple modes of fundamentally interconnected dominations, performing in this way a vital social function; but it does not *produce* a politics.

BETWEEN THE SCHOLAR AND THE TECHNICIAN: FRANKFURT SCHOOL "POLITICS"

The moment of the actualization of philosophy—that is to say, the moment of the world revolution—was "missed ... after the attempt to change the world

---

[81] Malm, *Progress of this Storm*.
[82] Malm, *Progress of this Storm*.
[83] Malm, *Corona, Climate, Chronic Emergency*.
[84] Theodor Adorno, *History and Freedom: Lectures 1964–1965*, ed. Rolf Tiedemann, trans. Rodney Livingstone (Cambridge, UK: Polity Press, 2006), 152.

miscarried."[85] As we've just seen, this observation is crucial for thinking socio-ecological critique today. This claim was, in origin though, a specific reaction to the First World War. A fairly conventional reading of Marx, especially alongside the corrective and globalizing work of Rosa Luxemburg, Lenin, and others on the question of imperialism and the role of colonies in the perpetuation of crisis-prone capitalism, seemed for many Marxist intellectuals and political actors across Europe to be playing out in the advent of a war between the competing bourgeois, imperialist powers.[86] The contradictions of this "late" stage of capitalism seemed poised to bring about the end of pre-history; conditions were precisely what had been predicted. The moment for revolution had arrived. But the solidarity of the Second International failed. With a few notable exceptions (not least the Bolsheviks), not only did most socialist parties either capitulate to or join the war effort, but, to varying degrees, masses across Europe swung toward their respective nationalist causes. Furthermore, the Bolshevik revolution—which could be seen as the course correction back to the initial missed moment—failed to spark a world revolution. And in the wake of catastrophic war and revolutionary impasse, new political movements, in particular fascism, offered a new kind of modern, mass politics.

Both this relation to WWI and the parallels noted earlier between not only Bolshevism but many Marxisms *outside* the European frame suggest a fairly different mapping of "Western Marxism" than what Perry Anderson argues for in *Considerations on Western Marxism*. Rather, there are plural splits all pivoting on whether WWI and the failure of world revolution as predicted required critique of what was dogmatic, lacking, or incomplete in Marxism or whether it was simply a stage or bump in the road to the ongoing development of the Marxist project. In this way, critical theory—despite its political paralyses—is better understood as fundamentally similar to Leninism, Maoism, and a wide range of anti-colonial Marxisms in the Global South in seeing Marxism as requiring not modest but fundamental revision (even if many would argue that theirs was the "real" Marxism).[87] In addition to other parallels, it is of course obvious that while, say, Bolshevism turned to working out this dilemma in, eventually, geopolitical logics, critical theory (with Benjamin possibly excepted, at least in theory) turned exclusively to

---

[85] Adorno, *Negative Dialectics*, 3.
[86] This was of course *not* the position embraced by Kautsky et al., who embraced an expansive, paternalistic imperialism in line with the professed ideals of their respective national-imperial bourgeoisies.
[87] Although I have previously pursued a similar line in my comparison of Walter Benjamin and Jalal Al-e Ahmad (and, as a shadow case, Adorno and Ali Shariati), I am far from alone in noting this affinity. For just two examples, see Susan Buck-Morss, *Thinking Past Terror: Islamism and Critical Theory on the Left* and Christian Fuchs, "M. N. Roy and the Frankfurt School."

both critique and reformulation. There were actually a broad range of politics throughout the Frankfurt School but none logically flowed from its analyses.

One place to see the paradoxes of critical theory and politics is in the encounter between Adorno and Angela Davis. Adorno famously disagreed with Davis on her plan to abandon a dissertation project with Adorno in Germany to return to the United States and engage in political activism, but he nonetheless assisted her in securing a formal university position studying with his former Institute for Social Research colleague, Herbert Marcuse.[88] Disappointed, Adorno would compare her shift from philosophy to active politics derisively—to his mind—as akin to shifting from being a "media studies scholar" to a "radio technician."[89] In contrast, Davis argued that "my ability to accomplish anything was directly dependent on my ability to contribute something concrete to the struggle."[90]

It can be easy to mythologize or dismiss this minor anecdote. It accurately reflects the distance that, in this case, Adorno saw between critical theory at that moment and political possibility. But there was hardly a unified politics within the Frankfurt School. It is unquestionably the case that Horkheimer grew increasingly conservative over the course of his life and particularly after the Second World War. Someone like Franz Neumann was a young participant in the 1919 revolution before joining the SPD later in the Weimar period as a constant critic from its left. Similarly, Otto Kirchheimer was a member of the German Communist Party (KPD) in the 1920s and 1930s. After the war, Neumann would argue quite differently from Horkheimer for a mode of political Spinozism "as a theory of an opposition that feels its strength and that hopes soon to transform its social power into political power."[91] Marcuse was also a participant in the Spartacist uprising and of course famously after the war was a well-known supporter of the various movements of the New Left. Benjamin—who relished the Nazi-imposed label of "Cultural Bolshevik"—famously never joined any party but in all his mature work expressed an open communism in a Marxist-Leninist mode.[92] None of this implies that critical theory, though, had or has a single cogent politics.

At the same time, the Davis/Adorno episode is incredibly instructive. The critical theorist today must be *both* a "media studies scholar" and a "radio

---

[88] Angela Y. Davis, *Angela Davis: An Autobiography* (New York: Random House, 1974), 145.
[89] Angela Y. Davis, "Marcuse's Legacies," in *Herbert Marcuse: A Critical Reader*, ed. John Abromeit and W. Mark Cobb (New York/London: Routledge, 2003), 8.
[90] Angela Davis, "Marcuse's Legacies," 8.
[91] Franz Neumann, "Change in the Function of Law in Modern Society," in *The Democratic and the Authoritarian State*, ed. Herbert Marcuse, trans. Peter Gay (New York: The Free Press, 1964), 104.
[92] See innumerable essays, but specifically the letter from Benjamin to Max Rychner, 1934, in *The Correspondence of Walter Benjamin*, 372–73.

technician." This is not an argument against some kind of division of labor but rather that present conditions require more than the studied distance many early Frankfurt School theorists employed in regard to practical political activity. A few could be considered engaged in the kind of explicit politics that Davis was, from the Black Panthers, the Communist Party, and later to prison abolition and Palestine solidarity movements. Davis is of course not alone in this; may others engaged in active political life while also continuing some practice of critical theory.[93] But Davis does provide something of a model; while she knew her political activity marked a break with some aspects of the critical theoretical "tradition," she simultaneously embraced not only the fundamental methodological foundations of critical theory but also engaged in theorization and critique from (and often toward) precisely the space of semi-autonomy that first-generation Frankfurt School theorists valorized.

In works like her *Blues Legacies and Black Feminism*,[94] Davis would argue for example—perhaps ironically given Adorno's famous aversion to popular music and jazz—that Black music was precisely the kind of quasi-autonomous space from which a radical aesthetic, however incomplete, was possible. At the same time, these quasi-autonomous spaces do not escape the social totality of capitalism; the Black spiritual might have served as space for social critique and fleeting relief from the relentless domination of slavery, but it also became an institution for modes of Black political quiescence and conservatism. She characterizes the blues as a kind of collective avant-garde alighting on the aesthetic question that animated both Benjamin and Adorno: the activity and passivity of the audience and, therein, the possibilities of generating political consciousness.[95] She engages Marcuse's "aesthetic dimension" but she historicizes it in an Adornian mode.[96] The music of Billie Holiday reflects the unreality of the real. Through artifice it performs the distortion and suppression of actual possibilities in social life. In it, "political agency"—in this case, that of Black women—"is nurtured by, and in turn, nurtures aesthetic agency."[97] Her critique is—although of course not exclusively—a critical continuation, expansion, and redefinition of critical theory.

---

[93] In my own understanding of critical theory, Habermas' work from the mid-70s onward is no longer critical theory in any sense of the word, since those works no longer ascribe to any of the key methodological or substantive lineaments. However, earlier works such as *The Structural Transformation of the Public Sphere* or *Legitimation Crisis* are clearly within that tradition.

[94] Angela Y. Davis, *Blues Legacies and Black Feminism: Gertrude "Ma" Rainey, Bessie Smith, and Billie Holiday* (New York: Vintage Books, 1999).

[95] Angela Y. Davis, "I Used to be Your Sweet Mama," in *Blues Legacies,* footnote 10; see also Raymond Guess, *Idea of a Critical Theory: Habermas and the Frankfurt School* (Cambridge, UK: Cambridge University Press, 1981), 63, for how this is a particularly Adornian move.

[96] See Davis, *Blues Legacies.*

[97] Davis, *Blues Legacies,* 164.

Although Davis drew her political praxis from the Panthers and the Communist Party, she saw the value in the kind of work critical theory is capable of. What's more, her political activism *spurred* her interest, even as she was initially drawn to critical theory for its own complementary radicalities. Not only does she not "denounce" critical theory or refrain from drawing on other "heterodox" influences and arguments, her political point of view is advanced through the active engagement of theory. Further, Davis does not choose to ignore the realities that critical theory sought to explicate. For example, while discussing the relations between gender, race, capital, and the family, Davis recapitulates (and develops) the cornerstone of Frankfurt School pessimism:

> A progressively increasing fragmentation among human beings has accompanied an ever more developed capitalism. In the era of advanced capitalism, the insularity is virtually complete. A salient example can be seen in the recently escalated flight toward the suburbs. Workers, especially white workers, have also joined in this exodus. The closed-in cubicle-like housing is a material extension of the ever-increasing distance which dissevers them from their fellow producers . . . . The worker must thus surmount many insurmountable barriers before he can become aware that he and all other producers are the wellspring of the society. The achievement of solidarity, thus of a revolutionary class consciousness, has never been so difficult as during the present era.[98]

Davis emphasizes how little access people have to "objective" social reality. This is not elitist dismissal but reckoning with the world of actually existing capitalism. Here, Davis talks about the reification of individuals including, but not limited to, the proletariat. Through a mediation that is near total and an "insularity" that is "virtually complete," capital has integrated the potential political force that Marxist theory had proposed would be its undoing. Pessimism, though, needn't be attached to practical paralysis. In a 1995 interview, Davis elaborates:

> Studying with both Adorno and Marcuse allowed me to think early on about the relationship between theory and practice, between intellectual work and activist work. Adorno tended to dismiss intellectual work that was connected with political activism. He argued that the revolution had failed, not so much because of problems presenting themselves in the practical implementation of revolutionary theory, but rather because the theory itself was flawed, perhaps even fundamentally flawed. He therefore insisted that the only sure way to move

---

[98] Angela Y. Davis, *The Angela Y. Davis Reader*, ed. Joy James (Malden, MA/Oxford, UK: Blackwell Publishers, 1998), 181–82.

along a revolutionary continuum was to effect, for the present, a retreat into theory . . . . Interestingly enough, many of Horkheimer's and Adorno's ideas were mobilized in challenging this advocacy of theory as the only possible mode of practice. I was involved, in fact, in the production of a pirate edition of *Dialectic of Enlightenment*, which Adorno and Horkheimer were not yet willing to republish. We typed the text on stencils, mimeographed it, and sold it for the cost of its production.[99]

Although it is widely known that she would eventually gravitate toward Marcuse, Davis' summary of Adorno's argument is remarkably similar to her own position. However, Davis' continued engagement with new modes of political praxis doesn't require his particular ascesis. She simply does not see the condition of failed revolution as justifying the claim that theory is the "*only* possible mode of practice."

Davis further distinguishes between the theorists and the theory. Adorno and even more so Horkheimer may have been troubled by the particular form of enthusiastic reception *Dialectic of Enlightenment* received among radicals, but this does not itself bare much relationship to the actual theory itself. One of the conceptual strengths of critical theory is that is has not—successful to its own program—inculcated a cult-of-the-master, hermeneutical stance. Davis has remarked that encountering Marcuse, and specifically reading Adorno and Horkheimer, not only encouraged her to study in Frankfurt but helped her recognize her own nascent radicalism as a young Black woman in the United States.[100] This is an archetypical example of how, not only in the socially popular and more empirically engaged forms, but even in its most maddeningly, seemingly inscrutable instantiations, Frankfurt School critical theory *worked*. Finally, critical theory opened up possibilities that seemed closed in traditional Marxism, even if it also demands its own radical reconsideration.

It did so not only for the students Davis discusses in the above comments. But rather, as she later put it:

Critical Theory, as formulated and founded by the Frankfurt School—which included Horkheimer and Marcuse—has as its goal the transformation of society, not simply of ideas, but social transformation and thus the reduction and elimination of human misery. It was on the basis of this insistence on the

---

[99] Angela Y. Davis, *Angela Davis Reader*, 317.
[100] Angela Y. Davis, *Angela Davis Reader*, 307.

social implementation of critical ideas that I was able to envision a relationship between philosophy and Black liberation.[101]

In confronting dogma within supposedly materialist Marxism, critical theory helped create space—akin to Frantz Fanon's arguments about the "stretching" of Marxism to fully address the possibility of decolonization—for new critique centered on other modes and forms of domination.

What Davis provides us, in addition to clarity around what critical theory can do and what indeed theory is for, is a kind of balancing act between the demands of critical theory and the realities of political practice. In contrast, Adorno was elusive in his commentary on current events and avoided direct political intervention. As with the episode with Davis, he maintained—perhaps to an almost hyperbolic level—the idea of critical theory's formal and political independence as paramount. Adorno saw his primary public intellectual role as pedagogical. Adorno was aghast to discover, upon his return to Germany, the generally "apolitical" attitude of students and even of society as a whole.[102] The shallow, pseudo-democratic present lightly painted over a repressed but ever-present fascist past. Through an engagement with mass media (particularly radio), Adorno was pivotal in reintroducing Marxism into general conversation as well as highlighting the fascist elements that permeated the nascent federal republic. Although we have already seen critical theory's origins in Benjamin, and systematic definitions in Horkheimer, it was Adorno in this period who crystalized both its more philosophical and avant-garde side in *Minima Moralia* as well as its more critical social scientific mode in a series of lectures and publications on sociology. Adorno's public intellectual work attracted vast interest among younger Germans, and particularly a broad social base of those uneasy about present German society.[103] Adorno's seminars overflowed even with some of the same students who would famously repudiate Adorno by the end of the 1960s. As Davis noted, there was simply no place "more conducive to philosophical studies" for people like her than Frankfurt in that era.[104]

In his 1968 lecture "Industrial Society or Late Capitalism?" Adorno delivered an uncharacteristically open discussion of the present situation for Marxism. Capitalism had not been replaced by some new, generic "industrial

---

[101] "Angela Y. Davis," in George Yancy, ed., *African-American Philosophers: 17 Conversations* (New York/London: Routledge, 1998), 22.
[102] Stefan Müller-Doohm, *Adorno: A Biography,* Part IV, trans. Rodney Livingstone (Cambridge, UK: Polity Press, 2005).
[103] Recall that Horkheimer tried to block Habermas' career on grounds of his being too politically radical; Adorno would not only help Habermas continue forward by recommending him to the more stringent Marxist scholar Wolfgang Abendroth, but he would invite figures like Abendroth and Marcuse to lecture at the Institute for Social Research.
[104] Davis, *Autobiography*, 145.

society," but rather an industrial society stamped with the characteristics of capitalist domination was the "means of production" that expressed "late capitalism's" underlying social structures.[105] "People are now totally controlled,"[106] far more than in Marx's day, and not simply the industrial proletariat but the whole of society, including intellectuals. While Adorno did not share a "thesis of the affluent society" as Marcuse did, he did think that general standards of living in what we would now call the Global North had rendered ever-present poverty—even when visible—ignorable, while capitalism in these geographies "has been strengthened by the process of integration."[107] In other words, if, in the developed world, state-managed capitalism could prevent "economic catastrophes," it could not prevent these myriad forms of "social enlightenment" from making demands which were no longer "utopian" concerning new forms of emancipation. At the same time, Adorno observed that "theories of imperialism have not been rendered obsolete by the great powers' withdrawal from their colonies."[108] Rather, imperialism lived on in the new global system and, Adorno speculated, "class relations were displaced onto the relations between the leading industrial states, on the one hand, and the vigorously courted underdeveloped nations, on the other."[109] Adorno, sadly, cuts himself off from this train of thought in which a *practical* politics of decolonization not only characterizes the question of emancipation in the Global South but increasingly, although differently, in the Global North as well.

Instead, Adorno returns to the theme of "the totality of the process of mediation" in which "no overall social subject exists."[110] Elsewhere Adorno discusses a possible "global subject" that in many ways takes the logic of self-preservation that had been so central to the *critique* in *Dialectic of Enlightenment* and redeems self-preservation not in an alienated individual but as a quality of a universal social subject. "The forms of humanity's own global societal consciousness threaten its life, if a self-conscious global subject does not develop and intervene. The possibility of progress, of averting the most extreme total disaster, has migrated to this global subject. "[111] This concept has proved tantalizing for ecologically minded theorists like Malm and Cook (and others), not only because of the way in which Adorno's description so well matches contemporary climate questions, but because

---

[105] Theodor Adorno, "Late Capitalism or Industrial Society?" in *Can One Live After Auschwitz?*
[106] Adorno, "Late Capitalism," 117.
[107] Adorno, "Late Capitalism," 118.
[108] Adorno, "Late Capitalism," 116.
[109] Adorno, "Late Capitalism," 117.
[110] Adorno, "Late Capitalism," 125.
[111] Theodor W. Adorno, *Critical Models: Interventions and Catchwords*, trans. Henry Pickford (New York: Columbia University Press, 1998), 144.

freedom is posited here precisely as that which is realized within the very real laws of nature. The idea of the "global subject" is bound within the very matrix of critical theory through negative dialectics. He even argues in *Negative Dialectics* that a practical task of critique is to foster "the idea of a solidarity transcending individual interests,"[112] even while the "global subject" is in no way a "collective" subject. It simultaneously shifts self-preservation to a self-conscious species level, but it is also comprised entirely of fully differentiated individuals. The whole conditionality of negative dialectics is foisted upon the "global subject" such that it is both a philosophical and political impossibility. What Adorno cannot grant—because it would indeed be brutal, instrumental practice—is that the "fear" he talks about is not a "universal feeling." Such feelings, as I have demonstrated elsewhere, are specifically *not* universally shared.[113] More simply, as he argues in the "Late Capitalism..." essay, no such subject seems apparent.

In private, Adorno was more politically adventurous. In the abortive project with Horkheimer now called *Towards a New Manifesto*,[114] Adorno openly advances the idea that a "new manifesto" should be "strictly Leninist," and remain faithful to "Marx, Engels, and Lenin" without conceding that theoretical ground to Stalinism. As we have seen, Adorno notes the affinity between early Bolshevik thought concerning subjectivity and critical theory, arguing that Lenin was the first to develop a deep theory of Marxist subjectivity that took the effects of capitalism on people "down to the very fibre of their being" seriously.[115] In lectures well toward the end of his life, Adorno would cite the inherent contradiction between formal democracy and economic and social domination, particularly around the ever-concentrating nature and power of capital, as a continuous foundation for fascist politics as well as holding back the inherent minimal emancipation possible within existing productive capacity.[116] And yet Adorno's critique cuts itself off from political praxis. As Buck-Morss notes: "In the name of revolution, thought could never acknowledge a revolutionary situation, in the name of utopia, it could never work for utopia's realization."[117] The conditions set on something like the global subject could never be met. Adorno was a Leninist without revolutionaries.

---

[112] Adorno, *Negative Dialectics*, 282.
[113] Ajay Singh Chaudhary, "Subjectivity, Affect, Exhaustion: The Political Theology of the Anthropocene," *Political Theology Network*, February 25, 2019.
[114] A project conversation recorded and transcribed by Gretel Adorno, a biologist turned essentially in-house editor, whose influence on critical theory is consistently underplayed.
[115] Adorno and Horkheimer, *Towards a New Manifesto*, 12.
[116] See Theodor Adorno, *Aspects of the New Right-Wing Extremism*, trans. Wieland Hoban (Cambridge, UK: Polity Press, 2020); Adorno, "Late capitalism."
[117] Susan Buck-Morss, *The Origin of Negative Dialectics: Theodor W. Adorno, Walter Benjamin, and the Frankfurt Institute* (New York: The Free Press, 1977), 187.

Adorno failed to see what Davis could: critical theory might be incapable of producing a politics, but this is not necessarily a bad thing. It can enhance or even set foundations for a different politics, all the while maintaining the possibility for the continued critique that was needed. Critical theory took many forms—the social scientific study, the philosophical treatise, the aphoristic fragment, or the explication of "the implacable logic of world historical disaster" which "is always counterposed... by the conviction that it could be otherwise."[118] The initial impetus for ideology critique has not vanished. As Geuss writes: "Critical Theory aims at emancipation and enlightenment, at making agents aware of hidden coercion, thereby freeing them from that coercion and putting them in a position to determine where their true interests lie."[119] These interests are altered by contemporary socio-ecological realities, but this hardly dispels the need for critique.

Early in WWII, a younger Adorno (and seemingly Horkheimer at almost the same time) had argued that critical theory's best hope, as Adorno would characterize it, was to create *"Flaschenposten,"* "messages in a bottle."[120] These messages, as Buck-Morss puts it, are characterized by "robbing the present of its ideological justification."[121] They were provocations, not grounded in some kind of transhistorical aporetic truth but rather in the contradictions of actually existing society. Adorno's *Minima Moralia*—with its scathing critique of the whole of modern capitalist life, written not in any academic form and not for any academic purpose—stands alongside Benjamin's essays as the quintessential example of this kind of theorizing (it is worth remembering that none of the theorists were professional academics until well after the war, except for Horkheimer). Far from mandarin and specialized detachment, the fragments, observations, arguments, and aphorisms elicit a critical response, help stir a nascent political subject where one was absent through the "ruthless criticism" of society. From one corner of the totally administered world, the critical theorist lobs such a bottle into another, hopeful that it will find a reader.

In the contemporary moment, then, it is actually ideal for Malm to ask "Where is that global subject? Who is it?" in theorizing an eco-Leninism.[122] Just as ecosocialist thought and other critical ecological thought are riddled

---

[118] Irving Wohlfrath, cited in Richard Leppert, "Introduction," in Theodor Adorno, *Essays on Music*, ed. Richard Leppert, trans. Susan H. Gillespie (Berkeley: University of California Press, 2002), 70.
[119] Geuss, *The Idea of a Critical Theory* (Cambridge, UK: Cambridge University Press, 1981), 55.
[120] Leppert in Adorno, *Essays on Music*, 70; Müller-Doohm, *Adorno: A Biography*, 262.
[121] Buck-Morss, *Origin of Negative Dialectics*, 36.
[122] Malm, *Corona, Climate, Chronic Emergency*; my own *political theory* of climate politics is better characterized as an eco-Fanonism, but that is *not* a question for *Critical Theory*.

with such "messages," precisely this is what they were supposed to do, even if many critical theorists kept their distance from the results in the late 1960s.[123] As we can see with Davis, though, the theoretical concept of the "message in the bottle" contains a radical, substantive democratic concept: critique is potentially for *anyone*. And again, as Adorno would surely condemn in such crudely practical language, it *works*.

But works at what? It works—in far more Benjaminian terms—to jar thought, to prompt critical consciousness, further critique, demystify ideology. This is hardly something which needs to be left behind. The political project at hand needs it as much as "the dictatorial side" of politics. Critical theory, even in some of its most seemingly abstruse forms, has provided a road to social consciousness for many, or an opening for previous social consciousness and experience into new radical ideas.

ORGANIZING PESSIMISM AND THE LIBERATION OF THE NEGATIVE

A concrete analysis of the concrete situation today argues for a radical emancipatory politics that confirms and departs from critical theory, just

---

[123] That radical emancipatory premise that ran through critical theory was not lost on the radical student movements of the late 1960s either. The breakdown of this relationship is complex and, in some ways, overinflated. The reception of works like *Dialectic of Enlightenment* and *Minima Moralia* by young radicals, while ultimately repudiated by Horkheimer and Adorno, proves as a kind of case in point of this very concept of theoretical praxis. The "New Left"—coalescing around many broader notions of domination that critical theory was helping both recover from within Marxism and expand beyond its "orthodox" horizons at that time—flocked to critical theory. More "traditional" Marxists, like the aforementioned Abendroth and the lesser-known "Marburg School" he was associated with, rejected the New Left and new social movements outside "the worker's movement" more broadly (see Lothar Peter, *Marx on Campus: A Short History of the Marburg School*, trans. Loren Balhorn (Leiden/Boston: Brill, 2019), 10–11). This was broadly reflective of the reaction of the Marxist left across the developed world. Younger Institute members like Oskar Negt and Habermas spoke out, initially, in favor of student protest movements, as did Marcuse and, initially although with more circumspection, Adorno. Adorno was often an invited keynote speaker and introduced major events of the nascent New Left, judged the war in Vietnam as a form of the continued existence of Auschwitz, condemned police murder, particularly of students and particularly of politically engaged students, and was sometimes the only major intellectual to even visit SDS occupations (see Müller-Doohm, *Adorno: A Biography*). Adorno's ultimate rejection of the New Left was, ironically, on similar grounds as that of more "traditional" Marxists: it lacked a sufficient class basis. In "a concrete analysis of the concrete situation," and in the light of failed emancipatory movements, Adorno went further: a petit-bourgeois movement that will not allow space for critical reflection and theory, and is divorced from a broader social base, will likely instantiate the very "technocratic domination" it seeks to overthrow. From the famous "culture industry" section of *Dialectic of Enlightenment*, to the discussion of radical theory itself in *Minima Moralia*, to his correspondence with Marcuse, Adorno was always aware that modern capitalist society could subsume critical elements into its own functioning. He had argued this many times. What he didn't seem to understand was that this was a success not a misunderstanding of their own theory. Marcuse—even though he shared the fundamental situational analysis—preferred engagement.

as it confirms and departs from Marxist revolution more broadly. Planetary boundaries are all too real while scarcity is still socially produced. Benjamin argued in 1929, witnessing and anticipating a different set of catastrophes, for an "organization of pessimism." As he wrote:

> And that means pessimism all down the line. Absolutely. Mistrust in the fate of literature, mistrust in the fate of freedom, mistrust in the fate of European humanity, but three times mistrust in all reconciliation: between classes, between nations, between individuals. And unlimited trust only in IG Farben and the peaceful perfection of the airforce. But what now? What next?[124]

Climate catastrophe is not the apocalypse; fatalism or nihilism is useless. Pessimism is the mode best matched to conditions of an already catastrophic condition—in which politics is precisely as Benjamin always thought: a gamble (and against a house with a stacked deck). There is no universal fear. For some there is opportunity and for others there is exhaustion. The *politics* of climate change are not about some theoretical future but paradoxically about meeting so many of the wants, needs, and desires generated through extraction, exploitation, expropriation, and exhaustion today. It is a politics "nourished by the image of enslaved ancestors rather than the ideal of liberated grandchildren."[125] Although Benjamin—unlike critical theory in general—has much to add to a *political theory* of climate change, he is certainly not the only voice.

What we have explored here is about critical theory in relation to that project. *Flaschenposten* still have their value, but the time for restricting critical theory to only such modes is inarguably past (and was likely insufficient already since much of the latter half of the twentieth century). Critical theory played a vital role in proponing the critique of progress which is sine-qua-non for understanding climate change and also, indeed, its politics. Contemporary conditions demand nothing short of what I have called a left-wing climate realism, an emancipatory climate politics predicated on a zero-sum political conflict.[126] A critical theory that works *with* such a politics has much to offer in terms of social theory, methodology, ideology critique, and still critical provocation. But there are two other ways that I wish to conclude with, in which a critical theory reconsidered on contemporary socio-ecological conditions should play a role: what the utopian imagination considered through determinate negation can mean today, and how posing the absolutely negative is more vital in conjunction with such a project, how it can even be liberating.

---

[124] Benjamin, *Selected Writings, Volume 2: Part I*, 217.
[125] Benjamin, *Selected Writings, Volume 4*, 394.
[126] Chaudhary, "Not in This."

For Edward Said, Adorno was "the dominating intellectual conscience of the middle twentieth century."[127] Said's praise was based not only on his consideration of Adorno's acumen but on his absolute, unwavering commitment to critique and in his representation of "the intellectual as permanent exile, dodging both old and new with equal dexterity."[128] Said was particularly interested in Adorno's situating exile and homelessness—themes all too familiar to Said—as a kind of fundamental quality of the modern capitalist era. Ecological catastrophe is a daily experience. The irrationality of the extractive circuit is a daily experience. Social domination in nearly every form provokes mass mobilization the world over. Societies break down, new solidarities are possible never before imagined, because, regardless of outcome, we're all living through the process of becoming homeless at home. The ground has shifted and promises to keep moving, even if our best hopes are realized. Said, following Adorno's original argument which culminates in the famous aphorism "wrong life cannot be lived rightly," thinks that while this is a brilliant argument, it misses "the pleasures of exile, those different arrangements of living and eccentric angles of vision it can afford."[129] Said is perhaps right in terms of the fragment he is examining, but he has missed moments where exile becomes a rootless utopian moment in determinate negation of the present.

It is precisely to those that Aaron Benanav, thinking of what a post-growth, post-scarcity society might promise in a new imagination, turns to a different moment in *Minima Moralia*. Benanav posits that such a condition might be considered equivalent to Marx's realm of freedom, only posed slightly differently.

> Of course, the realm of freedom is about having time for both socializing and solitude, for engaging in hobbies and doing nothing at all—"*rien faire comme une bete*, lying on water and looking peacefully at the sky." Frankfurt School critical theorist Theodor Adorno's phrase is suggestive of a world in which material dispossession and the existential insecurity to which it gives rise have been universally abolished.[130]

This is a pleasure of exile, especially when considered as the determinate negation of the socio-ecological exhaustions of the present moment.

---

[127] Edward Said, *Representations of the Intellectual: The 1993 Reith Lectures* (New York: Vintage Books, 1996), 54.
[128] Said, *Representations*, 56.
[129] Said, *Representations*, 59.
[130] Benanav, *Automation and the Future of Work*, 90.

Although small, even wispy, it expresses rest and relief, even if we can hardly say we are at home.

We see a similar, if less poetic, moment in Alfred Schmidt's *The Concept of Nature in Marx*. Schmidt rejects Ernst Bloch's positive and romantic utopian vision of a totally "non-mathematical and qualitative" relation to nature. In the added preface to the 1970 English edition, Schmidt reformulated his view of Marx via Benjamin arguing that "Marx wanted to achieve something qualitatively new: mastery by the whole of society of society's mastery of nature."[131] Just as Benanav reformulates freedom as against real natural limit, Schmidt here makes an argument that is perhaps more radical that he realizes. The realm of freedom is found in the purposeful determining of limitations on human freedom. There are the enabling conditions for undominated life. Or as he responds to Bloch:

> What could be salvaged from the idea of such a very naïve relation to nature, without quantification and calculation, is the hope that when men are no longer led by their form of society to regard each other primarily from the point of view of economic advantage, they will be able to restore to external things something of their independence, their "reality" in Brecht's sense. In such a society, men's view of natural things would lose its tenseness, it would have something of the rest and composure which surrounds the word "nature" in Spinoza.[132]

Determinate negation need not be limited to recapitulating classical critical theory ideas through new lenses. In the light of this moment in the Anthropocene, it can also be practiced through Benjamin's "constellations": quite literally digging through the past for all those possibilities all over the world lost to "the storm of progress" which speak to the socio-ecological wants, needs, and desires of an ecological niche released from the extractive circuit, not into the revolution as Marxists envisioned it, but something unexpectedly different. Negation in such a constellation would unquestionably have to cross boundaries of geography, culture, and time, to name but a few elements, and would require disciplines and ideas far beyond even a reconstituted critical theory. The goal is of course not some anarcho-primitivism or "naïve" fantasy as Schmidt dismisses above, but rather those lost alternative emancipatory moments and visions which speak to this moment. This time in full technicolor, just as with Benjamin's resurrections of Fourier: through the literal negation of the current catastrophic ecological niche, painting the possible Anthropocenic present with the architecture, design, art, science,

---

[131] Alfred Schmidt, *The Concept of Nature in Marx* (New York/London: Verso, 2014), 12.
[132] Schmidt, *The Concept of Nature*, 158.

and practice of alterative modernisms, suppressed knowledges, and unrealized visions.

Finally, as we reconsider critical theory in conjunction with the kind of political project at hand here, we should reaffirm the demand for purely negative critique that is "suspicious of the very categories of better, useful, appropriate, productive, and valuable." We should consider the still prevalent notion that critique must be accompanied by a "positive solution" as sheer barbarism. It is the most bourgeois value—and one of the most pernicious—to deny people access to criticism simply because a "solution" is not apparent. A crucial value of critical theory remains precisely to always pose again the question of the negative; not to generate some kind of Nietzschean "bad consciousness" or cultivate what Spinoza once called the "sad passions" but precisely to illuminate latent possibilities—whether technical, theoretical, or even affective—as set between any given phenomenon and the always limited view of social totality.

An engagement with a politics that will be so thoroughly instrumental, so unquestionably violent demands not the retreat of critique but its intensification. This mode of critical theory in light of such a project reminds us of just how limited even a project as radical as this is; just how much its brutality is, in crude language that would offend classic critical theorists, a means and not an end; just how dehumanizing it all is. We can get a sense of this in Alberto Toscano's characterization of Malm's eco-Leninism as "tragic instrumentalism."[133] In the terms I am describing here, this involves the embrace of instrumentality toward the arrest of progress. Self-preservation for the exhausted, molded so well by the extractive circuit, in naked usurpation. At the same time, contemporary radical thought is often plagued by impossible moralisms or revolutionary absolutes that are as crippling as the thorniest Frankfurt School dialectical puzzle. Here, we can speak of the liberation of the negative. Not only to remind us of distance between our view and a limited view of social totality, or between this project and "the point of view of redemption," but to remind us that this is not a project which can meet such perfection. To free political actors from a guilt, they should not have had and remind them of the humanity they are trying to preserve.

BIBLIOGRAPHY

Adorno, Theodor W. *Aspects of the New Right-Wing Extremism*. Translated by Wieland Hoban. Cambridge, UK: Polity Press, 2020.

---

[133] Toscano, Alberto. "The State of the Pandemic," *Historical Materialism* 28, no. 4 (2020): 20.

Adorno, Theodor W. *Can One Live After Auschwitz?* Edited by Rolf Tiedemann, translated by Rodney Livingstone et al. Stanford: Stanford University Press, 2003.

Adorno, Theodor W. *Critical Models: Interventions and Catchwords.* Translated by Henry Pickford. New York: Columbia University Press, 1998.

Adorno, Theodor W. *Essays on Music.* Edited by Richard Leppert, translated by Susan H. Gillespie. Berkeley: University of California Press, 2002.

Adorno, Theodor W. *Hegel: Three Studies.* Translated by Shierry Weber Nicholsen. Cambridge, MA/London: MIT Press, 1993.

Adorno, Theodor W. *History and Freedom: Lectures 1964–1965.* Edited by Rolf Tiedemann, translated by Rodney Livingstone. Cambridge, UK: Polity Press, 2006.

Adorno, Theodor W. *Negative Dialectics.* Translated by E.B. Ashton. New York/London: Continuum, 2007.

Adorno, Theodor W., and Max Horkheimer. *Dialectic of Enlightenment.* Edited by Gunzelin Schmid Noerr, translated by Edmund Jephcott. Stanford: Stanford University Press, 2002.

Adorno, Theodor W., and Max Horkheimer. *Towards a New Manifesto.* Translated by Rodney Livingstone. New York/London: Verso, 2011.

Ajl, Max. "The Hypertrophic City versus The Planet of Fields." In *Implosions/Explosions: Towards a Study of Planetary Urbanization*, edited by Neil Brenner, 533–50. Berlin: JOVIS, 2014.

Akuno, Kali, and Ajamu Nangwaya, eds. *Jackson Rising: The Struggle for Economic Democracy and Black Self-Determination in Jackson, Mississippi.* Cantley, QC: Daraja Press, 2017.

Altieri, Miguel, and Peter Rosset. *Agroecology: Science and Politics.* Winnipeg: Fernwood, 2017.

Azmanova, Albena. *Capitalism on Edge.* New York: Columbia University Press, 2020.

Battistoni, Alyssa. "Ways of Making a Living: Revaluing the Work of Social and Ecological Reproduction." *Socialist Register* 56 (Oct 2019): 182–98.

Benanav, Aaron. *Automation and the Future of Work.* New York/London: Verso, 2020.

Benjamin, Walter. *One-Way Street.* Edited by Michael W. Jennings, translated by Edmund Jephcott. Cambridge, MA: Belknap Press, 2016.

Benjamin, Walter. *Selected Writings, Volume 2: Part 1: 1927–1930.* Edited by Michael W. Jennings, Howard Eiland, and Gary Smith. Cambridge, MA: Belknap Press, 2005.

Benjamin, Walter. *Selected Writings, 4: 1938–1940.* Edited by Howard Eiland and Michael W. Jennings. Cambridge, MA: Belknap Press, 2006.

Benjamin, Walter. *The Correspondence of Walter Benjamin.* Edited by Gershom Scholem, Theodor W. Adorno et al. Chicago: University of Chicago Press, 1994.

Buck-Morss, Susan. *Dreamworld and Catastrophe: The Passing of Mass Utopia in East and Ways of Making a LivingWest.* Cambridge, MA: MIT Press, 2000.

Buck-Morss, Susan. *The Origin of Negative Dialectics: Theodor W. Adorno, Walter Benjamin, and the Frankfurt Institute.* New York: The Free Press, 1977.

Buck-Morss, Susan. *Thinking Past Terror: Islamism and Critical Theory on the Left.* New York/London: Verso, 2006.
Cassegård, Carl. "Eco-Marxism and the Critical Theory of Nature: Two Perspectives on Ecology and Dialectics." *Distinktion: Journal of Social Theory* 18, no. 3 (2017): 314–32.
Chaudhary, Ajay Singh. "It's Already Here." *n+1*, October 10, 2018.
Chaudhary, Ajay Singh. "Religions of Doubt: Religion, Critique, and Modernity in Jalal Al-e Ahmad and Walter Benjamin." Phd diss., Columbia University, 2013.
Chaudhary, Ajay Singh. "Subjectivity, Affect, Exhaustion: The Political Theology of the Anthropocene." *Political Theology Network*, February 25, 2019.
Chaudhary, Ajay Singh. "Sustaining What? Capitalism, Socialism, and Climate Change." In *Capital, Democracy, Socialism: Critical Debates.* Edited by Albena Azmanova and James Chamberlain, Cham: Springer, forthcoming.
Chaudhary, Ajay Singh. "The Climate of Socialism." *Socialist Forum* (Winter 2019).
Chaudhary, Ajay Singh. "We're Not in This Together." *The Baffler* 51 (April 2020).
Cook, Deborah. *Adorno on Nature.* New York/London: Routledge, 2011.
Davis, Angela Y. *Angela Davis: An Autobiography.* New York: Random House, 1974.
Davis, Angela Y. *The Angela Y. Davis Reader.* Edited by Joy James. Malden, MA/ Oxford, UK: Blackwell Publishers, 1998.
Davis, Angela Y. *Blues Legacies and Black Feminism: Gertrude "Ma" Rainey, Bessie Smith, and Billie Holiday.* New York: Vintage Books, 1999.
Davis, Angela Y. "Marcuse's Legacies." In *Herbert Marcuse: A Critical Reader*, edited by John Abromeit and W. Mark Cobb, 43–50. New York/London: Routledge, 2004.
Davis, Mike. *Late Victorian Holocausts: El Niño Famines and the Making of the Third World.* New York/London: Verso, 2017.
Douglas Kellner. *Critical Theory, Marxism, and Modernity.* Baltimore: Johns Hopkins University Press, 1989.
Fisher, Mark. "How to kill a zombie: strategizing the end of neoliberalism." *openDemocracy*, July 18, 2013.
Foster, John Bellamy. *Marx's Ecology: Materialism and Nature.* New York: Monthly Review Press, 2000.
Fraser, Nancy. "Behind Marx's Hidden Abode." *New Left Review* 86 (Mar/Apr 2014): 55–72.
Fraser, Nancy. "Expropriation and Exploitation in Racialized Capitalism: A Reply to Michael Dawson." *Critical Historical Studies* 3, no. 1 (2016): 163–78.
Fuchs, Christian. "Critical Social Theory and Sustainable Development: The Role of Class, Capitalism and Domination in a Dialectical Analysis of Un/Sustainability." *Sustainable Development* 25, no. 5 (Sept/Oct 2017): 443–58.
Fuchs, Christian. "M. N. Roy and the Frankfurt School: Socialist Humanism and the Critical Analysis of Communication, Culture, Technology, Fascism and Nationalism." *tripleC* 17, no. 2 (2019): 249–86.
Geuss, Raymond. "Dialectics and the Revolutionary Impulse." In *The Cambridge Companion to Critical Theory,* edited by Fred Rush, 103–38. Cambridge, UK: Cambridge University Press, 2004.

Geuss, Raymond. *The Idea of a Critical Theory: Habermas and the Frankfurt School.* Cambridge, UK: Cambridge University Press, 1981.

Geuss, Raymond. *Philosophy and Real Politics.* Princeton: Princeton University Press, 2008.

Gramsci, Antonio. *Selections from the Prison Notebooks.* Edited and translated by Quintin Hoare and Geoffrey Nowell Smith. New York: International Publishers, 1971.

Hansen, Miriam. *Cinema and Experience: Siegfried Kracauer, Walter Benjamin and Theodor W. Adorno.* Berkeley: University of California Press, 2011.

Haraway, Donna J. "The Transformation of the Left in Science: Radical Associations in Britain in the 30s and the U.S.A. in the 60s." *Surroundings: An Interdisciplinary Journal* 58, no. 4 (Winter 1975): 441–62.

Heller, Patrick. *The Labor of Development: Workers and the Transformation of Capitalism in Kerala, India.* Ithaca: Cornell University Press, 1999.

Hickel, Jason, and Giorgios Kallis. "Is Green Growth Possible?" *New Political Economy* 25, no. 4 (2020): 469–86.

Horkheimer, Max. *Critical Theory: Selected Essays.* Translated by Matthew J. O'Connel et al. New York: Continuum, 2002.

Jaffe, Sarah. "Zombie Neoliberalism: How 'There Is No Alternative' Gave Us Donald Trump." *Dissent,* Fall 2017.

Lewontin, Richard, and Richard Levins. "The Problem of Lysenkoism." In *The Radicalisation of Science,* edited by Hilary Rose and Steven Rose, 32–64. London: Macmillan, 1976.

Malm, Andreas. *Corona, Climate, Chronic Emergency: War Communism in the Twenty-First Century.* New York/London: Verso, 2020.

Malm, Andreas. "Ecology & Marxism." Reading guide, *Historical Materialism,* https://www.historicalmaterialism.org/reading-guides/ecology-marxism-andreas-malm.

Malm, Andreas. *Fossil Capital: The Rise of Steam Power and the Roots of Global Warming.* New York: Verso, 2016.

Malm, Andreas. *The Progress of This Storm: Nature and Society in a Warming World.* New York/London: Verso, 2020.

McPhearson, Timon, Christopher M. Raymond, Natalie Gulsrud, Christian Albert, Neil Coles, Nora Fagerholm, Michiru Nagatsu, Anton Stahl Olafsson, Niko Soininen, and Kati Vierikko. "Radical Changes Are Needed for Transformations to a Good Anthropocene." *npj Urban Sustain* 1, no. 5 (2021): 1–13.

Moore, Jason W. *Capitalism in the Web of Life: Ecology and the Accumulation of Capital.* New York/London: Verso, 2015.

Müller-Doohm, Stefan. *Adorno: A Biography.* Translated by Rodney Livingstone. Cambridge, UK: Polity Press, 2005.

Neilson, David and Thomas Stubbs. "Relative Surplus Population and Uneven Development in the Neoliberal Era: Theory and Empirical Application." *Capital and Class* 35, no. 3 (2011): 435–53.

Neumann, Franz. "Change in the Function of Law in Modern Society." In *The Democratic and the Authoritarian State,* edited by Herbert Marcuse, translated by Peter Gay. New York: The Free Press, 1964.

Oberle, Eric. *Theodor Adorno and the Century of Negative Identity.* Stanford: Stanford University Press, 2018.
O'Neill, Daniel, Andrew L. Fanning, William F. Lamb, and Julia K. Steinberger. "A Good Life for All within Planetary Boundaries." *Nature Sustainability* 1 (2018): 88–95.
Peter, Lothar. *Marx on Campus: A Short History of the Marburg School.* Translated by Loren Balhorn. Leiden/Boston: Brill, 2019.
Pirgmaier, Elke and Julia K. Steinberger. "Roots, Riots, and Radical Change—A Road Less Travelled for Ecological Economics." *Sustainability,* 11, no. 7 (2019): 1–18.
Przeworski, Adam. *Capitalism and Social Democracy.* Cambridge, UK: Cambridge University Press, 1985.
Raine, Barnaby. "The Anti-Colonial Revolt Was Key to Lenin's Vision of Revolution." *Jacobin,* March 1, 2021.
Rockström, Johan, et al. "A Safe Operating Space for Humanity." *Nature* 461 (2009): 472–75.
Sallah, Ariel. *Ecofeminism as Politics: Nature, Marx and the Postmodern.* London: Zed Books, 1997.
Said, Edward W. *Representations of the Intellectual: The 1993 Reith Lectures.* New York: Vintage Books, 1996.
Saito, Kohei. *Karl Marx's Ecosocialism.* New York: Monthly Review Press, 2017.
Schmidt, Alfred. *The Concept of Nature in Marx.* New York/London: Verso, 2014.
Steffen, Will, et al. "Trajectories of the Earth System in the Anthropocene." *PNAS* 115, no. 33 (2018): 8252–59.
Toscano, Alberto. "The State of the Pandemic." *Historical Materialism* 28, no. 4 (2020): 3–23.
Tsing, Anna Lowenhaupt. *The Mushroom at the End of the World: On the Possibility of Life in Capitalist Ruins.* Princeton: Princeton University Press, 2017.
Wark, McKenzie. *Molecular Red: Theory for the Anthropocene.* New York/London: Verso, 2015.
Wiedmann, Thomas, Manfred Lenzen, Lorenz T. Keyßer, and Julia K. Steinberger. "Scientists' Warning on Affluence." *Nature Communications* 11, no. 3107 (2020): 1–10.
Wilson, Edmund O. "The Attempt to Suppress Human Behavioral Genetics." *J Gen Educ* 29, no. 4 (Winter 1980): 277–87.
Yancy, George, ed. *African-American Philosophers: 17 Conversations.* New York/London: Routledge, 1998.
Yussof, Kathryn. *A Billion Black Anthropocenes or None.* Minneapolis: University of Minnesota Press, 2019.

Chapter 8

Renewing Critical Theory in an Ultra-Conservative Context

Between the Social Sciences, Political Philosophy, and Emancipatory Engagement

Philippe Corcuff
Translated by Daniel Benson

This chapter joins current attempts to reconfigure critical theory within the social sciences and political philosophy in order to address specific intellectual and political concerns of the twenty-first century.[1] It subscribes to critical theory as elaborated by the "Frankfurt School" in the 1920s and 1930s, whereby social critique is linked to a project of emancipation.[2] However, I seek to provide a reformulation that is both *comprehensive* (attentive to the meaning that individuals give to their actions in intersubjective frameworks, in a Weberian sense) and *pragmatic* (attentive to the capacities that social actors use in their situated actions, in the perspective of French pragmatic sociology initiated by Luc Boltanski and Laurent Thévenot in the late 1980s). In this general framework, I will explore the intellectual disarray that has disjoined academic critique from an emancipatory horizon, and then lay out possible ways to respond to this disarray. The exploration of the negative and the positive will allow me to trace out the possibilities of a reassociation between critical sociology and emancipation. I understand "reassociation"

---

[1] See for instance Luc Boltanski, *On Critique: A Sociology of Emancipation*, trans. Gregory Elliot (Malden, MA: Polity Press, 2011); Philippe Corcuff, *Où est passé la critique sociale? Penser le global au croisement des savoirs* (Paris: La Découverte, 2012); Manuel Cervera-Marzal, *Miguel Abensour, critique de la domination, pensée de l'émancipation* (Paris: Sens & Tonka, 2013); Bruno Frère, ed., *Le tournant de la théorie critique* (Paris: Desclée de Brouwer, 2015); as well as the dialogue between Luc Boltanski and Nancy Fraser in the current volume.

[2] Max Horkheimer, "Traditional and Critical Theory," in *Critical Theory: Selected Essays*, trans. Matthew J. O'Connell et al. (New York: Continuum, 2002), 188–243.

in a non-Hegelian sense. The goal is not to "overcome" a contradiction into a superior entity, but to preserve the awareness of the tensions within it. I take inspiration for this method from the overlooked critique of the Hegelian dialectic by the forerunner of anarchism, Pierre-Joseph Proudhon. Proudhon takes the notion of antinomy as the primary category, rather than that of the "overcoming" of contradictions.[3] And he formulates an epistemologically interesting formulation with his expression of a "balancing of oppositions" [*équilibration des contraires*].[4]

I will first indicate some of the prominent characteristics of my reading of the relation between social critique and emancipation in the current context. Modern social critique, emerging at the end of the eighteenth century and subsequently constituting one of the intellectual pillars of what came to be recognized internationally as "the left" in the twentieth century, arose to point out *negative* aspects of an existing social order within the horizon of a *positive* goal, emancipation. I understand *emancipation* in the meaning it acquired toward the end of the eighteenth century in Europe: to "use one's intellect without the direction of another," according to Immanuel Kant's expression used to define the Enlightenment.[5] Today, the question of emancipation has benefited from the perspectives of the worker and socialist movement, the feminist movement, the anti-colonial movement, and, moreover, can draw from the contributions of modern social sciences. It is also possible to integrate the way in which Cornelius Castoriadis placed the question of autonomy at the center of an emancipatory perspective. Initially, then, we can consider emancipation as an exit from various dominations in view of an individual and collective autonomy that implies the construction of specific social conditions.

My hypothesis is that the modern aim of social critique based on emancipation has become disrupted. Moreover, this disruption is not a purely academic phenomenon, and equally affects the political field globally. It can be seen from both ends of the political spectrum that had claimed the couplet critique social/emancipation for their political projects. On the one hand, the Stalinist impasse and the fall of the Berlin Wall have stymied what was called "communism" and have brought their lot of disenchantments and doubts to its emancipatory horizon. On the other hand, the conversion beginning in the

---

[3] Pierre-Joseph Proudhon, *De la justice dans la révolution et dans l'église*, vol. 1 (Paris: Fayard, 1988), 35–36, 567.
[4] See Pierre-Joseph Proudhon, *Théorie de la propriété* (Paris: l'Harmattan, 1997), 206, and Philippe Corcuff, "Antinomies et analogies comme outils transversaux en sociologie: en partant de Proudhon et de Passeron," *SociologieS*, November 2, 2015, http://journals.openedition.org/sociologies/5154.
[5] Immanuel Kant, "An Answer to the Question: What Is Enlightenment?" in *Towards Perpetual Peace and Other Writings on Politics, Peace, and History*, ed. Pauline Kleingeld (New Haven: Yale University Press, 2006), 17.

1980s of social democratic organizations to economic neoliberalism, thus adopting the form of *social liberalism*, has also contributed to the severance of emancipation from critique.

It should be noted that this trend of disassociation between social critique and emancipation, in both the intellectual and political fields, has left an open terrain for the rise of ultra-conservative usages of critique. This trend is visible throughout Europe (especially in Hungary, Poland, Bulgaria, Latvia, Norway, Slovakia, Switzerland, Italy...), and in France. For instance, currently in France, ultra-conservative social critique seems to be greater in volume on the internet and social media than leftist critique,[6] as the former benefits from the political crisis affecting the two historically dominant organizations of the left, the Socialist Party and the Communist Party, and from the ideological crisis more broadly of the notion of the "left" itself. Marine Le Pen, candidate of the far-right National Front (now called the National Rally), received 36.9 percent of the vote in the second round of the French presidential elections of 2017. This is roughly twice that of her father, Jean-Marie Le Pen, in 2002. During the European elections of May 2019 (with a single round of voting), the list of the National Rally arrived in front of all the thirty-four lists submitted, with 23.31 percent of the vote, beating out the list supported by the President of the Republic, Emmanuel Macron, who was victorious over Marine Le Pen in 2017. Outside of Europe, the extreme right won the U.S. presidency in 2016 (with a certain "Trumpism" likely to outlast Trump's electoral defeat in 2020), and in Brazil in 2018, with the election of Jair Bolsonaro.

We thus observe the rise of ideological configurations across the globe that associate hypercriticism (in the form of a vague "anti-system" language) and discrimination (xenophobic, sexist, homophobic, etc.) within a nationalist framework.[7] Ultra-conservative tendencies notably promote *identitarianist* theses, especially relative to closed visions of "national identity" in a triple opposition to the multicultural character of their societies, to migrants generally, and to Islam particularly, more or less associated, depending on the country, with a certain relegitimization of anti-semitism. This tendency

---

[6] See for instance the study by Antoine Bevort on the most visited political websites in France in October 2016. The first is the "anti-system" and anti-semitic site of Alain Soral (8 million visits per month) and the second is an Islamophobic site, equally hypercritical, *Fdesouche* (4.5 million visits per month). Leftist websites are not listed in the top ten. Antoine Bevort, "Les trente sites politiques français ayant le plus d'audience sur le web," *Mediapart* (blog), October 21, 2016, https://blogs.mediapart.fr/antoine-bevort/blog/211016/les-trente-sites-politiques-francais-ayant-le-plus-d-audience-surle-web-0.

[7] See Luc Boltanski and Arnaud Esquerre, *Vers l'extrême: extension des domaines de la droite* (Bellevaux: Éditions Dehors, 2014); Philippe Corcuff, *Les années 30 reviennent et la gauche est dans le brouillard* (Paris: Textuel, 2014); and Enzo Traverso, *The New Faces of Fascism: Populism and the Far Right*, trans. David Broder (New York: Verso, 2019).

benefits from the extension of domains of ideological confusionism, understood as spaces that allow for rhetorical passageways between themes of the extreme right, the right, and the left, often by recourse to a rhetoric of conspiracy.[8]

One of the pressing political issues of the current period consists in attempting to rearticulate social critique and emancipation, thereby opening possibilities for the reinvention of a critical theory tied to an emancipatory horizon and the re-emergence of an emancipatory left, in order to stem the danger of marginalization confronting both configurations. In this perspective, a new critical theory should be rethought with regard to the challenges of the moment, without diminishing the tensions between the "critical" pole and the "emancipatory" pole: tensions that have been prominently brought to light given their current uncoupling. I will concentrate, in order to explore these problems and possible ways forward, on the French context.

To do so, I will employ tools drawn from the social sciences and political philosophy, and associate them with my experience of political engagement, which ranges from a leftist current of social democracy to the alter-globalist, anti-capitalist, anarchist, and pragmatist left.[9] Within this overall approach, the three poles—sociology, political philosophy, and radical militancy—will intersect and interact on the basis of their respective autonomy. I envision them as "language games," as defined by Ludwig Wittgenstein, that is, inserted within (at least partially) different "forms of life" and "activity."[10] In this cross-border dialogue between "language games," the language games of sociology and political philosophy are considered to be "knowledge games," meaning language games principally oriented toward knowledge.[11]

ACADEMIC MISADVENTURES OF CRITIQUE WITHIN FRENCH SOCIOLOGY

The current tendency toward ultra-specialization in the social sciences—through the logic of disciplinary and subdisciplinary divisions, and through

---

[8] See Philippe Corcuff, "Après le Brexit et Trump: confusionnisme à gauche et extrême droitisation idéologique," *Les Possibles*, no. 12, 2017, https://france.attac.org/nos-publications/les-possibles/numero-12-hiver-2017/dossier-la-droitisation-des-politiques/article/apres-le-brexit-et-trump-confusionnisme-a-gauche-et-extreme-droitisation, and Philippe Corcuff, *La grande confusion. Comment l'extrême droite gagne la bataille des idées* (Paris: Textuel, 2021).
[9] Philippe Corcuff, *Enjeux libertaires pour le XXIe siècle par un anarchiste néophyte* (Paris: Éditions du Monde libertaire, 2015).
[10] Ludwig Wittgenstein, *Philosophical Investigations*, 4th ed., ed. and trans. G.E.M Anscombe, P.M.S. Hacker, and Joachim Schulte (Oxford: Wiley-Blackwell, 2010), part 1, § 23 and 39.
[11] Henri Atlan, *Enlightenment to Enlightenment: Intercritique of Science and Myth*, trans. Lenn J. Schramm (Albany: SUNY Press, 1993), 298–330.

the routinization of privileged objects of study together with their associated modalities of academic conformism—plays a part, in France, in the silent uncoupling of sociology from any explicit references to emancipation. The theme of "ethical neutrality" has taken hold of the field, gaining ground since the 1980s with the marginalization of Marxism in the university. It functions as a magical reference that defends the scientificity of the discipline, even though its epistemological grounds are barely mentioned, and contributes to the above disassociation by rendering it unconscious. Certain texts, however, give visibility to what usually remains hidden. I will take two significant examples: the epistemological positions of the sociologist Nathalie Heinich and the epistemological divergences between two other sociologists, Bernard Lahire and Geoffroy de Lagasnerie.

The Anti-Critical (and Hardly Neutral) Neutrality of Nathalie Heinich

The sociologist Nathalie Heinich comes from the tradition of critical sociology initiated by Pierre Bourdieu (who was her thesis advisor). She is one of the few sociologists in France to have attempted to systematically argue for the theme, inspired by Max Weber, of "ethical neutrality," beginning with her book of 1998 *Ce que l'art fait à la sociologie* (What art does to sociology). In it, she defends "an engaged neutrality" associated with an "acritical posture" that claims to avoid "any discourse relating to the nature or the value of things."[12] However, her body of work includes numerous deviations from the nuances and tensions that are present in Weber's analyses.[13]

Firstly, Weber attacks the thesis of a social science "without presuppositions," since "only a *part* of concrete reality is interesting and *significant* to us, because only it is related to the *cultural values* with which we approach reality."[14] From this emerges the idea of a "relevance to values" in "the selection of a given subject matter and the problems of an empirical analysis," which, for Weber, is in tension with the necessity to avoid judgments of value.[15] Julien Freund initially translated Weber's expression of *Wertfreiheit*

---

[12] Nathalie Heinich, *Ce que l'art fait à la sociologie* (Paris: Minuit, 1998), 77. See also 71–82 and 23–29. For the concept of ethical neutrality in Weber, see Max Weber, "The Meaning of 'Ethical Neutrality' in Sociology and Economics," in *The Methodology of the Social Sciences*, ed. and trans. Edward A. Shils and Henry A. Finch (Glencoe, IL: The Free Press, 1949), 1–47.

[13] Philippe Corcuff, "Le bêtisier sociologique et philosophique de Nathalie Heinich," *Lectures*, July 9, 2018, https://journals.openedition.org/lectures/25494.

[14] Max Weber, "'Objectivity' in Social Science and Social Policy," in *The Methodology of the Social Sciences*, ed. and trans. Edward A. Shils and Henry A. Finch (Glencoe, IL: The Free Press, 1949), 78.

[15] Weber, "Ethical Neutrality, 22.

into French as "axiological neutrality" [*neutralité axiologique*], which Weber presents as

> the intrinsically simple demand that the investigator and teacher should keep unconditionally separate the establishment of empirical facts . . . and *his* own practical evaluations, i.e., his evaluation of these facts as satisfactory or unsatisfactory . . . . These two things are logically different and to deal with them as though they were the same represents a confusion of entirely heterogeneous problems.[16]

The new French translation of the term *Wertfreiheit* proposed by Isabelle Kalinowski is "non-imposition of values," [*non-imposition des valeurs*] which better captures the nuances in Weber's analysis and orients us to another route than that taken by Heinich.[17] Weber seeks above all to caution us (and especially himself, in his reflexive methodology) against adopting a position of pedagogical authority. This is why, he does not forbid scholars "the possibility of expressing in value judgments the ideals which motivate them," so long as they "keep the readers and themselves sharply aware at every moment of the standards by which they judge reality and from which the value judgment is derived."[18]

Weber's more nuanced position on this issue is visible in his defense of recruiting an anarchist legal expert for a university position, not *in spite of* the fact that the individual is an anarchist, but *because of it*: the anarchist is "situated outside of conventions and suppositions that seem so evident to us." Thus, according to Weber, an anarchist legal expert would be able to "perceive problems in the fundamental postulates of legal theory which escape those who take them for granted."[19] We are very far from Heinich's vocabulary to avoid "any discourse relating to the nature or the value of things," which she continues to employ and even adopts a harder stance in a recent book written on the subject of values.[20]

And yet, the spheres of factual judgments and value judgments are not so neatly separated in Heinich's work itself. Consider the "social role" attributed to "engaged neutrality" in *Ce que l'art fait à la sociologie* "a role of mediation, of the construction of compromise between the interests and the values

---

[16] Weber, "Ethical Neutrality," 11.
[17] Isabelle Kalinowski, "Leçons wébériennes sur la science et la propagande," in *La science, profession & vocation*, by Max Weber (Marseille: Agone, 2005), 199.
[18] Max Weber, "Objectivity," 59.
[19] Weber, "Ethical Neutrality," 7.
[20] Heinich, *Ce que l'art fait*, 77. For more recent usage of this vocabulary, see Nathalie Heinich, *Des valeurs. Une approche sociologique* (Paris: Gallimard, 2017), 18.

in play, indeed the refoundation of a consensus."²¹ This role resonates with a certain normative conception of politics and democracy, closer to the "communicative action" of Jürgen Habermas, aiming at consensus, than the notion of "disagreement" of Jacques Rancière, which valorizes dissensus.

More recently, Heinich has also hardened her attacks against critical sociology, as defended by Pierre Bourdieu and Luc Boltanski in particular, through her participation in a more general controversy launched by a number of sociologists in November 2017 in the non-academic press (notably in *Le Débat*, October–November 2017 and *Le Monde*, November 24, 2017). In this debate, she goes so far as to qualify "gender studies" as "international garbage from academic mediocrity" and a 2017 book by Luc Boltanski and Arnaud Esquerre, *Enrichment: A Critique of Commodities*, as the "equivalent of creationist thought"!²² Clearly, her "ethical neutrality" is not particularly "neutral." Her critique of the "discredit lumped on whatever seeks to attenuate or surpass conflicts, through neutrality or universality, as stemming from strategies of domination" thus reveals the normative components at work in her promotion (itself legitimate, but controversial at the normative level) of searching for the "attenuation" or the "surpassing" of conflicts in social life through "neutrality" and "universality."²³

Confused Critical Sociology: Divergences between Bernard Lahire and Geoffroy de Lagasnerie

The question of "ethical neutrality" also reveals tensions within French critical sociology. This is particularly evident in the case of Bernard Lahire and Geoffroy de Lagasnerie.

Bernard Lahire is currently one of the representatives of a quality critical sociology, at the crossroads of empirical research and theoretical elaboration, situated within the university institution. In a book defending sociology against public stigmatizations of the field, he highlights "two distinct plans: the first is non-normative, and is the domain of scientific knowledge; the second is normative, and is the domain of justice, of the police, of prison, etc."²⁴ He employs Weber to make his argument, though in a manner that is more nuanced than Heinich's usage:

---

[21] Heinich, *Ce que l'art fait*, 81.
[22] Nathalie Heinich, "Misères de la sociologie critique," *Le débat* 197, no. 5 (2017): 122, 125.
[23] Heinich, "Misères," 121.
[24] Bernard Lahire, *Pour la sociologie. Et pour finir avec une prétendue "culture de l'excuse."* (Paris: La Découverte, 2016), 35.

Max Weber rightfully attempted to distinguish "judgments of value" and "relation to values": if the researcher necessarily expresses their "relation to values" by the choice of their objects of study and the way in which they conceive them, their work as such does not consist in saying what is "good" or "bad."[25]

In the conclusion to his work, however, he underlines the historical link between the social sciences and the Enlightenment, just as he links the social sciences to democracy in the contemporary context.[26] He thus continues to grasp only partially the complicated links between the scientific and the normative by remaining within the dominant perspective among sociologists of "ethical neutrality."

Geoffroy de Lagasnerie is a young critical theorist, both a sociologist and a philosopher, situated on the periphery of the university institution though benefiting from a certain public recognition. In a book of 2007, he elucidated his epistemological bearings. He criticizes certain shortcomings of scientific autonomy that curbs intellectual inventiveness: he writes of the "academic distribution of powers" as a factor of "conservatism," and attacks the "effects of censorship," of "disciplinary routines," and the "self-sustaining routinization of a discipline."[27] More recently, he has expanded his epistemological criticism "in the name of the values of knowledge and science," and condemns the "growing academic normalization and disciplinary logics" associated with the "reappearance of an ethic of neutrality."[28]

Lagasnerie helps us to understand better how the opening of fields in the social sciences to exterior questioning, including that of militant or artistic engagements, can counter the conformist tendencies that are generated by academic institutions. In so doing, he takes distance from Pierre Bourdieu's principal inclination to defend the autonomy of the scientific field, who underestimated the shortcomings produced by academic logic.[29]

However, Lagasnerie often bends the stick in the other direction, and thus weakens his critique of the blind spots of academic autonomization. He even flirts with epistemological relativism, when he writes: "It is necessary to break with the idea that there are fundamental differences, and thus differences of value, between a book of research, a philosophical treatise, an essay, an intervention in the press, or even between a demonstration or a political

---

[25] Lahire, *Pour la sociologie*, 39.
[26] Lahire, *Pour la sociologie*, 117–28.
[27] Geoffroy de Lagasnerie, *L'empire de l'université. Sur Bourdieu, les intellectuels et le journalisme* (Paris: Éditions Amsterdam, 2007), 61, 64, 75, 82.
[28] Geoffroy de Lagasnerie, *Juger. L'État pénal face à la sociologie* (Paris: Fayard, 2016), 274, 273, 275.
[29] Pierre Bourdieu, *Science of Science and Reflexivity*, trans. Richard Nice (Chicago: University of Chicago Press, 2004).

tract."[30] He also presents an overly unilateral critique of the place of empirical research in the social sciences, as if the latter was not one of the two lungs of scientific work (though admittedly restricted by disciplinary specializations), in its back and forth movement with theoretical elaboration.[31]

It would be more nuanced and pragmatic to recognize both that university institutions and disciplinary rules secure a certain autonomy and a certain intellectual rigor, and at the same time inhibit sociological imagination with their conformist tendencies.

TENSIONS BETWEEN THE CRITICAL SOCIOLOGY OF PIERRE BOURDIEU AND THE PHILOSOPHY OF EMANCIPATION OF JACQUES RANCIÈRE

The tension between the critical sociology of Pierre Bourdieu and the philosophy of emancipation by Jacques Rancière constitutes a singular expression of the problems encountered in the first part of this text. It offers a displaced expression, however, for it integrates the perspective of a philosophy of emancipation and thus allows us to broaden our view beyond the internal "knowledge game" of sociology. In this way, it helps us sketch out possibilities for a reassociation of emancipation and sociological critique.

A Broad Overview of the Tension between Bourdieu and Rancière

Pierre Bourdieu profoundly reinvented critical theories of domination in a way that could be qualified as "post-Marxist" insofar as he deciphers a plurality of forms of domination beyond that of capital over labor.[32] Two concepts establish the axes of his sociological approach to forms of domination: *habitus* (social relations borne in bodies and minds) and *fields* (social relations borne in institutions and conceived spatially).

With *habitus*, he follows the unconscious traces of social dominations in the bodies and minds of individuals. I will cite a significant passage on this concept in his book *Pascalian Meditations*:

> The practical recognition through which the dominated, often unwittingly, contribute to their own domination by tacitly accepting, in advance, the limits imposed on them, often takes the form of bodily emotion (shame, timidity,

---

[30] Lagasnerie, *L'empire de l'université*, 102.
[31] For this critique, see Lagasnerie, *Juger*, 267–96.
[32] Philippe Corcuff, *Bourdieu autrement: fragilité d'un sociologue de combat* (Paris: Textuel, 2003).

anxiety, guilt) . . . . It is betrayed in visible manifestations, such as blushing, inarticulacy, clumsiness, trembling, all ways of submitting, however reluctantly, to the dominant judgment.[33]

Bourdieu here brings to light how social experiences of domination are unconsciously imprinted in bodies, escaping the will of individuals to the point of hindering their potential. The external constraints of social fields organized according to specific modes of domination (for instance, in the economic, political, or cultural fields) only add to the weight of internalized oppressions. Bourdieu thus provides us with one of the most systematic forms of structural social critique of the second half of the twentieth century, within the academic sphere.

However, certain unformulated assumptions of this view of social relations through domination have been identified by Jacques Rancière, from a radically democratic emancipatory perspective. In an interview published in 2009, Rancière helps us clarify the problem of the relationship between critical theories of domination and philosophies of emancipation, by questioning the situationist critique of the "society of the spectacle" by Guy Debord and the sociological critique of Pierre Bourdieu. He writes:

> The entire critical/Marxist revolutionary tradition has absorbed a certain number of inegalitarian presuppositions, like the notion that some are active and others passive, that some see while others know. In sum, the idea that some are capable and others incapable. Once that's in place, a number of strategies become available: someone might think that what's needed is an avant-garde, composed of course of the capable, and tasked with inculcating the incapable with the means of pulling themselves out.[34]

For Rancière, philosophers of emancipation begin with the possibility of equality by building on the capacities of the oppressed, whereas classical critical theories begin with inequality, thus, from the oppressed considered as "incapable," their capacities crushed by their sordid situation. Yet there is a risk that domination becomes the exclusive focus of these classical critical theories, with the dominated conceived as totally subjected to domination and "alienated." In this invasive inequality of critical theories, the very efforts of the dominated toward emancipation tend to be described as the effects of a "manipulation" or of a "recuperation" by the "system," or else as an

---

[33] Pierre Bourdieu, *Pascalian Meditations*, trans. Richard Nice (Stanford: Stanford University Press, 2000), 169.
[34] Jacques Rancière, "Critique of the Critique of the 'Spectacle,'" in *Dissenting Words: Interviews with Jacques Rancière,* ed. and trans. Emiliano Battista (New York: Bloomsbury, 2017), 258.

inept reproduction of dominant stereotypes. The oppressed would thus be definitively trapped in the iron cages of domination, and their emancipation, while declared as the political goal (for Debord as for Bourdieu), becomes practically impossible, continually held in abeyance under the pretext of being subject to the cunning of domination. As Rancière states, "the master always keeps a piece of learning—that is to say, a piece of the student's ignorance—up his sleeve" by endlessly pushing away the moment of equality and emancipation.[35]

Rancière here highlights an occurrence of the surreptitious, and frequent, slippage of the pronominal verb *to emancipate oneself* (in the sense of "the emancipation of the working classes must be conquered by the working classes themselves," in the statutes of the International Working Men's Association of 1864, written by Marx) to the transitive verb *to emancipate* (in the sense of masters emancipating their slaves in the American slave system). This displacement, often unconscious, to a tutelary approach of emancipation has taken many different historical shapes in the political sphere: in the past, the Leninist revolutionary avant-garde or the French republican school teacher emancipating pupils from the prejudice of "tradition"; today, the alter-globalist denouncing "media propaganda" in order to guide citizens out of Plato's cavern, or old-school feminists claiming to liberate veiled Muslim women or prostitutes from themselves, or ecological prophets from their "unalienated" outposts denouncing "consumer society."

Rancière's analysis leads him to distrust the terrain of critical theories of domination in the classical sense of highlighting the structural constraints that bear down on individuals and their representations of the world. He writes: "Collective understanding of emancipation is not the comprehension of a total process of subjugation. It is the collectivization of the capacities invested in scenes of dissensus."[36] He thus privileges the philosophy of emancipation over the structural social critique of domination. However, doesn't emancipation presuppose, at least implicitly, domination, since it acts as an emancipation *from* domination? Why fear saying too much about one of the poles in the pair? Is it really possible to think emancipation by marginalizing critical understanding of domination? It seems rather difficult.

If Rancière thus elucidates certain blind spots in Bourdieu's work, Bourdieu can reciprocally do the same for Rancière's analysis, notably when the sociologist points out the unconscious ways dominations insinuate themselves in the bodies of individuals and paralyze their capacities, in the form of uncontrolled emotions such as shame or blushing.

---

[35] Jacques Rancière, *The Ignorant Schoolmaster: Five Lessons in Intellectual Emancipation*, trans. Kristin Ross (Stanford: Stanford University Press, 1991), 21.

[36] Jacques Rancière, *The Emancipated Spectator*, trans. Gregory Elliot (New York: Verso, 2009), 49.

After this broad analysis of the tension between the sociology of Bourdieu and the philosophy of Rancière, I will consider a particular instance, among others, that can serve to refine the analysis.

An Ambivalent Allodoxia between Bourdieu and Rancière

In *Distinction*, Bourdieu puts forward the notion of *allodoxia* from ancient Greek: "allo" from the word *allos*, that is, "other", and "doxia" from the word *doxa*, "opinion."[37] For Bourdieu, it refers to an error of identification, where given social criteria are unsuited to the instituted cultural hierarchy. It is thus a notion marked with the veil of ignorance, as it indicates the culturally awkward character, despite their "cultural goodwill," of those who are outside the circle of the dominant cultural norm. This notion is firstly aimed at the petite bourgeoisie, but can also apply to certain sectors of the working classes (such as the self-taught or activists). *Allodoxia* presents itself as a "misapprehension" and is the domain of "imitation": it is a question of confusing, for example, imitation leather with real leather.

Conversely, for Rancière, the itineraries of the first representatives of working-class speech around 1830 reveal that this *allodoxia* does not condemn them to the iron cages of domination, but instead allows for an opening of a process of emancipation. He thus writes: "The first worker-militants began by taking themselves for poets or knights, priests or dandies. An allodoxia that is the only way to heterodoxia. Borrowed passions using the only words that make reappropriation possible: borrowed words."[38] This is why, the approach of the critical sociologist is accused of maintaining a continual error, stigmatizing such efforts as a sort of "false" emancipation. The sociological posture establishes suspicion "everywhere there had been the image of division and equivocality."[39] For Rancière, in order to deny "that the subject of democracy can ever happen, sociological critique speaks of the eternal reign of the slight difference."[40]

To shed light on this question, I will take an example from field research: an empirical study undertaken for my thesis, which involved a local ethnography of railway worker unionism.[41] It is an extract of a semi-directive interview with Pierre Dubois (April 1986), age 58 at the time, a retired union activist. His

---

[37] On the notion of allodoxia, see Pierre Bourdieu, *Distinction: A Social Critique of the Judgement of Taste*, trans. Richard Nice (Cambridge, MA: Harvard University Press, 1984), 323, 326–27, 459.
[38] Jacques Rancière, *The Philosopher and His Poor*, ed. Andrew Parker, trans. John Drury, Corrine Oster, and Andrew Parker (Durham: Duke University Press, 2004), 200.
[39] Rancière, *The Philosopher*, 201.
[40] Rancière, *The Philosopher*, 214.
[41] Philippe Corcuff, "Constructions du mouvement ouvrier. Activités cognitives, pratiques unificatrices et conflits dans un syndicat de cheminots" (Phd diss., EHESS, 1991).

father began as an unskilled worker and ended as a railway monitor. Dubois himself was a certified metalworker, and then passed an in-house training course with the SNCF (Société nationale des chemins de fer français) to begin his career as a specialist metalworker. He then became a railway monitor, and eventually manager, entering retirement at 52. During retirement, he resumed his studies: first by taking night courses at the labor exchange, and then by enrolling in the university where he obtained a degree in communication and journalism. Here is the critical way, based on his late university experience, in which he sees the "intellectual" in opposition to the "practical approach":

> Let's say that there's a lot of hot air in the pure intellectual, you know, always rummaging for the master idea, the idea that will take shape, drag something in . . . . In other words, I find that they're not very, well, they don't have a pragmatic enough mind . . . . A mind that loses itself with theories, in possibilities, with combinations, no, I say it's not right. But someone who has a practical mind, they say to themselves: "That's just not worth it" and they get on with it, they channel an operational way of thinking and do things right away.[42]

At another moment, however, he recognizes the importance of "contemplative work" and he qualifies his two years of university life as "beneficial at a personal level." He also notes how this dimension tends to be "lacking in the working class."[43] But the limitations he identifies in the working class have symmetrical counterparts in the limitations of intellectuals.

The danger for the intellectual would thus be to "lose themselves" in a multiplicity of "possibilities" and "combinations," thus the need for "channeling." For Pierre Dubois, the "practical mind"—arising from his familial, professional, and militant experience—constitutes a safeguard in the face of the vertigo of intellectual reflection, which, at its extreme, could even lead to despair:

> I would like to get into astronomy, but that leads to a reflection on infinity, and I just can't go there, I'd lose my mental equilibrium, it makes my stomach turn, I can't do it. Think about infinity—first you have a lid, than the box [he shows a box], and then nothingness, and then . . . . To imagine infinity, what never ends, for me, that remains inaccessible to humanity, I can't do it. No no, it makes be sick, just sick, it makes me crazy. It's really the point that just bothers me the most.[44]

---

[42] Corcuff, *critique sociale*, 53.
[43] Corcuff, *critique sociale*, 53.
[44] Corcuff, *critique sociale*, 53–54.

It would be easy to interpret the discourse of Pierre Dubois as one of *allodoxia*, following Bourdieu, in the sense of a misapprehension of intellectual work from an autodidact, for example in the connection he makes between "philosophical reflection" and a "queasy stomach." But doing so would involve a pitiful flattening of his experiences and his relationship to the world expressed in his words. What if we took Pierre Dubois more seriously, and consider the way he establishes a singular relationship to the intellectual world? Can't we see, in the tensions between the "practical" and the "intellectual" pole, a displacement of the traditionally dominant cultural hierarchy? We can clearly observe, in such trial and error, an emancipatory logic that involves "borrowings," in Rancière's words, and hybridizations. We thus move away from the elitist tendency of Bourdieu's notion of *allodoxia* that is quick to cast doubt on the intellectual authenticity of popular discourses, the self-taught, or the petite bourgeoisie.

This does not mean our perspective is situated in an unreal, peaceful world and neglects the significance of constraints of domination. It appears appropriate to integrate, here, an element of truth from sociological critique, lest we forget about other characteristics of Pierre Dubois' experience as seen through his discourse. Indeed, the constraints of domination are visible in his speech: there is both a distancing and a reverence in his relationship to the intellectual world. And Pierre Dubois willingly recognizes himself to be clumsy with respect to the resources and the procedures of a world that was originally foreign to him. The initial gap between social worlds is clearly acknowledged. And the physical distress he feels in his discussion of intellectual reflection on infinity reveals the corporal imprint of such initial discrepancies in relation to the intellectual realm. Bourdieu rightly insisted on the importance of the body regarding dominant norms and widely divergent social worlds. The passage I cited earlier from *Pascalian Meditations* is relevant to this aspect of the involuntary character of "bodily emotion (shame, timidity, anxiety, guilt)."

Emancipatory borrowings and hybridizations, on the one hand, and embedded constraints of dominations, on the other: we shouldn't seek to reduce one or the other, but rather assume the tension between them, in order to understand the ambivalences of experience.

Rancière/Bourdieu: Two Partial Approaches to Emancipation

At this stage of the analysis, it seems useful to pause a moment in order to compare the privileged images of emancipation in Rancière and Bourdieu's work.

For Rancière, the image of emancipation consists in the crossing of social division, notably in borrowings from dominant social milieux, allowing for the possibility of equality within social worlds marked by inequality. Thus, there is emancipation, according to Rancière, "when the egalitarian contingency disrupts the natural pecking order."[45] He further notes that emancipation is related to the "blurring of the boundary between those who act and those who look."[46] This still leaves rather murky, however, the element of emancipatory logic that acts to breach the objective and internalized weight of dominations.

There are also paths to emancipation in Bourdieu, even if they are more marginal than for Rancière (for whom emancipation is a principle theme) and less visible in the framework of his sociology. Bourdieu takes inspiration form the Spinozist model of relative liberty through understanding determinations.[47] Emancipation would thus be principally associated with the knowledge of one's own social determinants, at both the individual and collective level. This tends, however, to give an intellectual and elitist tint to emancipation.

These two partial images of emancipation are not necessarily mutually exclusive. We can imagine, as in the case of Pierre Dubois, that emancipatory borrowings can be enriched with knowledge, without any shame, of the limitations against which one is confronted. Bourdieu speaks to this effect in the postscript to the collective work *The Weight of the World*, when he invokes the possibility of "allowing those who suffer to find out that their suffering can be imputed to social causes and thus to feel exonerated."[48] The point, though, is to avoid letting critical analysis of social determinants swallow the entirety of experience in the dynamic of a generalized suspicion. Tension here again!

Putting the critical sociology of Bourdieu in tension with the philosophy of emancipation of Rancière allows us to grasp the question from both ends: from the capacities of the oppressed *and* by their incapacities, in order to build new approaches that are both critical *and* pragmatic-comprehensive. In this perspective, a critical sociology of domination would not necessarily be an obstacle to the logic of emancipation, but a dynamic space of tensions could open up between them. Tensions would remain, of course, because the two poles remain irreconcilable. There is no definitive harmony possible between critique and emancipation, just as there is no Hegelian "end of history."

---

[45] Jacques Rancière, *Disagreement: Politics and Philosophy*, trans. Julie Rose (Minneapolis: University of Minnesota Press, 1999), 18.
[46] Rancière, *The Emancipated Spectator*, 19.
[47] Benedict de Spinoza, *Ethic,* trans. William Hale White (London: Trubner & Co, 1883), Part III, proposition II, 108–12, and Part V, proposition X, 260–62.
[48] Pierre Bourdieu, ed., *The Weight of the World: Social Suffering in Contemporary Society*, trans. Priscilla Parkhurst Ferguson (Stanford: Stanford University Press, 1999), 629.

RETHINKING EMANCIPATION IN LIGHT OF CURRENT ISSUES: INDIVIDUALITY, THE IDENTITARIANIST CHALLENGE, AND THE POLITICS OF OPEN BEING

To reassociate social critique and emancipation in a renewed critical theory, at the crossroads of the social sciences and political philosophy, calls for at least three major areas of work, of which I propose only a partial treatment here: the domain of critical sociology, addressed in the first part of the article; the relationship between sociological critique and the philosophy of emancipation, addressed in the second part; and that of political philosophy, which I will address in this third and last section. I will privilege the angle of individual singularity understood in a relationist perspective, that is, within social relations.

Individual Singularity as the Basis for Emancipatory Social Critique

Individuality, as singularity, has been an important support for social critique with an emancipatory horizon since the end of the eighteenth century, as heir to the modern history of the self in the Western tradition.[49] A link was then established in various ways between the perspective of individual self-governance and that of the collective self-governance of human groups, which Cornelius Castoriadis systematized in the second half of the twentieth century by centering the thought of emancipation around the question of autonomy.[50] But it is an autonomy grasped in a relationalist way, integrating the contributions of the social sciences, and conceived in the course of historically situated social relations, and not in a monadic and timeless way as tends to be the case in the tradition of political liberalism. Moreover, the Western world does not have a monopoly on individuality, as other civilizations have also constructed figures of individual singularity.[51] And today, in a more globalized world, hybrid forms are developing in the interplay between relations of domination and resistance. Individuality does not therefore constitute a universal, but could constitute a universalizable horizon on the basis of intercultural dialogue.

---

[49] Charles Taylor, *Sources of the Self: The Making of the Modern Identity* (Cambridge: Cambridge University Press, 1992).
[50] Cornelius Castoriadis, *The Imaginary Institution of Society*, trans. Kathleen Blamey (Cambridge, MA: MIT Press, 1997).
[51] Emmanuel Lozerand, ed., *Drôles d'individus. De la singularité individuelle dans le Reste-du-monde* (Paris: Klincksieck, 2014).

However, in the first half of the twentieth century, the level of individual emancipation was made secondary, even marginalized, in the dominant currents of the labor and socialist movement, outside the anarchist sectors, in favor of what I call "collectivist programing." North America should be treated as an exception, where the individualist component has remained more prominent on the left.

In increasingly individualized contemporary societies, though, individual singularity could constitute an even more important emancipatory element for a radical critique of capitalism. For the contradiction *capital/individuality*, partially developed in Marx's analyses,[52] is central to the functioning of capitalism, especially its contemporary variant which valorizes the figure of the entrepreneurial "individual."[53] Capitalism contributes, on the one hand, to nourishing contemporary individualism (in interaction with other social logics that cannot be reduced to capitalism, such as the consolidation of personal intimacy, the recognition of individual rights, or the transformations of the patriarchal family) and stimulates desires for personal fulfillment. On the other, capitalism ultimately limits and truncates individuality through commodification and the division of labor. It thus gives rise to desires for self-realization that it cannot really satisfy within the dynamics of capital accumulation via the profit motive. By encouraging dreams of individual fulfillment and personal recognition, capitalism ultimately creates frustrations. Wounded individualities could constitute potential levers for the subversion of capitalism; these could be politicized through language and action that is political in a broad sense, rather than narrowly partisan.

But for a convergence of multiple forms of contestation to capitalism to arise, the question of individuality must implicitly be linked to the "social question," referring to the production and distribution of resources (economic and cultural in particular). In his ethics of the face, Emmanuel Levinas offers pathways to establish this relationship (though such a relation needs to be based on an infinite tension by taking inspiration from Proudhon, discussed below).[54] He immediately grasps individual singularity in a relationalist manner through the face of the other, in its incomparable uniqueness. But the question of social justice, and thus of the space of the comparable, is also

---

[52] Philippe Corcuff, "Individualité et contradictions du néocapitalisme," *SociologieS*, October 22, 2006, http://sociologies.revues.org/document462.html.
[53] Luc Boltanski and Eve Chiapello, *The New Spirit of Capitalism*, trans. Gregory Elliott (New York: Verso, 2018).
[54] Philippe Corcuff, "Repères libertaires et pragmatiques pour des coalitions altermondialistes," *Politiques de coalition. Penser et se mobiliser avec Judith Butler/Politics of Coalition. Thinking Collective Action with Judith Butler*, ed. Delphine Gardey and Cynthia Kraus (Zurich: Seismo, 2016), 194–219.

present in the figure of the "third" [*tiers*]. In the following passage, he suggests a possible connection between the incomparable and the comparable:

> How is it that there is justice? I answer that it is the fact of the multiplicity of men and the presence of someone else next to the Other, which condition the laws and establish justice. If I am alone with the Other, I owe him everything, but there is someone else . . . . It is consequently necessary to weigh, to think, to judge, in comparing the incomparable.[55]

Levinas thus provides an initial framework to understand the necessary and irreconcilable tension between the incommensurability of individual singularity, under the modality of the other's face, on the one hand, and the common space of measurement and social justice, on the other. The formula "comparing the incomparable" appears to be a particularly heuristic way of dealing with the relationship between the question of individuality and the social question.

Emancipation and Contemporary Identitarianist Politics

Another angle on the question of emancipation in the early twenty-first century needs to be considered here. For the horizon of individual and collective autonomy as an escape from subordinating relations of domination within historically situated social relations, in the tradition of Kant to Castoriadis, cannot suffice to characterize emancipation in the face of mounting identitarianist tendencies. In the introduction, I mentioned the rise of ultraconservative and xenophobic uses of national identity in Europe, the United States, and Brazil. But other, very different modalities of association between authoritarianism (of varying degrees), conservatism, and identity (nationalist and/or religious) make up significant political forces around the world. These include the various forms of more or less authoritarian Islamic conservatism (from the political regimes of Iran and the Gulf monarchies to the softer forms of Islamism heading the Moroccan government or participating in the Tunisian government, without forgetting the increasingly repressive Islamic government of Turkey's Recep Tayyip Erdogan) to its most extreme, murderous forms (jihadism); and various forms of nationalism, incarnated by Vladimir Putin in Russia, the radicalized and colonizing right-wing authority of Benjamin Netanyahu in Israel, or the Hindu nationalism in power in India. China has seen the stabilization since the 1990s of a particular socio-political

---

[55] Emmanuel Levinas and Philippe Nemo, *Ethics and Infinity*, trans. Richard A. Cohen (Pittsburgh, PA: Duquesne University Press, 1985), 89–90.

configuration combining unbridled capitalism, nationalistic rhetoric, and the authoritarian political power of a single party, the Chinese Communist Party.

To criticize *identitarianisms* is not to deny any place to individual and collective identities in politics, but to question the political focus on a single, homogenous, and closed identity in the understanding of an individual or a group. It is the logic of identity closure that is targeted. Identitarianism is a form of essentialism, since it tends to transform individual and collective identities into singular, sealed entities. It is of course legitimate to defend minority cultural identities in the promotion of cultural pluralism to oppose cultural domination (which is often associated with economic and political domination, for example in colonial, neocolonial, and postcolonial situations). The passage from fully justified identity claims to dangerous identitarianist logics takes place when the identities in question are considered to be closed, policed by identitarian gatekeepers, for example in the face of migrations seen as "threatening," and when the diverse alluviums constitutive of identity-in-movement are ignored.[56]

Rethinking the place of individual singularity in a politics of emancipation also means being equipped to disarm such identitarianist traps. In a relationalist approach, individuality is conceived as a place of crossing and hybridization of a variety of collective affiliations and experiences; even if its socially and historically constituted uniqueness makes it irreducible to each of them.

Levinas: Resources for a Politics of Open Being

Here again, Levinas provides us with tools to refine our analysis of how individual singularity can be used against identitarian confinement.[57] He does not deny the weight of stabilized identities, but he puts them in tension with the possibility of "getting out of being," which is part of the human condition. He does so by using several images he constructed over the course of his intellectual career, such as "escape," "the caress," and "the face of the other."

In an early text of 1935 on "escape," Levinas questions identitarianist tendencies in theoretical and political reflections on being: "Being is: ...this...is precisely what one states when one speaks of the identity of being. Identity...

---

[56] Faced with the risk of oppressed groups fixing themselves into rigid identities, two figures that have marked postcolonial thought, Palestinian Edward Saïd and Jamaican-born Briton Stuart Hall, emphasized the interpenetration and hybrid character of cultures in general and dominated cultures in particular. See Edward W. Said, "Introduction," *Culture and Imperialism* (New York: Vintage, 1994), xii–xxviii, and Stuart Hall, "The Multi-cultural Question," *Un/Settled Multiculturalisms: Diasporas, Entanglement, Transruptions*, ed. Barnor Hesse (London: Zed Books, 2000), 209–41.

[57] Philippe Corcuff, "Levinas-Abensour contre Spinoza-Lordon. Ressources libertaires pour s'émanciper des pensées de l'identité en contexte ultra-conservateur," *Réfractions. Recherches et expressions anarchistes*, no. 39 (Winter 2017): 109–22 and Philippe Corcuff, *Réinventer l'émancipation* (Paris: Seuil, 2022).

expresses the sufficiency of the fact of being, whose absolute and definitive character no one, it seems, could place in doubt."[58] He contrasts this conception of being with his notion of escape as "getting out of being,"[59] a notion that has generated much scholarly discussion. Miguel Abensour, a thinker of emancipation and utopia, writes: "From what is the escape from? From being as such, from its limits. For being itself, in its completeness, is imprisonment, confinement."[60] Abensour is one of the few critical thinkers to put Levinas to political use, by drawing utopian resources from him against the identitarian weight of being, whereas Levinas is often apprehended within the academic limits of moral philosophy, far removed from politics.

In a text published after the Second World War, Levinas explores the notion of the caress. In terms of the dominant socio-historical imaginary in the West, the caress can be associated with a "feminine" erotic—in contrast to the erotic of "seizing" and "possessing," associated with the dominant socio-historical imaginary of the "masculine" erotic. He thus writes:

> The seeking of the caress constitutes its essence by the fact that the caress does not know what it seeks. This "not knowing," this fundamental disorder, is essential. It is like a game with something slipping away, a game absolutely without project or plan, not with what can become ours or us, but with something other, always other, always inaccessible, and always to come [à venir].
>
> Can this relationship with the other through Eros be characterized as a failure? Once again, the answer is yes, if one adopts the terminology of current descriptions, if one wants to characterize the erotic by "grasping," "possessing," or "knowing." But there is nothing of all this, or the failure of all this, in eros. If one could possess, grasp, and know the other, it would not be other. Possessing, knowing, and grasping are synonyms of power.[61]

The movement *elsewhere* of the caress is an infinite exploration, without aiming at a final realization. The figure of the caress can be used metaphorically to enrich a politics of emancipation: utopia is not a state one reaches, but an endless movement toward the "unattainable." Utopia cannot be realized in a definitive way, it is always "to come." In this sense, as Miguel Abensour writes, utopia is "beyond this or that particular project."[62] The utopian caress

---

[58] Emmanuel Levinas, *On Escape*, trans. Bettina Bergo (Stanford: Stanford University Press, 2003), 51.
[59] Levinas, *On Escape*, 73.
[60] Miguel Abensour, "L'extravagante hypothèse," *Levinas,* ed. Danielle Cohen-Levinas (Paris: Bayard, 2006), 78.
[61] Emmanuel Levinas, *Time and the Other*, trans. Richard A. Cohen (Pittsburgh, PA: Duquesne University Press, 1987), 89–90.
[62] Miguel Abensour, *Utopia from Thomas More to Walter Benjamin*, trans. Raymond N. MacKenzie (Minneapolis: Univocal Publishing, 2017), 51.

is perpetual discovery, a constantly renewed sense of change. For Levinas, utopia, particularly in the form of caress, is a fundamental characteristic of human beings in their movement of escape from being, even if the logic of a return to being constantly restrains such escape (a logic which is perhaps more pervasive, but less specific to the human condition). The return of being in this case takes the form of "power," understood as a claim to total mastery and knowledge of the other. But there is something in the other that necessarily escapes me, that only allows me to take partial control, that "escapes" my claim to have total control. If this were not the case, the other would not be *other*, it would be the *same*. The reduction of the other to the same, to identity, is precisely one of the hallmarks of "power" for Levinas.

Totality and Infinity and *Otherwise than Being*[63] are Levinas' two major books of philosophical maturity, in which he employs the figure of the face of the other as the expression of a singular distress that calls for my responsibility. Levinas here shifts his emphasis toward the impossibility of completely *comprehending* the other, in the double meaning of the word: to know them completely *and* to encompass them. For there is something in the other that escapes my totalizing grasp: the irreducible uniqueness of their face. Levinas thus speaks of "ethics as that disruption of our being-in-the-world which opens us to the other."[64] The figure of the self does not disappear, but it loses its pretension to be the fundamental and exclusive expression of personal singularity by becoming decentralized in the inter-human relationship: "I become a responsible or ethical 'I' to the extent that I agree to depose or dethrone myself—to abdicate my position of centrality—in favour of the vulnerable other."[65]

These three figures—escape, the caress, and the face of the other—thus allow us to consider emancipation in terms of emancipation from identitarian closures. A policy of open, exploratory, and adventurous identities could then take shape: open to fear, open to anxiety, open to what is not them, open to hybridization and transformation, open to the new, held together by relative stabilizations. Such a perspective would both arise from identity and subvert it, avoiding the pitfalls of identitarianism. Judith Butler, a thinker who has done much to integrate Levinasian resources into critical theory, grasps this as "the constitution of the subject by and in alterity."[66]

---

[63] Emmanuel Levinas, *Totality and Infinity: An Essay on Exteriority*, trans. Alphonso Lingis (Pittsburgh, PA: Duquesne University Press, 1969) and Emmanuel Levinas, *Otherwise Than Being, Or Beyond Essence*, trans. Alphonso Lingis (Pittsburgh, PA: Duquesne University Press, 1998).
[64] Emmanuel Levinas, "Ethics of the Infinite: Interview with Richard Kearney," in *Dialogues with Contemporary Continental Thinkers: The Phenomenological Heritage*, ed. Richard Kearney (Manchester: Manchester University Press), 59.
[65] Emmanuel Levinas, "Ethics of the Infinite," 63.
[66] Judith Butler, *Parting Ways: Jewishness and the Critique of Zionism* (New York: Columbia University Press, 2012), 39.

Other Images for a Politics of Open Being

Other intellectual resources can be drawn on to enrich Levinas' repertory in order to challenge identitarian closure and work toward the reinvention of emancipatory thought in the contemporary moment. Jacques Rancière's philosophy of political subjectivation constitutes another resource, whereby the dominant social order is disrupted through his conception of democracy. In his critique of Bourdieu discussed earlier, Rancière emphasizes the borrowing and blurring of preconstituted social identities that are part of an emancipatory logic. In his critical dialogue with Axel Honneth, he provides a more theoretical perspective on this point: his concept of "disidentification" allows for an escape from dominant assigned identities, avoiding "frustration," and thus constitutes an important dimension of an emancipatory dynamic.[67]

Another theoretical perspective is that of Judith Butler in *Gender Trouble*,[68] with her stimulating use of Levinas' philosophy mentioned earlier. By destabilizing "gender" and then calling on feminist political theory to break with "identity politics," Butler provides other possible bifurcations for a politics of identity openness.

Finally, within postcolonial studies, the analysis of the sociologist Abdellali Hajjat is pertinent, particularly her critique of the pitfalls of "inverted essentialism" present in certain forms of mobilization against racial discrimination and stigmatization, for instance by the *Indigènes de la République* in France. Without putting the essentialism of the dominant and the essentialism of the dominated on the exact same level, her analysis provides an outline for a decolonial and intersectional politics of open being.[69] The risk of "inverted essentialism" involves the marginalization of individual singularity (as a place where a diversity of collective threads intersect) in favor of constituted collectivities, whereby representatives of subordinate groups are fetishized and their culture hermetically sealed off.[70]

---

[67] Axel Honneth and Jacques Rancière, *Recognition or Disagreement: A Critical Encounter on the Politics of Freedom, Equality, and Identity*, ed. Jean-Philppe Deranty and Katia Genel (New York: Columbia University Press, 2016), 92–95, 119–20, 122, 126–27.

[68] Judith Butler, *Gender Trouble: Feminism and the Subversion of Identity* (New York: Routledge, 2011).

[69] Abdellali Hajjat, "Les dilemmes de l'autonomie : assimilation, indigénisme et libération," *Quartiers XXI*, October 7, 2015, http://quartiersxxi.org/les-dilemmes-de-l-autonomie-assimilation-indigenisme-et-liberation.

[70] See Pierre Bourdieu, "Delegation and Political Fetishism," *Language and Symbolic Power*, ed. John B. Thompson, trans. Gino Raymond and Matthew Adamson (Cambridge, MA: Harvard University Press, 1991), 203–19.

CONCLUSION: TOWARD A NEW APPROACH TO THEORY

After exploring the current academic misadventures of critical theory within French sociology, and confronting Pierre Bourdieu's critical sociology with Jacques Rancière's philosophy of emancipation, and, finally, attempting to enrich political philosophy of emancipation through Levinas, I will not conclude by proposing a new critical theory with a unified emancipatory horizon. Rather, I have attempted to sketch out a new approach to theory (and what is meant by theory). This approach takes distance from the most traditional relationship to conceptualization: that of a systematic (or totalizing) style, in the sense of Hegel's "philosophical system," or the body of works brought together to constitute "Marxism" (which is far removed from the more composite and shifting writings of Marx himself).

Instead, I propose an elliptical style of theory that would take its inspiration from the idea of "theory as a toolkit" promoted and practiced by Michel Foucault, emphasizing the mobility of the questioning and the conceptual tools used to confront problems.[71] This type of theory seeks to delineate problems and areas of tension, rather than build hierarchical and integrated systems of concepts. Areas of tension remain, because it is not only a question of articulating problems and concepts between themselves, as it was classically, but also of thinking through the antinomies at work in the problems explored, without trying to resolve them in a theoretical system. To this end, Proudhon's notion of "balancing oppositions" is useful, in its opposition to the Hegelian-inspired notion of overcoming contradictions.

Anarchist militant and self-taught philosopher of the nineteenth century, Pierre-Joseph Proudhon[72] produced a little-known critique of the Hegelian dialectic, or rather a critique of the simplified version of it expressed in the triad thesis–antithesis–synthesis taught in what Merleau-Ponty called "textbook Hegel."[73] In *De la Justice dans la Révolution et dans l'Église* (On justice in revolution and church), Proudhon writes:

> The Hegelian formula [thesis–antithesis–synthesis] is a triad only for the good pleasure or error of the master, who counts three terms where there are really

---

[71] Michel Foucault, "Power and Strategies," *Power/Knowledge: Selected Interviews and Other Writings, 1972–1977*, ed. by Colin Gordon, trans. Colin Gordon et al. (New York: Pantheon Books, 1980), 145.

[72] We should not overlook, however, the repeated sexist statements and the few, much rarer, traces of anti-semitism that Proudhon draws from the stereotypes of his era. It is the mark of the weaknesses of a mind that was otherwise quite lucid about the prejudices of its time.

[73] Maurice Merleau-Ponty, *Sense and Non-Sense*, trans. Hubert L. Dreyfus and Patricia Allen Dreyfus (Evanston, IL: Northwestern University Press, 1964), 81.

only two, and who does not see that antinomy is not resolved, but instead indicates an oscillation or antagonism susceptible only of equilibrium.[74]

Antinomy would thus be primary, in the form of an unstable and shifting balance. In Proudhon's work, the principle of antinomy replaces the Hegelian-inspired principle of overcoming, that is, the overcoming of contradictions into a unifying entity or "synthesis." In a posthumous book published shortly after his death in 1866, *Théorie de la propriété* (The theory of property), he states:

> I recognized that if antinomy is a law of nature and intelligence, like all the notions it affects, it cannot be resolved; it remains eternally what it is, first cause of all movement, principle of all life and evolution, through the contradiction of its terms; antinomy can only be balanced, either through the balancing of oppositions [*équilibration des contraires*], or through its opposition to other antinomies.[75]

Here Proudhon's text takes on an ontological dimension: antinomy is presented as "a law of nature" and therefore "the first cause of all movement, principle of all life and evolution." Appearing together with the notion of antinomy is the notion of "balancing of oppositions," which constitutes for Proudhon a particular modality of antinomy, and presents for us perhaps an even more heuristic formula, as it opens up in particular an original conception of political spaces emancipated from the predominance of the One.

My hybrid personal itinerary, as an academic and as an anti-capitalist, libertarian, and alter-globalist activist, has nourished my approach to critical theory. Openness *to* the outside world—through the diffusion and hybridization of academic work—and openness *toward* the outside world—toward views abandoned by the academic world and toward critical questions about its functioning and its productions—both call for dialogue, cooperation, cross-fertilization, and reciprocal critique. Such an approach is facilitated by the fact that we can already see, in our societies, the existence of an intermixing between scholarly knowledge and ordinary knowledge, inserted in a dynamic of interrelationships, continuities and discontinuities, similarities and differences. At the same time, this type of approach must not ignore the irreducible antinomy between scholarly knowledge and ordinary logic, or between scientific distance and militant engagements. My experience in hybrid circles situated in the in-between—such as being part of the Scientific

---

[74] Proudhon, *De la justice*, 35.
[75] Proudhon, *Théorie de la propriété*, 206.

Council of the alter-globalist association ATTAC, participating in alternative popular universities, contributing to the journal *ContreTemps* led by the Marxist activist and philosopher Daniel Bensaïd, or my involvement in the militant and anarchist research seminar ETAPE (Explorations Théoriques Anarchistes Pragmatistes pour l'Emancipation)—has been a useful reminder of this permanently unstable balance.

In this renewed theoretical perspective, something like an incomplete, constantly moving constellation can emerge. Its results would always be provisional, and would not appear as a closed "whole." And they certainly would not be limited to verified and verifiable knowledge, since a more global orientation is sought. For it is useful to situate the various types of knowledge produced in the course of an investigation (in this case, a critical theory with an emancipatory aim) within a more global landscape, thus avoiding the fragmentation of increasingly specialized knowledge, but without claiming to see "everything." In so doing, a global compass would both feed specific inquiries and look beyond their scope, thus opening up new paths for other investigations, which in turn would be capable of shifting the compass coordinates. This approach would lead to theoretical constructions in motion, provisional, partial, wrought with inevitable tensions, associating problems in a variable way rather than casting them into a common structure.

The pathways leading to a renewed critical theory today cannot follow the totalizing inclinations of yesterday. The numerous observations regarding the diversification of knowledge and the fragility of human understanding lead us away from this direction, though it still arouses a great deal of nostalgia among contemporary thinkers. We must not, however, abandon a global compass, by remaining too immersed in specialized divisions or by giving in to the infinite dissipation of meaning initiated by postmodernism. New critical theories must remain committed to the global, without subscribing to the uncontrolled charms of the total.

BIBLIOGRAPHY

Abensour, Miguel. *Utopia from Thomas More to Walter Benjamin.* Translated by Raymond N. MacKenzie. Minneapolis: Univocal Publishing, 2017.

Abensour, Miguel. "L'extravagante hypothèse." In *Levinas,* edited by Danielle Cohen-Levinas, 55–84. Paris: Bayard, 2006.

Atlan, Henri. *Enlightenment to Enlightenment: Intercritique of Science and Myth.* Translated by Lenn J. Schramm. Albany: SUNY Press, 1993.

Boltanski, Luc. *On Critique: A Sociology of Emancipation.* Translated by Gregory Elliot. Malden, MA: Polity Press, 2011.

Boltanski, Luc, and Eve Chiapello. *The New Spirit of Capitalism.* Translated by Gregory Elliott. New York: Verso, 2018.

Boltanski, Luc, Philippe Corcuff, and Nancy Fraser. *Domination et émancipation. Pour un renouveau de la critique sociale* (Lyon: Presses Universitaires de Lyon, 2014).

Boltanski, Luc, and Arnaud Esquerre. *Vers l'extrême: extension des domaines de la droite.* Bellevaux: Éditions Dehors, 2014.

Boltanski, Luc, and Arnaud Esquerre. *Enrichment: A Critique of Commodities.* Translated by Catherine Porter. Medford, MA: Polity Press, 2020.

Bourdieu, Pierre. *Distinction: A Social Critique of the Judgement of Taste.* Translated by Richard Nice. Cambridge, MA: Harvard University Press, 1984.

Bourdieu, Pierre. "Delegation and Political Fetishism." In *Language and Symbolic Power*, edited by John B. Thompson, translated by Gino Raymond and Matthew Adamson, 203–19. Cambridge, MA: Harvard University Press, 1991.

Bourdieu, Pierre. *Pascalian Meditations.* Translated by Richard Nice. Stanford: Stanford University Press, 2000.

Bourdieu, Pierre. *Science of Science and Reflexivity.* Translated by Richard Nice. Chicago: University of Chicago Press, 2004.

Bourdieu, Pierre, ed. *The Weight of the World: Social Suffering in Contemporary Society.* Translated by Priscilla Parkhurst Ferguson. Stanford: Stanford University Press, 1999.

Butler, Judith. *Gender Trouble: Feminism and the Subversion of Identity.* New York: Routledge, 2011.

Butler, Judith. *Parting Ways: Jewishness and the Critique of Zionism.* New York: Columbia University Press, 2012.

Castoriadis, Cornelius. *The Imaginary Institution of Society.* Translated by Kathleen Blamey. Cambridge, MA: MIT Press, 1997.

Cervera-Marzal, Manuel. *Miguel Abensour, critique de la domination, pensée de l'émancipation.* Paris: Sens & Tonka, 2013.

Corcuff, Philippe. *Les années 30 reviennent et la gauche est dans le brouillard.* Paris: Textuel, 2014.

Corcuff, Philippe. "Antinomies et analogies comme outils transversaux en sociologie: en partant de Proudhon et de Passeron." *SociologieS*, November 2, 2015. http://journals.openedition.org/sociologies/5154.

Corcuff, Philippe. "Après le Brexit et Trump: confusionnisme à gauche et extrême droitisation idéologique." *Les Possibles*, no. 12 (February 2017): 51–62. https://france.attac.org/nos-publications/les-possibles/numero-12-hiver-2017/dossier-la-droitisation-des-politiques/article/apres-le-brexit-et-trump-confusionnisme-a-gauche-et-extreme-droitisation.

Corcuff, Philippe. "Le bêtisier sociologique et philosophique de Nathalie Heinich." *Lectures*, July 9, 2018. https://journals.openedition.org/lectures/25494.

Corcuff, Philippe. *Bourdieu autrement: fragilité d'un sociologue de combat.* Paris: Textuel, 2003.

Corcuff, Philippe. "Constructions du mouvement ouvrier. Activités cognitives, pratiques unificatrices et conflits dans un syndicat de cheminots." Phd diss., EHESS, 1991.

Corcuff, Philippe. *Enjeux libertaires pour le XXIe siècle par un anarchiste néophyte.* Paris: Éditions du Monde libertaire, 2015.
Corcuff, Philippe. *La grande confusion. Comment l'extrême droite gagne la bataille des idées.* Paris: Textuel, 2021.
Corcuff, Philippe, "Levinas-Abensour contre Spinoza-Lordon. Ressources libertaires pour s'émanciper des pensées de l'identité en contexte ultra-conservateur." *Réfractions. Recherches et expressions anarchistes*, no. 39 (Winter 2017): 109–22.
Corcuff, Philippe. "Individualité et contradictions du néocapitalisme." *SociologieS*, October 22, 2006. http://sociologies.revues.org/document462.html.
Corcuff, Philippe. *Où est passé la critique sociale? Penser le global au croisement des savoirs.* Paris: La Découverte, 2012.
Corcuff, Philippe. *Réinventer l'émancipation.* Paris: Scuil, 2022.
Corcuff, Philippe. "Repères libertaires et pragmatiques pour des coalitions altermondialistes." In *Politiques de coalition. Penser et se mobiliser avec Judith Butler/ Politics of Coalition. Thinking Collective Action with Judith Butler*, edited by Delphine Gardey and Cynthia Kraus, 194–219. Zurich: Seismo, 2016.
Foucault, Michel. "Power and Strategies." In *Power/Knowledge: Selected Interviews and Other Writings, 1972–1977*, edited by Colin Gordon, translated by Colin Gordon, Leo Marshall, John Mepham, and Kate Soper, 134–45. New York: Pantheon Books, 1980.
Frère, Bruno, ed. *Le tournant de la théorie critique.* Paris: Desclée de Brouwer, 2015.
Hajjat, Abdellali. "Les dilemmes de l'autonomie: assimilation, indigénisme et libération." *Quartiers XXI*, October 7, 2015. http://quartiersxxi.org/les-dilemmes-de-l-autonomie-assimilation-indigenisme-et-liberation.
Hall, Stuart. "The Multi-cultural Question." In *Un/Settled Multiculturalisms: Diasporas, Entanglement, Transruptions*, edited by Barnor Hesse, 209–41. London: Zed Books, 2000.
Heinich, Nathalie. *Ce que l'art fait à la sociologie.* Paris: Minuit, 1998.
Heinich, Nathalie. "Misères de la sociologie critique." *Le débat* 197, no. 5 (2017): 119–26.
Heinich, Nathalie. *Des valeurs. Une approche sociologique.* Paris: Gallimard, 2017.
Honneth, Axel, and Jacques Rancière. *Recognition or Disagreement: A Critical Encounter on the Politics of Freedom, Equality, and Identity.* Edited by Jean-Philpe Deranty and Katia Genel. New York: Columbia University Press, 2016.
Horkheimer, Max. "Traditional and Critical Theory." In *Critical Theory: Selected Essays*, translated by Matthew J. O'Connel et al., 188–243. New York: Continuum, 2002.
Kalinowski, Isabelle. "Leçons wébériennes sur la science et la propagande." In *La science, profession & vocation*, by Max Weber, 61–173. Marseille: Agone, 2005.
Kant, Immanuel. "An Answer to the Question: What Is Enlightenment?" In *Towards Perpetual Peace and Other Writings on Politics, Peace, and History*, edited by Pauline Kleingeld, 17–23. New Haven: Yale University Press, 2006.
"La sociologie au risque d'un dévoiement." *Le débat* 197, no. 5 (2017): 113–41.
Lagasnerie Geoffroy de. *L'empire de l'université. Sur Bourdieu, les intellectuels et le journalisme.* Paris: Éditions Amsterdam, 2007.

Lagasnerie, Geoffroy de. *Juger. L'État pénal face à la sociologie.* Paris: Fayard, 2016.

Lahire, Bernard. *Pour la sociologie. Et pour finir avec une prétendue "culture de l'excuse."* Paris: La Découverte, 2016.

"Les fractures intellectuelles de la sociologie française." *Le Monde*, November 24, 2017.

Levinas, Emmanuel. "Ethics of the Infinite: Interview with Richard Kearney." In *Dialogues with Contemporary Continental Thinkers: The Phenomenological Heritage,* edited by Richard Kearney, 47–70. Manchester: Manchester University Press, 1984.

Levinas, Emmanuel. *On Escape.* Translated by Bettina Bergo. Stanford: Stanford University Press, 2003.

Levinas, Emmanuel. *Otherwise Than Being, Or Beyond Essence.* Translated by Alphonso Lingis. Pittsburgh, PA: Duquesne University Press, 1998.

Levinas, Emmanuel. *Time and the Other.* Translated by Richard A. Cohen. Pittsburgh, PA: Duquesne University Press, 1987.

Levinas, Emmanuel. *Totality and Infinity: An Essay on Exteriority.* Translated by Alphonso Lingis. Pittsburgh, PA: Duquesne University Press, 1969.

Levinas, Emmanuel, and Philippe Nemo. *Ethics and Infinity.* Translated by Richard A. Cohen. Pittsburgh, PA: Duquesne University Press, 1985.

Lozerand, Emmanuel, ed. *Drôles d'individus. De la singularité individuelle dans le Reste-du-monde.* Paris: Klincksieck, 2014.

Merleau-Ponty, Maurice. *Sense and Non-Sense.* Translated by Hubert L. Dreyfus and Patricia Allen Dreyfus. Evanston, IL: Northwestern University Press, 1964.

Proudhon, Pierre-Joseph. *De la justice dans la révolution et dans l'église.* 4 vols. Paris: Fayard, 1988.

Proudhon, Pierre-Joseph. *Théorie de la propriété.* Paris: L'Harmattan, 1997.

Rancière, Jacques. "Critique of the Critique of the 'Spectacle.'" In *Dissenting Words: Interviews with Jacques Rancière,* edited and translated by Emiliano Battista, 255–71. New York: Bloomsbury, 2017.

Rancière, Jacques. *Disagreement: Politics and Philosophy.* Translated by Julie Rose. Minneapolis: University of Minnesota Press, 1999.

Rancière, Jacques. *The Emancipated Spectator.* Translated by Gregory Elliot. New York: Verso, 2009.

Rancière, Jacques. *The Ignorant Schoolmaster: Five Lessons in Intellectual Emancipation. T* Translated by Kristin Ross. Stanford: Stanford University Press, 1991.

Rancière, Jacques. *The Philosopher and His Poor.* Edited by Andrew Parker, translated by John Drury, Corrine Oster, and Andrew Parker. Durham: Duke University Press, 2004.

Said, Edward W. *Culture and Imperialism.* New York: Vintage, 1994.

Séminaire ETAPE. *Explorations libertaires. Pour une pensée critique et émancipatrice.* Lyon: Atelier de création libertaire. 2019.

Spinoza, Benedict de. *Ethic.* Translated by William Hale White. London: Trubner & Co, 1883.

Taylor, Charles. *Sources of the Self: The Making of the Modern Identity*. Cambridge: Cambridge University Press, 1992.

Traverso, Enzo. *The New Faces of Fascism: Populism and the Far Right*. Translated by David Broder. New York: Verso, 2019.

Weber, Max. "'Objectivity' in Social Science and Social Policy." In *The Methodology of the Social Sciences*, edited and translated by Edward A. Shils and Henry A. Finch, 49–112. Glencoe, IL: The Free Press, 1949.

Weber, Max. "The Meaning of 'Ethical Neutrality' in Sociology and Economics." In *The Methodology of the Social Sciences*, edited and translated by Edward A. Shils and Henry A. Finch, 1–47. Glencoe, IL: The Free Press, 1949.

Weber, Max. "Politics as a Vocation." In *From Max Weber*, edited and translated by Hans H. Gerth and C. Wright Mills, 77–128. New York: Oxford University Press, 1946.

Wittgenstein, Ludwig. *Philosophical Investigations*. 4th ed. Edited and translated by G.E.M Anscombe, P.M.S. Hacker, and Joachim Schulte. Oxford: Wiley-Blackwell, 2010.

Chapter 9

Politics in Tensions. Counter-Currents for a Postcritical Age

Yves Citton

Translated by Daniel Benson

DOMINATION WITHOUT EMANCIPATION: TIME FOR POSTCRITICAL POLITICS?[1]

A radical critique of domination will lead to emancipation: over the past centuries, such a hope has fueled decades of (often successful) political struggles, and thus deserves much respect and gratitude. Should it continue to structure our current conception of political activism? That is much less clear. Many voices and many arguments seem to undermine our faith in this typically "modern" take on politics. The leftist critique of domination marching toward ever more freedom and equality seems to have lost a great deal of its traction over the past four decades. At best, it has slowed down, to the point of almost complete stasis. At worst, it has largely derailed into a new form of conservatism. Should the traditional heralds and heroes of emancipation see in this pause an opportunity to gather their forces, before resuming their triumphant march forward toward social progress? Or should they suspect their very banner to have become somewhat obsolete?

While acknowledging the proven merits of the critique of domination toward emancipation, this article suggests supplementing—not necessarily replacing—this traditional triangle with a *politics of tensions* more closely articulated with our contemporary economy of attention. It will be left to the reader to decide whether this politics of tensions is just another form of politics, able to help us renew our intellectual and practical toolkit to intervene more

---

[1] This section, parts of the section "Eighteen Political Counter-Currents," and the final section "What's Left in a Politics of Tensions and Counter-Currents?" were originally written in English. The rest of the chapter is my translation from the French, slightly revised and augmented by the author.—Ed.

effectively in the current and future evolutions of our ever-changing societies, or whether what is proposed here is the very negation (and denial) of what politics is, and should be, all about. I, for one, humbly confess to see equally good reasons to defend both of these apparently incompatible opinions.

But before sketching this proposal of supplementation, let us briefly survey some of the good reasons that can make us weary of the current valences of each of the three corners of the modernist triangle.

Domination clearly is the least objectionable of the three. The domination of capital over workers has rarely been so absolute and shameless. The domination of colonizing nations and populations over the rest of the world has certainly altered its modalities over the last hundred years, but it maintains a world order in which people of European descent keep exploiting the labor, resources, and cultures of the Global South, with important (but not yet game-changing) challenges coming from the far East. Within the Global North, while the status of women and racial and gender minorities has nominally improved over the last fifty years, social and economic domination proves dramatically persistent under the thin shellac of legal equality. Furthering the struggles against domination launched at the end of the eighteen century with the Haitian Revolution and the *Declaration of the Rights of Women* clearly remains on the order of the day.

Of course, conceptions of domination (most prominently in the work of French sociologist Pierre Bourdieu) often run the risk of reducing dominated parts of the population to the status of merely passive victims: but only minor adjustments are necessary to correct this. For half a century, cultural studies have taught us to pay more attention to the multiple forms of (often surprising, creative, and inspiring) agency developed among those who constantly invent new ways to deflect, dodge, neutralize, ridicule, and counteract the power used to oppress them.

Emancipation will be harder to salvage. Three major objections can be turned against its promise, a promise that has been so efficient in empowering disenfranchised populations with hopes of a better future. First, of course, the track records of supposedly emancipated societies have not been as convincing as one had initially hoped for. The USSR, Communist China, Cuba, Cambodia, North Korea, and Venezuela could hardly be depicted for very long as external models to emulate. When milder forms of socialist parties have managed to democratically come to power (in France in 1981, in post-Franco Spain, or Syriza in Greece in 2015), their realist turn while in government has quickly deflated any serious promise of emancipation. But this typical "postmodern" distrust of political will is by far the most rehashed and the least interesting objection of the three.

The second objection does not stress the abyss that separates the ideals from their realizations, but questions the validity of the ideal itself. Why in the world would one want to be "emancipated"? Slaves, serfs, servants, and children, for sure, crave to no longer be kept "under the authoritative hand" (*mancipatio* or *mancipium*) of a master or a patriarch. And, metaphorically, anybody put under the institutional tutelage of another person may legitimately desire to become autonomous from this dependence. Several recent thinkers, however, have raised doubts about the ideal of "individual autonomy" that has played such a central role in modernist political philosophy. Bruno Latour stresses the importance of the "attachments" which bind us together, simultaneously tying us to each other (i.e., restricting my individual freedom to choose whatever pleases me) and providing us with the collective strength that constitutes our necessarily interrelated agency (i.e., empowering me actually to do, with the help of others, what I choose). Donna Haraway, Anna Tsing, and Karen Barad, among many other ecofeminist thinkers, and along with Tim Ingold, show how "entangled" we are in the web of life, and how the very notion of each individual "giving himself his own law" (autonomy) is both unrealistic and dangerous. Bernard Aspe or Jason Read turns to Gilbert Simondon's concept of transindividuality to better understand our necessary co-evolution with other humans and non-humans (technical objects in particular), within complex milieus of co-action, taking us quite far from the imaginary of self-mastery made to shine at the horizon of political emancipation.[2]

The third objection to the ideal of emancipation comes from considering the unsustainability of our modern conception of the economy, which has been denounced by a renewed wave of environmentalism. In a recent essay,[3] French philosopher Pierre Charbonnier has retraced the historical conjuncture in which a certain conception of freedom developed that was based on the presupposition of a limitless availability of natural resources (Jason Moore's "cheap nature"[4]). To make a long story short, the ideal of political emancipation is heavily indebted to an economic fantasy of unlimited growth that proves more damning every day.

For at least these three sets of reasons, our contemporary challenge may be to conceive of political actions that fight the countless injustices of domination without being in a position to make any promise of future

---

[2] See for instance, Bruno Latour, *An Inquiry into the Modes of Existence*, trans. Catherine Porter (Harvard University Press, 2012); Karen Barad, *Meeting the Universe Halfway. On the Entanglement of Matter and Meaning* (Durham: Duke University Press, 2007); Jason Read, *The Politics of Transindividuality* (Chicago: Haymarket, 2016).

[3] Pierre Charbonnier, *Abondance et liberté. Une histoire environnementale des idées politiques* (Paris: La Découverte, 2020).

[4] Jason W. Moore, "The End of Cheap Nature. Or How I Learned to Stop Worrying about 'the' Environment and Love the Crisis of Capitalism," *Structures of the World Political Economy and The Future of Global Conflict and Cooperation*, ed. Christian Suter and Christopher Chase-Dunn (Berlin: Lit Verlag, 2014).

emancipation—since growing out of the legal *mancipatio* of a human tutor can in no way "free" us from our mutual attachments, from the meshwork of intra-dependences that entangle us within our environments, nor from the finite resources that necessarily limit the extension of our freedom.

The third corner of the modernist triangle, the practice of *critique* to denounce, analyze, understand, and ultimately tear down domination, can also be subjected to a series of three reproaches: its arrogance, its misuse, and its counter-productivity.[5] Whoever criticizes someone or something tends to place himself above the person, the institution, or the event that is being criticized: the critique "knows better" what could and should have been done. There is thus something inherently arrogant in a gesture that can only be made from above, from the superior point of view of better knowledge toward the inferior status of a lesser understanding. Hence, a somewhat contradictory posture within modernist politics: domination is denounced from a domineering position of critique; emancipation is promoted with the *mancipium* of a superior authority.

While this structural contradiction could in principle be neutralized by a careful practice of respectful (constructive) criticism, twentieth-century leftist politics have amply demonstrated a poisonous tendency for critique to corrode, splinter, and undermine the opportunities to gather forces around a common cause. Ideologues and theorists have reserved their sharpest and most violent critiques for the faction that was closest to their overall position, driving dynamics of inner divisions and splits that have considerably weakened these movements. Most critiques waste everybody's time, either by raising objections that the criticized person (and his/her readers) were already well aware of, but could not address within the limits of their statement, or by reproaching them not to have done or said something different than what they did or said (thus frequently ignoring what they actually put forth). Our intellectual conversations would be much richer if we were to stick to two basic rules of interaction: (a) in each particular thing one encounters, let us try and take what is good and fruitful in it (Spinoza, *Ethics*, V, 10); (b) instead of condemning others for writing or doing what they did, let us show and teach by example what and how one can do better.

Finally, probably as a result of its arrogance and its misuses, critique can often be shown to be counter-productive. A common reproach made to politics as usual, as practiced in Parliaments and reflected in the media, concerns its drift toward bickering. "People" are *not* stupid, even those fed on Fox News: people—i.e., we—know very well that most of what politicians throw

---

[5] A recent book directed by Laurent de Sutter, ed., *Postcritique* (Paris: PUF, 2019) has collected a few arguments for the shift toward a postcritical age. See also, by the same author, *Indignation totale* (Paris: Editions de l'Observatoire, 2019).

at each other is disingenuous, overly critical posturing, largely disconnected from the substantive issues at hand. More importantly, even a most superficial understanding of the attention economy should teach us the "Mae West" lesson: "there is no such thing as bad publicity" (more accurately attributed to nineteenth-century publicist Phineas T. Barnum). To criticize someone or something results in fueling it with more attention than it deserves; by doing so, one often strengthens what one intends to denounce. Here again, proposing better alternatives is much more important than locking the debate on the terms chosen by one's adversary. More generally, the productive part of critique is its capacity to expose, explain, and thus counter-effect, the causes that allow for a certain form of domination to impose its oppressive effects. Even if our understanding is intrinsically linked to our judgment, we would generally be much better off without the accusations and condemnations that litter our political conversations.

What could politics look like, after the necessary attempts to counter oppressive forms of domination have got rid of the lures of emancipation, as well as of the traps of critique? It is such a tentative postcritical and post-emancipatory politics that the following sections will try and sketch.

PARTY LINES AND UNDERCURRENTS

The storming of the Republican presidential primaries by a media-obsessed businessman in the Unites States, along with the victories of the Marchers [*La République en marche!*] in France or the Five-Star Movement in Italy, are often interpreted as heralding the end of twentieth-century-styled political parties (that is, parties supported by an ideology, based on a coherent vision of the world, and precisely identifiable on a political spectrum moving from the far left to the far right). Such an interpretation forgets—or refuses to acknowledge—that for a long time already a democrat in the U.S. South can hold positions that are more conservative than a republican from Massachusetts. Or that the French Socialist Party has been persistently divided and energized by a huge variety of currents, eventually debilitated by the obligation to form a toothless "synthesis" (an insipid art most infamously practiced by former President François Hollande).

If the present decomposition of the European "Left" indicates anything, it may be that *the most pertinent level for analyzing contemporary political evolutions is not so much that of the parties, but that of underlying currents.* The two levels are not of course mutually exclusive. If currents remain scattered and divided, they are shuttered from the framework of representative politics inherited from the nineteenth century; the major challenge of the art of politics is to assemble a cluster of currents into a party in a consistent, dynamic, and galvanizing (i.e., not toothless and insipid) way. The "Left" has been doubly incapable of overcoming this challenge, which has led to its contemporary decay, thus opening a two-lane street for the advance of the "far center" (pro-business Marchers in France, liberal-democrats everywhere), soon to be overtaken by the far right (xenophobic Frontists, nationalists, and white supremacists).

We can turn to common language to better understand the distinction between party lines and undercurrents. Like any other common language—insofar as it carries the fine grain of popular wisdom resulting from centuries of cooperative practices, social frictions, mediated conflicts, and innovative adjustments—the French language indicates a suggestive way to understand how political parties neutralize political dynamics as much as they embody them. The expression *en prendre son parti*, literally "to take one's party" (roughly equivalent to the English expression "to accept one's lot"), refers to a moment of resignation, wherein what was originally undesirable, or even unacceptable, ends up being seen as the only option left. "To take one's party" thus amounts to renouncing one's ambition, desire, or rightful claims, in order to follow the path of least resistance or of most achievable second best.

Contrary to the organic unity the Communist Party had hoped to achieve during a few decades of the twentieth century (with some real successes, but at an overall heavy price)—an unrealistic dream that eventually led the left to fragment itself in a ridiculous plethora of microscopic sectarian entities spending most of their energy in internecine quarrels and fraternal detestation—contemporary parties may be best considered as opportunistic coalitions among various currents who continuously try to pull it in their direction, resulting in a "party line" drawn just before the breaking point.

The past four decades have witnessed, on the face of it, a dramatic backlash in terms of the traditional left vs. right mapping of politics. In Europe, socialists have discredited themselves by endorsing neoliberal "reforms" (privatization of public services, disassembling of the welfare state, "tough-on-crime" policies, indifference toward the evils of social inequalities), capitulating to the economic and financial flows induced by globalized capitalism. They certainly acted politically, even if it led to avoiding politics altogether (beyond its managerial form). But their narrative of irresistible globalized flows has emptied institutional politics of its very foundation (the possibility of opposition). In other words, the neoliberal backlash imposed itself by promoting the image of a world of flows devoid of counter-currents.

It's not surprising that representative politics dissolve in such a world (as demonstrated by the rise in abstention rates), since everyone is called on to resign oneself [*en prendre son parti*] to a single party line, already drawn by the calculations of orthodox economists. Party politics has reduced itself to promoting the acceptance of an inescapably unfair collective destiny, in which everyone is the rival of everyone else, but in which a happy few seem positioned to win-it-all at the expenses of too many. Such a (non) choice can only lead to an explosive mixture of acrimony and indifference, between which our contemporary political affects dangerously oscillate, with a strong inclination for tilting toward fascistoid reactions in times of collapse.

At the same time, however, very lively cultural undercurrents have deeply altered the way the majority of our populations see themselves. With considerable independence and mistrust toward political parties, social movements driven by other forms of activism have successfully promoted and spread a number of struggles against long-lasting forms of domination, in terms of racial equality, women's rights, gay rights, animal rights, environmental awareness, and neurodiversity. All these undercurrents are opposed to a certain circulation of capital and power flows among us. Nowadays, *politics lives by counter-currents that refuse to "take the party"* [en prendre leur parti] *of domination.* They are perceived as political insofar as they *counter* a certain flow of domination. Indeed, it is precisely *against* a preexisting current that a gesture or a collective acquires form and consistency in a political landscape.

EIGHTEEN POLITICAL COUNTER-CURRENTS

An initial image of a *politics of currents* would identify the basic unit of institutional politics with activist sensibilities that are attuned to the basic currents that animate and antagonize social life.[6] I have proposed a rough (and partisan) mapping of such currents and counter-currents in my 2018 book entitled *Political Counter-Currents*, identifying eighteen polarities that offer a poetic cartography of the material and mental energies whose contradictions structure our present and future.[7] I will list and characterize them here very concisely, in order to illustrate what types of currents I have in mind. It would of course be useful to refine their characterization, and especially to identify others.

Even if the book was published a few months before the Yellow Vests movement took to the streets of France in 2018, triggered by a mobilization against an increase in gas prices and speed limits on country roads, my first

---

[6] Bruno Latour's 2018 essay *Down to Earth: Politics in the New Climatic Regime*, trans. Catherine Porter (Cambridge: Polity Press, 2018) attempts to reorient our vision of the political landscape by spinning a 90° turn on the traditional left vs. right opposition, integrating both within a new polarity where Earthbound people need to build coalitions against the humans who ravage our environment.

[7] Yves Citton, *Contre-courants politiques* (Paris: Fayard, 2018). The present article is an augmented and modified version of the conclusion of the book. The author expresses his deep gratitude to Daniel Benson, for the careful translation, generous discussion, and considerable improvements he provided to this article.

polarity contrasted the *Automobilists*, who think in terms of individual will, seeing the world from behind their windshield and steering wheel, considering others as rivals for parking spaces and obstacles to faster driving, and listening to hate radio while stuck in traffic jams during their daily commute, with the *Medialists*, who approach the world in terms of common causes and of the social conditioning of reality by the media/milieu. A second polarity opposed the *Sovereignists*, eager to assert their personal and national mastery over themselves, building walls to make sure foreign influences be kept at bay, to *Dividualists*, who conceive of their personal and collective identities (personhood, nationality, ethnicity) as inherently divided, partial, and inescapably schizophrenic. A third polarity divided the world between *SlowDownists*, who resent and denounce the absurd speed imposed upon us, in all aspects of our existence, by an imperative to think, communicate, and work ever faster than before, and *Accelerationists*, who blame our exhaustion and burn-out on the fundamentally backward nature of capitalist domination, stuck as it is on obsolete rules of property that prevent our sociopolitical relations to keep in sync with our technological potentials for emancipation. The fourth polarity distinguished *HomeOwnerists*, defending their right to keep their home, backyard and way of life insulated from the outside world by walls, gates, and locks, from *Inseparationists*, who stress the impossibility (and undesirability) of tightly separating the constantly interpenetrating spheres of our existence on the surface of this one planet.

A fifth polarity set the *Transparentists*, who expect all processes to be transparent, documented, accountable, paper-trailed, against the *Opacists*, who consider a certain amount of opacity as a precondition for privacy and diversity. A sixth polarity contrasted the *(Anti-)Terrorists*, who either resort to terror-inducing tactics or legitimate counter-terror in the name of defending our safety against whomever is accused to threaten it, with the *Desirists*, who believe the best way to safeguard and nurture our sociability is to foster desires rather than to propagate fears. A seventh polarity opposed the *Extractivists*, who approach our social and natural world as being full of itemizable resources ready to be exploited to our profit, to the *Lyannajists*,[8] who see our only real strengths and wealth in the solidary entanglements that tie us to each other across species. As an eighth polarity, the *Competivists*, who place financial competitiveness and rivalry for limited resources as the only (Darwinist) rule of survival between individuals and nations, are contrasted with the *Pollinists*, who locate our most important sources of wealth in

---

[8] The term *lyannaj*, in Creole, has been made famous during the 2009 social movement led in Guadeloupe by the collective *Liyannaj Kont Pwofitasyon*. It is well presented in Dénètem Touam Bona, "Lignes de fuite du marronnage. Le 'lyannaj' ou l'esprit de la forêt," *Multitudes* 70, no. 1 (2018): 177–85.

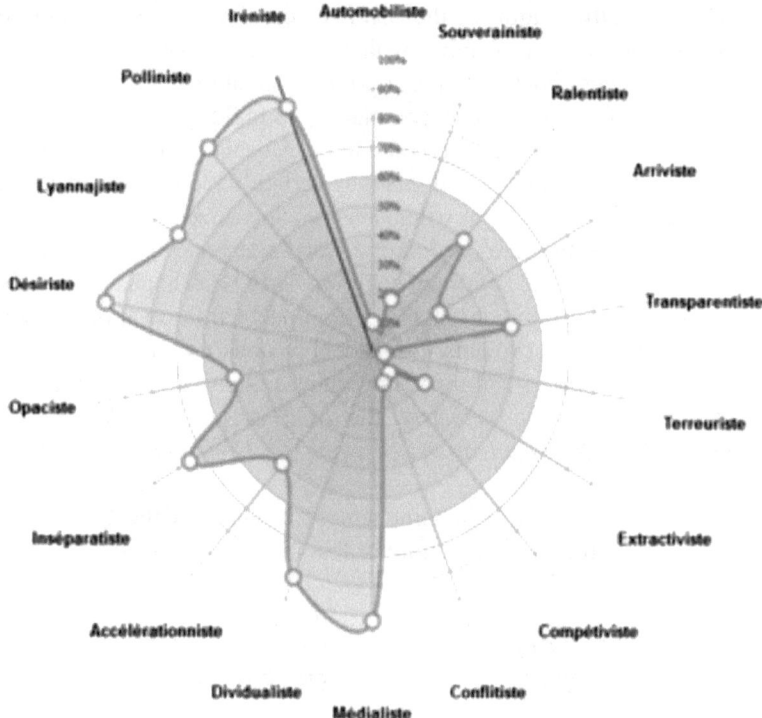

Figure 9.1 Self-perceived ideological profile of the author, according to Jonathan Favre-Lamarine's visualization device.

activities of pollination that are generally unaccounted for in the price indicators that skew our dominant perception of competition. The ninth and final polarity opposed *Conflictualists*, who believe political change can only be carried out through confrontations and power struggles, to the *Irenists*,[9] who are most weary of avoiding war, most aware of our common interdependence, and most eager to defuse conflicts through creative lines of flight.

After the book was published, Jonathan Favre-Lamarine, a Swiss designer, devised a clever tool that invited readers to position themselves somewhere along the continuum sketched by these nine polarities, generating a graphic representation of each person's (self-perceived) multidimensional ideological profile.[10] While the visual result can easily be translated into the traditional polarity of left vs. right (figure 9.1 revealing a clearly leftist inclination, for

---

[9] *Irènè* is a Greek word for "peace", and *irénisme*, in French, usually refers to a naïve confidence in the possibility to pacify all conflicts.
[10] This tool is available at https://jfavlam.gitlab.io/contre-courants-politiques/#/about. I am deeply grateful to Jonathan Favre-Lamarine for taking the time to develop it.

instance), the multiplication of the contrasts can be used to fine-tune this rough opposition, which probably remains decisive, but which hides as many features as it reveals about our current political situations.

One of our most urgent challenges may be to build up common fronts of resistance, through coalitions that would unite us behind a selected number of largely consensual demands—and this may certainly recompose a battlefield between a left wing and a right wing. This much needed task, however, will have to be aware of the variety of currents and counter-currents that always threaten to undermine and split such coalitions. My book hoped to contribute to this preliminary mapping through a certain poetical renewal of our political vocabulary—which explains, but probably does not suffice to excuse, why other more obvious, and more important, polarities were omitted, like the *Equalists* vs. the *Supremacists*, the *LGBTists* vs. the *Patriarcalists*, the *Veganists* vs. the *Omnivorists*, or even the *Undercommonists* vs. the *Governalists*.

Whatever the labels, my main point here is to understand the dynamics that are at work below the surface of more or less cleverly designed party lines.

THE ECONOMY OF ATTENTION AND THE POLITICS OF TENSIONS

In its recent European use, the label "populist" serves to disqualify anyone who refuses to consent to the supposedly scientific laws of markets and financial flows. With a banker at their head, the French Marchers are the standard-bearers of the financial markets [*marchés*], drumming up the competitive beat to which we're all expected to march [*marcher*]—under the recurrent whip of endless "reforms" designed to make us work more efficiently. But the apathy brought about by the mantra of TINA (There is no alternative) has given an unhoped-for visibility to any movement claiming to counteract market domination. Assuming the position of a counter-current to the biased party line of flows has become the proof of political authenticity.

The most reactionary and conservative currents and parties easily profit from this situation, since their hallmark is to position themselves against the movement of time as well as against any form of becoming that upsets the well-engrained modes of domination. They can simultaneously win on two fronts: on the one hand, they denounce financial globalization as a transnational attack on national sovereignty; on the other, they defend traditional values against inner enemies portrayed as foreign agents. Xenophobia, patriotism, religious fundamentalism (Christian or Hindu, as much as Islamic), intolerant fetishization of the patriarchal family, of the police order, of secularism [*Laïcité*]: all such marks of identitarian difference to the party line of flows become powerful attractors of attention and affectivity by crowning themselves with the magical aura of resistance.

"Populism" needs to be understood in its causes, rather than simply disqualified and condemned. The often superficial and simple analyses that are articulated under the heading of *the economy of attention* would benefit from a more profound sensitivity to the valid reasons that push our affects to embrace "bad" causes. Of course, we should not underestimate the media enthrallments created by the various entertainment industries.[11] From the old-fashioned daily press to cinema, radio, and television, all the way to digital platforms that target us through the aid of self-learning algorithms, our attention is constantly being attracted, captivated, magnetized, and enlisted in the desire for name-brand products (Nespresso), in the fear of certain populations (African-American young men, Latinos, Roma, veiled women), or in the acceptance of certain fetishes (anti-terrorism, employment, GDP growth).

If we look at the stock value of Google and Facebook, attentional flows constitute the merchandise that generates the highest profit rates. But the very real exploitation of the economy of attention should not obscure the underlying importance, and still underestimated potential, of *the politics of tensions*. The first perspective considers the attraction that an image, a story, or a slogan exerts on a particular public at a given moment in terms of bait (a hook, an attractor, as "priming"), which localizes the problem on an intermittent relationship between a particular (attracting) object and a particular (attracted) subject, all considered and accounted for in terms of flows (click flows, re-tweets, investment flows). But this attraction can also, in a more interesting way, be envisioned from the perspective of *a magnetic field* that inscribes the attentive subject and the attentional object in the *electric tension* maintained by two opposing polarities. These opposite poles can easily remain hidden from view: their effects only become visible once a certain distance and altitude are taken toward them. Indeed, phenomena resulting from electromagnetic polarization affected human existence for thousands of years before we began to come to an understanding of their invisible causes (which only were discovered in the eighteenth century).

Our power of analysis thus benefits by substituting a vocabulary of *currents* for a (related but distinct) vocabulary of *flows*. To speak of *flows* invites us to imagine measurable quantities of various entities (liquids, raw materials, merchandise, labor force, money, information, images) moving from a point A to a point B within a certain period of time, which is a function of their travel speed. While air currents and marine currents follow the same

---

[11] For the notion of *media enthrallments*, see Yves Citton, *The Ecology of Attention*, trans. Barnaby Norman (Cambridge: Polity, 2017), and *Mediarchy*, trans. Andrew Brown (Cambridge: Polity, 2019).

imaginary, the model of an *electric current* has the particularity of turning our perception away from distances or speeds of electron flows (which we can scarcely imagine), and instead focuses our attention on the underlying presence of a stable polarity that structures surface circulations (figure 9.2). The electromagnetic imaginary, using the discourse of currents, makes us attentive to the permanence of the differentials that motivate and mobilize the exchange of words.

Addressing political questions from the perspective of the polarities that energize them allows for a double reframing of our tired and rather discouraging political spectacle. Firstly, one is no longer dazzled by the staging of political debates, since our attention moves from the (extremely repetitive) thematics that are discussed to the *modalities of their composition and framing* that determine what is being spoken of and in what terms. In other words: instead of seeing what is presented (such as the evolution of employment rates, public deficits, competitiveness), we instead look to the flashlight that chooses to illuminate a certain problem rather than another.

But a second displacement occurs that is just as important. Before posing the question of what the flashlight is illuminating, we should first ask ourselves what powers its light. And the response to this second question helps us respond more appropriately to the first. That is: before tearing ourselves to pieces over the unemployment curve or the reduction of the number

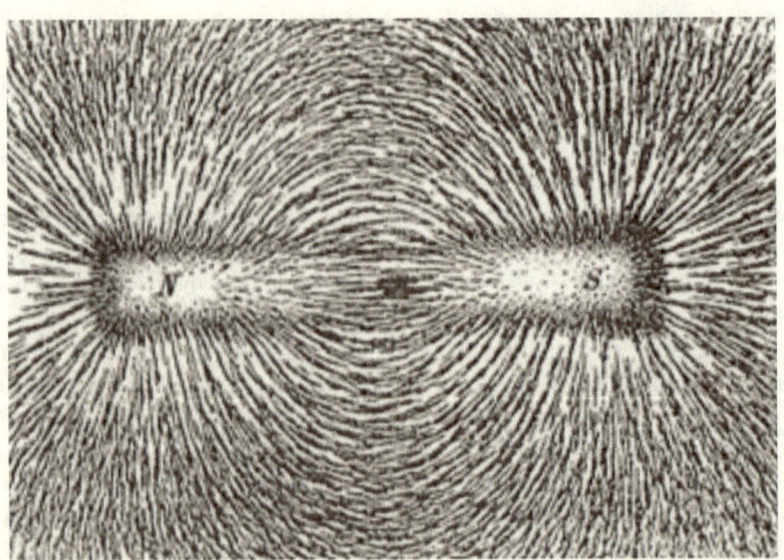

Figure 9.2 A magnetic field Newton Henry Black, Harvey N. Davis, Practical Physics, The MacMillan Co., 1913, p. 242. https://commons.wikimedia.org/w/index.php?curid=73846.*Source:* Public domain.

of civil servants, let's first observe not only the flashlight that illuminates the surrounding darkness, but also and especially the battery which supplies its current, as well as the nerve tensions of the person holding it. It is from the observation, selection, and interpretation of these multiple sources of tension—heterogenous but formidably interlinked—that we can better understand our attentions and inattentions of the moment. The economy of attention needs to be completed with a politics of tensions, since the latter is what powers the former (electrically, magnetically, affectively).

MEDIA ELECTRIFICATIONS AND POLITICAL COUNTER-CURRENTS

The reader will have grasped by now that the insistent recourse to electromagnetic metaphors (battery, pole, flashlight, current, tension, attraction, magnetization) is not purely analogical, even if they were elaborated with poetic license and literary freedom. The materialist study of electronic currents that physically circulate between us, as well as within us, runs parallel to the interpretative study of the symbolic magnetizations that influence our behavior. It's clear that behind each televised image or photograph posted on Instagram is a camera, the nerve tension of a finger which releases the shutter, and the brain that anticipates the effect of a particular framing. But there is also the network of EDF [*électricité de France*] and the nuclear reactors of Areva—whose electric currents, economic interests, and political influence contribute to facilitate or inhibit the circulation of certain flows of images and currents of ideas over others.

A politics of tensions must strive to conceive the continuity, as well as the marge of relative autonomy, that both unite and distinguish—without ever really separating—the electrification of our technical apparatuses and the impulses of our nervous systems. If our collective mediatized attention chooses certain fragments of reality rather than others, in order to charge certain objects with political tensions, it happens according to the material polarizations that structure and reproduce (indirectly, and often through complex and pliable intermediaries) our institutions and social inequalities. At any given time period, the media electrifications that populate political imaginaries with their familiar figures (such as the President, the leader of the opposition, the CEO, the terrorist, the veiled woman, suburban youth, the unionist on strike, the traveler infuriated over another day of transportation strike) constitute a symbolic infrastructure in which polarization plays a role as fundamental as that of the + and the − in an electric battery.

Approaching institutional politics in terms of counter-currents means granting a double status to the notion of opposition. On the one hand, as mentioned earlier, it's clear that what moves without encountering (human) resistance is not part of the political sphere. A current of air in an empty room does not generate debate. Only in the context of constructing a dam does a waterway become political. Politics only exists, in this eminently modern viewpoint, through *counter*-currents. Interest arises only for those movements that *oppose* a particular current visible within a given circulation of flows.

But as we've just seen, the merit of an electromagnetic imaginary lies in its ability to conceive of opposition not as something occasional, but structural. From the perspective of a battery or an electric circuit, the positive pole does not come *before* a negative pole, which would only come later as a reaction to a preexisting feature of the world. Resistance is not reactive but constitutive of electric tension. The two poles + and − are strictly contemporary, co-present, intrinsically linked to each other like two sides of the same coin. Even if they "oppose" each other, it would be absurd to "choose" one at the exclusion of the other, since neither would exist without its opposite. Their opposition does not arise from an exclusive rivalry, but from a constitutive and dynamic *tension*.

This is the way to understand and use the eighteen polarities sketched earlier. The political counter-currents conceived in terms of these polarities do not correspond to separate political parties (on the model of territorial partitions), which would ask us to choose our exclusive belonging to one or the other among the terms in opposition. The pairing of *Transparentists* vs. *Opacists*, for instance, puts in tension two counter-currents that certainly oppose each other, but whose existence nonetheless depends on each other in the form of a *contrast*. They are constituted in their contradictory co-presence: they only exist as counter-currents to each other, without either one having primacy over the other—though within a certain magnetic field that has been greatly altered over the recent years by the development of big data, face recognition, and surveillance capitalism.

The model presented here is not one of an exclusive partition, but of a participative sharing [*partage*], understood in the sense of slicing different parts of a cake for those who partake in the same shared meal. Individually as well as collectively, we are necessarily divided between two poles, in the same way that, wherever we live on the planet, we necessarily live at a certain distance from the North Pole and from the South Pole, since life is impossible to sustain while residing on one of the poles themselves. Politics of tension constitute our condition of existence, as human consumption (unequally concentrated among a few rich nations) exceeds the limits of the planet in an increasingly patent and preoccupying manner. We can't learn to live on this planet, necessarily and willingly together, unless we manage to *adjust*—in the sense of regulating, but especially in the sense of making more just—the tensions that a participative sharing imposes on us. Mapping the political counter-currents that move through us, at the individual as well as global level, may provide a useful prelude to this work of adjustment.

POSTCRITICAL VECTORIALIST POWER AND THE TRIUMPH OF HINGERY

So what sort of politics do the previous pages speak of? The politics presented on TV programs? The politics that happen during the daily negotiations of Ms. Mayor? The politics that get decided when a lobbyist enters a legislator's office? The politics of putting one's physical well-being at risk to face off riot police come to evict a ZAD [*zone à défendre*]? The polarities and counter-currents mentioned above span all these scenarios, precisely because they all participate in the same fields of tension and are articulated within them.

Concerning standard "party politics," they are certainly exasperating when they bore us with empty slogans, sometimes denounced as such, other times piously dissected by a clique of exegetes of our common stupidity. But even when reduced to the personal affairs of media-friendly figures, whose scandals and outrageous behavior exhaust our attention and insult our collective intelligence, contemporary party politics reveal important underlying tensions—though not without bringing about a significant loss of meaning, among other calamitous effects. Given the way our current electrified media world functions (and it could function differently), the personalization of politics is harmful but perhaps inevitable. The best thing to do is to push it further, rather than powerlessly lament it. As nauseating (and/or ridiculous) as they can be, "scandals" and "affairs" that implicate political figures at least have the merit of bringing to light the source of the circulation of certain currents that feed political electrification. They effectively produce the displacement mentioned above, if only we get into the habit of turning our attention away from the visible theme (what a President says) toward the flashlight which illuminates it (what a President does, in favor of whose interests).

The key to take this mediatized politics of tensions to a higher level—and not to repeat the self-defeating righteous mistakes of the Trump years—is to adopt a radically postcritical stance: *Never criticize what your opponent says* (no matter how outrageous it may be)! The Mae West lesson ("There is no such thing as bad publicity") is central to any proper understanding of the attention economy. When denouncing your opponent's idiocy, you strengthen his position, by the very fact of attracting more attention toward the agenda that he dictated with his statement. No better way to get buffoons elected into White Houses. Ignore your opponents, never respond to them, always be on the attack! Uncover what they do but wouldn't want too many people to know! Disclose who supports them, for what motives, with what returns on investments! In other words: choose *your* tensions—don't let anybody entrap you in theirs!

Plenty of interesting questions arise, even in the most stultifying affairs that debase politics to politicking, once our attention has been sharpened to what Emily Apter has cleverly analyzed as *Unexceptional Politics*.[12] From what position in the field of socio-economic tensions does a particular legislative initiative, or gridlock, emerge? Which power source allows the initiative to make visible a particular issue by attempting to address it? Personal scandals tend to hide actual political problems, while often revealing the true problems of the politics of tensions. The idiocy of mediatized affairs—understood in the etymological sense of the Greek term *idiôtès,* which doesn't mean an "imbecile," but a "private individual"—actually help to conceive the politics of tensions in another way. Entering into the details of who contacted whom, at what time, exerting what sort of pressure on them, to obtain what in exchange, takes us from the abstract sky of ideas into the concrete realities of power. Indeed, for better (softening ever-too-rigid rules) or worse (taking advantage of loopholes for personal gain), the realities of power are rarely based on questions of principle, and most often arise from practical handiwork.

What obstacle can be put in place to obstruct a harmful action to the community? How to encourage beneficial behavior? What wrench can be thrown to block which part of a nefarious machine? In other words: where should a levee be erected, and with what material? Where should a backdoor be opened, and to what end? Or, as is more often the case: what is the criteria for opening the door or closing it? In other words, in its concrete exercise, *politics is an affair of hinges* [*une histoire de gonds*].[13]

For a number of years now, McKenzie Wark has drawn our attention to the crucial role played by "vectors" in our intensely electrified societies—to the point of toying with the idea that the capitalist class is now being overtaken by a "vectorialist class."[14] Vectorialist power comes from owning and controlling the vectors through which our communications take place. And since what is communicated among us draws its value from those who devote some of their attention to it, the vectorialist class effectively controls the production of value in our society.

---

[12] Emily Apter, *Unexceptional Politics. On Obstruction, Impasse and the Impolitics* (New York: Verso Press, 2017).

[13] In the original French version, this whole section plays with the phonic proximity between the word *gond* ("hinge") and the word *con* ("idiot"). Many tongue-in-cheek sentences in the following paragraphs invite the reader to a double interpretation of political *gonnerie* (a word made up by the author) as meaning both political "hingery" and political "bullshit" (*connerie*).

[14] McKenzie Wark, *Capital Is Dead. Is This Something Worse?* (New York: Verso, 2019).

How does one control a vector? In our world of currents and counter-currents, vectorialist power decides to interrupt the flows or to let them pass, reverse their course, tilt them this way or that way, to the left or right, diminish or accelerate their output, filter their content. In the space inhabited by human bodies, these operations occur through walls, doors, roads, stairs, turnstiles, barriers. In the electronic world, they occur through microprocessors, switches, gates, cables, servers, and platforms. Between national borders as between computers, only in rare cases does nothing pass (an impassable wall?), and equally rare are those in which everything can pass without any constraint (a limitless public square?). Most often we arrange our living environments around gates, which we can, according to the needs of the moment, keep *more or less* open or closed. *Hinges* are thus central, though little celebrated, elements of our ways of living and sharing our territories of existence. Hinges are the main power tools of vectorialist domination.

Our microprocessors are nothing other than stripes of little hinges. They are conceived to be switched between an *on* mode, in which a current passes, and an *off* mode, in which it doesn't. Ubiquitous digitalization—which penetrates ever more intimately our territories and physical existence, by saturating them with sensors and switches that monitor and control our every gesture and action—involves implanting an army of little hinges around us, and soon within us. The enormous equipment currently being employed on behalf of artificial intelligence is an enormous "hingery" [gonnerie].

From this discussion, we can arrive at a very general definition of *politics in the vectorialist age*: that which decides on the implantation and the operational modalities of hinges. This applies to every level of our existence, from microprocessors to bathroom doors (figure 9.3) and all the way to the thousands of kilometers traced by the frontier between Mexico and the United States. And whether they speak of the economy, of finance, of security, of censorship, of the job market, of taxes, or of welfare programs, *politicians' talk is a talk of hingery* [les politiciens disent des gonneries]. Such is their function within our representative democracies: to give voice to the desires, fears, interests, and hopes of seeing barriers more or less open or closed in various instances.

Of course, professional politicians are not the only ones to talk of hingery. Striking workers and students who block university campuses are also involved in hingery, by letting in certain employees, negotiators, students, teachers, administrative personnel, or journalists, based on their function within a particular place. Facebook engineers apply hingery when they reconfigure the terms of service regulating the access to our (supposedly) personal data: they selectively open or close the door to such data and determine the price of entry. If, as Jeremy Rifkin observed, our societies have entered the "age of access," then our era is likely to see the triumph of hingery.

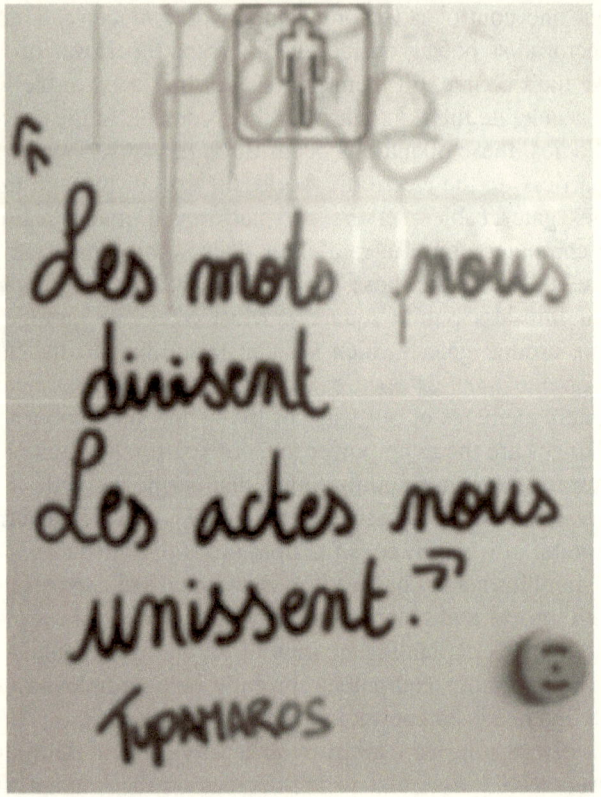

Figure 9.3 Bathroom door at the University of Paris 8 with a graffiti: "Words divide us. Acts unite us." (2018) (photo by Yves Citton).

Currently, the vectorialist triumph of hingery is also *the triumph of bullshit*. According to the technical definition provided in 1986 by Harry G. Frankfurt, "bullshit" is spoken whenever the speaker does not care whether what is said is true or false, because the only thing that matters is the impact it will have on the listener/reader, an impact that is expected to flow in the interest of the bullshitter.[15] Frankfurt's theory has recently experienced a revival, due to its uncanny illustration by the flows of bulltweetting emitted from the White House. But its validity extends to the vectorialist class as a whole: Facebook, Twitter, Apple, Amazon, Verizon, or Orange don't care whether what passes through their vectors is true or false, right or wrong, good or bad, as long as it

---

[15] Harry G. Frankfurt, "On Bullshit," *Raritan Quarterly Review* 6, no. 2 (1986): 81–100. The article came out as a book, under the same title, published by Princeton University Press in 2005 and translated into French as *De l'art de dire des conneries* (Paris: 10/18, 2006).

attracts attention, and rakes up profits. Vectorialist power, based on hingery, can thus be considered as *intrinsically postcritical*.

BINARISTS AND POTENTIALISTS

To see (or hallucinate) hinges everywhere is not, however, sufficient to advance our understanding of the politics of tension. The most important thing to remember is that *not all hinges/bullshits are born equal*. This inequality will allow me to conclude by analyzing a tenth and final political polarity, whose contrast helps us grasp the tension that is likely to become central with the expansion of digitization.

The electrification of our everyday lives is based on devices whose functionality is essentially binary: powered *on* (the device is switched on, the current passes) or powered *off* (the device is switched off, the current doesn't pass). This mechanical logic of all or nothing still regulates the elementary components of our computers (at least until quantum computation arrives, which is only in its first stages): everything ultimately rests on the transition from *on* to *off*, on the discrete (discontinuous) alternation of 0 and 1.

But the nerve electrification of the sensory systems responsible for human thought is based on swarm behavior that seems irreducible to (and of a higher complexity than) our (current) microprocessors—at least as far as we can tell, and as far as we're unwilling to project the mechanical model of cybernetics onto the biological functioning of our brain.

Two abstract models of hingery emerge from this opposition (which goes beyond simply registering the distinction between the mechanical and the biological). They distinguish two broad types of machines, living or otherwise, according to their level of organization. The first model functions according to the strictly binary choice of *on* or *off*, 1 or 0, yes or not, present or absent, black or white. In this model, hinges only serve to switch the door from an open state to a closed state, and vice versa. There is no third possibility.

The second model allows for an organism to modulate its reactions according to perceived *nuances* within a continuum, with threshold effects arising according to given sampling ratio. This means, for example, that it can produce a sound moving from one octave to the one above it, without any audible interruption, or alter itself continuously form purple to red within a rainbow. Hinges here allow for a *relative* opening of the gate, in such a way that *more or less* current can pass according to need, where the door will often be neither completely open nor completely closed, but (a little) open and (a little) closed at the same time.

It should be clear that the distinction between these two models of hingery is of crucial importance for possible conceptualizations of the politics of tension.[16] Likewise for the status of the other polarities presented above.

The *Binarists*—close travel companions of the *Conflictualists*—rightly emphasize that, sooner or later, politics consists in choosing to do or not to do, to accept or to oppose, to vote *for* or *against*. For them, hinges ultimately mean open or closed doors. This seems to be the case as soon as we look at the concrete details of particular cases. From an abstract point of view, a border is certainly meant to be permeable (neither completely open nor completely closed), such that the door is left partially open and capable of moving on its hinges. But when abstraction hits the concrete ground, the binary nature of politics becomes dramatically clear, for instance when anyone approaches the arrival counter at any U.S. or Schengen area border control without a visa.[17]

In the eyes of *Binarists*, modulations appear as illusions of abstraction, or as a luxury of the rich. Observed from the fine grain of their concreteness, sociopolitical realities are determined by switches and circuit breakers, whose rigidity is only exacerbated by ubiquitous digitization. *Binarists* are no cheerleaders of binary: they are the first to deplore its absurdities or cruelties. But they lay claim to a realism that considers these effects as ineluctable—even more in a digital age of ubiquitous computation ultimately based on current passing or not passing within a microprocessor.

At the other pole, enthusiasts of modulation could present themselves as *Potentialists*. They are not satisfied with reducing the continuum of the rainbow to the discontinuity of a limited set of pre-programmed colors, which will impose a response *for* or *against* to any conceivable question. Their instrument of choice is the *potentiometer* which, similar to the volume control on an audio device, allows for the modulation of the effective power of an operation within a given potential. The potentiometer appears as the instrument of adjustment *par excellence*—the magic button of political wizardry. Contrary to common wisdom, the *Potentialists* claim the superiority of the analog.[18]

Their fundamental demands involve using the potentiometer to quell the most menacing tensions, and also to clear a path for claiming new rights. The first and last gesture of political hingery consists, according to the *Potentialists,* to put a foot in a door that is about to close, or to block a

---

[16] Franco "Bifo" Berardi has very suggestively contrasted the *connective* (digital) mode of relations between beings to the *conjunctive* (analog) mode in *And: A Phenomenology of the End* (Los Angeles: Semiotext(e), 2015).

[17] Strong *Binarist* arguments can be found in Alain Badiou, *Logics of Worlds*, trans. Alberto Toscano (London: Bloomsbury, 2013) or in Bernard Aspe, *Les mots et les actes* (Caen: Éditions Nous, 2011).

[18] See Brian Massumi, "On the Superiority of the Analog," *Parables* for the *Virtual: Movement, Affect, Sensation* (Durham: Duke University Press, 2002). The same author provides strong *Potentialist* arguments in *The Power at the end of the Economy* (Durham: Duke University Press, 2014).

current that exerts a harmful action, in order to put in its place a modulator that allows for the reinvention of the dividing lines between the "open" and the "closed." Following this logic, each implantation of a potentiometer leads to the emergence of a new potential. Collective political power does not arise from a simple stocking up of force, nor from the mere interruption of flows, but from the refinement of our mutual capacities of adjustment.

According to *Binarists*, the two poles in opposition are attractors. Every political action ultimately tends toward one of them, since any action is constrained by the exclusive choices that are forced on us by the given state of our concrete realities. According to *Potentialists*, the poles are the two extremes that mark the limits between which each of us has to situate himself/herself, always somewhere between the two—though not necessarily in the middle. The first group calls on us to choose our party between the counter-currents sketched above; the second invites us, less toward compromise, and more toward the challenge of "disparity" [*la disparation*]. The philosopher of technology Gilbert Simondon defined the latter as the stereoscopic ability to make emerge, from two contradictory images (that which my left eye receives and that which my right eye receives), a third dimension (depth), thus allowing the apparent contradiction to be resolved with creativity.[19]

Of course, the very notion of counter-currents, as it was presented in the earlier sections of this article, pays tribute to Binarists, as the eighteen neologisms were organized around clearly contradictory polarities. These polarities impel us, sooner or later, to consider the basis of our everyday decisions, to vindicate one pole rather than the other—as soon as one leaves the poetic sphere of a thought experiment in order to confront the painful dilemmas generated by the various forms of domination that brutalize our social realities. However, multiple occasions in the preceding pages have subscribed to the Potentialist faith. The above polarities have been presented as reference points, rather than calls to adhere to one pole at the exclusion of the other. The visual dashboard provided earlier by Jonathan Favre-Lamarine (figure 9.1) invites the reader to evaluate how far he/she is ready to go in each of the opposed directions. It operates as a potentiometer insofar as it allows the user to finely modulate his/her position in the tensional field drawn by each polarity.

---

[19] See Gilbert Simondon, *L'Individu et sa genèse physico-biologique* (Grenoble: Jérôme Millon, 1995), 206.

COMPLICATE POLITICS, POLITICIZE COMPLEXITY

How, then, can such a politics of tensions contribute to our political orientation? By drowning us in twenty counter-currents, each dressed up in far-fetched neologisms? Doesn't it render the map of our political engagements even more illegible than the actual chaos of the party system? If one is serious about overcoming our current impotence, *shouldn't our politics be about simplifying things*?

Beneath their diversity, the belief in the need for simplification may be what unites the first group of the ten polarities represented on the right side of the dashboard. The Automobilists, the Sovereignists, the SlowDownists, the HomeOwnerists, the Transparentists, the (Anti-)Terrorists, the Extractivists, the Competivists, the Conflictualists, the Binarists all will find, each for different reasons and each in a different way, that the counter-currents sketched out in this book blur politics through an extravagant literary fantasy that uselessly complicates what should instead be made accessible by clear explanations and simpler means. And they would be right.

For the past half century, the discourses on the necessary consideration of "complexity"—however true and stimulating that they can be—have certainly had a demobilizing effect. Since everything is so maddeningly entangled, triggering the worst unexpected consequences even when the original intentions were noble and generous, how presumptuous can one be to even attempt to radically transform our societies? All we can do is throw our arms in the air, hope for the best, pity the victims, and provide humanitarian aid to appease momentarily the most intolerable catastrophes.

Discourses of complexity did bring to light the violence done by the simple responses, inherited from traditional ideologies, when they are cut and pasted onto the fragile subtlety of the multiple, interlinked layers that compose social realities and political problems. Of course, the social sciences should continue to devote all their efforts to explain social effects by their necessarily multiple causes. It is indeed urgent to grant them (at least) as much attention (and funding) as to the "harder" techno-scientific disciplines, since our very survival depends on them as much as on technical or managerial innovation. The true problem, however, is to measure to what degree the awareness of the complexity of the social leads to a political paralysis, inhibiting any action whose results may easily backfire on the best of intentions.

Not everyone is paralyzed. We know of hyperactive politicians, who hurriedly reform in every direction, without concern for the social calamities incurred by the simplistic dogmas in the name of which they justify their reforms, who progressively reduce public liberties to tighten their grip on the power apparatus, or who eagerly dismantle environmental regulation to make sure their friends in the business world can fully profit from the last drops of prosperity before our common collapse. Their immunity to ethical apprehension relative to complexity no doubt arises from their stubborn faith in constructing markets into self-regulating mechanisms, in traditional hierarchies of domination, or in the idea that self-interest is never so well served as by oneself.

If the Medialists, the Dividualists, the Accelerationists, the Inseparatists, the Opacists, the Desirists, the Lyannajists, the Pollinists, the Irenists, and the Potentialists share a common belief—which is far from certain—it may be that they concern themselves with the inevitability of complexity. In their eyes, a carefree simplification of our scruples toward complexity can only worsen problems, never find (sustainably satisfactory) solutions. The shared sensibility that aligns these currents is no doubt their bias in favor of an AND... AND... logic, one which attempts to avoid, for as long as possible, responding to any injunction that would be imprisoned in an exclusive choice of the type OR...OR.

The tension between these two constellations of counter-currents thus appears in all its cunning irony. If one decides to follow the second group in their reluctance to take sides for or against, one effectively makes a (binary) decision to side with those currents that refuse to take sides—thereby ruling in favor of the first group!

Thus, there is no final realignment possible of the twenty counter-currents around the traditional left vs. right divide. It is healthy to lament complication, and to work on clearing a path to more simplicity. But while it is important not to suffer complexity like a curse, it may be crucial to reclaim it as a fundamental issue and as a most urgent imperative. It thus may be necessary to begin by complicating politics (a little), in order to be in a position to *politicize complexity*. This, in any case, is the gamble of what I have presented above. Politicizing complexity means seeing the plurality of counter-currents that animate our (sometimes contradictory) engagements as a mark and motor of a future politics, rather than as a simple obstacle to be overcome. Politicizing complexity means putting the tensions that result from this pluralism as the source, the finality, and the dynamic basis for future forms of activism.

WHAT'S LEFT IN A POLITICS OF TENSIONS AND COUNTER-CURRENTS?

A strong objection can be raised to the politicization of complexity as well as to the whole reasoning proposed in this article: the lack of traction that has characterized leftist politics over the past decades is due to too much talking and not enough acting. As succinctly stated by a graffiti tagged on a bathroom door of the University of Paris 8 at Saint-Denis, *Words divide us, actions unite us* (figure 9.3). If one is expected to measure all the possible unintended consequences of one's action, one is paralyzed. More concretely in the case of leftist politics: the left needs to spend much less of its energy on intellectual speculation in academic journals, and much more time on political organization in the social territories that are so badly mistreated by ecocidal and sociocidal capitalism.

The next phase of a strong leftist revival—which may very well be accelerating in the wake of COVID-19 pandemic—should be devoted to taking an active part, at the grassroots level, in the many conflicts that are currently brewing on social and environmental issues; to organizing wide coalitions beyond and above the tensions and turmoil of our conflicting counter-currents; and to enacting the mediatization of such coalitions in the viral forms of communication made so powerful by the internet and social media.[20] The (impossible?) challenge of such a program would be to build such a revival, not on the denial and obfuscation of the tensions, fragilities, and ambivalences delineated in this article, but on their very dynamics.

To prepare for this, and as a summary to this very preliminary reflection, I could imagine the resurrection of a reference to the political left on at least three grounds. Firstly, and least problematically, a postcritical left would continue to push forward the demands for equality traditionally identified with social progress. Taking into account the "redshift" which, for two centuries, has led yesterday's progressives to become today's centrists and tomorrow's conservatives, the egalitarian front now encompasses not only political rights and economic welfare, but also gender and racial issues, cultural diversity, vectorialist power, postnational migrations, anti-speciesism, and environmentalism. This first definition of the left would be fairly comfortable insofar as it keeps pushing the modernization front beyond the current limitations and inconsistencies of the modernist project.

A second definition, however, could elevate the acceptance of the fragilities and uncertainties linked to the increasing complexity of our social systems to the status of a new marker for what it means to stand on the left side of politics. As indicated above, most of the polarities located on the right side of Jonathan Favre-Lamarine's graph have in common the desire to hold on to reassuring well-accepted solutions and worldviews, while those on its left side tend to run against well-established and dominant common opinions. This second criterion is much more disturbing than the first, since the willingness to confront the mindboggling complexities of our entanglements, and the readiness to acknowledge the tentative nature of the explanations and

---

[20] This is the program I attempt to sketch in Yves Citton, *Faire face aux ruptures. Conflits, coalitions, contagions* (Paris: Les Liens qui Libèrent, 2021).

solutions one promotes, may lead to redrawing the ideological divide quite far from its traditional distribution along clear party lines. According to this second criterion, an article from the (neoliberal) *Economist* weekly may be situated to the left of an editorial by a Trotskyite columnist, while certain legitimate denunciations of social injustices may end up to the right of the spectrum, due to their authoritative tone or to their oversimplification of the complexities at hand.

A third, and even more destabilizing, possible redefinition of the left would push one notch further the Capitalocenic challenge of confronting the tensions that tear us *from the inside*—tensions for which the term "complexity" is in fact a rather weak expression, and for which "schizophrenia" would no doubt be much more accurate. This challenge involves learning to live and situate oneself in a world of contradictory counter-currents, where each and every one—with a degree of exposure to risk very unequally allocated—is not so much expected to take sides, as to negotiate the inner and exterior tensions resulting from our unstable and multidimensional positioning, somewhere along the continuums that the twenty polarities described above barely begin to map. In the maelstrom of our world economy more and more narrowly constrained by the limits of our global ecology, we are all called to identify, simultaneously and alternatively, with the fish in the whirlpools, with the constructors of the dams that kill the fish, with the consumers of the electricity generated from the dam, with the fishermen robbed of their job by the disappearance of the fish, if not with the fishermen's dogs who enjoy their unemployed companion to stay home and walk them more often. If they help to identify some of the multiple dimensions of this maelstrom, the twenty neologisms presented here might not be superfluous. What they attempt to map out is less a political landscape than a deeply disorienting schizophrenia. And one way of redefining the left might be to identify it with the (embarrassed and embarrassing) willingness to acknowledge the schizophrenic nature of our modes of living and thinking.

Hence, a postcritical list of open questions, ruling out the very possibility to close this reflection on a self-assured conclusion designed to assert an indisputable truth. Can the counter-currents, nerve tensions, and magnetic fields discussed in the previous sections result in anything that could look like a politics? Or are they bound to paralyze our political agency even further, emblematizing a denial of politics rather than its renewal? Can an openly schizophrenic left become a powerful attractor for a newly politicized people that is currently emerging? Has such a people been cruelly missing only because of a refusal to face its intrinsically ambivalent constitution? Or is it our very schizophrenia that prevents us from devising a leftist politics with actual traction in our actual world, which is dramatically drifting into the arms of right-wing rulers leading it (and us) toward self-destruction? Does seeing allies as well as enemies each time we look at ourselves in the mirror signal the mutation of politics to a higher level of complexity? Or does it ring its failure and demise? Should we lament and mourn such a demise, or rejoice in it?

Could the recent electroshock triggered by COVID-19 pandemic help us see that confrontational politics, traditionally conceived upon a model of war between enemies, needs to be complemented with *viral* politics, where bits of code are successful when they manage to be accepted and reproduced within their hosts?[21] Can such a "viropolitics" generate new models of understanding and new modes of intervention by inquiring and exploiting the superposition of three deeply interrelated forms of virality—*biological* virality (COVID-19), *software* virality (WannaCry ransomware), and *media* virality ("going viral" on social media)? Aren't the relations between a guest and its host a promising field of study and experimentation for such a viropolitics in a world of tensions and counter-currents dominated by the hosting power of the vectorialist class?

If what's left in viropolitics asks to be articulated in terms of furthering equality, of addressing the challenges of complexity, and of acknowledging our schizophrenic ambivalences, can it content itself with merely asking questions upon questions? Shouldn't it require its proponents to launch empirical investigations, targeted interventions, insidious penetrations, victorious contaminations? Could it count on you to join in?

BIBLIOGRAPHY

Apter, Emily. *Unexceptional Politics. On Obstruction, Impasse and the Impolitics.* New York: Verso Press, 2017.

Aspe, Bernard. *Les mots et les actes.* Caen: Éditions Nous, 2011.

Badiou, Alain. *Logics of Worlds.* Translated by Alberto Toscano. London: Bloomsbury, 2013.

Barad, Karen. *Meeting the Universe Halfway. On the Entanglement of Matter and Meaning.* Durham: Duke University Press, 2007.

Bardini, Thierry. *Capitalisme génétique.* Paris: Les Liens qui Libèrent, 2021.

Berardi, Franco. *And: A Phenomenology of the End.* Los Angeles: Semiotext(e), 2015.

Bisson, Frédéric. *Virus Couronné. Prolégomènes à toute viropolitique future qui voudra se présenter comme science.* Paris: Questions Théoriques, 2020.

---

[21] For a first approach to such viral politics, see Frédéric Bisson, *Virus Couronné. Prolégomènes à toute viropolitique future qui voudra se présenter comme science* (Paris: Questions Théoriques, 2020); Pierre Cassou-Noguès, *Virusland* (Paris: Le Cerf, 2020); Thierry Bardini, *Capitalisme génétique* (Paris: Les Liens qui Libèrent, 2021).

Bona, Dénètem Touam. "Lignes de fuite du marronnage. Le 'lyannaj' ou l'esprit de la forêt." *Multitudes* 70, no. 1 (2018): 177–85.
Cassou-Noguès, Pierre. *Virusland.* Paris: Le Cerf, 2020.
Charbonnier, Pierre. *Abondance et liberté. Une histoire environnementale des idées politiques.* Paris: La Découverte, 2020.
Citton, Yves. *Contre-courants politiques.* Paris: Fayard, 2018.
Citton, Yves. *The Ecology of Attention.* Translated by Barnaby Norman. Cambridge: Polity, 2017.
Citton, Yves. *Faire face aux ruptures. Conflits, coalitions, contagions.* Paris: Les Liens qui Libèrent, 2021.
Citton, Yves. *Mediarchy.* Translated by Andrew Brown. Cambridge: Polity, 2019.
Frankfurt, Harry G. "On Bullshit." *Raritan Quarterly Review* 6, no. 2 (1986): 81–100.
Latour, Bruno. *Down to Earth: Politics in the New Climatic Regime.* Translated by Catherine Porter. Cambridge: Polity Press, 2018.
Latour, Bruno. *An Inquiry into the Modes of Existence.* Translated by Catherine Porter. Harvard University Press, 2012.
Massumi, Brian. "On the Superiority of the Analog," *Parables* for the *Virtual: Movement, Affect, Sensation.* Durham: Duke University Press, 2002.
Massumi, Brian. *The Power at the end of the Economy.* Durham: Duke University Press, 2014.
Moore, Jason W. "The End of Cheap Nature. Or How I Learned to Stop Worrying about 'the' Environment and Love the Crisis of Capitalism." In *Structures of the World Political Economy and The Future of Global Conflict and Cooperation*, edited by Christian Suter and Christopher Chase-Dunn, 285–314. Berlin, Lit Verlag, 2014.
Read, Jason. *The Politics of Transindividuality.* Chicago: Haymarket, 2016.
Simondon, Gilbert. *L'Individu et sa genèse physico-biologique.* Grenoble: Jérôme Millon, 1995.
Sutter, Laurent de. *Indignation totale.* Paris: Editions de l'Observatoire, 2019.
Sutter, Laurent de, ed. *Postcritique.* Paris: PUF, 2019.
Wark, McKenzie. *Capital Is Dead. Is This Something Worse?* New York: Verso, 2019.

Index

Adorno, Theodor, xviii, xx, 123, 124, 124n20, 125n23, 127–35, 127n30, 130n47, 135n69, 137–39, 187–92, 194, 195–96, 198–200, 205, 206–7, 209, 210n87, 211–19, 219n123, 221
Africa, xvn17, xix, 84, 173, 177, 186
African, 172–74, 177, 179
African-American, 99, 152, 164–66, 171, 205n67, 269
agency, xviii, 4, 39–40, 60, 90–93, 96, 102, 110, 113, 121, 189, 191n23, 197, 201, 212, 260–61, 283; agency (research), 135, 155n145; state agency, 100. *See also* Central Intelligence Agency (CIA)
allodoxia, 240, 240n37, 242
Althusser, Louis, xvii, 61, 77, 134
anarchism, xvii, xxi, 56, 230
Anthropocene, 168, 175–76, 186–87, 191, 204, 222
anti-semitism, 13, 205n67, 231, 251n72
Arab Spring, xiv, xvn17, 31, 33
authoritarian/authoritarianism, xvn17, xiii, xvi–xvii, 40, 45, 48–49, 51–52, 59, 110, 131, 144n100, 153, 192, 246–47
autonomy, 7–8, 20, 22, 85, 144n100, 212, 230, 232, 236–37, 244, 246, 261
avant-garde, 16, 35, 58, 212, 215, 238–39

Badiou, Alain, xvii, 56, 61–62, 80–82, 84, 85n47, 87
Bandung Conference, xiv, xix, 165
Bauer, Bruno, 74–75, 134
Benhabib, Seyla, 140, 197
Benjamin, Walter, 37, 56, 124n20, 138, 185–87, 189–90, 189n14, 194–96, 196n40, 196n43, 200, 205, 209–12, 210n87, 215, 218–20, 222
Berlin Wall, xiv, 140, 230
Black Panther Party, xx, 60, 139, 148, 164, 167, 212
Bolshevik, 45n25, 49–50, 60, 123n16, 128n35, 150n124, 210–11, 217
Bolshevism, 48, 196, 196n40, 210
Boltanski, Luc, xv–xvi, 5–6, 8–9, 11, 15, 17, 20–22, 31, 34, 42, 58, 152, 229, 235
Bourdieu, Pierre, xx, 34, 37, 42, 61, 233, 235–40, 242–43, 250–51, 260
Butler, Judith, xx, 42, 50, 59, 111, 249–50

capitalism: critique of, 15–16, 22–23, 28, 57, 144n100, 245; new spirit of, 7; racial capitalism, 164, 167–69, 172–73, 175, 177
Capitalocene, xix, 176, 283
CCF. *See* Congress for Cultural Freedom

Central Intelligence Agency (CIA), 45, 53, 124–26, 124n21, 125n23, 128, 131–32, 134–36, 135n69
Césaire, Aimé, 144–45, 165
civil society, 20, 74–76, 86
class: class struggle, xix, 32–33, 39–40, 49, 52, 52n37, 54, 54n42, 59–61, 84, 112, 134, 144, 149, 151–52, 156, 193; dominant/ruling class, 25, 34, 40, 44, 46–47, 51–52, 59, 76, 86, 141, 193, 274; vectorialist class, 274, 276, 284; working class, xvii, xix, 7, 14, 35, 38, 45n25, 48, 51, 53, 79, 98, 111n32, 120, 120n8, 126n28, 133, 146n109, 149–50, 153n134, 194n30, 195, 199, 239–41
climate change, 57, 186–88, 190, 199, 201, 202, 204, 209, 220; climate politics, 191–92, 201, 220; climate science, xx, 186–87, 201, 202n58, 204n65, 206
colonialism, 86, 101, 141, 145, 164, 166, 171; French colonialism, 40, 165
communism/communist, xiv, xviii, xx, 14–15, 34n5, 42, 44, 44n23, 45n24, 46–47, 54, 58, 62, 82, 87, 120, 124n20, 127, 129–30, 129n40, 131–32, 134–36, 134n67, 139, 149–51, 154, 154n139, 165, 170, 193, 203n63, 211–13, 230, 260, 264; anti-communism/anti-communist, 33, 44, 60, 62, 62n54, 118, 128, 129n40, 132, 136, 147, 154n141, 170; Chinese Communist Party, 247; French Communist Party, 231; German Communist Party, 211
Congress for Cultural Freedom (CCF), 134–36, 135n69. *See also* Central Intelligence Agency (CIA)
consumerism, 167
Cuba, xiii, 44n23, 45, 52, 154n139, 196, 203, 260; Federation of Cuban Women, 151
Cuban Revolution, xiv, xix, 40, 134n67, 148, 164

Davis, Angela, xx, 138–39, 140n89, 188, 197, 199, 211–15, 218–19
decolonization, xiii–xiv, 170, 174, 177, 180, 215–16
Derrida, Jacques, 37–38, 38n11, 61, 154n141
dialectics/dialectical, 76, 98, 102, 121, 130, 130n47, 146, 156, 189, 199, 200, 203–4, 206–7, 223; dialectical critique, 190; dialectical materialism, 202, 206n71; *Dialectic of Enlightenment*, 124n21, 188, 191, 205nn67–68, 214, 216, 219n123; dialectic of scission, 81; Hegelian dialectic, 77, 230, 251; negative dialectics, 217

ecological, xiv, xxi, 14, 22, 27, 33, 57–58, 152n132, 156, 186–87, 190–91, 197–98, 200–201, 204, 206, 207n76, 208–9, 208n78, 216, 218, 221, 239; agroecological, 203; ecological critique, 208, 210; ecological economics, 204–5; socio-ecological, 188, 190–92, 196, 210, 218, 220, 221–22
economy of attention, xxi, 259, 269, 271
emancipation: emancipatory horizon, xii, xiv, xx–xxi, 229–30, 232, 244, 251; political emancipation, 74, 76, 85, 261; real emancipation, xvii, 74, 76–77, 79; self-emancipation, 17–18, 20–22, 50, 71, 73–74, 82, 86; subject of, xvii, xviin23, 70, 73, 79
Engels, Friedrich, 81, 83, 119, 121, 121n11, 149, 151, 169, 193, 217
Enlightenment, 24, 56, 58, 71, 76, 84–85, 141, 189, 191, 199, 207n76, 216, 218, 230, 236. *See also Dialectic of Enlightenment*
equality, xiii, 43, 60, 70, 73, 75, 82, 99, 145, 150n124, 152, 165, 168, 202, 238–39, 243, 259–60, 282, 284; racial, 265; sexual, 149
Eurocentrism, xviii, 85–86, 85n47, 155n146

Index

exploitation, xix, 14, 27, 96, 100, 113, 117, 138n79, 141, 144, 168–69, 175, 189–90, 204, 207n76, 220, 269
EZLN. *See* Zapatista National Liberation Army

feminism/feminist, xiii, xxi, 4, 13, 22, 27, 41–42, 45, 50, 57–58, 110–11, 111n32, 137, 147, 150–51, 153n134, 154n140, 165, 167, 171–72, 197, 203n60, 208, 212, 230, 239, 250; ecofeminism, 205, 207n76, 261; feminist movement, xiii, 110, 172, 230
financial crisis, 2008, xi, xvi, 14, 15, 22, 31, 48
First World War. *See* World War I
Flaschenposten, 134, 188, 218, 220
Forst, Rainer, 140
Foucault, Michel, 16, 37–38, 38n12, 42, 61n53, 178, 251; Foucauldian, xv, 61
Frankfurt School, xv, xviii–xx, 30, 61–62, 117–18, 121–23, 126n28, 127–28, 133–40, 135n70, 138n83, 140n89, 142, 147, 155, 187, 193, 200–201, 206, 207n76, 211–12, 213–14, 221, 223, 229; Frankfurt scholars, 124n20, 126, 131, 134, 134n67, 136
Fraser, Nancy, xvi, xviii, 3, 5, 8–9, 11, 14–15, 17, 20–22, 31, 32n1, 42, 58–59, 111, 140, 143, 147–48, 148n117, 150–55, 154nn140–41, 197, 199
fundamentalism, 268

globalization, 32, 44, 53, 142, 192n24, 268
the Global North, 96, 194, 198–99, 216, 260; North/South inequalities, 5
the Global South, 5, 96, 164–65, 196, 210, 216, 260
Gramsci, Antonio, 32, 34, 61, 193
Gramscian, 34, 199

Habermas, Jürgen, xin3, xviii, 127–30, 129n42, 130n43, 137, 139–43, 141n90, 142n92, 143n94, 146, 147, 149, 149n117, 193, 197, 207, 212n93, 215n103, 219n123, 235
Habermasian, 62, 139, 143, 144n100, 147–49, 199
Hegel, G. W. F., 74, 76–77, 133, 196n43, 251
Hegelian, xx–xxi, 82, 138, 201, 230, 243, 251–52
hegemony, 32, 34–36, 39, 148; economic hegemony, 166; neoliberal hegemony, xvi, 32
history: historical process, xvi–xvii, 28, 74, 77–79, 83, 120n8; historicization, 6; subject of history, 77–79, 81
homophobia, xii, 36
Honneth, Axel, xviii, 42, 140, 143–46, 143n94, 144n100, 146n109, 148, 250
Horkheimer, Max, xv, xviii, 121–29, 122nn13–14, 123n18, 124n21, 127n30, 128n36, 129n41, 131n50, 133–39, 133n60, 135n70, 138n79, 140n89, 187, 189, 191, 194–95, 207, 207n76, 209, 211, 214–15, 215n103, 217–18, 219n123
human rights, 174

identity: cultural identity, 91; identitarian, xx, 51, 90, 111, 148, 247–49, 268; identitarianism, 247, 249; identitarianist, 231, 246–47; identity politics, xvii–xviii, xxi, 48, 51–52, 60, 89–92, 110, 250
ideology, 24, 33, 40, 44, 59–60, 78, 129n40, 139, 146, 148, 156, 167, 169, 188, 190, 192, 194n30, 207, 218–20, 263; dominant ideology, 24, 33–34, 54, 126, 139; *The German Ideology*, 78
imperialism, xii, xiv, xviii, 45, 52, 59, 122n14, 137, 141–42, 155, 164–65, 167, 171, 175, 195, 208–10, 210n86, 216
India, xvii, 31, 84, 192, 192n24, 246; Indian state of Kerala, xiii, 196, 203

individualism, 146, 245
inequality, xvi, 19, 33, 75, 96, 155, 197, 200, 204, 238, 243, 277
internationalism, 41, 45, 48, 51

Kant, Immanuel, xii, 71, 118n2, 133, 230, 246
Kantian, 188

Latour, Bruno, xii–xiii, 37, 57, 261, 265n6
the left: American Left, 136; left wing/left-wing, xx–xxi, 147, 188, 194n32, 195, 199, 208, 220, 268; New Left, 4–5, 11, 131, 133, 138, 196, 199, 207–8, 208n79, 211, 219n23; Old Left, 133, 207–8
Lenin, Vladimir Ilyich, 39, 54, 120, 149–50, 194n30, 195–96, 210, 217
Leninist/Leninism, 35, 50, 122n12, 210, 217, 239; anti-Leninist, 42; eco-Leninism, 218, 223; Leninism and critical theory, 197; Marxist-Leninist, 211
liberalism, xi, 11, 24, 33, 145, 192–93; economic liberalism, 8, 11, 22–23, 57; political liberalism, 8–9, 11, 20, 23, 50, 57, 244; social liberalism, 19, 231. *See also* neoliberalism
liberation, xivn13, xix, 59, 70–72, 128, 137, 149, 165, 167, 188, 215, 223
libertarian, 9, 20–21, 43, 49, 58, 118n2, 252

Marcuse, Herbert, 123, 126, 126n30, 127n32, 130, 131n50, 133, 136, 138–39, 140n89, 196, 199, 207, 207n76, 211–14, 216, 219n123
Marx, Karl, xii, xiv, xvii, xix, 51, 57, 62, 73–86, 119–21, 120nn7–8, 133–34, 146, 149–51, 173, 186, 189, 189n14, 193, 196, 200, 203, 205–6, 206n70, 217, 222, 239, 245, 251
May 68, 16

nationalism, 246
nation-state, 5, 9–10, 19, 25, 43, 47–48, 94, 113, 122n14, 194
NATO, 129, 129n42
negative liberty, 9–10
neoliberalism, xii, xvi, 3–5, 9–11, 13–14, 19–20, 22–23, 25, 27, 32–33, 32n2, 36, 40–41, 48, 51, 57, 112, 177, 192, 231
North American Free Trade Agreement (NAFTA), 97, 112

organizing (political), xviii, 33, 41, 45–46, 49, 53, 90–92, 111, 128n35, 207, 282

politics of tensions, xxi, 259, 269, 271, 273–74, 280
populism, xxi, 269
populist, 268
postcolonial, 4, 27, 55, 58, 165, 167, 169–71, 177, 247, 247n56, 250
postmodernism, 253
postmodernist, 33, 42, 94
Proudhon, Pierre-Joseph, xxi, 51, 230, 245, 251–51, 251n72

racism, xiv, 55, 164, 171, 204, 205n67, 208; anti-racism, 41–42, 45, 150–51, 165
racist, 9, 33, 99, 129, 137, 207n74
Rancière, Jacques, xiv, xx, 37, 42–43, 61, 235, 237–40, 242–43, 250–51
republicanism: French republicanism, 4, 11, 13, 24
Réunion Island, xix, 164–65, 169–70
revolution: Bolivarian Revolution, 148; Burkina Faso Revolution, 148; Chinese Revolution, 167n67, 196; French Revolution, 24, 85; Haitian Revolution, 85–86, 85n47, 179, 197, 260; revolutionary theory, 33, 62, 84, 120n6, 121, 133, 156, 213; revolution/reform, 48–49, 186, 188; Russian Revolution, xin2, 38n12, 50. *See also* Cuban Revolution

the right: extreme right, xx, 5, 13, 13n21, 24, 31, 34–36, 131–32, 231–32; French right, 13

Said, Edward, 137, 221
Sanders, Bernie, 46–48, 154n140
Scientists and Engineers for Social and Political Action (SEPSA), 207
Second World War. *See* World War II
slavery, xix, 72–73, 76, 83–85, 129, 141, 149, 152, 166, 172–75, 179, 212
social democracy, 4, 19–20, 41, 46, 154, 232
socialism, xiv, xvii, 15, 31–33, 37, 40, 44–47, 44n23, 52n37, 55, 58–62, 120–23, 131, 136, 140, 146n109, 147, 153–54, 194–95, 199, 201, 203; ecosocialist, 187–88, 200, 218; revolutionary socialism, xvii, 31, 33, 46, 59; Socialist Party (France), 11n16, 20, 41, 231, 263
social movement, xv, xvii, 4, 8, 12, 15–16, 28, 35–36, 48, 110, 112–13, 133, 138, 147, 153, 199, 207, 219n123, 265, 266n8
social protection, xvi, 3–5, 8–10, 20–21, 112, 152
social security, 8, 10, 154
sociology: critical sociology, xx, 42, 229, 233, 235, 237, 243–44, 251
the South. *See* the Global South
Soviet Union. *See* USSR
Spinoza, 191, 222–23, 262
Spinozist, 243
Stalinism, 48, 147, 217
state: statism, 3, 5, 8, 11, 43, 49; welfare state, 3–5, 7, 24, 32, 48, 140, 153, 264
strategy: political, xi, 41, 49–50, 177, 180; strategy and tactics, 47
subject: political subject, xvii–xviii, 70, 77, 79–80, 82–84, 91, 93, 193, 196–97, 218; political subjectivation, 250; political subjectivity, 86, 191, 197. *See also* emancipation, subject of

teleology, xvii, 77, 79, 82–83
Thatcher, Margaret, 14, 23, 169
There is no alternative (TINA), 14, 169, 268
totalitarian, 37, 39, 48, 59, 124n20, 144n100
totalitarianism, 56
Trotsky, Leon, 122–23, 197
Trotskyist, 42, 46–47, 52, 283

USSR, xiv, 32, 44, 45n25, 52, 129, 131, 196, 203, 260
utopian, xvi, 120n8, 140–41, 147, 153n134, 179, 188, 201, 209, 216, 220–22, 248

Weber, Max, 61, 133, 233–36
Weberian, xx, 229
the West, xiv, 12, 61, 129, 140, 143, 153, 167–68, 174, 244, 248; Western academy, 123; Western intelligentsia, 33, 61, 136, 146n109, 147–48
women's movement, 111, 199. *See also* feminism, feminist movement
World War I/First World War, xix, 185, 189, 197, 210
World War II/Second World War, xin2, xix, xx, 4, 6, 8, 125n23, 174, 194, 211, 218, 248

xenophobia/xenophobic, 6, 9, 13, 24, 36, 231, 246, 264

Yellow Vests, xvi, 31, 35–37, 39–40, 43, 193, 265

Zapatista National Liberation Army (EZLN), 112

Notes on Contributors

Daniel Benson is an assistant professor of Foreign Languages and International Cultural Studies at St. Francis College. His writing has appeared in journals including *Diacritics, Critical Review of Contemporary French Fixxion*, and *Left History*.

Luc Boltanski is Directeur d'Études at the Écoles des Hautes Études en Sciences Sociales (EHESS) and member of the Institut de Recherche Interdisciplinaire sur les Enjeux Sociaux (IRIS). Recent books include *Enrichment: A Critique of Commodities,* co-authored with Arnaud Esquerre (Polity Press, 2020), *Mysteries and Conspiracies* (Polity Press, 2014), and *On Critique: A Sociology of Emancipation* (Polity Press, 2011).

Ajay Singh Chaudhary is the executive director of the Brooklyn Institute for Social Research and its core faculty member specializing in social and political theory. He has written for the *The Guardian, The Nation, The Baffler, n+1, Los Angeles Review of Books, Social Text, Dialectical Anthropology, The Hedgehog Review, Filmmaker Magazine,* and *3quarksdaily*, among other venues. Ajay is currently writing a manuscript on the politics of climate change.

Yves Citton is a professor of Literature and Media at the University of Paris-8 Vincennes-Saint Denis. He is the Director of the l'École Universitaire de Recherche (EUR) ArTeC and co-editor of the journal *Multitudes*. His books include *Faire avec. Conflits, coalitions, contagions* (Les Liens qui Libèrent, 2021), *Générations collapsonautes* (Seuil, 2020, in collaboration with Jacopo Rasmi), *Mediarchy,* (Polity Press, 2019), and *Contre-courants politiques* (Fayard, 2018).

Philippe Corcuff is an associate professor of Political Science at the Institut d'Études Politique de Lyon and a member of the sociological laboratory CERLIS (Centre de Recherche sur les Liens Sociaux, CNRS-Université de Paris-Université Sorbonne Nouvelle). He is politically engaged in anti-capitalist, pragmatic, and alter-globalist anarchism and is the co-director of the libertarian and militant research seminar ETAPE (Explorations Théoriques Anarchistes Pragmatistes pour l'Émancipation).

Nancy Fraser is the Henry and Louise A. Loeb professor of Philosophy and Politics at the New School for Social Research. Recent books include *Feminism for the 99%: A Manifesto* (Verso, 2019), co-authored with Cinzia Arruzza and Tithi Bhattacharya, *Capitalism: A Conversation in Critical Theory* (Polity, 2018), co-authored with Rahel Jaeggi, and *Fortunes of Feminism: From State-Managed Capitalism to Neoliberal Crisis* (Verso, 2013).

Asad Haider is a founding editor of *Viewpoint Magazine*, author of *Mistaken Identity: Race and Class in the Age of Trump* (Verso, 2018), and co-editor of *Black Radical Tradition: A Reader* (Verso, forthcoming). His writing can be found in *The Baffler*, *n+1*, *The Point*, *Salon*, and elsewhere.

Gabriel Rockhill is the founding director of the Critical Theory Workshop/Atelier de Théorie Critique, Professor of Philosophy at Villanova University, and an anti-capitalist activist. Recent books include *Contre-histoire du temps présent* (CNRS, 2017), *Interventions in Contemporary Thought* (Edinburgh UP, 2016) and *Radical History and the Politics of Art* (Columbia UP, 2014).

Rosaura Sánchez is an emeritus professor of Latin American Literature and Chicano Literature at the University of California, San Diego. *Spatial and Discursive Violence,* co-authored with Beatrice Pita, is soon to appear from Duke University Press.

Françoise Vergès is a founding member of the Decolonize the Arts collective and a decolonial feminist, anti-racist activist, and independent curator. Recent books include *The Wombs of Women. Capitalism, Race, Gender* (Duke UP, 2020), *Une théorie féministe de la violence* (La Fabrique, 2020), and *A Decolonial Feminism* (Pluto, forthcoming).

www.ingramcontent.com/pod-product-compliance
Lightning Source LLC
Chambersburg PA
CBHW022010300426
44117CB00005B/107